EVERYMAN'S LIBRARY

EVERYMAN,
I WILL GO WITH THEE,
AND BE THY GUIDE,
IN THY MOST NEED
TO GO BY THY SIDE

JAMES BALDWIN

THE FIRE NEXT TIME

NOBODY KNOWS MY NAME

NO NAME IN THE STREET

THE DEVIL FINDS WORK

WITH AN INTRODUCTION
BY EDDIE S. GLAUDE JR.

EVERYMAN'S LIBRARY
Alfred A. Knopf   New York   London   Toronto

THIS IS A BORZOI BOOK
PUBLISHED BY ALFRED A. KNOPF

First included in Everyman's Library, 2024

Nobody Knows My Name
Copyright © 1961 by James Baldwin
Copyright © 1954, 1956, 1958, 1959, 1960 by James Baldwin
Copyright renewed 1988, 1989 by Gloria Baldwin Karefa-Smart

The Fire Next Time
Copyright © 1962, 1963 by James Baldwin
Copyright renewed 1990, 1991 by Gloria Baldwin Karefa-Smart

No Name in the Street
Copyright © 1972 by James Baldwin
Copyright renewed 2000 by Gloria Baldwin Karefa-Smart

The Devil Finds Work
Copyright © 1976 by James Baldwin
Copyright renewed 2004 by Gloria Baldwin Karefa-Smart

All rights reserved including the right of reproduction in whole or part in any form. This edition published by arrangement with the James Baldwin Estate.

Introduction copyright © 2024 by Eddie S. Glaude, Jr.
Bibliography and Chronology copyright © 2016 by Everyman's Library

All rights reserved. Published in the United States by Alfred A. Knopf, a division of Penguin Random House LLC, New York, and distributed in Canada by Penguin Random House Canada Limited, Toronto. Distributed by Penguin Random House LLC, New York. Published in the United Kingdom by Everyman's Library, 50 Albemarle Street, London W1S 4BD and distributed by Penguin Random House UK, 20 Vauxhall Bridge Road, London SW1V 2SA.

Originally published by The Dial Press, New York in
1961 (*Nobody Knows My Name*), 1963 (*The Fire Next Time*),
1972 (*No Name in the Street*), 1976 (*The Devil Finds Work*).

The Acknowledgments on pages 487–8 constitutes an extension of this copyright page.

everymanslibrary.com
www.everymanslibrary.co.uk

ISBN: 978-1-101-90847-1 (US)
978-1-84159-424-8 (UK)

A CIP catalogue reference for this book is available from the British Library

Typography by Peter B. Willberg

Book design by Barbara de Wilde and Carol Devine Carson

Typeset in the UK by Input Data Services Ltd, Bridgwater, Somerset
Printed and bound in Germany by GGP Media GmbH, Pössneck

CONTENTS

Introduction vii
Select Bibliography xix
Chronology xx

The Fire Next Time (1963) 1
Nobody Knows My Name (1961) 71
No Name in the Street (1972) 239
The Devil Finds Work (1976) 377
Acknowledgments 487

INTRODUCTION

James Baldwin as Essayist

In 1986, about a year before his death, James Baldwin sat down with David C. Estes for the *New Orleans Review* to talk about his latest book, *The Evidence of Things Not Seen*. It was a wide-ranging interview, a kind of retrospective of Baldwin's career as a writer and a reflection, in light of the new book, on his career as an essayist. It is in the context of this discussion that the question of how he became an essayist emerged.

How did he think about the form? How did he see himself as someone who inhabited the genre at the highest level? After all, at this point in his career Baldwin had stood for some time as one of America's greatest essayists. In his non-fiction writing, particularly in the books collected here, Baldwin offered the most searing and insightful commentary on the vital questions of race, culture, and American democracy. His prose gave the nation a language in which to think about itself differently, loosed from the shackles of ideas of American exceptionalism and the illusions of whiteness that led some to believe that somehow, no matter what God said, the color of one's skin accorded one value above or below every other human being. On the page, he forced a confrontation with the ugliness of who we are, and he did it in such a way that might have made Montaigne nod his head in recognition. Simply put, Baldwin had mastered the form.

In this interview with Estes, however, Baldwin admitted that he "never intended to become an essayist."* It was working with Saul Levitas at *The New Leader* and with Robert Warshow at *Commentary* when he was in his early twenties that helped him find his feet in the genre. His first inspiration came from the flaccid race books he had to review every week at *The New*

---

* David C. Estes, "An Interview with James Baldwin," in *Conversations with James Baldwin*, eds. Fred L. Standley and Louis H. Pratt (Jackson: University Press of Mississippi, 1989), 274.

JAMES BALDWIN

Leader, which made clear to him that he could not write from the vantage point of a victim. Baldwin developed his approach to the question of race and American democracy in contrast to the all-too-common stale sociology and tangled web of social statistics that purported to reveal the problems of American race relations. As a young man writing reviews for *The New Leader*, he had his fill of such books. Sentimental accounts that treated Black people as victims. Books that refused to attend to the complexity of peoples' lives only, in the end, to tell us to "be kind to niggers" and "be kind to Jews."* Instead, Baldwin took his readers beneath the surface of the country's malaise to tap the root. There he asked the *moral* question of who we take ourselves to be as individuals and as Americans. In doing so, he forced a painful encounter with experience (with life), historical and present. That honest encounter, he insisted, could free us to deal with who we might possibly become by releasing us from the straitjacket of our national illusions. A confrontation with what torments the nation and with the pain and wounds that move us about meant keeping track of the material conditions of American life *and* the inner lives of those who had to bear it all. For Baldwin, and these essays make the point explicit, the unwillingness of Americans to reckon with the suffering at the heart of the country's identity—to evade the history that makes them who they are—has made them monstrous.

Americans often long for the illusions of safety that trap us in categories while we retreat into sentimentality that gums up our ability to feel. "Sentimentality, the ostentatious parading of excessive and spurious emotion," Baldwin wrote in "Everybody's Protest Novel" (1949), "is the mark of dishonesty, the inability to feel; the wet eyes of the sentimentalist betray his aversion to experience, his fear of life, his arid heart; and it is always, therefore, the signal of secret and violent inhumanity, the mask of cruelty."† Baldwin published those words when he was twenty-four years old. He would echo the sentiment some twenty-plus years later in *No Name in the Street* with a description of the "wet eyes" of a powerful white man in the South, "staring up at [his]

---

* Estes, "Interview with James Baldwin," 276.
† James Baldwin, *Notes of a Native Son* (Boston: Beacon Press, 1984), 14.

INTRODUCTION

face, and his wet hands groping for [Baldwin's] cock, we were both, abruptly, in history's ass-pocket." Race, desire, and emptiness felt in an unwanted touch.

But, again, reading Baldwin requires more than tracking the pain and suffering of the nation and of himself. He does not speak as a victim. Baldwin is a poet in Emerson's sense: that person who "shall draw us with love and terror" and "chaunt[s] our own times and social circumstance."* He is an artist, a writer, in conversation with a wide range of influences (inheritances and ancestors) that shape what he sees and how he inhabits the genre. To read him is a demanding practice: to track how the language and blues sensibilities of Black folk in the United States shape the writing; to sit with the ways the King James Bible and the homiletic structure of Black preaching influence the form; and to trace his references and invocations (to see, for example, the influence of Henry James in his sentence structure and the ongoing engagement with the themes that animated James's novels like *The Ambassadors*, or how he riffs on Emerson's essay "Self-Reliance," and Marcel Proust's reflections on time and memory), and to do this work across a wide-ranging corpus of close to seven thousand pages.

This collection begins in 1961 with *Nobody Knows My Name* and ends with *The Devil Finds Work*, published in 1976. From the height of the civil rights movement with student sit-ins, the March on Washington, and the peak of his fame with his face on the cover of *Time* Magazine to the stain of Watergate, the election of Jimmy Carter, and the burden of being a celebrity artist now in his fifties with a political movement in ruins, these essays offer the reader a sense of the complex arc of Baldwin's witness and craft.

With the publication of *The Evidence of Things Not Seen* in 1985, the "old man" had occasion to look back and to look forward. As he resisted Estes's question about the New Journalism and the distinct form of *Evidence*, he recalled a lesson learned from Saul Bellow. "I'm speaking only for myself . . . I don't think a writer ever should show off, anyway. Saul Bellow would say to me years

---

* Ralph Waldo Emerson, "The Poet" in *Emerson: Essays and Lectures*, ed. Joel Porte (New York: The Library of America, 1983), 465.

and years ago, 'Get that fancy footwork out of there.'"* A lesson for writers, still. In this short interview, Baldwin revealed what sits at the heart of his essay writing, how that journey began, and how just a year before his death it ended. This Everyman's Library edition, implicitly framed by Baldwin's first and last books, takes up what happened in between, a writer who finds his voice on the page and, by extension, in the world.

In the late 1940s, Baldwin learned from the editorial pen of Warshow that, if he was not going to lie on the page, he had to confront his own fears and terrors. He had to deal with the overbearing presence and image of his stepfather. He had to grapple with desire; not only his sexual desire but his desire to be loved. He had to face the rage deposited in his gut by a world that announced from his birth that he was inferior simply because of the color of his skin, and he had to admit, if he was to assert his right to live fully, that at one point in his life he tragically believed what the world said about him. Baldwin had to plumb the depths of his own perspective, which required he find out exactly what his perspective was. "I couldn't talk about 'them' and 'us,'" he said to Estes. "So I had to use 'we' and let the reader figure out who 'we' is. That was the only possible choice of pronoun. It had to be 'we.' And we had to figure out who 'we' was, or who 'we' is."† The slight and playful shift to Black English, "who we is," reveals how, for him, Black people reside at the heart of the answer to that question. Autobiography became a ready-to-hand resource, not because his life was interesting—everybody suffers; everyone must make choices that are theirs alone—but, as he put it, "in my social situation ... I had to use my personal dilemma to illuminate something. I repeat, I am not speaking from the point of view of the victim. I am speaking as a person who has a right to be here."‡ That insistence combined with a fearless interrogation of the circumstances that shaped his life, both materially (he grew up poor in Harlem) and in his most private, interior moments (where love and desire co-mingled with race), gave his essays

---

* Estes, 273.
† Estes, 275.
‡ Estes, 277.

INTRODUCTION

a sense of urgency and power that continues to inspire and unsettle.

In the end, Baldwin took himself to be a witness and from that perch he tackled the social and moral questions that confronted the nation and confront each of us. As such, these books offer biting commentary on the state of American life and are deeply personal. I have no doubt Baldwin would agree with Virginia Woolf—another literary stylist and social critic—that the principle guiding the essay must be that of pleasure. But it also demands more. Woolf writes that the essay "should lay us under a spell with its first word, and we should only wake, refreshed, with its last. . . . The essay must lap us about and draw its curtain across the world."* That is how Baldwin brings us such clarity. He wrote not for pleasure alone, but that we might, in the end, become better human beings. The moral concern is the beating heart of Baldwin's prose.

The open form of the genre of the essay requires a kind of candor that often escapes our talk of race in the United States. Americans lie to themselves repeatedly, and that self-deception immobilizes the country, as Baldwin told Estes, "with a past it cannot explain away."† That complicated history is habitually buried beneath tidy self-representations that declare, despite our national sins, we are always on the road to a more perfect union. But Baldwin's essays rend the country's illusions by demanding an honest assessment of the way race distorts and disfigures not only the nation but individuals, white and black alike. His sentences sometimes rage. They cry out like the prophets of old. And yet, as I have suggested, something deeply personal and private is at work here. Confessional even. To be sure, Baldwin's essays are about the nation and the difficult questions of race, culture, and democracy, but they are also extraordinary efforts at self-creation, where the poor child of Harlem, born on August 2, 1924 to Emma Berdis Jones, who managed to survive the rages of his stepfather, David Baldwin, wills himself, with the aid of the likes of Beauford Delaney and others, to become one

---

* "The Modern Essay," in *The Complete Works of Virginia Woolf*, Kindle edition, 1071–2.
† Estes, 280.

of the world's greatest writers. He inhabits the genre of the essay as both prophet and romantic, as one who warns of the fires to come and as the writer who declares near the end of his life, "I have nothing to prove. The world also belongs to me."* Here insight reaches towards the world and towards the soul—a kind of soul-making prose.

These essays are, at once, intimate and expansive, vulnerable and relentless in their demands of the reader. They challenge and upset. Something close to the heart is happening on the page. In *The Fire Next Time*, for example, readers are allowed to eavesdrop on a conversation that happens behind the veil, behind a closed door in places that white folk rarely, if ever, enter. "To be loved, baby, hard, at once, and forever, to strengthen you against the loveless world," Baldwin wrote to his nephew. "Remember that: I know how black it looks today, for you. It looked bad that day, too, yes, we were trembling. We have not stopped trembling yet, but if we had not loved each other none of us would have survived. And now you must survive because we love you, and for the sake of your children and your children's children." This is intimate knowledge being passed from one generation to the next. Something akin to what my father told me as the shadow of the veil fell over my own teenage eyes.

In the introduction to *Nobody Knows My Name*, Baldwin wrote, "In America, the color of my skin had stood between myself and me . . . [T]he question of who I was was not solved because I had removed myself from the social forces which menaced me—anyway, these forces had become interior, and I had dragged them across the ocean with me. The question of who I was had at last become a personal question, and the answer was to be found in me." The introduction in *Nobody* orients the reader to what follows and, perhaps more importantly, attempts *to create that reader* who is able to attend, all at once, to the social, aesthetic, political and moral stakes of the matter—which include the person writing and the individual reading.

Reading these books together one can trace the themes that

---

* "Go the Way Your Blood Beats: An Interview with James Baldwin" with Richard Goldstein in *James Baldwin: The Last Interview and Other Conversations* (Brooklyn: Melville House, 2014), 73.

INTRODUCTION

animate Baldwin's essays across the body of his work. The idea here is not to read him in a straight line as if he was at the height of his powers in 1963 and, by 1976, he is an old man gone bad in the teeth as celebrity has dulled his pen. Instead, it is better to see Baldwin's work as constantly folding back on itself, where earlier formulations are revised in the full light of what he has seen and experienced. How has the shift in the material conditions of Black life and struggle affected the substance of what he sees and feels? Reading *The Fire Next Time* next to *No Name in the Street*, for example, allows us to see how his thinking about history, identity, and American democracy shifts, and the way he experiments with form to capture those changes. *No Name in the Street* is a marvelous meditation on memory and trauma. Baldwin represents the fragmentation of memory in the very way in which he structures the book. Recollections cannot be trusted. Memories fade but redound in our current living. But the book also takes up the substance of previous claims.

Think for a moment about this formulation in *The Fire Next Time*:

Color is not a human or a personal reality; it is a political reality. But this is a distinction so extremely hard to make that the West has not been able to make it yet. And at the center of this dreadful storm, this vast confusion, stand the black people of this nation, who must now share the fate of a nation that has never accepted them, to which they were brought in chains.

Here race talk confounds our self-understanding; it is a political reality that must be addressed if we are finally to leave behind the confusion that leads Americans "to take refuge in any delusion—and the value placed on the color of the skin is always and everywhere and forever a delusion." But in *No Name in the Street*, at first glance, Baldwin seems to reject this view:

And as the black glories in his newfound color, which is *his* at last, and asserts, not always with the very greatest politeness, the unanswerable validity and power of his being—even in the shadow of death—the white is very often affronted and very often made afraid. He has his reasons, after all, not only for being weary of the entire concept of color,

JAMES BALDWIN

but fearful as to what may be made of this concept once it has fallen, as it were, into the wrong hands. And one may indeed be wary, but the point is that it was inevitable that black and white should arrive at this dizzying height of tension. Only when we have passed this moment will we know what our history has made of us.

One might read this as an embrace of the concept of color—that Baldwin has fallen for the siren song of those young radicals of Black Power. But, instead, we can read this passage as a kind of *layering*, where Baldwin has taken the earlier formulation in *The Fire Next Time* and layered it with the disappointments and rage that birthed Black Power and with what he has seen and lived (the murders of Medgar Evers, Malcolm X, and Martin Luther King, Jr.). The result is a deeper questioning and an insistence on a kind of dialectical tension that has brought us to the moment in 1972 that he is desperately trying to explain.

Reading *The Devil Finds Work* we can see Baldwin take up, once again, the story of his life, but this time with film as his aide. And like *No Name in the Street*, which includes his reflections on policing, incarceration, and race that foreshadow the scholarship to come, *The Devil Finds Work* does something similar with film as Baldwin explores and examines the workings of the movies in the making and remaking of race in America. That exploration also helps us to see his own effort at self-creation, the shifts in how he accounts for his stepfather and in how he possesses his own story, and what it all means not only for himself but for the nation. "The eldest can be, God knows, as much a burden as a help," he writes, "and is doomed to be something of a mystery for those growing up behind him—a mystery when not, indeed, an intolerable exasperation. *I*, nevertheless, was the eldest, a responsibility I did not intend to fail, and my first calculation as to how to go about defeating the world's intentions for me and mine began on that Saturday afternoon in what we called *the movies*, but which was actually my first entrance into the cinema of my mind." A familiar note with a seasoned pen.

My own encounters with Baldwin over the years come with a torrent of emotions. (And this goes beyond my utter shock, as someone from the coast of Mississippi, that he did not like grits, with or without sugar.) Reading him I am left angry at the

INTRODUCTION

country's state of affairs *and* called to love. I am pushed to examine my pain and wounds—to run towards my fears, to resist the damning comfort of safety—*and* urged to show mercy and grace. Reading him feels at times like being swept up by the gale-force winds of a raging storm *and* being held by a lover who tends, with soft hands, to the soul. His sentences carry the weight of it all. Elegant and rhythmic. Emotional and tender. Never bitter, even when piping hot. As Toni Morrison said, Baldwin gifted us (me) "a language to dwell in." All the while he spoke with what Matthew Arnold described as "fire and strength" to a nation that refused to grow up. On the day of his funeral at the Cathedral Church of St. John the Divine in Manhattan in December of 1987, Morrison called attention to the courage of Baldwin's witness:

Yours was the courage to live life in and from its belly as well as beyond its edges, to see and say what it was, to recognize and identify evil but never fear or stand in awe of it. It is a courage that came from a ruthless intelligence married to a pity so profound it could convince anyone who cared to know that those who despised us "need the moral authority of their former slaves, who are the only people in the world who know anything about them and who may be, indeed, the only people in the world who really care about them."*

To read Baldwin's essays is to confront honestly and without flinching the country, the world, *and* oneself—and, as the reader will see, that is no cakewalk.

It seems to me that reading Baldwin, returning to him again and again, offers us an opportunity to engage in the soul craft his essays demand. We do so not as a narcissistic preoccupation apart from the world and its ugliness; we do so because we realize the world desperately needs better human beings, and that requires a willingness to confront the ugliness in us.

---

* Toni Morrison, "James Baldwin: His Voice Remembered; His Life in Language," in *The New York Times*, December 20, 1987, Sunday edition, 27. https://archive.nytimes.com/www.nytimes.com/books/98/03/29/specials/baldwin-morrison.html

JAMES BALDWIN

You survive this and in some terrible way, which I suppose no one can ever describe, you are compelled, you are corralled, you are bullwhipped into dealing with whatever it is that hurt you. And what is crucial here is that if it hurt you, that is not what's important. Everybody's hurt. What is important, what corrals you, what bullwhips you, what drives you, torments you, is that you must find some way of using this to connect you with everyone else alive. . . . You must understand that your pain is trivial except insofar as you can use it to connect with other people's pain; and insofar as you can do that . . . you can be released from it, and then hopefully it works the other way around too; insofar as I can tell you what it is to suffer, perhaps I can help you to suffer less.*

Baldwin's writings urge us to descend into the belly of life, to step beyond the edges of the world, to imagine that world as it could be (to imagine ourselves as we could be), and to do the hard work, with love, in making it all real and felt in the marrow of the bone.

*

Paris in December is dreary. The sun sulks behind clouds. The cold hints that soon, in a matter of days, it will become bitter, the startling benediction of warm fires and oversized coats. The dreariness doesn't stop the Christmas shopping or dim the holiday lights. Throngs of people move about the shops and cafés. Some smile. Some hold hands. Others have the typical look of Parisian disregard. An older man, with a beard brown with cigarette smoke and a large cross dangling from his neck amid layers of clothes, sits on the subway steps begging. Politely. It feels familiar. No one stops as he asks for money. Above ground, a young Indian couple rub noses as their eyes glimmer with love. Another older man stands with his grandchild for a photograph against the lighted backdrop of the Galeries Lafayette. A Muslim woman sits on the sidewalk with her child wrapped in a heavy shawl. Their cheeks chapped red. She quietly asks for food.

    I wonder how James Baldwin survived here in 1948. Young, Black, queer, and poor. He had never traveled outside of the

---

* James Baldwin, "The Artist's Struggle for Integrity," in James Baldwin, *The Cross of Redemption: Uncollected Writings*, ed. Randall Kenan (New York: Vintage International, 2011), 52.

INTRODUCTION

United States and did not speak the language. The periodic silence gifted a different kind of perception. "The City of Light" afforded him an occasion to escape the horrors of American life—to leave behind, so he thought, the assumptions that sought to suffocate his dreams and force him to believe what the world said about him. In America, he was, and could only be, a "nigger." In Paris, Baldwin fashioned himself into the writer— the poet—he imagined himself to be. But he refused to trade the American fantasy for another soporific French one—that race somehow didn't matter here. The brown faces of Algerians betrayed that lie. No more sleepwalking. His big eyes were now wide open. Paris gave Baldwin the space to breathe fully; it helped unleash the thinking about the place called America that, whatever it was or could be, belonged to him. That journey from Harlem to Paris and back again gave the world a body of writing that is, at once, unsettling and beautiful.

Eddie S. Glaude Jr.
Paris, December 2023

EDDIE S. GLAUDE JR. is the James S. McDonnell Distinguished University Professor at Princeton University. He is the author of several books, including *We Are the Leaders We Have Been Looking For*, *Democracy in Black*, and the *New York Times* bestseller, *Begin Again: James Baldwin's America and its Urgent Lessons for Our Own*, winner of the Harriet Beecher Stowe Book Prize. He is a native of Moss Point, Mississippi.

SELECT BIBLIOGRAPHY

JAMES CAMPBELL, *Talking at the Gates: A Life of James Baldwin*, Viking, 1991; Faber, 1991.
DAVID LEEMING, *James Baldwin: A Biography*, Alfred A. Knopf, Inc., 1994; Michael Joseph, 1994.
HERB BOYD, *Baldwin's Harlem: A Biography of James Baldwin*, Atria Press, 2008.
DOUGLAS FIELD, ed., *A Historical Guide to James Baldwin*, Oxford University Press, 2009.
DOUGLAS FIELD, *All Those Strangers: The Art and Lives of James Baldwin*, Oxford University Press, 2015.
MICHELE ELAM, ed., *The Cambridge Companion to James Baldwin*, Cambridge University Press, 2015.

CHRONOLOGY

DATE	AUTHOR'S LIFE	LITERARY CONTEXT
1924	James Arthur Jones born in Harlem, New York (August 2), to Emma Berdis Jones.	O'Neill: *Desire Under the Elms*. Forster: *A Passage to India*. Neruda: *Twenty Love Poems*.
1925		Harold Ross founds *The New Yorker*. Fitzgerald: *The Great Gatsby*. Cullen: *Color*. ed. Locke: *The New Negro*. Gide: *The Counterfeiters*.
1926		Hemingway: *The Sun Also Rises*. Hughes: *The Weary Blues*.
1927	Baldwin's mother marries Reverend David Baldwin, a factory worker and lay preacher, who adopts James. Over the next sixteen years the couple have eight children.	Proust: *In Search of Lost Time*. Wilder: *The Bridge of San Luis Rey*.
1928		Lawrence: *Lady Chatterley's Lover*. McKay: *Home to Harlem*.
1929	Attends Public School 24 in Harlem. Begins writing and reading avidly.	Faulkner: *The Sound and the Fury*. Hemingway: *A Farewell to Arms*. Larsen: *Passing*. Cocteau: *The Terrible Children*.
1930		Faulkner: *As I Lay Dying*. Hammett: *The Maltese Falcon*. Hughes: *Not Without Laughter*. Johnson: *Black Manhattan*.
1931		Schuyler: *Black No More*.
1932		Caldwell: *Tobacco Road*. Faulkner: *Light in August*. Huxley: *Brave New World*. Runyon: *Guys and Dolls*.
1933		Stein: *The Autobiography of Alice B. Toklas*.
1934		Fitzgerald: *Tender Is the Night*. H. Miller: *Tropic of Cancer*. Hughes: *The Ways of White Folk*. Malraux: *Man's Fate*.

HISTORICAL EVENTS

Death of Lenin. Indian Citizenship Act gives indigenous people right to US citizenship.

Ku Klux Klan marches in Washington.

Germany admitted to League of Nations.

Lindbergh's solo Atlantic flight. First "talkie," *The Jazz Singer*.

Hoover elected US president. Fleming discovers penicillin.

Wall Street Crash. Period of worldwide Depression begins.

Mahatma Gandhi begins civil disobedience movement in India.

US unemployment reaches 8 million. British Commonwealth founded. Roosevelt elected US president.

Roosevelt announces New Deal. Prohibition repealed. Billie Holiday's first recording.
Stalin's purge of the Communist Party begins. Hitler becomes dictator of Germany.

JAMES BALDWIN

DATE	AUTHOR'S LIFE	LITERARY CONTEXT
1935	Starts at Frederick Douglass Junior High School where he is taught by Countee Cullen, poet and one of the leading figures of the Harlem Renaissance.	Lewis: *It Can't Happen Here*. Steinbeck: *Tortilla Flat*. Du Bois: *Black Reconstruction in America*.
1936		Eliot: *Collected Poems*. Faulkner: *Absalom, Absalom!* Mitchell: *Gone with the Wind*.
1937		Hemingway: *To Have and Have Not*. Hurston: *Their Eyes Were Watching God*. Steinbeck: *Of Mice and Men*.
1938	Begins preaching as a junior minister at Fireside Pentecostal Assembly, Harlem. Attends the prestigious DeWitt Clinton High School in the Bronx where he edits *The Magpie*, the school's literary journal, working alongside Richard Avedon, later one of America's best known photographers.	Dos Passos: *USA*. Wright: *Uncle Tom's Children*. Sartre: *Nausea*.
1939		Joyce: *Finnegans Wake*. Steinbeck: *The Grapes of Wrath*.
1940	The painter Beauford Delaney becomes his mentor.	Hemingway: *For Whom the Bell Tolls*. Wright: *Native Son*. Du Bois: *Dusk of Dawn*. Hughes: *The Big Sea*.
1941		Fitzgerald: *The Last Tycoon*. O'Neill: *Long Day's Journey into Night*.
1942	Graduates from DeWitt Clinton High School. Renounces the ministry.	Camus: *The Outsider*. Eliot: *Four Quartets*.
1943	Death of his stepfather. Moves to Greenwich Village, New York. Begins writing first novel, taking odd jobs to support himself.	Sartre: *Being and Nothingness*. Saint-Exupéry: *The Little Prince*.
1944	Meets writer Richard Wright.	Myrdal: *An American Dilemma*. Smith: *Strange Fruit*. Williams: *The Glass Menagerie*. Borges: *Fictions*.

CHRONOLOGY

HISTORICAL EVENTS

National Labor Relations Act gives US workers right to join unions. Penguin publishes first paperbacks. Gershwin's *Porgy and Bess* opens in New York.

Spanish Civil War (to 1939). Black American athlete Jesse Owens wins four gold medals at Olympic Games in Berlin.

Japanese invasion of China. *Hindenburg* airship explodes in New Jersey.

Germany annexes Austria; Munich crisis. Actor Orson Welles causes panic in US with radio broadcast of *The War of the Worlds*.

Nazi–Soviet Pact; Hitler invades Poland. World War II begins.

Churchill prime minister in UK. Fall of France. Battle of Britain.

Japan attacks Pearl Harbor; US enters war. Hitler invades Soviet Union.

North African campaign. Battle of Midway. First nuclear reactor constructed at University of Chicago. *Billboard* magazine publishes "Harlem Hit Parade," the first Black record chart.
Allies land in Italy. Jitterbug dance becomes popular in US.

Allied (D-Day) landings in Normandy. Liberation of Paris.

JAMES BALDWIN

DATE	AUTHOR'S LIFE	LITERARY CONTEXT
1945		Orwell: *Animal Farm*. Sartre: *The Age of Reason*. Waugh: *Brideshead Revisited*. Wright: *Black Boy*.
1946	First book review published in *The Nation*, on Maxim Gorki. Wins Eugene F. Saxton Memorial Trust Fellowship.	Isherwood: *The Berlin Stories*. O'Neill: *The Iceman Cometh*.
1947		Williams: *A Streetcar Named Desire*. Camus: *The Plague*. Sartre: *Existentialism and Humanism*.
1948	First short story, "Previous Condition," published in *Commentary*. Wins a Rosenwald Foundation Fellowship. Leaves the US to escape discrimination and settles in Paris.	Greene: *The Heart of the Matter*. Mailer: *The Naked and the Dead*.
1949	First essay, "Everybody's Protest Novel," published in *Partisan Review*.	Beauvoir: *The Second Sex*. A. Miller: *Death of a Salesman*. Orwell: *Nineteen Eighty-Four*.
1950		Ionesco: *The Bald Prima Donna*.
1951		Salinger: *The Catcher in the Rye*. Hughes: *Montage of a Dream Deferred*. Yourcenar: *Memoirs of Hadrian*.
1952	Returns, briefly, to America.	Beckett: *Waiting for Godot*. Ellison: *Invisible Man*. A. Miller: *The Crucible*. Steinbeck: *East of Eden*.
1953	First novel, *Go Tell It on the Mountain*, published by Knopf to rave reviews.	Bellow: *The Adventures of Augie March*. Wright: *The Outsider*.
1954	Wins a Guggenheim Fellowship. Second novel, *Giovanni's Room*, rejected by Knopf because of homosexual content.	K. Amis: *Lucky Jim*. Sagan: *Bonjour Tristesse*.
1955	*Notes of a Native Son* (essays) published. First play, *The Amen Corner*, produced at Howard University.	Nabokov: *Lolita*. Williams: *Cat on a Hot Tin Roof*.
1956	After several more rejections, *Giovanni's Room* is published by Dial. Begins writing *Another*	Ginsberg: *Howl and Other Poems*. Wright: *The Color Curtain*.

CHRONOLOGY

HISTORICAL EVENTS

Roosevelt dies; Truman president. Unconditional surrender of Germany. US drops atomic bombs on Hiroshima and Nagasaki. End of World War II. Wave of strikes in America (to 1946). United Nations founded.

USSR extends influence in Eastern Europe. Beginning of Cold War. Indochina War.

Independence of India and Pakistan. Central Intelligence Agency (CIA) created in US.

Jewish state of Israel founded. Arab–Israeli War. Assassination of Gandhi in India. Apartheid introduced in South Africa. US military allows Black and white soldiers to serve together. The *Empire Windrush* brings one of the first large groups of immigrants from the Caribbean to Britain.

Communists win Chinese Civil War. North Atlantic Treaty signed.

Korean War begins (to 1953). Beginning of McCarthy's campaign against communists in US.

Eisenhower elected US president. Accession of Elizabeth II in UK. Mau Mau rebellion against British colonial rule in Kenya.

Death of Stalin.

French withdraw from Vietnam; Vietnam War begins. Algerian War of Independence begins. Racial segregation in US schools declared unconstitutional.

Warsaw Pact between Soviet Union and several Eastern European countries. Rosa Parks refuses to give up her seat to a white person on a bus, leading to Montgomery Bus Boycott. Vietnam War

Soviets invade Hungary. Suez crisis.

JAMES BALDWIN

DATE	AUTHOR'S LIFE	LITERARY CONTEXT
1956 cont.	*Country* (novel). Wins award from National Institute of Arts and Letters and a Partisan Review Fellowship.	Osborne: *Look Back in Anger*.
1957	Travels through the Southern states of America, becomes involved in the civil rights movement, meets Martin Luther King and Malcolm X. "Sonny's Blues," one of Baldwin's best known short stories, published in *Partisan Review*.	Kerouac: *On the Road*. Wright: *White Man, Listen!* Camus: *Exile and the Kingdom*. Pasternak: *Doctor Zhivago*.
1958		Achebe: *Things Fall Apart*. Capote: *Breakfast at Tiffany's*. Genet: *The Blacks*.
1959	Wins a Ford Foundation grant.	Bellow: *Henderson the Rain King*. Burroughs: *Naked Lunch*. Queneau: *Zazie in the Metro*. Cortázar: "Blow-Up."
1960		Achebe: *No Longer at Ease*. Lee: *To Kill a Mockingbird*. Updike: *Rabbit, Run*.
1961	*Nobody Knows My Name* (essays) published. "The Black Boy Looks at the White Boy" in *Esquire*, replies to Norman Mailer's criticisms in *Advertisements for Myself*. Travels to Istanbul.	Heller: *Catch-22*. Naipaul: *A House for Mr. Biswas*. Fanon: *The Wretched of the Earth*.
1962	*Another Country* published. Travels to Africa. Receives the National Conference of Christian and Jews Brotherhood Award.	Nabokov: *Pale Fire*. Solzhenitsyn: *One Day in the Life of Ivan Denisovich*.
1963	The first half of "The Fire Next Time" (essay) is published in the *New Yorker* and the other in the *Progressive*. As a book, it becomes the first essay to spend 41 weeks in the top five of the *New York Times* Bestseller List. Meets with Robert Kennedy. Leads civil rights demonstration in Paris. Makes a prominent appearance at Martin Luther King's speech	Plath: *The Bell Jar*. Pynchon. *V*. Cortázar: *Hopscotch*.

CHRONOLOGY

HISTORICAL EVENTS

Civil Rights Commission established to safeguard voting rights in US. Ghana becomes first sub-Saharan African colony to achieve independence from Britain (all but one – Namibia – of the others gain independence by 1966). USSR launches Sputnik satellite.

Race riots in Notting Hill (London) and Nottingham. Alaska becomes 49th state of the US. First stereo record is introduced.

Castro seizes power in Cuba.

John F. Kennedy elected US president. African-American students stage sit-ins in North Carolina. British prime minister Harold Macmillan's "Wind of Change" speech accepts inevitable wind-down of British empire. Sharpeville massacre in South Africa. Vietcong formed in Hanoi. Contraceptive pill approved for use in the US (UK 1961).
Massacre of Algerian demonstrators by Paris police. Erection of Berlin Wall. Bay of Pigs invasion. US gives military assistance to South Vietnam. Freedom Rides organized by the Congress of Racial Equality in US southern states.

Cuban missile crisis. Algeria gains independence from France. Illinois becomes the first US state to decriminalize homosexual acts between consenting adults. Independence of Jamaica and of Trinidad and Tobago. Death of actress Marilyn Monroe.
Assassination of President Kennedy. Martin Luther King's March on Washington features his "I Have a Dream Speech." Church bombing in Birmingham, Alabama.

JAMES BALDWIN

DATE	AUTHOR'S LIFE	LITERARY CONTEXT
1963 cont.	during the March on Washington. Second trip to Africa. Wins George Polk Award and is featured on the cover of *Time Magazine*.	
1964	*Blues for Mister Charlie* (play) produced and published. Wins Foreign Drama Critics Award. *Nothing Personal* (collaboration with Richard Avedon) published.	Achebe: *Arrow of God*. Bellow: *Herzog*. Ellison: *Shadow and Act*.
1965	*Going to Meet the Man* (short stories) published. Debates with William F. Buckley Jr. at Cambridge. Travels to Israel with production of *The Amen Corner*.	Malcolm X: *The Autobiography of Malcolm X*. Brown: *Manchild in the Promised Land*. King: *Why We Can't Wait*.
1966		Achebe: *A Man of the People*. Capote: *In Cold Blood*. Pynchon: *The Crying of Lot 49*.
1967		Márquez: *One Hundred Years of Solitude*. Styron: *The Confessions of Nat Turner*.
1968	*Tell Me How Long the Train's Been Gone* (novel) published. *Amen Corner* (play) published. Agrees to write screenplay of *The Autobiography of Malcolm X* for Columbia Pictures but later pulls out. Helps raise funds with Martin Luther King. Following King's assassination moves to St. Paul de Vence, France.	Cleaver: *Soul on Ice*. Solzhenitsyn: *Cancer Ward*.
1969		Angelou: *I Know Why the Caged Bird Sings*. Roth: *Portnoy's Complaint*. Vonnegut: *Slaughterhouse-Five*.
1970	Directs *Fortune and Men's Eyes*, a play by John Herbert, in Istanbul.	Morrison: *The Bluest Eye*.
1971	*A Rap on Race* (non-fiction), with anthropologist Margaret Mead, published.	Updike: *Rabbit Redux*. Welty: *The Optimist's Daughter*.
1972	*No Name in the Street* (essays) published. *A Dialogue* (with Nikki Giovanni) published.	

CHRONOLOGY

HISTORICAL EVENTS

Riots in Harlem, New Jersey, Chicago, and Philadelphia. US Civil Rights Act prohibits discrimination. Martin Luther King wins Nobel Peace Prize. Nelson Mandela begins life sentence in South Africa.

Malcolm X assassinated. Race riots in Los Angeles. Martin Luther King leads civil rights march from Selma to Montgomery. US Voting Rights Act. First US ground troops sent to Vietnam. US military intervention in Dominican Republic. First Race Relations Act in UK.

Start of Cultural Revolution, Maoist purge in China (to 1976). First transgender riot in San Francisco. Formation of the "Black Power" Black Panthers Party in US.
Arab–Israeli Six-Day War. President Johnson commissions a report on racial violence in US. Escalation of anti-war protests in US. Supreme Court overrules laws forbidding interracial marriage. Branch of Black Panthers formed in UK.
Student unrest in US and Europe; national strike in France. My Lai massacre. Assassination of Martin Luther King. Soviet invasion of Czechoslovakia. Robert Kennedy assassinated. Riots at Democratic National Convention in Chicago. Nixon elected US president. US Fair Housing Act bans discrimination in housing. Tory MP Enoch Powell's incendiary anti-immigration "Rivers of Blood" speech in Birmingham, UK.

Americans land first man on the moon. Gay community in Greenwich Village riots after police raid on the Stonewall Inn.

World Trade Center in New York becomes the world's tallest building. First Gay Pride march in New York.

Death of Louis Armstrong.

USSR and USA sign Strategic Arms Limitation Treaty (SALT). Nixon makes historic visit to China. President Idi Amin expells Ugandan Asians.

JAMES BALDWIN

DATE	AUTHOR'S LIFE	LITERARY CONTEXT
1973		Pynchon: *Gravity's Rainbow*. Solzhenitsyn: *The Gulag Archipelago* (to 1975).
1974	*If Beale Street Could Talk* (novel) published.	
1975		Levi: *The Periodic Table*.
1976	*The Devil Finds Work* (essays) published. Collaborates with Yoran Cazac on *Little Man, Little Man: A Story of Childhood* (children's book).	Haley: *Roots: The Saga of an American Family*. Carver: *Will You Please Be Quiet Please?* Walker: *Meridian*.
1977		Morrison: *Song of Solomon*. Wright: *American Hunger*.
1978		Irving: *The World According to Garp*.
1979	*Just Above My Head* (novel) published. Travels to Russia for a symposium of American and Soviet writers.	Gordimer: *Burger's Daughter*. Phillips: *Black Tickets*. Calvino: *If on a winter's night a traveler*.
1980		Eco: *The Name of the Rose*.
1981		Rushdie: *Midnight's Children*. Updike: *Rabbit Is Rich*. Márquez: *Chronicle of a Death Foretold*.
1982		Walker: *The Color Purple*. Allende: *The House of the Spirits*.
1983	*Jimmy's Blues* (poems) published. Takes up Professorship of Literature and Afro-American Studies at Five College Network in Amherst, Massachusetts.	Wilson: *Fences*.
1984		Updike: *The Witches of Eastwick*.
1985	*The Evidence of Things Not Seen* (essays) and *The Price of the Ticket* (essays) published.	Atwood: *The Handmaid's Tale*. DeLillo: *White Noise*. Márquez: *Love in the Time of Cholera*.
1986	Awarded Légion d'honneur by President Mitterrand of France. Makes second trip to Russia and meets Mikhail Gorbachev.	
1987	Dies of stomach cancer in France (December 1). Thousands attend funeral service in New York.	Achebe: *Anthills of the Savannah*. Morrison: *Beloved*. Wilson: *The Piano Lesson*. Wolfe: *The Bonfire of the Vanities*.

CHRONOLOGY

HISTORICAL EVENTS

Yom Kippur War. Oil crisis. Legalization of abortion in US. Ceasefire signed; last US troops leave Vietnam.

Nixon resigns in wake of Watergate scandal.

Saigon falls to the Vietcong. End of Vietnam War. G6 Group founded (becomes G7 1975, G8 1997).
Death of Mao Tse-Tung. Carter elected US president. Commission for Racial Equality set up in UK.

First Apple computers go on sale. Death of Elvis Presley.

Camp David agreement between US, Egypt and Israel.

Carter and Brezhnev sign SALT-2 Arms Limitation Treaty. Soviets occupy Afghanistan. Iranian revolution; Iran hostage crisis.

Reagan US president. Former Beatle John Lennon shot dead in New York. Egyptian president Sadat assassinated. First cases of AIDS detected in US. Race riots in Brixton, London, Toxteth (Liverpool), Chapeltown (Leeds), and Handsworth (Birmingham).

Falklands War.

US troops invade Grenada. Vanessa Williams becomes first Black Miss America.

Famine in Ethiopia. Indira Gandhi assassinated.
Gorbachev becomes General Secretary of the Communist Party in USSR. Vaal Uprising in apartheid South Africa.

Gorbachev–Reagan summit. State of Emergency in South Africa. Chernobyl nuclear power accident.

"Black Monday" – stock markets crash around the world. In the UK, four MPs from ethnic minorities are elected, the first since 1929.

THE FIRE
NEXT TIME

for James
 James
 Luc James

*"God gave Noah the rainbow sign,
No more water, the fire next time!"*

CONTENTS

MY DUNGEON SHOOK:
*Letter to My Nephew on the
One Hundredth Anniversary
of the Emancipation*   7

DOWN AT THE CROSS:
Letter from a Region in My Mind   15

MY DUNGEON SHOOK

Letter to My Nephew
on the One Hundredth Anniversary
of the Emancipation

Dear James:

I HAVE BEGUN this letter five times and torn it up five times. I keep seeing your face, which is also the face of your father and my brother. Like him, you are tough, dark, vulnerable, moody—with a very definite tendency to sound truculent because you want no one to think you are soft. You may be like your grandfather in this, I don't know, but certainly both you and your father resemble him very much physically. Well, he is dead, he never saw you, and he had a terrible life; he was defeated long before he died because, at the bottom of his heart, he really believed what white people said about him. This is one of the reasons that he became so holy. I am sure that your father has told you something about all that. Neither you nor your father exhibit any tendency towards holiness: you really *are* of another era, part of what happened when the Negro left the land and came into what the late E. Franklin Frazier called "the cities of destruction." You can only be destroyed by believing that you really are what the white world calls a *nigger*. I tell you this because I love you, and please don't you ever forget it.

I have known both of you all your lives, have carried your Daddy in my arms and on my shoulders, kissed and spanked him and watched him learn to walk. I don't know if you've known anybody from that far back; if you've loved anybody that long, first as an infant, then as a child, then as a man, you gain a strange perspective on time and human pain and effort. Other people cannot see what I see whenever I look into your father's face, for behind your father's face as it is today are all those other faces which were his. Let him laugh and I see a cellar your father does not remember and a house he does not remember and I hear in his present laughter his laughter as a child. Let him curse and I remember him falling down the cellar steps, and howling, and I remember, with pain, his tears, which my hand or your grandmother's so easily wiped away. But no one's hand can wipe away those tears he sheds invisibly today, which one hears in his laughter and in his speech and in his songs. I know what the world has done to my brother and how narrowly he has survived it. And I know, which is much worse, and this is the crime of which I accuse my country and my countrymen, and for which neither I nor time nor history will ever forgive them, that they have destroyed and are destroying hundreds of thousands of lives and do not know it and do not want to know it. One can be, indeed one must strive to become, tough and philosophical concerning destruction and death, for this is what most of mankind has been best at since we have heard of man. (But remember: *most* of mankind is not *all* of mankind.) But it is not permissible that the authors of devastation should also be innocent. It is the innocence which constitutes the crime.

Now, my dear namesake, these innocent and well-meaning people, your countrymen, have caused you to be born under conditions not very far removed from those described for us by Charles Dickens in the London of more than a hundred years ago. (I hear the chorus of the innocents screaming, "No! This is not true! How *bitter* you are!"—but I am writing this letter to *you*, to try to tell you something about how to handle *them*, for most of them do not yet really know that you exist. I *know* the conditions under which you were born, for I was there. Your countrymen were *not* there, and haven't made it yet. Your grandmother was also there, and no one has ever accused her of being bitter. I suggest that the innocents check with her. She isn't hard to find. Your countrymen don't know that *she* exists, either, though she has been working for them all their lives.)

Well, you were born, here you came, something like fifteen years ago; and though your father and mother and grandmother, looking about the streets through which they were carrying you, staring at the walls into which they brought you, had every reason to be heavyhearted, yet they were not. For here you were, Big James, named for me—you were a big baby, I was not—here you were: to be loved. To be loved, baby, hard, at once, and forever, to strengthen you against the loveless world. Remember that: I know how black it looks today, for you. It looked bad that day, too, yes, we were trembling. We have not stopped trembling yet, but if we had not loved each other none of us would have survived. And now you must survive because we love you, and for the sake of your children and your children's children.

This innocent country set you down in a ghetto in which, in fact, it intended that you should perish. Let me spell out precisely what I mean by that, for the heart of the matter is here, and the root of my dispute with my country. You were born where you were born and faced the future that you faced because you were black and *for no other reason*. The limits of your ambition were, thus, expected to be set forever. You were born into a society which spelled out with brutal clarity, and in as many ways as possible, that you were a worthless human being. You were not expected to aspire to excellence: you were expected to make peace with mediocrity. Wherever you have turned, James, in your short time on this earth, you have been told where you could go and what you could do (and *how* you could do it) and where you could live and whom you could marry. I know your countrymen do not agree with me about this, and I hear them saying, "You exaggerate." They do not know Harlem, and I do. So do you. Take no one's word for anything, including mine—but trust your experience. Know whence you came. If you know whence you came, there is really no limit to where you can go. The details and symbols of your life have been deliberately constructed to make you believe what white people say about you. Please try to remember that what they believe, as well as what they do and cause you to endure, does not testify to your inferiority but to their inhumanity and fear. Please try to be clear, dear James, through the storm which rages about your youthful head today, about the reality which lies behind the words *acceptance* and *integration*. There is no reason for you to try to become like white people and there is no basis whatever for their impertinent assumption that *they* must accept *you*. The really terrible thing, old buddy, is that *you* must accept *them*. And I mean that very seriously.

You must accept them and accept them with love. For these innocent people have no other hope. They are, in effect, still trapped in a history which they do not understand; and until they understand it, they cannot be released from it. They have had to believe for many years, and for innumerable reasons, that black men are inferior to white men. Many of them, indeed, know better, but, as you will discover, people find it very difficult to act on what they know. To act is to be committed, and to be committed is to be in danger. In this case, the danger, in the minds of most white Americans, is the loss of their identity. Try to imagine how you would feel if you woke up one morning to find the sun shining and all the stars aflame. You would be frightened because it is out of the order of nature. Any upheaval in the universe is terrifying because it so profoundly attacks one's sense of one's own reality. Well, the black man has functioned in the white man's world as a fixed star, as an immovable pillar: and as he moves out of his place, heaven and earth are shaken to their foundations. You, don't be afraid. I said that it was intended that you should perish in the ghetto, perish by never being allowed to go behind the white man's definitions, by never being allowed to spell your proper name. You have, and many of us have, defeated this intention; and, by a terrible law, a terrible paradox, those innocents who believed that your imprisonment made them safe are losing their grasp of reality. But these men are your brothers—your lost, younger brothers. And if the word *integration* means anything, this is what it means: that we, with love, shall force our brothers to see themselves as they are, to cease fleeing from reality and begin to change it. For this is your home, my friend, do not be driven from it; great men have done great things here, and will again, and we can make America what America must become. It will be hard, James, but you come from sturdy, peasant stock, men who picked cotton and dammed rivers and built railroads, and, in the teeth of the most terrifying odds, achieved an unassailable and monumental dignity. You come from a long line of great poets, some of the greatest poets since Homer. One of them said, *The very time I thought I was lost, My dungeon shook and my chains fell off.*

You know, and I know, that the country is celebrating one hundred years of freedom one hundred years too soon. We cannot be free until they are free. God bless you, James, and Godspeed.

Your uncle,
James

DOWN AT THE CROSS

Letter from a Region in My Mind

Take up the White Man's burden—
Ye dare not stoop to less—
Nor call too loud on Freedom
To cloak your weariness;
By all ye cry or whisper,
By all ye leave or do,
The silent, sullen peoples
Shall weigh your Gods and you.
—KIPLING

Down at the cross where my Saviour died,
Down where for cleansing from sin I cried,
There to my heart was the blood applied,
Singing glory to His name!
—HYMN

I UNDERWENT, DURING the summer that I became fourteen, a prolonged religious crisis. I use the word "religious" in the common, and arbitrary, sense, meaning that I then discovered God, His saints and angels, and His blazing Hell. And since I had been born in a Christian nation, I accepted this Deity as the only one. I supposed Him to exist only within the walls of a church—in fact, of *our* church—and I also supposed that God and safety were synonymous. The word "safety" brings us to the real meaning of the word "religious" as we use it. Therefore, to state it in another, more accurate way, I became, during my fourteenth year, for the first time in my life, afraid—afraid of the evil within me and afraid of the evil without. What I saw around me that summer in Harlem was what I had always seen; nothing had changed. But now, without any warning, the whores and pimps and racketeers on the Avenue had become a personal menace. It had not before occurred to me that I could become one of them, but now I realized that we had been produced by the same circumstances. Many of my comrades were clearly headed for the Avenue, and my father said that I was headed that way, too. My friends began to drink and smoke, and embarked—at first avid, then groaning—on their sexual careers. Girls, only slightly older than I was, who sang in the choir or taught Sunday school, the children of holy parents, underwent, before my eyes, their incredible metamorphosis, of which the most bewildering aspect was not their budding breasts or their rounding behinds but something deeper and more subtle, in their eyes, their heat, their odor, and the inflection of their voices. Like the strangers on the Avenue, they became, in the twinkling of an eye, unutterably different and fantastically *present*. Owing to the way I had been raised, the abrupt discomfort that all this aroused in me and the fact that

I had no idea what my voice or my mind or my body was likely to do next caused me to consider myself one of the most depraved people on earth. Matters were not helped by the fact that these holy girls seemed rather to enjoy my terrified lapses, our grim, guilty, tormented experiments, which were at once as chill and joyless as the Russian steppes and hotter, by far, than all the fires of Hell.

Yet there was something deeper than these changes, and less definable, that frightened me. It was real in both the boys and the girls, but it was, somehow, more vivid in the boys. In the case of the girls, one watched them turning into matrons before they had become women. They began to manifest a curious and really rather terrifying single-mindedness. It is hard to say exactly how this was conveyed: something implacable in the set of the lips, something farseeing (seeing what?) in the eyes, some new and crushing determination in the walk, something peremptory in the voice. They did not tease us, the boys, any more; they reprimanded us sharply, saying, "You better be thinking about your soul!" For the girls also saw the evidence on the Avenue, knew what the price would be, for them, of one misstep, knew that they had to be protected and that we were the only protection there was. They understood that they must act as God's decoys, saving the souls of the boys for Jesus and binding the bodies of the boys in marriage. For this was the beginning of our burning time, and "It is better," said St. Paul—who elsewhere, with a most unusual and stunning exactness, described himself as a "wretched man"—"to marry than to burn." And I began to feel in the boys a curious, wary, bewildered despair, as though they were now settling in for the long, hard winter of life. I did not know then what it was that I was reacting to; I put it to myself that they were letting themselves go. In the same way that the girls were destined to gain as much weight as their mothers, the boys, it was clear, would rise no higher than their fathers. School began to reveal itself, therefore, as a child's game that one could not win, and boys dropped out of school and went to work. My father wanted me to do the same. I refused, even though I no longer had any illusions about what an education could do for me; I had already encountered too many college-graduate handymen. My friends were now "downtown," busy, as they put it, "fighting the man." They began to care less about the way they looked, the way they dressed, the things they did; presently, one found them in twos and threes and fours, in a hallway, sharing a jug of wine or a bottle of whiskey, talking, cursing, fighting, sometimes weeping: lost, and unable to say what it was that oppressed them, except that they knew it was "the man"—the white man. And there seemed to be no way whatever to remove this cloud that stood between them and the sun, between them and love and life and power, between them and whatever it was that they wanted. One did not have to be very bright to realize how little one could do to change one's situation; one did not have to be abnormally sensitive to be worn down to a cutting edge by the incessant and gratuitous humiliation and danger one encountered every working day, all day long. The humiliation did not apply merely to working days, or workers; I was thirteen and was crossing Fifth Avenue on my way to the Forty-second Street library, and the cop in the middle of the street muttered as I passed him, "Why don't you niggers stay uptown where you belong?" When I was ten, and didn't look, certainly, any older, two policemen amused themselves with me by frisking me, making comic (and terrifying) speculations concerning my ancestry and probable sexual prowess, and for good measure, leaving me flat on my back in one of Harlem's empty lots. Just before and then during the Second World War, many of my friends fled into the service, all to be changed there, and rarely for the better, many to be ruined, and many to die. Others fled to other states and cities—that is, to other ghettos. Some went on wine or whiskey or the needle, and are still on it. And others, like me, fled into the church.

For the wages of sin were visible everywhere, in every wine-stained and urine-splashed hallway, in every clanging ambulance bell, in every scar on the faces of the pimps and their whores, in every helpless, newborn baby being brought into this danger, in every knife and pistol fight on the Avenue, and in every disastrous bulletin: a cousin, mother of six, suddenly gone mad, the children parceled out here and there; an indestructible aunt rewarded for years of hard labor by a slow, agonizing death in a terrible small room; someone's bright son blown into eternity by his own hand; another turned robber and carried off to jail. It was a summer of dreadful speculations and discoveries, of which these were not the worst. Crime became real, for example—for the first time—not as *a* possibility but as *the* possibility. One would never defeat one's circumstances by working and saving one's pennies; one would never, by working, acquire that many pennies, and, besides, the social treatment accorded even the most successful Negroes proved that one needed, in order to be free, something more than a bank account. One needed a handle, a lever, a means of inspiring fear. It was absolutely clear that the police would whip you and take you in as long as they could get away with it, and that everyone else—housewives, taxi-drivers, elevator boys, dishwashers, bartenders, lawyers, judges, doctors, and grocers—would never, by the operation of any generous human feeling, cease to use you as an outlet for his frustrations and hostilities. Neither civilized reason nor Christian love would cause any of those people to treat you as they presumably wanted to be treated; only the fear of your power to retaliate would cause them to do that, or to seem to do it, which was (and is) good enough. There appears to be a vast amount of confusion on this point, but I do not know many Negroes who are eager to be "accepted" by white people, still less to be loved by them; they, the blacks, simply don't wish to be beaten over the head by the whites every instant of our brief passage on this planet. White people in this country will have quite enough to do in learning how to accept and love themselves and each other, and when they have achieved this—which will not be tomorrow and may very well be never—the Negro problem will no longer exist, for it will no longer be needed.

People more advantageously placed than we in Harlem were, and are, will no doubt find the psychology and the view of human nature sketched above dismal and shocking in the extreme. But the Negro's experience of the white world cannot possibly create in him any respect for the standards by which the white world claims to live. His own condition is overwhelming proof that white people do not live by these standards. Negro servants have been smuggling odds and ends out of white homes for generations, and white people have been delighted to have them do it, because it has assuaged a dim guilt and testified to the intrinsic superiority of white people. Even the most doltish and servile Negro could scarcely fail to be impressed by the disparity between his situation and that of the people for whom he worked; Negroes who were neither doltish nor servile did not feel that they were doing anything wrong when they robbed white people. In spite of the Puritan-Yankee equation of virtue with well-being, Negroes had excellent reasons for doubting that money was made or kept by any very striking adherence to the Christian virtues; it certainly did not work that way for black Christians. In any case, white people, who had robbed black people of their liberty and who profited by this theft every hour that they lived, had no moral ground on which to stand. They had the judges, the juries, the shotguns, the law—in a word, power. But it was a criminal power, to be feared but not respected, and to be outwitted in any way whatever. And those virtues preached but not practiced by the white world were merely another means of holding Negroes in subjection.

It turned out, then, that summer, that the moral barriers that I had supposed to exist between me and the dangers of a criminal career were so tenuous as to be nearly nonexistent. I certainly could not discover any principled reason for not becoming a criminal, and it is not my poor, God-fearing parents who are to be indicted for the lack but this society. I was icily determined—more determined, really, than I then knew—never to make my peace with the ghetto but to die and go to Hell before I would let any white man spit on me, before I would accept my "place" in this republic. I did not intend to allow the white people of this country to tell me who I was, and limit me that way, and polish me off that way. And yet, of course, at the same time, I *was* being spat on and defined and described and limited, and could have been polished off with no effort whatever. Every Negro boy—in my situation during those years, at least—who reaches this point realizes, at once, profoundly, because he wants to live, that he stands in great peril and must find, with speed, a "thing," a gimmick, to lift him out, to start him on his way. *And it does not matter what the gimmick is.* It was this last realization that terrified me and—since it revealed that the door opened on so many dangers—helped to hurl me into the church. And, by an unforeseeable paradox, it was my career in the church that turned out, precisely, to be my gimmick.

For when I tried to assess my capabilities, I realized that I had almost none. In order to achieve the life I wanted, I had been dealt, it seemed to me, the worst possible hand. I could not become a prizefighter—many of us tried but very few succeeded. I could not sing. I could not dance. I had been well conditioned by the world in which I grew up, so I did not yet dare take the idea of becoming a writer seriously. The only other possibility seemed to involve my becoming one of the sordid people on the Avenue, who were not really as sordid as I then imagined but who frightened me terribly, both because I did not want to live that life and because of what they made me feel. Everything inflamed me, and that was bad enough, but I myself had also become a source of fire and temptation. I had been far too well raised, alas, to suppose that any of the extremely explicit overtures made to me that summer, sometimes by boys and girls but also, more alarmingly, by older men and women, had anything to do with my attractiveness. On the contrary, since the Harlem idea of seduction is, to put it mildly, blunt, whatever these people saw in me merely confirmed my sense of my depravity.

It is certainly sad that the awakening of one's senses should lead to such a merciless judgment of oneself—to say nothing of the time and anguish one spends in the effort to arrive at any other—but it is also inevitable that a literal attempt to mortify the flesh should be made among black people like those with whom I grew up. Negroes in this country—and Negroes do not, strictly or legally speaking, exist in any other—are taught really to despise themselves from the moment their eyes open on the world. This world is white and they are black. White people hold the power, which means that they are superior to blacks (intrinsically, that is: God decreed it so), and the world has innumerable ways of making this difference known and felt and feared. Long before the Negro child perceives this difference, and even longer before he understands it, he has begun to react to it, he has begun to be controlled by it. Every effort made by the child's elders to prepare him for a fate from which they cannot protect him causes him secretly, in terror, to begin to await, without knowing that he is doing so, his mysterious and inexorable punishment. He must be "good" not only in order to please his parents and not only to avoid being punished by them; behind their authority stands another, nameless and impersonal, infinitely harder to please, and bottomlessly cruel. And this filters into the child's consciousness through his parents' tone of voice as he is being exhorted, punished, or loved; in the sudden, uncontrollable note of fear heard in his mother's or his father's voice when he has strayed beyond some particular boundary. He does not know what the boundary is, and he can get no explanation of it, which is frightening enough, but the fear he hears in the voices of his elders is more frightening still. The fear that I heard in my father's voice, for example, when he realized that I really *believed* I could do anything a white boy could do, and had every intention of proving it, was not at all like the fear I heard when one of us was ill or had fallen down the stairs or strayed too far from the house. It was another fear, a fear that the child, in challenging the white world's assumptions, was putting himself in the path of destruction. A child cannot, thank Heaven, know how vast and how merciless is the nature of power, with what unbelievable cruelty people treat each other. He reacts to the fear in his parents' voices because his parents hold up the world for him and he has no protection without them. I defended myself, as I imagined, against the fear my father made me feel by remembering that he was very old-fashioned. Also, I prided myself on the fact that I already knew how to outwit him. To defend oneself against a fear is simply to insure that one will, one day, be conquered by it; fears must be faced. As for one's wits, it is just not true that one can live by them—not, that is, if one wishes really to live. That summer, in any case, all the fears with which I had grown up, and which were now a part of me and controlled my vision of the world, rose up like a wall between the world and me, and drove me into the church.

As I look back, everything I did seems curiously deliberate, though it certainly did not seem deliberate then. For example, I did not join the church of which my father was a member and in which he preached. My best friend in school, who attended a different church, had already "surrendered his life to the Lord," and he was very anxious about my soul's salvation. (I wasn't, but any human attention was better than none.) One Saturday afternoon, he took me to his church. There were no services that day, and the church was empty, except for some women cleaning and some other women praying. My friend took me into the back room to meet his pastor—a woman. There she sat, in her robes, smiling, an extremely proud and handsome woman, with Africa, Europe, and the America of the American Indian blended in her face. She was perhaps forty-five or fifty at this time, and in our world she was a very celebrated woman. My friend was about to introduce me when she looked at me and smiled and said, "Whose little boy are you?" Now this, unbelievably, was precisely the phrase used by pimps and racketeers on the Avenue when they suggested, both humorously and intensely, that I "hang out" with them. Perhaps part of the terror they had caused me to feel came from the fact that I unquestionably wanted to be *somebody's* little boy. I was so frightened, and at the mercy of so many conundrums, that inevitably, that summer, *someone* would have taken me over; one doesn't, in Harlem, long remain standing on any auction block. It was my good luck—perhaps—that I found myself in the church racket instead of some other, and surrendered to a spiritual seduction long before I came to any carnal knowledge. For when the pastor asked me, with that marvelous smile, "Whose little boy are you?" my heart replied at once, "Why, yours."

The summer wore on, and things got worse. I became more guilty and more frightened, and kept all this bottled up inside me, and naturally, inescapably, one night, when this woman had finished preaching, everything came roaring, screaming, crying out, and I fell to the ground before the altar. It was the strangest sensation I have ever had in my life—up to that time, or since. I had not known that it was going to happen, or that it could happen. One moment I was on my feet, singing and clapping and, at the same time, working out in my head the plot of a play I was working on then; the next moment, with no transition, no sensation of falling, I was on my back, with the lights beating down into my face and all the vertical saints above me. I did not know what I was doing down so low, or how I had got there. And the anguish that filled me cannot be described. It moved in me like one of those floods that devastate counties, tearing everything down, tearing children from their parents and lovers from each other, and making everything an unrecognizable waste. All I really remember is the pain, the unspeakable pain; it was as though I were yelling up to Heaven and Heaven would not hear me. And if Heaven would not hear me, if love could not descend from Heaven—to wash me, to make me clean—then utter disaster was my portion. Yes, it does indeed mean something—something unspeakable—to be born, in a white country, an Anglo-Teutonic, antisexual country, black. You very soon, without knowing it, give up all hope of communion. Black people, mainly, look down or look up but do not look at each other, not at you, and white people, mainly, look away. And the universe is simply a sounding drum; there is no way, no way whatever, so it seemed then and has sometimes seemed since, to get through a life, to love your wife and children, or your friends, or your mother and father, or to be loved. The universe, which is not merely the stars and the moon and the planets, flowers, grass, and trees, but *other people*, has evolved no terms for your existence, has made no room for you, and if love will not swing wide the gates, no other power will or can. And if one despairs—as who has not?—of human love, God's love alone is left. But God—and I felt this even then, so long ago, on that tremendous floor, unwillingly—is white. And if His love was so great, and if He loved all His children, why were we, the blacks, cast down so far? Why? In spite of all I said thereafter, I found no answer on the floor—not *that* answer, anyway—and I was on the floor all night. Over me, to bring me "through," the saints sang and rejoiced and prayed. And in the morning, when they raised me, they told me that I was "saved."

Well, indeed I was, in a way, for I was utterly drained and exhausted, and released, for the first time, from all my guilty torment. I was aware then only of my relief. For many years, I could not ask myself why human relief had to be achieved in a fashion at once so pagan and so desperate—in a fashion at once so unspeakably old and so unutterably new. And by the time I was able to ask myself this question, I was also able to see that the principles governing the rites and customs of the churches in which I grew up did not differ from the principles governing the rites and customs of other churches, white. The principles were Blindness, Loneliness, and Terror, the first principle necessarily and actively cultivated in order to deny the two others. I would love to believe that the principles were Faith, Hope, and Charity, but this is clearly not so for most Christians, or for what we call the Christian world.

I was saved. But at the same time, out of a deep, adolescent cunning I do not pretend to understand, I realized immediately that I could not remain in the church merely as another worshipper. I would have to give myself something to do, in order not to be too bored and find myself among all the wretched unsaved of the Avenue. And I don't doubt that I also intended to best my father on his own ground. Anyway, very shortly after I joined the church, I became a preacher—a Young Minister—and I remained in the pulpit for more than three years. My youth quickly made me a much bigger drawing card than my father. I pushed this advantage ruthlessly, for it was the most effective means I had found of breaking his hold over me. That was the most frightening time of my life, and quite the most dishonest, and the resulting hysteria lent great passion to my sermons—for a while. I relished the attention and the relative immunity from punishment that my new status gave me, and I relished, above all, the sudden right to privacy. It had to be recognized, after all, that I was still a schoolboy, with my schoolwork to do, and I was also expected to prepare at least one sermon a week. During what we may call my heyday,

I preached much more often than that. This meant that there were hours and even whole days when I could not be interrupted—not even by my father. I had immobilized him. It took rather more time for me to realize that I had also immobilized myself, and had escaped from nothing whatever.

The church was very exciting. It took a long time for me to disengage myself from this excitement, and on the blindest, most visceral level, I never really have, and never will. There is no music like that music, no drama like the drama of the saints rejoicing, the sinners moaning, the tambourines racing, and all those voices coming together and crying holy unto the Lord. There is still, for me, no pathos quite like the pathos of those multicolored, worn, somehow triumphant and transfigured faces, speaking from the depths of a visible, tangible, continuing despair of the goodness of the Lord. I have never seen anything to equal the fire and excitement that sometimes, without warning, fill a church, causing the church, as Leadbelly and so many others have testified, to "rock." Nothing that has happened to me since equals the power and the glory that I sometimes felt when, in the middle of a sermon, I knew that I was somehow, by some miracle, really carrying, as they said, "the Word"—when the church and I were one. Their pain and their joy were mine, and mine were theirs—they surrendered their pain and joy to me, I surrendered mine to them—and their cries of "Amen!" and "Hallelujah!" and "Yes, Lord!" and "Praise His name!" and "Preach it, brother!" sustained and whipped on my solos until we all became equal, wringing wet, singing and dancing, in anguish and rejoicing, at the foot of the altar. It was, for a long time, in spite of—or, not inconceivably, because of—the shabbiness of my motives, my only sustenance, my meat and drink. I rushed home from school, to the church, to the altar, to be alone there, to commune with Jesus, my dearest Friend, who would never fail me, who knew all the secrets of my heart. Perhaps He did, but I didn't, and the bargain we struck, actually, down there at the foot of the cross, was that He would never let me find out.

He failed His bargain. He was a much better Man than I took Him for. It happened, as things do, imperceptibly, in many ways at once. I date it—the slow crumbling of my faith, the pulverization of my fortress—from the time, about a year after I had begun to preach, when I began to read again. I justified this desire by the fact that I was still in school, and I began, fatally, with Dostoevski. By this time, I was in a high school that was predominantly Jewish. This meant that I was surrounded by people who were, by definition, beyond any hope of salvation, who laughed at the tracts and leaflets I brought to school, and who pointed out that the Gospels had been written long after the death of Christ. This might not have been so distressing if it had not forced me to read the tracts and leaflets myself, for they were indeed, unless one believed their message already, impossible to believe. I remember feeling dimly that there was a kind of blackmail in it. People, I felt, ought to love the Lord *because* they loved Him, and not because they were afraid of going to Hell. I was forced, reluctantly, to realize that the Bible itself had been written by men, and translated by men out of languages I could not read, and I was already, without quite admitting it to myself, terribly involved with the effort of putting words on paper. Of course, I had the rebuttal ready: These men had all been operating under divine inspiration. *Had* they? *All* of them? And I also knew by now, alas, far more about divine inspiration than I dared admit, for I knew how I worked myself up into my own visions, and how frequently—indeed, incessantly—the visions God granted to me differed from the visions He granted to my father. I did not understand the dreams I had at night, but I knew that they were not holy. For that matter, I knew that my waking hours were far from holy. I spent most of my time in a state of repentance for things I had vividly desired to do but had not done. The fact that I was dealing with Jews brought the whole question of color, which I had been desperately avoiding, into the terrified center of my mind. I realized that the Bible had been written by white men. I knew that, according to many Christians, I was a descendant of Ham, who had been cursed, and that I was therefore predestined to be a slave. This had nothing to do with anything I was, or contained, or could become; my fate had been sealed forever, from the beginning of time. And it seemed, indeed, when one looked out over Christendom, that this was what Christendom effectively believed. It was certainly the way it behaved. I remembered the Italian priests and bishops blessing Italian boys who were on their way to Ethiopia.

Again, the Jewish boys in high school were troubling because I could find no point of connection between them and the Jewish pawnbrokers and landlords and grocery-store owners in Harlem. I knew that these people were Jews—God knows I was told it often enough—but I thought of them only as white. Jews, as such, until I got to high school, were all incarcerated in the Old Testament, and their names were Abraham, Moses, Daniel, Ezekiel, and Job, and Shadrach, Meshach, and Abednego. It was bewildering to find them so many miles and centuries out of Egypt, and so far from the fiery furnace. My best friend in high school was a Jew. He came to our house once, and afterward my father asked, as he asked about everyone, "Is he a Christian?"—by which he meant "Is he saved?" I really do not know whether my answer came out of innocence or venom, but I said coldly, "No. He's Jewish." My father slammed me across the face with his great palm, and in that moment everything flooded back—all the hatred and all the fear, and the depth of a merciless resolve to kill my father rather than allow my father to kill me—and I knew that all those sermons and tears and all that repentance and rejoicing had changed nothing. I wondered if I was expected to be glad that a friend of mine, or anyone, was to be tormented forever in Hell, and I also thought, suddenly, of the Jews in another Christian nation, Germany. They were not so far from the fiery furnace after all, and my best friend might have been one of them. I told my father, "He's a better Christian than you are," and walked out of the house. The battle between us was in the open, but that was all right; it was almost a relief. A more deadly struggle had begun.

Being in the pulpit was like being in the theater; I was behind the scenes and knew how the illusion was worked. I knew the other ministers and knew the quality of their lives. And I don't mean to suggest by this the "Elmer Gantry" sort of hypocrisy concerning sensuality; it was a deeper, deadlier, and more subtle hypocrisy than that, and a little honest sensuality, or a lot, would have been like water in an extremely bitter desert. I knew how to work on a congregation until the last dime was surrendered—it was not very hard to do—and I knew where the money for "the Lord's work" went. I knew, though I did not wish to know it, that I had no respect for the people with whom I worked. I could not have said it then, but I also knew that if I continued I would soon have no respect for myself. And the fact that I was "the young Brother Baldwin" increased my value with those same pimps and racketeers who had helped to stampede me into the church in the first place. They still saw the little boy they intended to take over. They were waiting for me to come to my senses and realize that I was in a very lucrative business. They knew that I did not yet realize this, and also that I had not yet begun to suspect where my own needs, *coming up* (they were very patient), could drive me. They themselves did know the score, and they knew that the odds were in their favor. And, really, I knew it, too. I was even lonelier and more vulnerable than I had been before. And the blood of the Lamb had not cleansed me in any way whatever. I was just as black as I had been the day that I was born. Therefore, when I faced a congregation, it began to take all the strength I had not to stammer, not to curse, not to tell them to throw away their Bibles and get off their knees and go home and organize, for example, a rent strike. When I watched all the children, their copper, brown, and beige faces staring up at me as I taught Sunday school, I felt that I was committing a crime in talking about the gentle Jesus, in telling them to reconcile themselves to their misery on earth in order to gain the crown of eternal life. Were only Negroes to gain this crown? Was Heaven, then, to be merely another ghetto? Perhaps I might have been able to reconcile myself even to this if I had been able to believe that there was any loving-kindness to be found in the haven I represented. But I had been in the pulpit too long and I had seen too many monstrous things. I don't refer merely to the glaring fact that the minister eventually acquires houses and Cadillacs while the faithful continue to scrub floors and drop their dimes and quarters and dollars into the plate.

I really mean that there was no love in the church. It was a mask for hatred and self-hatred and despair. The transfiguring power of the Holy Ghost ended when the service ended, and salvation stopped at the church door. When we were told to love everybody, I had thought that that meant *everybody*. But no. It applied only to those who believed as we did, and it did not apply to white people at all. I was told by a minister, for example, that I should never, on any public conveyance, under any circumstances, rise and give my seat to a white woman. White men never rose for Negro women. Well, that was true enough, in the main—I saw his point. But what was the point, the purpose, of *my* salvation if it did not permit me to behave with love toward others, no matter how they behaved toward me? What others did was their responsibility, for which they would answer when the judgment trumpet sounded. But what *I* did was *my* responsibility, and I would have to answer, too—unless, of course, there was also in Heaven a special dispensation for the benighted black, who was not to be judged in the same way as other human beings, or angels. It probably occurred to me around this time that the vision people hold of the world to come is but a reflection, with predictable wishful distortions, of the world in which they live. And this did not apply only to Negroes, who were no more "simple" or "spontaneous" or "Christian" than anybody else—who were merely more oppressed. In the same way that we, for white people, were the descendants of Ham, and were cursed forever, white people were, for us, the descendants of Cain. And the passion with which we loved the Lord was a measure of how deeply we feared and distrusted and, in the end, hated almost all strangers, always, and avoided and despised ourselves.

But I cannot leave it at that; there is more to it than that. In spite of everything, there was in the life I fled a zest and a joy and a capacity for facing and surviving disaster that are very moving and very rare. Perhaps we were, all of us—pimps, whores, racketeers, church members, and children—bound together by the nature of our oppression, the specific and peculiar complex of risks we had to run; if so, within these limits we sometimes achieved with each other a freedom that was close to love. I remember, anyway, church suppers and outings, and, later, after I left the church, rent and waistline parties where rage and sorrow sat in the darkness and did not stir, and we ate and drank and talked and laughed and danced and forgot all about "the man." We had the liquor, the chicken, the music, and each other, and had no need to pretend to be what we were not. This is the freedom that one hears in some gospel songs, for example, and in jazz. In all jazz, and especially in the blues, there is something tart and ironic, authoritative and double-edged. White Americans seem to feel that happy songs are *happy* and sad songs are *sad*, and that, God help us, is exactly the way most white Americans sing them—sounding, in both cases, so helplessly, defenselessly fatuous that one dare not speculate on the temperature of the deep freeze from which issue their brave and sexless little voices. Only people who have been "down the line," as the song puts it, know what this music is about. I think it was Big Bill Broonzy who used to sing "I Feel So Good," a really joyful song about a man who is on his way to the railroad station to meet his girl. She's coming home. It is the singer's incredibly moving exuberance that makes one realize how leaden the time must have been while she was gone. There is no guarantee that she will stay this time, either, as the singer clearly knows, and, in fact, she has not yet actually arrived. Tonight, or tomorrow, or within the next five minutes, he may very well be singing "Lonesome in My Bedroom," or insisting, "Ain't we, ain't we, going to make it all right? Well, if we don't today, we will tomorrow night." White Americans do not understand the depths out of which such an ironic tenacity comes, but they suspect that the force is sensual, and they are terrified of sensuality and do not any longer understand it. The word "sensual" is not intended to bring to mind quivering dusky maidens or priapic black studs. I am referring to something much simpler and much less fanciful. To be sensual, I think, is to respect and rejoice in the force of life, of life itself, and to be *present* in all that one does, from the effort of loving to the breaking of bread. It will be a great day for America, incidentally, when we begin to eat bread again, instead of the blasphemous and tasteless foam rubber that we have substituted for it. And I am not being frivolous now, either. Something very sinister happens to the people of a country when they begin to distrust their own reactions as deeply as they do here, and become as joyless as they have become. It is this individual uncertainty on the part of white American men and women, this inability to renew themselves at the fountain of their own lives, that makes the discussion, let alone elucidation, of any conundrum—that is, any reality—so supremely difficult. The person who distrusts himself has no touchstone for reality—for this touchstone can be only oneself. Such a person interposes between himself and reality nothing less than a labyrinth of attitudes. And these attitudes, furthermore, though the person is usually unaware of it (is unaware of so much!), are historical and public attitudes. They do not relate to the present any more than they relate to the person. Therefore, whatever white people do not know about Negroes reveals, precisely and inexorably, what they do not know about themselves.

White Christians have also forgotten several elementary historical details. They have forgotten that the religion that is now identified with their virtue and their power—"God is on our side," says Dr. Verwoerd—came out of a rocky piece of ground in what is now known as the Middle East before color was invented, and that in order for the Christian church to be established, Christ had to be put to death, by Rome, and that the real architect of the Christian church was not the disreputable, sun-baked Hebrew who gave it his name but the mercilessly fanatical and self-righteous St. Paul. The energy that was buried with the rise of the Christian nations must come back into the world; nothing can prevent it. Many of us, I think, both long to see this happen and are terrified of it, for though this transformation contains the hope of liberation, it also imposes a necessity for great change. But in order to deal with the untapped and dormant force of the previously subjugated, in order to survive as a human, moving, moral weight in the world, America and all the Western nations will be forced to re-examine themselves and release themselves from many things that are now taken to be sacred, and to discard nearly all the assumptions that have been used to justify their lives and their anguish and their crimes so long.

"The white man's Heaven," sings a Black Muslim minister, "is the black man's Hell." One may object—possibly—that this puts the matter somewhat too simply, but the song is true, and it has been true for as long as white men have ruled the world. The Africans put it another way: When the white man came to Africa, the white man had the Bible and the African had the land, but now it is the white man who is being, reluctantly and bloodily, separated from the land, and the African who is still attempting to digest or to vomit up the Bible. The struggle, therefore, that now begins in the world is extremely complex, involving the historical role of Christianity in the realm of power—that is, politics—and in the realm of morals. In the realm of power, Christianity has operated with an unmitigated arrogance and cruelty—necessarily, since a religion ordinarily imposes on those who have discovered the true faith the spiritual duty of liberating the infidels. This particular true faith, moreover, is more deeply concerned about the soul than it is about the body, to which fact the flesh (and the corpses) of countless infidels bears witness. It goes without saying, then, that whoever questions the authority of the true faith also contests the right of the nations that hold this faith to rule over him—contests, in short, their title to his land. The spreading of the Gospel, regardless of the motives or the integrity or the heroism of some of the missionaries, was an absolutely indispensable justification for the planting of the flag. Priests and nuns and school-teachers helped to protect and sanctify the power that was so ruthlessly being used by people who were indeed seeking a city, but not one in the heavens, and one to be made, very definitely, by captive hands. The Christian church itself—again, as distinguished from some of its ministers—sanctified and rejoiced in the conquests of the flag, and encouraged, if it did not formulate, the belief that conquest, with the resulting relative well-being of the Western populations, was proof of the favor of God. God had come a long way from the desert—but then so had Allah, though in a very different direction. God, going north, and rising on the wings of power, had become white, and Allah, out of power, and on the dark side of Heaven, had become—for all practical purposes, anyway—black. Thus, in the realm of morals the role of Christianity has been, at best, ambivalent. Even leaving out of account the remarkable arrogance that assumed that the ways and morals of others were inferior to those of Christians, and that they therefore had every right, and could use any means, to change them, the collision between cultures—and the schizophrenia in the mind of Christendom—had rendered the domain of morals as chartless as the sea once was, and as treacherous as the sea still is. It is not too much to say that whoever wishes to become a truly moral human being (and let us not ask whether or not this is possible; I think we must *believe* that it is possible) must first divorce himself from all the prohibitions, crimes, and hypocrisies of the Christian church. If the concept of God has any validity or any use, it can only be to make us larger, freer, and more loving. If God cannot do this, then it is time we got rid of Him.

I had heard a great deal, long before I finally met him, of the Honorable Elijah Muhammad, and of the Nation of Islam movement, of which he is the leader. I paid very little attention to what I heard, because the burden of his message did not strike me as being very original; I had been hearing variations of it all my life. I sometimes found myself in Harlem on Saturday nights, and I stood in the crowds, at 125th Street and Seventh Avenue, and listened to the Muslim speakers. But I had heard hundreds of such speeches—or so it seemed to me at first. Anyway, I have long had a very definite tendency to tune out the moment I come anywhere near either a pulpit or a soapbox. What these men were saying about white people I had often heard before. And I dismissed the Nation of Islam's demand for a separate black economy in America, which I had also heard before, as willful, and even mischievous, nonsense. Then two things caused me to begin to listen to the speeches, and one was the behavior of the police. After all, I had seen men dragged from their platforms on this very corner for saying less virulent things, and I had seen many crowds dispersed by policemen, with clubs or on horseback. But the policemen were doing nothing now. Obviously, this was not because they had become more human but because they were under orders and because they were afraid. And indeed they were, and I was delighted to see it. There they stood, in twos and threes and fours, in their Cub Scout uniforms and with their Cub Scout faces, totally unprepared, as is the way with American he-men, for anything that could not be settled with a club or a fist or a gun. I might have pitied them if I had not found myself in their hands so often and discovered, through ugly experience, what they were like when *they* held the power and what they were like when *you* held the power. The behavior of the crowd, its silent intensity, was the other thing that forced me to reassess the speakers and their message. I sometimes think, with despair, that Americans will swallow whole any political speech whatever—we've been doing very little else, these last, bad years—so it may not mean anything to say that this sense of integrity, after what Harlem, especially, has been through in the way of demagogues, was a very startling change. Still, the speakers had an air of utter dedication, and the people looked toward them with a kind of intelligence of hope on their faces—not as though they were being consoled or drugged but as though they were being jolted.

Power was the subject of the speeches I heard. We were offered, as Nation of Islam doctrine, historical and divine proof that all white people are cursed, and are devils, and are about to be brought down. This has been revealed by Allah Himself to His prophet, the Honorable Elijah Muhammad. The white man's rule will be ended forever in ten or fifteen years (and it must be conceded that all present signs would seem to bear witness to the accuracy of the prophet's statement). The crowd seemed to swallow this theology with no effort—all crowds do swallow theology this way, I gather, in both sides of Jerusalem, in Istanbul, and in Rome—and, as theology goes, it was no more indigestible than the more familiar brand asserting that there is a curse on the sons of Ham. No more, and no less, and it had been designed for the same purpose; namely, the sanctification of power. But very little time was spent on theology, for one did not need to prove to a Harlem audience that all white men were devils. They were merely glad to have, at last, divine corroboration of their experience, to hear—and it was a tremendous thing to hear—that they had been lied to for all these years and generations, and that their captivity was ending, for God was black. Why were they *hearing* it now, since this was not the first time it had been said? I had heard it many times, from various prophets, during all the years that I was growing up. Elijah Muhammad himself has now been carrying the same message for more than thirty years; he is not an overnight sensation, and we owe his ministry, I am told, to the fact that when he was a child of six or so, his father was lynched before his eyes. (So much for states' rights.) And now, suddenly, people who have never before been able to hear this message hear it, and believe it, and are changed. Elijah Muhammad has been able to do what generations of welfare workers and committees and resolutions and reports and housing projects and playgrounds have failed to do: to heal and redeem drunkards and junkies, to convert people who have come out of prison and to keep them out, to make men chaste and women virtuous, and to invest both the male and the female with a pride and a serenity that hang about them like an unfailing light. He has done all these things, which our Christian church has spectacularly failed to do. How has Elijah managed it?

Well, in a way—and I have no wish to minimize his peculiar role and his peculiar achievement—it is not he who has done it but time. Time catches up with kingdoms and crushes them, gets its teeth into doctrines and rends them; time reveals the foundations on which any kingdom rests, and eats at those foundations, and it destroys doctrines by proving them to be untrue. In those days, not so very long ago, when the priests of that church which stands in Rome gave God's blessing to Italian boys being sent out to ravage a defenseless black country—which until that event, incidentally, had not considered itself to be black—it was not possible to believe in a black God. To entertain such a belief would have been to entertain madness. But time has passed, and in that time the Christian world has revealed itself as morally bankrupt and politically unstable. The Tunisians were quite right in 1956—and it was a very significant moment in Western (and African) history—when they countered the French justification for remaining in North Africa with the question "Are the *French* ready for self-government?" Again, the terms "civilized" and "Christian" begin to have a very strange ring, particularly in the ears of those who have been judged to be neither civilized nor Christian, when a Christian nation surrenders to a foul and violent orgy, as Germany did during the Third Reich. For the crime of their ancestry, millions of people in the middle of the twentieth century, and in the heart of Europe—God's citadel—were sent to a death so calculated, so hideous, and so prolonged that no age before this enlightened one had been able to imagine it, much less achieve and record it. Furthermore, those beneath the Western heel, unlike those within the West, are aware that Germany's current role in Europe is to act as a bulwark against the "uncivilized" hordes, and since power is what the powerless want, they understand very well what we of the West want to keep, and are not deluded by our talk of a freedom that we have never been willing to share with them. From my own point of view, the fact of the Third Reich alone makes obsolete forever any question of Christian superiority, except in technological terms. White people were, and are, astounded by the holocaust in Germany. They did not know that they could act that way. But I very much doubt whether black people were astounded—at least, in the same way. For my part, the fate of the Jews, and the world's indifference to it, frightened me very much. I could not but feel, in those sorrowful years, that this human indifference, concerning which I knew so much already, would be my portion on the day that the United States decided to murder its Negroes systematically instead of little by little and catch-as-catch-can. I was, of course, authoritatively assured that what had happened to the Jews in Germany could not happen to the Negroes in America, but I thought, bleakly, that the German Jews had probably believed similar counselors, and, again, I could not share the white man's vision of himself for the very good reason that white men in America do not behave toward black men the way they behave toward each other. When a white man faces a black man, especially if the black man is helpless, terrible things are revealed. I know. I have been carried into precinct basements often enough, and I have seen and heard and endured the secrets of desperate white men and women, which they knew were safe with me, because even if I should speak, no one would believe me. And they would not believe me precisely because they would know that what I said was true.

The treatment accorded the Negro during the Second World War marks, for me, a turning point in the Negro's relation to America. To put it briefly, and somewhat too simply, a certain hope died, a certain respect for white Americans faded. One began to pity them, or to hate them. You must put yourself in the skin of a man who is wearing the uniform of his country, is a candidate for death in its defense, and who is called a "nigger" by his comrades-in-arms and his officers; who is almost always given the hardest, ugliest, most menial work to do; who knows that the white G.I. has informed the Europeans that he is sub-human (so much for the American male's sexual security); who does not dance at the U.S.O. the night white soldiers dance there, and does not drink in the same bars white soldiers drink in; and who watches German prisoners of war being treated by Americans with more human dignity than he has ever received at their hands. And who, at the same time, as a human being, is far freer in a strange land than he has ever been at home. *Home!* The very word begins to have a despairing and diabolical ring. You must consider what happens to this citizen, after all he has endured, when he returns—home: search, in his shoes, for a job, for a place to live; ride, in his skin, on segregated buses; see, with his eyes, the signs saying "White" and "Colored," and especially the signs that say "White Ladies" and "Colored *Women*"; look into the eyes of his wife; look into the eyes of his son; listen, with his ears, to political speeches, North and South; imagine yourself being told to "wait." And all this is happening in the richest and freest country in the world, and in the middle of the twentieth century. The subtle and deadly change of heart that might occur in you would be involved with the realization that a civilization is not destroyed by wicked people;

it is not necessary that people be wicked but only that they be spineless. I and two Negro acquaintances, all of us well past thirty, and looking it, were in the bar of Chicago's O'Hare Airport several months ago, and the bartender refused to serve us, because, he said, we looked too young. It took a vast amount of patience not to strangle him, and great insistence and some luck to get the manager, who defended his bartender on the ground that he was "new" and had not yet, presumably, learned how to distinguish between a Negro boy of twenty and a Negro "boy" of thirty-seven. Well, we were served, finally, of course, but by this time no amount of Scotch would have helped us. The bar was very crowded, and our altercation had been extremely noisy; not one customer in the bar had done anything to help us. When it was over, and the three of us stood at the bar trembling with rage and frustration, and drinking—and trapped, now, in the airport, for we had deliberately come early in order to have a few drinks and to eat—a young white man standing near us asked if we were students. I suppose he thought that this was the only possible explanation for our putting up a fight. I told him that he hadn't wanted to talk to us earlier and we didn't want to talk to him now. The reply visibly hurt his feelings, and this, in turn, caused me to despise him. But when one of us, a Korean War veteran, told this young man that the fight we had been having in the bar had been his fight, too, the young man said, "I lost my conscience a long time ago," and turned and walked out. I know that one would rather not think so, but this young man is typical. So, on the basis of the evidence, had everyone else in the bar lost *his* conscience. A few years ago, I would have hated these people with all my heart. Now I pitied them, pitied them in order not to despise them. And this is not the happiest way to feel toward one's countrymen.

But, in the end, it is the threat of universal extinction hanging over all the world today that changes, totally and forever, the nature of reality and brings into devastating question the true meaning of man's history. We human beings now have the power to exterminate ourselves; this seems to be the entire sum of our achievement. We have taken this journey and arrived at this place in God's name. This, then, is the best that God (the white God) can do. If that is so, then it is time to replace Him—replace Him with what? And this void, this despair, this torment is felt everywhere in the West, from the streets of Stockholm to the churches of New Orleans and the sidewalks of Harlem.

God is black. All black men belong to Islam; they have been chosen. And Islam shall rule the world. The dream, the sentiment is old; only the color is new. And it is this dream, this sweet possibility, that thousands of oppressed black men and women in this country now carry away with them after the Muslim minister has spoken, through the dark, noisome ghetto streets, into the hovels where so many have perished. The white God has not delivered them; perhaps the Black God will.

While I was in Chicago last summer, the Honorable Elijah Muhammad invited me to have dinner at his home. This is a stately mansion on Chicago's South Side, and it is the headquarters of the Nation of Islam movement. I had not gone to Chicago to meet Elijah Muhammad—he was not in my thoughts at all—but the moment I received the invitation, it occurred to me that I ought to have expected it. In a way, I owe the invitation to the incredible, abysmal, and really cowardly obtuseness of white liberals. Whether in private debate or in public, any attempt I made to explain how the Black Muslim movement came about, and how it has achieved such force, was met with a blankness that revealed the little connection that the liberals' attitudes have with their perceptions or their lives, or even their knowledge—revealed, in fact, that they could deal with the Negro as a symbol or a victim but had no sense of him as a man. When Malcolm X, who is considered the movement's second-in-command, and heir apparent, points out that the cry of "violence" was not raised, for example, when the Israelis fought to regain Israel, and, indeed, is raised only when black men indicate that they will fight for *their* rights, he is speaking the truth. The conquests of England, every single one of them bloody, are part of what Americans have in mind when they speak of England's glory. In the United States, violence and heroism have been made synonymous except when it comes to blacks, and the only way to defeat Malcolm's point is to concede it and then ask oneself why this is so. Malcolm's statement is *not* answered by references to the triumphs of the N.A.A.C.P., the more particularly since very few liberals have any notion of how long, how costly, and how heartbreaking a task it is to gather the evidence that one can carry into court, or how long such court battles take. Neither is it answered by references to the student sit-in-movement, if only because not all Negroes are students and not all of them live in the South. I, in any case, certainly refuse to be put in the position of denying the truth of Malcolm's statements simply because I disagree with his conclusions, or in order to pacify the liberal conscience. Things are as bad as the Muslims say they are—in fact, they are worse, and the Muslims do not help matters—but there *is* no reason that black men should be expected to be more patient, more forbearing, more farseeing than whites; indeed, quite the contrary. The real reason that non-violence is considered to be a virtue in Negroes—I am not speaking now of its racial value, another matter altogether—is that white men do not want their lives, their self-image, or their property threatened. One wishes they would say so more often. At the end of a television program on which Malcolm X and I both appeared, Malcolm was stopped by a white member of the audience who said, "I have a thousand dollars and an acre of land. What's going to happen to me?" I admired the directness of the man's question, but I didn't hear Malcolm's reply, because I was trying to explain to someone else that the situation of the Irish a hundred years ago and the situation of the Negro today cannot very usefully be compared. Negroes were brought here in chains long before the Irish ever thought of leaving Ireland; what manner of consolation is it to be told that emigrants arriving here— voluntarily—long after you did have risen far above you? In the hall, as I was waiting for the elevator, someone shook my hand and said, "Goodbye, Mr. James Baldwin. We'll soon be addressing you as Mr. James X." And I thought, for an awful moment, My God, if this goes on much longer, you probably will. Elijah Muhammad had seen this show, I think, or another one, and he had been told about me. Therefore, late on a hot Sunday afternoon, I presented myself at his door.

I was frightened, because I had, in effect, been summoned into a royal presence. I was frightened for another reason, too. I knew the tension in me between love and power, between pain and rage, and the curious, the grinding way I remained extended between these poles—perpetually attempting to choose the better rather than the worse. But this choice was a choice in terms of a personal, a private better (I was, after all, a writer); what was its relevance in terms of a social worse? Here was the South Side—a million in captivity—stretching from this doorstep as far as the eye could see. And they didn't even read; depressed populations don't have the time or energy to spare. The affluent populations, which should have been their help, didn't, as far as could be discovered, read, either—they merely bought books and devoured them, but not in order to learn: in order to learn new attitudes. Also, I knew that once I had entered the house, I couldn't smoke or drink, and I felt guilty about the cigarettes in my pocket, as I had felt years ago when my friend first took me into his church. I was half an hour late, having got lost on the way here, and I felt as deserving of a scolding as a schoolboy.

The young man who came to the door—he was about thirty, perhaps, with a handsome, smiling face—didn't seem to find my lateness offensive, and led me into a large room. On one side of the room sat half a dozen women, all in white; they were much occupied with a beautiful baby, who seemed to belong to the youngest of the women. On the other side of the room sat seven or eight men, young, dressed in dark suits, very much at ease, and very imposing. The sunlight came into the room with the peacefulness one remembers from rooms in one's early childhood—a sunlight encountered later only in one's dreams. I remember being astounded by the quietness, the ease, the peace, the taste. I was introduced, they greeted me with a genuine cordiality and respect—and the respect increased my fright, for it meant that they expected something of me that I knew in my heart, for their sakes, I could not give—and we sat down. Elijah Muhammad was not in the room. Conversation was slow, but not as stiff as I had feared it would be. They kept it going, for I simply did not know which subjects I could acceptably bring up. They knew more about me, and had read more of what I had written, than I had expected, and I wondered what they made of it all, what they took my usefulness to be. The women were carrying on their own conversation, in low tones; I gathered that they were not expected to take part in male conversations. A few women kept coming in and out of the room, apparently making preparations for dinner. We, the men, did not plunge deeply into any subject, for, clearly, we were all waiting for the appearance of Elijah. Presently, the men, one by one, left the room and returned. Then I was asked if I would like to wash, and I, too, walked down the hall to the bathroom. Shortly after I came back, we stood up, and Elijah entered.

I do not know what I had expected to see. I had read some of his speeches, and had heard fragments of others on the radio and on television, so I associated him with ferocity. But, no—the man who came into the room was small and slender, really very delicately put together, with a thin face, large, warm eyes, and a most winning smile. Something came into the room with him—his disciples' joy at seeing him, his joy at seeing them. It was the kind of encounter one watches with a smile simply because it is so rare that people enjoy one another. He teased the women, like a father, with no hint of that ugly and unctuous flirtatiousness I knew so well from other churches, and they responded like that, with great freedom and yet from a great and loving distance. He had seen me when he came into the room, I knew, though he had not looked my way. I had the feeling, as he talked and laughed with the others, whom I could only think of as his children, that he was sizing me up, deciding something. Now he turned toward me, to welcome me, with that marvelous smile, and carried me back nearly twenty-four years, to that moment when the pastor had smiled at me and said, "Whose little boy are you?" I did not respond now as I had responded then, because there are some things (not many, alas!) that one cannot do twice. But I knew what he made me feel, how I was drawn toward his peculiar authority, how his smile promised to take the burden of my life off my shoulders. *Take your burdens to the Lord and leave them there.* The central quality in Elijah's face is pain, and his smile is a witness to it—pain so old and deep and black that it becomes personal and particular only when he smiles. One wonders what he would sound like if he could sing. He turned to me, with that smile, and said something like "I've got a lot to say to *you*, but we'll wait until we sit *down*." And I laughed. He made me think of my father and me as we might have been if we had been friends.

In the dining room, there were two long tables; the men sat at one and the women at the other. Elijah was at the head of our table, and I was seated at his left. I can scarcely remember what we ate, except that it was plentiful, sane, and simple—so sane and simple that it made me feel extremely decadent, and I think that I drank, therefore, two glasses of milk. Elijah mentioned having seen me on television and said that it seemed to him that I was not yet brainwashed and was trying to become myself. He said this in a curiously unnerving way, his eyes looking into mine and one hand half hiding his lips, as though he were trying to conceal bad teeth. But his teeth were not bad. Then I remembered hearing that he had spent time in prison. I suppose that I *would* like to become myself, whatever that may mean, but I knew that Elijah's meaning and mine were not the same. I said yes, I was trying to be me, but I did not know how to say more than that, and so I waited.

Whenever Elijah spoke, a kind of chorus arose from the table, saying "Yes, that's right." This began to set my teeth on edge. And Elijah himself had a further, unnerving habit, which was to ricochet his questions and comments off someone else on their way to you. Now, turning to the man on his right, he began to speak of the white devils with whom I had last appeared on TV: What had they made *him* (me) feel? I could not answer this and was not absolutely certain that I was expected to. The people referred to had certainly made me feel exasperated and useless, but I did not think of them as devils. Elijah went on about the crimes of white people, to this endless chorus of "Yes, that's right." Someone at the table said, "The white man sure *is* a devil. He proves that by his own actions." I looked around. It was a very young man who had said this, scarcely more than a boy—very dark and sober, very bitter. Elijah began to speak of the Christian religion, of Christians, in the same soft, joking way. I began to see that Elijah's power came from his single-mindedness. There is nothing calculated about him; he means every word he says. The real reason, according to Elijah, that I failed to realize that the white man was a devil was that I had been too long exposed to white teaching and had never received true instruction. "The so-called American Negro" is the only reason Allah has permitted the United States to endure so long; the white man's time was up in 1913, but it is the will of Allah that this lost black nation, the black men of this country, be redeemed from their white masters and returned to the true faith, which is Islam. Until this is done—and it will be accomplished very soon—the total destruction of the white man is being delayed. Elijah's mission is to return "the so-called Negro" to Islam, to separate the chosen of Allah from this doomed nation. Furthermore, the white man knows his history, knows himself to be a devil, and knows that his time is running out, and all his technology, psychology, science, and "tricknology" are being expended in the effort to prevent black men from hearing the truth. This truth is that at the very beginning of time there was not one white face to be found in all the universe. Black men ruled the earth and the black man was perfect. This is the truth concerning the era that white men now refer to as prehistoric. They want black men to believe that they, like white men, once lived in caves and swung from trees and ate their meat raw and did not have the power of speech. But this is not true. Black men were never in such a condition. Allah allowed the Devil, through his scientists, to carry on infernal experiments, which resulted, finally, in the creation of the devil known as the white man, and later, even more disastrously, in the creation of the white woman. And it was decreed that these monstrous creatures should rule the earth for a certain number of years—I forget how many thousand, but, in any case, their rule now is ending, and Allah, who had never approved of the creation of the white man in the first place (who knows him, in fact, to be not a man at all but a devil), is anxious to restore the rule of peace that the rise of the white man totally destroyed. There is thus, by definition, no virtue in white people, and since they are another creation entirely and can no more, by breeding, become black than a cat, by breeding, can become a horse, there is no hope for them.

There is nothing new in this merciless formulation except the explicitness of its symbols and the candor of its hatred. Its emotional tone is as familiar to me as my own skin; it is but another way of saying that *sinners shall be bound in Hell a thousand years*. That sinners have always, for American Negroes, been white is a truth we needn't labor, and every American Negro, therefore, risks having the gates of paranoia close on him. In a society that is entirely hostile, and, by its nature, seems determined to cut you down—that has cut down so many in the past and cuts down so many every day—it begins to be almost impossible to distinguish a real from a fancied injury. One can very quickly cease to attempt this distinction, and, what is worse, one usually ceases to attempt it without realizing that one has done so. All doormen, for example, and all policemen have by now, for me, become exactly the same, and my style with them is designed simply to intimidate them before they can intimidate me. No doubt I am guilty of some injustice here, but it is irreducible, since I cannot risk assuming that the humanity of these people is more real to them than their uniforms. Most Negroes cannot risk assuming that the humanity of white people is more real to them than their color. And this leads, imperceptibly but inevitably, to a state of mind in which, having long ago learned to expect the worst, one finds it very easy to believe the worst. The brutality with which Negroes are treated in this country simply cannot be overstated, however unwilling white men may be to hear it. In the beginning—and neither can this be overstated—a Negro just cannot *believe* that white people are treating him as they do; he does not know what he has done to merit it. And when he realizes that the treatment accorded him has nothing to do with anything he has done, that the attempt of white people to destroy him—for that is what it is—is utterly gratuitous, it is not hard for him to think of white people as devils. For the horrors of the American Negro's life there has been almost no language. The privacy of his experience, which is only beginning to be recognized in language, and which is denied or ignored in official and popular speech—hence the Negro idiom—lends credibility to any system that pretends to clarify it. And, in fact, the truth about the black man, as a historical entity and as a human being, *has* been hidden from him, deliberately and cruelly; the power of the white world is threatened whenever a black man refuses to accept the white world's definitions. So every attempt is made to cut that black man down—not only was made yesterday but is made today. Who, then, is to say with authority where the root of so much anguish and evil lies? Why, then, is it not possible that all things began with the black man and that he was perfect—especially since this is precisely the claim that white people have put forward for themselves all these years? Furthermore, it is now absolutely clear that white people are a minority in the world—so severe a minority that they now look rather more like an invention—and that they cannot possibly hope to rule it any longer. If this is so, why is it not also possible that they achieved their original dominance by stealth and cunning and bloodshed and in opposition to the will of Heaven, and not, as they claim, by Heaven's will? And if *this* is so, then the sword they have used so long against others can now, without mercy, be used against them. Heavenly witnesses are a tricky lot, to be used by whoever is closest to Heaven at the time. And legend and theology, which are designed to sanctify our fears, crimes, and aspirations, also reveal them for what they are.

I said, at last, in answer to some other ricocheted questions, "I left the church twenty years ago and I haven't joined anything since." It was my way of saying that I did not intend to join their movement, either.

"And what are you now?" Elijah asked.

I was in something of a bind, for I really could not say—could not allow myself to be stampeded into saying—that I was a Christian. "I? Now? Nothing." This was not enough. "I'm a writer. I like doing things alone." I heard myself saying this. Elijah smiled at me. "I don't, anyway," I said, finally, "think about it a great deal."

Elijah said, to his right, "I think he ought to think about it *all* the deal," and with this the table agreed. But there was nothing malicious or condemnatory in it. I had the stifling feeling that *they* knew I belonged to them but knew that I did not know it yet, that I remained unready, and that they were simply waiting, patiently, and with assurance, for me to discover the truth for myself. For where else, after all, could I go? I was black, and therefore a part of Islam, and would be saved from the holocaust awaiting the white world whether I would or no. My weak, deluded scruples could avail nothing against the iron word of the prophet.

I felt that I was back in my father's house—as, indeed, in a way, I was—and I told Elijah that *I* did not care if white and black people married, and that I had many white friends. I would have no choice, if it came to it, but to perish with them, for (I said to myself, but not to Elijah), "I love a few people and they love me and some of them are white, and isn't love more important than color?"

Elijah looked at me with great kindness and affection, great pity, as though he were reading my heart, and indicated, skeptically, that I *might* have white friends, or think I did, and they *might* be trying to be decent—now—but their time was up. It was almost as though he were saying, "They had their chance, man, and they goofed!"

And I looked around the table. I certainly had no evidence to give them that would outweigh Elijah's authority or the evidence of their own lives or the reality of the streets outside. Yes, I knew two or three people, white, whom I would trust with my life, and I knew a few others, white, who were struggling as hard as they knew how, and with great effort and sweat and risk, to make the world more human. But how could I say this? One cannot argue with anyone's experience or decision or belief. All my evidence would be thrown out of court as irrelevant to the main body of the case, for I could cite only exceptions. The South Side proved the justice of the indictment; the state of the world proved the justice of the indictment. Everything else, stretching back throughout recorded time, was merely a history of those exceptions who had tried to change the world and had failed. Was this true? *Had* they failed? How much depended on the point of view? For it would seem that a certain category of exceptions never failed to make the world worse—that category, precisely, for whom power is more real than love. And yet power is real, and many things, including, very often, love, cannot be achieved without it. In the eeriest way possible, I suddenly had a glimpse of what white people must go through at a dinner table when they are trying to prove that Negroes are not subhuman. I had almost said, after all, "Well, take my friend Mary," and very nearly descended to a catalogue of those virtues that gave Mary the right to be alive. And in what hope? That Elijah and the others would nod their heads solemnly and say, at least, "Well, *she's* all right—but the *others!*"

And I looked again at the young faces around the table, and looked back at Elijah, who was saying that no people in history had ever been respected who had not owned their land. And the table said, "Yes, that's right." I could not deny the truth of this statement. For everyone else has, *is*, a nation, with a specific location and a flag—even, these days, the Jew. It is only "the so-called American Negro" who remains trapped, disinherited, and despised, in a nation that has kept him in bondage for nearly four hundred years and is still unable to recognize him as a human being. And the Black Muslims, along with many people who are not Muslims, no longer wish for a recognition so grudging and (should it ever be achieved) so tardy. Again, it cannot be denied that this point of view is abundantly justified by American Negro history. It is galling indeed to have stood so long, hat in hand, waiting for Americans to grow up enough to realize that you do not threaten them. On the other hand, how is the American Negro now to form himself into a separate nation? For this—and not only from the Muslim point of view—would seem to be his only hope of not perishing in the American backwater and being entirely and forever forgotten, as though he had never existed at all and his travail had been for nothing.

Elijah's intensity and the bitter isolation and disaffection of these young men and the despair of the streets outside had caused me to glimpse dimly what may now seem to be a fantasy, although, in an age so fantastical, I would hesitate to say precisely what a fantasy is. Let us say that the Muslims were to achieve the possession of the six or seven states that they claim are owed to Negroes by the United States as "back payment" for slave labor. Clearly, the United States would never surrender this territory, on any terms whatever, unless it found it impossible, for whatever reason, to hold it—unless, that is, the United States were to be reduced as a world power, exactly the way, and at the same degree of speed, that England has been forced to relinquish her Empire. (It is simply not true—and the state of her ex-colonies proves this—that England "always meant to go.") If the states were Southern states—and the Muslims seem to favor this—then the borders of a hostile Latin America would be raised, in effect, to, say, Maryland. Of the American borders on the sea, one would face toward a powerless Europe and the other toward an untrustworthy and non-white East, and on the North, after Canada, there would be only Alaska, which is a Russian border. The effect of this would be that the white people of the United States and Canada would find themselves marooned on a hostile continent, with the rest of the white world probably unwilling and certainly unable to come to their aid. All this is not, to my mind, the most imminent of possibilities, but if I were a Muslim, this is the possibility that I would find myself holding in the center of my mind, and driving toward. And if I were a Muslim, I would not hesitate to utilize—or, indeed, to exacerbate—the social and spiritual discontent that reigns here, for, at the very worst, I would merely have contributed to the destruction of a house I hated, and it would not matter if I perished, too. One has been perishing here so long!

And what were they thinking around the table? "I've come," said Elijah, "to give you something which can never be taken away from you." How solemn the table became then, and how great a light rose in the dark faces! This is the message that has spread through streets and tenements and prisons, through the narcotics wards, and past the filth and sadism of mental hospitals to a people from whom everything has been taken away, including, most crucially, their sense of their own worth. People cannot live without this sense; they will do anything whatever to regain it. This is why the most dangerous creation of any society is that man who has nothing to lose. You do not need ten such men—one will do. And Elijah, I should imagine, has had nothing to lose since the day he saw his father's blood rush out—rush down, and splash, so the legend has it, down through the leaves of a tree, on him. But neither did the other men around the table have anything to lose. "Return to your true religion," Elijah has written. "Throw off the chains of the slavemaster, the devil, and return to the fold. Stop drinking his alcohol, using his dope—protect your women—and forsake the filthy swine." I remembered my buddies of years ago, in the hallways, with their wine and their whiskey and their tears; in hallways still, frozen on the needle; and my brother saying to me once, "If Harlem didn't have so many churches and junkies, there'd be blood flowing in the streets." *Protect your women:* a difficult thing to do in a civilization sexually so pathetic that the white man's masculinity depends on a denial of the masculinity of the blacks. *Protect your women:* in a civilization that emasculates the male and abuses the female, and in which, moreover, the male is forced to depend on the female's bread-winning power. *Protect your women:* in the teeth of the white man's boast "We figure we're doing you folks a favor by pumping some white blood into your kids," and while facing the Southern shotgun and the Northern billy. Years ago, we used to say, "*Yes*, I'm black, goddammit, and I'm beautiful!"—in defiance, into the void. But now—now—African kings and heroes have come into the world, out of the past, the past that can now be put to the uses of power. And black has *become* a beautiful color—not because it is loved but because it is feared. And this urgency on the part of American Negroes is *not to be forgotten!* As they watch black men elsewhere rise, the promise held out, at last, that they may walk the earth with the authority with which white men walk, protected by the power that white men shall have no longer, is enough, and more than enough, to empty prisons and pull God down from Heaven. It has happened before, many times, before color was invented, and the hope of Heaven has always been a metaphor for the achievement of this particular state of grace. The song says, "I know my robe's going to fit me well. I tried it on at the gates of Hell."

It was time to leave, and we stood in the large living room, saying good night, with everything curiously and heavily unresolved. I could not help feeling that I had failed a test, in their eyes and in my own, or that I had failed to heed a warning. Elijah and I shook hands, and he asked me where I was going. Wherever it was, I would be driven there—"because, when we invite someone here," he said, "we take the responsibility of protecting him from the white devils until he gets wherever it is he's going." I was, in fact, going to have a drink with several white devils on the other side of town. I confess that for a fraction of a second I hesitated to give the address—the kind of address that in Chicago, as in all American cities, identified itself as a white address by virtue of its location. But I did give it, and Elijah and I walked out onto the steps, and one of the young men vanished to get the car. It was very strange to stand with Elijah for those few moments, facing those vivid, violent, so problematical streets. I felt very close to him, and really wished to be able to love and honor him as a witness, an ally, and a father. I felt that I knew something of his pain and his fury, and, yes, even his beauty. Yet precisely because of the reality and the nature of those streets—because of what he conceived as his responsibility and what I took to be mine—we would always be strangers, and possibly, one day, enemies. The car arrived—a gleaming, metallic, grossly American blue—and Elijah and I shook hands and said good night once more. He walked into his mansion and shut the door.

The driver and I started on our way through dark, murmuring—and, at this hour, strangely beautiful—Chicago, along the lake. We returned to the discussion of the land. How were we—Negroes—to get this land? I asked this of the dark boy who had said earlier, at the table, that the white man's actions proved him to be a devil. He spoke to me first of the Muslim temples that were being built, or were about to be built, in various parts of the United States, of the strength of the Muslim following, and of the amount of money that is annually at the disposal of Negroes—something like twenty billion dollars. "That alone shows you how strong we are," he said. But,

I persisted, cautiously, and in somewhat different terms, this twenty billion dollars, or whatever it is, depends on the total economy of the United States. What happens when the Negro is no longer a part of this economy? Leaving aside the fact that in order for this to happen the economy of the United States will itself have had to undergo radical and certainly disastrous changes, the American Negro's spending power will obviously no longer be the same. On what, then, will the economy of this separate nation be based? The boy gave me a rather strange look. I said hurriedly, "I'm not saying it *can't* be done—I just want to know *how* it's to be done." I was thinking, In order for this to happen, your entire frame of reference will have to change, and you will be forced to surrender many things that you now scarcely know you have. I didn't feel that the things I had in mind, such as the pseudo-elegant heap of tin in which we were riding, had any very great value. But life would be very different without them, and I wondered if he had thought of this.

How can one, however, dream of power in any other terms than in the symbols of power? The boy could see that freedom depended on the possession of land; he was persuaded that, in one way or another, Negroes must achieve this possession. In the meantime, he could walk the streets and fear nothing, because there were millions like him, coming soon, now, to power. He was held together, in short, by a dream—though it is just as well to remember that some dreams come true—and was united with his "brothers" on the basis of their color. Perhaps one cannot ask for more. People always seem to band together in accordance to a principle that has nothing to do with love, a principle that releases them from personal responsibility.

Yet I could have hoped that the Muslim movement had been able to inculcate in the demoralized Negro population a truer and more individual sense of its own worth, so that Negroes in the Northern ghettos could begin, in concrete terms, and at whatever price, to change their situation. But in order to change a situation one has first to see it for what it is: in the present case, to accept the fact, whatever one does with it thereafter, that the Negro has been formed by this nation, for better or for worse, and does not belong to any other—not to Africa, and certainly not to Islam. The paradox—and a fearful paradox it is—is that the American Negro can have no future anywhere, on any continent, as long as he is unwilling to accept his past. To accept one's past—one's history—is not the same thing as drowning in it; it is learning how to use it. An invented past can never be used; it cracks and crumbles under the pressures of life like clay in a season of drought. How can the American Negro's past be used? The unprecedented price demanded—and at this embattled hour of the world's history—is the transcendence of the realities of color, of nations, and of altars.

"Anyway," the boy said suddenly, after a very long silence, "things won't ever again be the way they used to be. I know *that*."

And so we arrived in enemy territory, and they set me down at the enemy's door.

No one seems to know where the Nation of Islam gets its money. A vast amount, of course, is contributed by Negroes, but there are rumors to the effect that people like Birchites and certain Texas oil millionaires look with favor on the movement. I have no way of knowing whether there is any truth to the rumors, though since these people make such a point of keeping the races separate, I wouldn't be surprised if for this smoke there was some fire. In any case, during a recent Muslim rally, George Lincoln Rockwell, the chief of the American Nazi party, made a point of contributing about twenty dollars to the cause, and he and Malcolm X decided that, racially speaking, anyway, they were in complete agreement. The glorification of one race and the consequent debasement of another—or others—always has been and always will be a recipe for murder. There is no way around this. If one is permitted to treat any group of people with special disfavor because of their race or the color of their skin, there is no limit to what one will force them to endure, and, since the entire race has been mysteriously indicted, no reason not to attempt to destroy it root and branch. This is precisely what the Nazis attempted. Their only originality lay in the means they used. It is scarcely worthwhile to attempt remembering how many times the sun has looked down on the slaughter of the innocents. I am very much concerned that American Negroes achieve their freedom here in the United States. But I am also concerned for their dignity, for the health of their souls, and must oppose any attempt that Negroes may make to do to others what has been done to them. I think I know—we see it around us every day—the spiritual wasteland to which that road leads. It is so simple a fact and one that is so hard, apparently, to grasp: *Whoever debases others is debasing himself.* That is not a mystical statement but a most realistic one, which is proved by the eyes of any Alabama sheriff—and I would not like to see Negroes ever arrive at so wretched a condition.

Now, it is extremely unlikely that Negroes will ever rise to power in the United States, because they are only approximately a ninth of this nation. They are not in the position of the Africans, who are attempting to reclaim their land and break the colonial yoke and recover from the colonial experience. The Negro situation is dangerous in a different way, both for the Negro qua Negro and for the country of which he forms so troubled and troubling a part. The American Negro is a unique creation; he has no counterpart anywhere, and no predecessors. The Muslims react to this fact by referring to the Negro as "the so-called American Negro" and substituting for the names inherited from slavery the letter "X." It is a fact that every American Negro bears a name that originally belonged to the white man whose chattel he was. I am called Baldwin because I was either sold by my African tribe or kidnapped out of it into the hands of a white Christian named Baldwin, who forced me to kneel at the foot of the cross. I am, then, both visibly and legally the descendant of slaves in a white, Protestant country, and this is what it means to be an American Negro, this is who he is—a kidnapped pagan, who was sold like an animal and treated like one, who was once defined by the American Constitution as "three-fifths" of a man, and who, according to the Dred Scott decision, had no rights that a white man was bound to respect. And today, a hundred years after his technical emancipation, he remains—with the possible exception of the American Indian—the most despised creature in his country. Now, there is simply no possibility of a real change in the Negro's situation without the most radical and far-reaching changes in the American political and social structure. And it is clear that white Americans are not simply unwilling to effect these changes; they are, in the main, so slothful have they become, unable even to envision them. It must be added that the Negro himself no longer believes in the good faith of white Americans—if, indeed, he ever could have. What the Negro *has* discovered, and on an international level, is that power to intimidate which he has always had privately but hitherto could manipulate only privately—for private ends often, for limited ends always. And therefore when the country speaks of a "new" Negro, which it has been doing every hour on the hour for decades, it is not really referring to a change in the Negro, which, in any case, it is quite incapable of assessing, but only to a new difficulty in keeping him in his place, to the fact that it encounters him (again! again!) barring yet another door to its spiritual and social ease. This is probably, hard and odd as it may sound, the most important thing that one human being can do for another—it is certainly *one* of the most important things; hence the torment and necessity of love—and this is the enormous contribution that the Negro has made to this otherwise shapeless and undiscovered country. Consequently, white Americans are in nothing more deluded than in supposing that Negroes could ever have imagined that white people would "give" them anything. It is rare indeed that people give. Most people guard and keep; they suppose that it is they themselves and what they identify with themselves that they are guarding and keeping, whereas what they are actually guarding and keeping is their system of reality and what they assume themselves to be. One can give nothing whatever without giving oneself—that is to say, risking oneself. If one cannot risk oneself, then one is simply incapable of giving. And, after all, one can give freedom only by setting someone free. This, in the case of the Negro, the American republic has never become sufficiently mature to do. White Americans have contented themselves with gestures that are now described as "tokenism." For hard example, white Americans congratulate themselves on the 1954 Supreme Court decision outlawing segregation in the schools; they suppose, in spite of the mountain of evidence that has since accumulated to the contrary, that this was proof of a change of heart—or, as they like to say, progress. Perhaps. It all depends on how one reads the word "progress." Most of the Negroes I know do not believe that this immense concession would ever have been made if it had not been for the competition of the Cold War, and the fact that Africa was clearly liberating herself and therefore had, for political reasons, to be wooed by the descendants of her former masters. Had it been a matter of love or justice, the 1954 decision would surely have occurred sooner; were it not for the realities of power in this difficult era, it might very well not have occurred yet. This seems an extremely harsh way of stating the case—ungrateful, as it were—but the evidence that supports this way of stating it is not easily refuted. I myself do not think that it can be refuted at all. In any event, the sloppy and fatuous nature of American good will can never be relied upon to deal with hard problems. These have been dealt with, when they have been dealt with at all, out of necessity—and in political terms, anyway, necessity means concessions made in order to stay on top. I think this is a fact, which it serves no purpose to deny, *but, whether it is a fact or not, this is what the black population of the world, including black Americans, really believe.* The word "independence" in Africa and the word "integration" here are almost equally meaningless; that is, Europe has not yet left Africa, and black men here are not yet free. And both of these last statements are undeniable facts, related facts, containing the gravest implications for us all. The Negroes of this country may never be able to rise to power, but they are very well placed indeed to precipitate chaos and ring down the curtain on the American dream.

This has everything to do, of course, with the nature of that dream and with the fact that we Americans, of whatever color, do not dare examine it and are far from having made it a reality. There are too many things we do not wish to know about ourselves. People are not, for example, terribly anxious to be equal (equal, after all, to what and to whom?) but they love the idea of being superior. And this human truth has an especially grinding force here, where identity is almost impossible to achieve and people are perpetually attempting to find their feet on the shifting sands of status. (Consider the history of labor in a country in which, spiritually speaking, there are no workers, only candidates for the hand of the boss's daughter.) Furthermore, I have met only a very few people—and most of these were not Americans—who had any real desire to be free. Freedom is hard to bear. It can be objected that I am speaking of political freedom in spiritual terms, but the political institutions of any nation are always menaced and are ultimately controlled by the spiritual state of that nation. We are controlled here by our confusion, far more than we know, and the American dream has therefore become something much more closely resembling a nightmare, on the private, domestic, and international levels. Privately, we cannot stand our lives and dare not examine them; domestically, we take no responsibility for (and no pride in) what goes on in our country; and, internationally, for many millions of people, we are an unmitigated disaster. Whoever doubts this last statement has only to open his ears, his heart, his mind, to the testimony of—for example—any Cuban peasant or any Spanish poet, and ask himself what *he* would feel about us if *he* were the victim of our performance in pre-Castro Cuba or in Spain. We defend our curious role in Spain by referring to the Russian menace and the necessity of protecting the free world. It has not occurred to us that we have simply been mesmerized by Russia, and that the only real advantage Russia has in what we think of as a struggle between the East and the West is the moral history of the Western world. Russia's secret weapon is the bewilderment and despair and hunger of millions of people of whose existence we are scarcely aware. The Russian Communists are not in the least concerned about these people. But our ignorance and indecision have had the effect, if not of delivering them into Russian hands, of plunging them very deeply in the Russian shadow, for which effect—and it is hard to blame them—the most articulate among them, and the most oppressed as well, distrust us all the more. Our power and our fear of change help bind these people to their misery and bewilderment, and insofar as they find this state intolerable we are intolerably menaced. For if they find their state intolerable, but are too heavily oppressed to change it, they are simply pawns in the hands of larger powers, which, in such a context, are always unscrupulous, and when, eventually, they do change their situation—as in Cuba—we are menaced more than ever, by the vacuum that succeeds all violent upheavals. We should certainly know by now that it is one thing to overthrow a dictator or repel an invader and quite another thing really to achieve a revolution. Time and time and time again, the people discover that they have merely betrayed themselves into the hands of yet another Pharaoh, who, since he was necessary to put the broken country together, will not let them go. Perhaps, people being the conundrums that they are, and having so little desire to shoulder the burden of their lives, this is what will always happen. But at the bottom of my heart I do not believe this. I think that people can be better than that, and I know that people can be better than they are. We are capable of bearing a great burden, once we discover that the burden is reality and arrive where reality is. Anyway, the point here is that we are living in an age of revolution, whether we will or no, and that America is the only Western nation with both the power and, as I hope to suggest, the experience that may help to make these revolutions real and minimize the human damage. Any attempt we make to oppose these outbursts of energy is tantamount to signing our death warrant.

Behind what we think of as the Russian menace lies what we do not wish to face, and what white Americans do not face when they regard a Negro: reality—the fact that life is tragic. Life is tragic simply because the earth turns and the sun inexorably rises and sets, and one day, for each of us, the sun will go down for the last, last time. Perhaps the whole root of our trouble, the human trouble, is that we will sacrifice all the beauty of our lives, will imprison ourselves in totems, taboos, crosses, blood sacrifices, steeples, mosques, races, armies, flags, nations, in order to deny the fact of death, which is the only fact we have. It seems to me that one ought to rejoice in the *fact* of death—ought to decide, indeed, to *earn* one's death by confronting with passion the conundrum of life. One is responsible to life: It is the small beacon in that terrifying darkness from which we come and to which we shall return. One must negotiate this passage as nobly as possible, for the sake of those who are coming after us. But white Americans do not believe in death, and this is why the darkness of my skin so intimidates them. And this is also why the presence of the Negro in this country can bring about its destruction. It is the responsibility of free men to trust and to celebrate what is constant—birth, struggle, and death are constant, and so is love, though we may not always think so—and to apprehend the nature of change, to be able and willing to change. I speak of change not on the surface but in the depths—change in the sense of renewal. But renewal becomes impossible if one supposes things to be constant that are not—safety, for example, or money, or power. One clings then to chimeras, by which one can only be betrayed, and the entire hope—the entire possibility—of freedom disappears. And by destruction I mean precisely the abdication by Americans of any effort really to be free. The Negro can precipitate this abdication because white Americans have never, in all their long history, been able to look on him as a man like themselves. This point need not be labored; it is proved over and over again by the Negro's continuing position here, and his indescribable struggle to defeat the stratagems that white Americans have used, and use, to deny him his humanity. America could have used in other ways the energy that both groups have expended in this conflict. America, of all the Western nations, has been best placed to prove the uselessness and the obsolescence of the concept of color. But it has not dared to accept this opportunity, or even to conceive of it as an opportunity. White Americans have thought of it as their shame, and have envied those more civilized and elegant European nations that were untroubled by the presence of black men on their shores. This is because white Americans have supposed "Europe" and "civilization" to be synonyms—which they are not—and have been distrustful of other standards and other sources of vitality, especially those produced in America itself, and have attempted to behave in all matters as though what was east for Europe was also east for them. What it comes to is that if we, who can scarcely be considered a white nation, persist in thinking of ourselves as one, we condemn ourselves, with the truly white nations, to sterility and decay, whereas if we could accept ourselves *as we are*, we might bring new life to the Western achievements, and transform them. The price of this transformation is the unconditional freedom of the Negro; it is not too much to say that he, who has been so long rejected, must now be embraced, and at no matter what psychic or social risk. He is *the* key figure in his country, and the American future is precisely as bright or as dark as his. And the Negro recognizes this, in a negative way. Hence the question: Do I really *want* to be integrated into a burning house?

White Americans find it as difficult as white people elsewhere do to divest themselves of the notion that they are in possession of some intrinsic value that black people need, or want. And this assumption—which, for example, makes the solution to the Negro problem depend on the speed with which Negroes accept and adopt white standards—is revealed in all kinds of striking ways, from Bobby Kennedy's assurance that a Negro can become President in forty years to the unfortunate tone of warm congratulation with which so many liberals address their Negro equals. It is the Negro, of course, who is presumed to have become equal—an achievement that not only proves the comforting fact that perseverance has no color but also overwhelmingly corroborates the white man's sense of his own value. Alas, this value can scarcely be corroborated in any other way; there is certainly little enough in the white man's public or private life that one should desire to imitate. White men, at the bottom of their hearts, know this. Therefore, a vast amount of the energy that goes into what we call the Negro problem is produced by the white man's profound desire not to be judged by those who are not white, not to be seen as he is, and at the same time a vast amount of the white anguish is rooted in the white man's equally profound need to be seen as he is, to be released from the tyranny of his mirror. All of us know, whether or not we are able to admit it, that mirrors can only lie, that death by drowning is all that awaits one there. It is for this reason that love is so desperately sought and so cunningly avoided. Love takes off the masks that we fear we cannot live without and know we cannot live within. I use the word "love" here not merely in the personal sense but as a state of being, or a state of grace—not in the infantile American sense of being made happy but in the tough and universal sense of quest and daring and growth. And I submit, then, that the racial tensions that menace Americans today have little to do with real antipathy—on the contrary, indeed—and are involved only symbolically with color. These tensions are rooted in the very same depths as those from which love springs, or murder. The white man's unadmitted—and apparently, to him, unspeakable—private fears and longings are projected onto the Negro. The only way he can be released from the Negro's tyrannical power over him is to consent, in effect, to become black himself, to become a part of that suffering and dancing country that he now watches wistfully from the heights of his lonely power and, armed with spiritual traveler's checks, visits surreptitiously after dark. How can one respect, let alone adopt, the values of a people who do not, on any level whatever, live the way they say they do, or the way they say they should? I cannot accept the proposition that the four-hundred-year travail of the American Negro should result merely in his attainment of the present level of the American civilization. I am far from convinced that being released from the African witch doctor was worthwhile if I am now—in order to support the moral contradictions and the spiritual aridity of my life—expected to become dependent on the American psychiatrist. It is a bargain I refuse. The only thing white people have that black people need, or should want, is power—and no one holds power forever. White people cannot, in the generality, be taken as models of how to live. Rather, the white man is himself in sore need of new standards, which will release him from his confusion and place him once again in fruitful communion with the depths of his own being. And I repeat: The price of the liberation of the white people is the liberation of the blacks—the total liberation, in the cities, in the towns, before the law, and in the mind. Why, for example—especially knowing the family as I do—I should *want* to marry your sister is a great mystery to me. But your sister and I have every right to marry if we wish to, and no one has the right to stop us. If she cannot raise me to her level, perhaps I can raise her to mine.

In short, we, the black and the white, deeply need each other here if we are really to become a nation—if we are really, that is, to achieve our identity, our maturity, as men and women. To create one nation has proved to be a hideously difficult task; there is certainly no need now to create two, one black and one white. But white men with far more political power than that possessed by the Nation of Islam movement have been advocating exactly this, in effect, for generations. If this sentiment is honored when it falls from the lips of Senator Byrd, then there is no reason it should not be honored when it falls from the lips of Malcolm X. And any Congressional committee wishing to investigate the latter must also be willing to investigate the former. They are expressing exactly the same sentiments and represent exactly the same danger. There is absolutely no reason to suppose that white people are better equipped to frame the laws by which I am to be governed than I am. It is entirely unacceptable that I should have no voice in the political affairs of my own country, for I am not a ward of America; I am one of the first Americans to arrive on these shores.

This past, the Negro's past, of rope, fire, torture, castration, infanticide, rape; death and humiliation; fear by day and night, fear as deep as the marrow of the bone; doubt that he was worthy of life, since everyone around him denied it; sorrow for his women, for his kinfolk, for his children, who needed his protection, and whom he could not protect; rage, hatred, and murder, hatred for white men so deep that it often turned against him and his own, and made all love, all trust, all joy impossible—this past, this endless struggle to achieve and reveal and confirm a human identity, human authority, yet contains, for all its horror, something very beautiful. I do not mean to be sentimental about suffering—enough is certainly as good as a feast—but people who cannot suffer can never grow up, can never discover who they are. That man who is forced each day to snatch his manhood, his identity, out of the fire of human cruelty that rages to destroy it knows, if he survives his effort, and even if he does not survive it, something about himself and human life that no school on earth—and, indeed, no church—can teach. He achieves his own authority, and that is unshakable. This is because, in order to save his life, he is forced to look beneath appearances, to take nothing for granted, to hear the meaning behind the words. If one is continually surviving the worst that life can bring, one eventually ceases to be controlled by a fear of what life can bring; whatever it brings must be borne. And at this level of experience one's bitterness begins to be palatable, and hatred becomes too heavy a sack to carry. The apprehension of life here so briefly and inadequately sketched has been the experience of generations of Negroes, and it helps to explain how they have endured and how they have been able to produce children of kindergarten age who can walk through mobs to get to school. It demands great force and great cunning continually to assault the mighty and indifferent fortress of white supremacy, as Negroes in this country have done so long. It demands great spiritual resilience not to hate the hater whose foot is on your neck, and an even greater miracle of perception and charity not to teach your child to hate. The Negro boys and girls who are facing mobs today come out of a long line of improbable aristocrats—the only genuine aristocrats this country has produced. I say "this country" because their frame of reference was totally American. They were hewing out of the mountain of white supremacy the stone of their individuality. I have great respect for that unsung army of black men and women who trudged down back lanes and entered back doors, saying "Yes, sir" and "No, Ma'am" in order to acquire a new roof for the schoolhouse, new books, a new chemistry lab, more beds for the dormitories, more dormitories. They did not like saying "Yes, sir" and "No Ma'am," but the country was in no hurry to educate Negroes, these black men and women knew that the job had to be done, and they put their pride in their pockets in order to do it. It is very hard to believe that they were in any way inferior to the white men and women who opened those back doors. It is very hard to believe that those men and women, raising their children, eating their greens, crying their curses, weeping their tears, singing their songs, making their love, as the sun rose, as the sun set, were in any way inferior to the white men and women who crept over to share these splendors after the sun went down. But we must avoid the European error; we must not suppose that, because the situation, the ways, the perceptions of black people so radically differed from those of whites, they were racially superior. I am proud of these people not because of their color but because of their intelligence and their spiritual force and their beauty. The country should be proud of them, too, but, alas, not many people in this country even know of their existence. And the reason for this ignorance is that a knowledge of the role these people played—and play—in American life would reveal more about America to Americans than Americans wish to know.

The American Negro has the great advantage of having never believed that collection of myths to which white Americans cling: that their ancestors were all freedom-loving heroes, that they were born in the greatest country the world has ever seen, or that Americans are invincible in battle and wise in peace, that Americans have always dealt honorably with Mexicans and Indians and all other neighbors or inferiors, that American men are the world's most direct and virile, that American women are pure. Negroes know far more about white Americans than that; it can almost be said, in fact, that they know about white Americans what parents—or, anyway, mothers—know about their children, and that they very often regard white Americans that way. And perhaps this attitude, held in spite of what they know and have endured, helps to explain why Negroes, on the whole, and until lately, have allowed themselves to feel so little hatred. The tendency has really been, insofar as this was possible, to dismiss white people as the slightly mad victims of their own brainwashing. One watched the lives they led. One could not be fooled about that; one watched the things they did and the excuses that they gave themselves, and if a white man was really in trouble, deep trouble, it was to the Negro's door that he came. And one felt that if one had had that white man's worldly advantages, one would never have become as bewildered and as joyless and as thoughtlessly cruel as he. The Negro came to the white man for a roof or for five dollars or for a letter to the judge; the white man came to the Negro for love. But he was not often able to give what he came seeking. The price was too high; he had too much to lose. And the Negro knew this, too. When one knows this about a man, it is impossible for one to hate him, but unless he becomes a man—becomes equal—it is also impossible for one to love him. Ultimately, one tends to avoid him, for the universal characteristic of children is to assume that they have a monopoly on trouble, and therefore a monopoly on *you*. (Ask any Negro what he knows about the white people with whom he works. And then ask the white people with whom he works what they know about *him*.)

How can the American Negro past be used? It is entirely possible that this dishonored past will rise up soon to smite all of us. There are some wars, for example (if anyone on the globe is still mad enough to go to war) that the American Negro will not support, however many of his people may be coerced—and there is a limit to the number of people any government can put in prison, and a rigid limit indeed to the practicality of such a course. A bill is coming in that I fear America is not prepared to pay. "The problem of the twentieth century," wrote W. E. B. Du Bois around sixty years ago, "is the problem of the color line." A fearful and delicate problem, which compromises, when it does not corrupt, all the American efforts to build a better world—here, there, or anywhere. It is for this reason that everything white Americans think they believe in must now be re-examined. What one would not like to see again is the consolidation of peoples on the basis of their color. But as long as we in the West place on color the value that we do, we make it impossible for the great unwashed to consolidate themselves according to any other principle. Color is not a human or a personal reality; it is a political reality. But this is a distinction so extremely hard to make that the West has not been able to make it yet. And at the center of this dreadful storm, this vast confusion, stand the black people of this nation, who must now share the fate of a nation that has never accepted them, to which they were brought in chains. Well, if this is so, one has no choice but to do all in one's power to change that fate, and at no matter what risk—eviction, imprisonment, torture, death. For the sake of one's children, in order to minimize the bill that *they* must pay, one must be careful not to take refuge in any delusion—and the value placed on the color of the skin is always and everywhere and forever a delusion. I know that what I am asking is impossible. But in our time, as in every time, the impossible is the least that one can demand—and one is, after all, emboldened by the spectacle of human history in general, and American Negro history in particular, for it testifies to nothing less than the perpetual achievement of the impossible.

When I was very young, and was dealing with my buddies in those wine- and urine-stained hallways, something in me wondered, *What will happen to all that beauty?* For black people, though I am aware that some of us, black and white, do not know it yet, are very beautiful. And when I sat at Elijah's table and watched the baby, the women, and the men, and we talked about God's—or Allah's—vengeance, I wondered, when that vengeance was achieved, *What will happen to all that beauty then?* I could also see that the intransigence and ignorance of the white world might make that vengeance inevitable—a vengeance that does not really depend on, and cannot really be executed by, any person or organization, and that cannot be prevented by any police force or army: historical vengeance, a cosmic vengeance, based on the law that we recognize when we say, "Whatever goes up must come down." And here we are, at the center of the arc, trapped in the gaudiest, most valuable, and most improbable water wheel the world has ever seen. Everything now, we must assume, is in our hands; we have no right to assume otherwise. If we—and now I mean the relatively conscious whites and the relatively conscious blacks, who must, like lovers, insist on, or create, the consciousness of the others—do not falter in our duty now, we may be able, handful that we are, to end the racial nightmare, and achieve our country, and change the history of the world. If we do not now dare everything, the fulfillment of that prophecy, re-created from the Bible in song by a slave, is upon us: *God gave Noah the rainbow sign, No more water, the fire next time!*

NOBODY KNOWS
MY NAME

MORE NOTES OF A NATIVE SON

for my brothers,
    George, Wilmer
    and
    David

CONTENTS

Introduction   75

PART ONE Sitting in the House . . .
1. The Discovery of What It Means to Be an American   81
2. Princes and Powers   87
3. Fifth Avenue, Uptown: a Letter from Harlem   115
4. East River, Downtown: Postscript to a Letter from Harlem   126
5. A Fly in Buttermilk   133
6. Nobody Knows My Name: a Letter from the South   143
7. Faulkner and Desegregation   156
8. In Search of a Majority: an Address   162

PART TWO . . . With Everything on My Mind
9. Notes for a Hypothetical Novel: an Address   171
10. The Male Prison   180
11. The Northern Protestant   186
12. Alas, Poor Richard   i. Eight Men   198
                           ii. The Exile   203
                           iii. Alas, Poor Richard   209
13. The Black Boy Looks at the White Boy   221

INTRODUCTION

THESE ESSAYS WERE written over the last six years, in various places and in many states of mind. These years seemed, on the whole, rather sad and aimless to me. My life in Europe was ending, not because I had decided that it should, but because it became clearer and clearer—as I dealt with the streets, the climate, and the temperament of Paris, fled to Spain and Corsica and Scandinavia—that something had ended for me. I rather think now, to tell the sober truth, that it was merely my youth, first youth, anyway, that was ending and I hated to see it go. In the context of my life, the end of my youth was signaled by the reluctant realization that I had, indeed, become a writer; so far, so good: now I would have to go the distance.

In America, the color of my skin had stood between myself and me; in Europe, that barrier was down. Nothing is more desirable than to be released from an affliction, but nothing is more frightening than to be divested of a crutch. It turned out that the question of who I was was not solved because I had removed myself from the social forces which menaced me—anyway, these forces had become interior, and I had dragged them across the ocean with me. The question of who I was had at last become a personal question, and the answer was to be found in me.

I think that there is always something frightening about this realization. I know it frightened me—that was one of the reasons that I dawdled in the European haven for so long. And yet, I could not escape the knowledge, though God knows I tried, that if I was still in need of havens, my journey had been for nothing. Havens are high-priced. The price exacted of the haven-dweller is that he contrive to delude himself into believing that he has found a haven. It would seem, unless one looks more deeply at the phenomenon, that most people are able to delude themselves and get through their lives quite happily. But I still believe that the unexamined life is not worth living: and I know that self-delusion, in the service of no matter what small or lofty cause, is a price no writer can afford. His subject is himself and the world and it requires every ounce of stamina he can summon to attempt to look on himself and the world as they are.

What it came to for me was that I no longer needed to fear leaving Europe, no longer needed to hide myself from the high and dangerous winds of the world. The world was enormous and I could go anywhere in it I chose—including America: and I decided to return here because I was afraid to. But the question which confronted me, nibbled at me, in my stony Corsican exile was: Am I afraid of returning to America? Or am I afraid of journeying any further with myself? Once this question had presented itself it would not be appeased, it had to be answered.

"Be careful what you set your heart upon," someone once said to me, "for it will surely be yours." Well, I had said that I was going to be a writer, God, Satan, and Mississippi notwithstanding, and that color did not matter, and that I was going to be free. And, here I was, left with only myself to deal with. It was entirely up to me.

These essays are a very small part of a private logbook. The question of color takes up much space in these pages, but the question of color, especially in this country, operates to hide the graver questions of the self. That is precisely why what we like to call "the Negro problem" is so tenacious in American life, and so dangerous. But my own experience proves to me that the connection between American whites and blacks is far deeper and more passionate than any of us like to think. And, even in icy Sweden, I found myself talking with a man whose endless questioning has given him himself, and who reminded me of black Baptist preachers. The questions which one asks oneself begin, at last, to illuminate the world, and become one's key to the experience of others. One can only face in others what one can face in oneself. On this confrontation depends the measure of our wisdom and compassion. This energy is all that one finds in the rubble of vanished civilizations, and the only hope for ours.

JAMES BALDWIN

PART ONE

SITTING IN THE HOUSE ...

1.
THE DISCOVERY OF WHAT IT MEANS TO BE AN AMERICAN

"IT IS A COMPLEX fate to be an American," Henry James observed, and the principal discovery an American writer makes in Europe is just how complex this fate is. America's history, her aspirations, her peculiar triumphs, her even more peculiar defeats, and her position in the world—yesterday and today—are all so profoundly and stubbornly unique that the very word "America" remains a new, almost completely undefined and extremely controversial proper noun. No one in the world seems to know exactly what it describes, not even we motley millions who call ourselves Americans.

I left America because I doubted my ability to survive the fury of the color problem here. (Sometimes I still do.) I wanted to prevent myself from becoming *merely* a Negro; or, even, merely a Negro writer. I wanted to find out in what way the *specialness* of my experience could be made to connect me with other people instead of dividing me from them. (I was as isolated from Negroes as I was from whites, which is what happens when a Negro begins, at bottom, to believe what white people say about him.)

In my necessity to find the terms on which my experience could be related to that of others, Negroes and whites, writers and non-writers, I proved, to my astonishment, to be as American as any Texas G.I. And I found my experience was shared by every American writer I knew in Paris. Like me, they had been divorced from their origins, and it turned out to make very little difference that the origins of white Americans were European and mine were African—they were no more at home in Europe than I was.

The fact that I was the son of a slave and they were the sons of free men meant less, by the time we confronted each other on European soil, than the fact that we were both searching for our separate identities. When we had found these, we seemed to be saying, why, then, we would no longer need to cling to the shame and bitterness which had divided us so long.

It became terribly clear in Europe, as it never had been here, that we knew more about each other than any European ever could. And it also became clear that, no matter where our fathers had been born, or what they had endured, the fact of Europe had formed us both was part of our identity and part of our inheritance.

I had been in Paris a couple of years before any of this became clear to me. When it did, I, like many a writer before me upon the discovery that his props have all been knocked out from under him, suffered a species of breakdown and was carried off to the mountains of Switzerland. There, in that absolutely alabaster landscape, armed with two Bessie Smith records and a typewriter, I began to try to re-create the life that I had first known as a child and from which I had spent so many years in flight.

It was Bessie Smith, through her tone and her cadence, who helped me to dig back to the way I myself must have spoken when I was a pickaninny, and to remember the things I had heard and seen and felt. I had buried them very deep. I had never listened to Bessie Smith in America (in the same way that, for years, I would not touch watermelon), but in Europe she helped to reconcile me to being a "nigger."

I do not think that I could have made this reconciliation here. Once I was able to accept my role—as distinguished, I must say, from my "place"—in the extraordinary drama which is America, I was released from the illusion that I hated America.

The story of what can happen to an American Negro writer in Europe simply illustrates, in some relief, what can happen to any American writer there. It is not meant, of course, to imply that it happens to them all, for Europe can be very crippling, too; and, anyway, a writer, when he has made his first breakthrough, has simply won a crucial skirmish in a dangerous, unending and unpredictable battle. Still, the breakthrough is important, and the point is that an American writer, in order to achieve it, very often has to leave this country.

The American writer, in Europe, is released, first of all, from the necessity of apologizing for himself. It is not until he *is* released from the habit of flexing his muscles and proving that he is just a "regular guy" that he realizes how crippling this habit has been. It is not necessary for him, there, to pretend to be something he is not, for the artist does not encounter in Europe the same suspicion he encounters here. Whatever the Europeans may actually think of artists, they have killed enough of them off by now to know that they are as real—and as persistent—as rain, snow, taxes or businessmen.

Of course, the reason for Europe's comparative clarity concerning the different functions of men in society is that European society has always been divided into classes in a way that American society never has been. A European writer considers himself to be part of an old and honorable tradition—of intellectual activity, of letters—and his choice of a vocation does not cause him any uneasy wonder as to whether or not it will cost him all his friends. But this tradition does not exist in America.

On the contrary, we have a very deep-seated distrust of real intellectual effort (probably because we suspect that it will destroy, as I hope it does, that myth of America to which we cling so desperately). An American writer fights his way to one of the lowest rungs on the American social ladder by means of pure bull-headedness and an indescribable series of odd jobs. He probably *has* been a "regular fellow" for much of his adult life, and it is not easy for him to step out of that lukewarm bath.

We must, however, consider a rather serious paradox: though American society is more mobile than Europe's, it is easier to cut across social and occupational lines there than it is here. This has something to do, I think, with the problem of status in American life. Where everyone has status, it is also perfectly possible, after all, that no one has. It seems inevitable, in any case, that a man may become uneasy as to just what his status is.

But Europeans have lived with the idea of status for a long time. A man can be as proud of being a good waiter as of being a good actor, and, in neither case, feel threatened. And this means that the actor and the waiter can have a freer and more genuinely friendly relationship in Europe than they are likely to have here. The waiter does not feel, with obscure resentment, that the actor has "made it," and the actor is not tormented by the fear that he may find himself, tomorrow, once again a waiter.

This lack of what may roughly be called social paranoia causes the American writer in Europe to feel—almost certainly for the first time in his life—that he can reach out to everyone, that he is accessible to everyone and open to everything. This is an extraordinary feeling. He feels, so to speak, his own weight, his own value.

It is as though he suddenly came out of a dark tunnel and found himself beneath the open sky. And, in fact, in Paris, I began to see the sky for what seemed to be the first time. It was borne in on me—and it did not make me feel melancholy—that this sky had been there before I was born and would be there when I was dead. And it was up to me, therefore, to make of my brief opportunity the most that could be made.

I was born in New York, but have lived only in pockets of it. In Paris, I lived in all parts of the city—on the Right Bank and the Left, among the bourgeoisie and among *les misérables*, and knew all kinds of people, from pimps and prostitutes in Pigalle to Egyptian bankers in Neuilly. This may sound extremely unprincipled or even obscurely immoral: I found it healthy. I love to talk to people, all kinds of people, and almost everyone, as I hope we still know, loves a man who loves to listen.

This perpetual dealing with people very different from myself caused a shattering in me of preconceptions I scarcely knew I held. The writer is meeting in Europe people who are not American, whose sense of reality is entirely different from his own. They may love or hate or admire or fear or envy this country—they see it, in any case, from another point of view, and this forces the writer to reconsider many things he had always taken for granted. This reassessment, which can be very painful, is also very valuable.

This freedom, like all freedom, has its dangers and its responsibilities. One day it begins to be borne in on the writer, and with great force, that he is living in Europe as an American. If he were living there as a European, he would be living on a different and far less attractive continent.

This crucial day may be the day on which an Algerian taxi-driver tells him how it feels to be an Algerian in Paris. It may be the day on which he passes a café terrace and catches a glimpse of the tense, intelligent and troubled face of Albert Camus. Or it may be the day on which someone asks him to explain Little Rock and he begins to feel that it would be simpler—and, corny as the words may sound, more honorable—to *go* to Little Rock than sit in Europe, on an American passport, trying to explain it.

This is a personal day, a terrible day, the day to which his entire sojourn has been tending. It is the day he realizes that there are no untroubled countries in this fearfully troubled world; that if he has been preparing himself for anything in Europe, he has been preparing himself—for America. In short, the freedom that the American writer finds in Europe brings him, full circle, back to himself, with the responsibility for his development where it always was: in his own hands.

Even the most incorrigible maverick has to be born somewhere. He may leave the group that produced him—he may be forced to—but nothing will efface his origins, the marks of which he carries with him everywhere. I think it is important to know this and even find it a matter for rejoicing, as the strongest people do, regardless of their station. On this acceptance, literally, the life of a writer depends.

The charge has often been made against American writers that they do not describe society, and have no interest in it. They only describe individuals in opposition to it, or isolated from it. Of course, what the American writer is describing is his own situation. But what is *Anna Karenina* describing if not the tragic fate of the isolated individual, at odds with her time and place?

The real difference is that Tolstoy was describing an old and dense society in which everything seemed—to the people in it, though not to Tolstoy—to be fixed forever. And the book is a masterpiece because Tolstoy was able to fathom, and make us see, the hidden laws which really governed this society and made Anna's doom inevitable.

American writers do not have a fixed society to describe. The only society they know is one in which nothing is fixed and in which the individual must fight for his identity. This is a rich confusion, indeed, and it creates for the American writer unprecedented opportunities.

That the tensions of American life, as well as the possibilities, are tremendous is certainly not even a question. But these are dealt with in contemporary literature mainly compulsively; that is, the book is more likely to be a symptom of our tension than an examination of it. The time has come, God knows, for us to examine ourselves, but we can only do this if we are willing to free ourselves of the myth of America and try to find out what is really happening here.

Every society is really governed by hidden laws, by unspoken but profound assumptions on the part of the people, and ours is no exception. It is up to the American writer to find out what these laws and assumptions are. In a society much given to smashing taboos without thereby managing to be liberated from them, it will be no easy matter.

It is no wonder, in the meantime, that the American writer keeps running off to Europe. He needs sustenance for his journey and the best models he can find. Europe has what we do not have yet, a sense of the mysterious and inexorable limits of life, a sense, in a word, of tragedy. And we have what they sorely need: a new sense of life's possibilities.

In this endeavor to wed the vision of the Old World with that of the New, it is the writer, not the statesman, who is our strongest arm. Though we do not wholly believe it yet, the interior life is a real life, and the intangible dreams of people have a tangible effect on the world.

2.

PRINCES AND POWERS

THE CONFERENCE OF Negro-African Writers and Artists (*Le Congrès des Ecrivains et Artistes Noirs*) opened on Wednesday, September 19, 1956, in the Sorbonne's Amphitheatre Descartes, in Paris. It was one of those bright, warm days which one likes to think of as typical of the atmosphere of the intellectual capital of the Western world. There were people on the café terraces, boys and girls on the boulevards, bicycles racing by on their fantastically urgent errands. Everyone and everything wore a cheerful aspect, even the houses of Paris, which did not show their age. Those who were unable to pay the steep rents of these houses were enabled, by the weather, to enjoy the streets, to sit, unnoticed, in the parks. The boys and girls and old men and women who had nowhere at all to go and nothing whatever to do, for whom no provision had been made, or could be, added to the beauty of the Paris scene by walking along the river. The newspaper vendors seemed cheerful; so did the people who bought the newspapers. Even the men and women queueing up before bakeries—for there was a bread strike in Paris—did so as though they had long been used to it.

The conference was to open at nine o'clock. By ten o'clock the lecture hall was already unbearably hot, people choked the entrances and covered the wooden steps. It was hectic with the activity attendant upon the setting up of tape recorders, with the testing of earphones, with the lighting of flash-bulbs. Electricity, in fact, filled the hall. Of the people there that first day, I should judge that not quite two-thirds were colored.

Behind the table at the front of the hall sat eight colored men. These included the American novelist Richard Wright; Alioune Diop, the editor of *Présence Africaine* and one of the principal organizers of the conference; poets Leopold Senghor, from Senegal, and Aimé Cesaire, from Martinique, and the poet and novelist Jacques Alexis, from Haiti. From Haiti, also, came the President of the conference, Dr. Price-Mars, a very old and very handsome man.

It was well past ten o'clock when the conference actually opened. Alioune Diop, who is tall, very dark and self-contained, and who rather resembles, in his extreme sobriety, an old-time Baptist minister, made the opening address. He referred to the present gathering as a kind of second Bandung. As at Bandung, the people gathered together here held in common the fact of their subjugation to Europe, or, at the very least, to the European vision of the world. Out of the fact that European well-being had been, for centuries, so crucially dependent on this subjugation had come that *racisme* from which all black men suffered. Then he spoke of the changes which had taken place during the last decade regarding the fate and the aspirations of non-European peoples, especially the blacks. "The blacks," he said, "whom history has treated in a rather cavalier fashion. I would even say that history has treated black men in a resolutely spiteful fashion were it not for the fact that this history with a large *H* is nothing more, after all, than the Western interpretation of the life of the world." He spoke of the variety of cultures the conference represented, saying that they were genuine cultures and that the ignorance of the West regarding them was largely a matter of convenience.

Yet, in speaking of the relation between politics and culture, he pointed out that the loss of vitality from which all Negro cultures were suffering was due to the fact that their political destinies were not in their hands. A people deprived of political sovereignty finds it very nearly impossible to re-create, for itself, the image of its past, this perpetual re-creation being an absolute necessity for, if not, indeed, the definition of a living culture. And one of the questions, then, said Diop, which would often be raised during this conference was the question of assimilation. Assimilation was frequently but another name for the very special brand of relations between human beings which had been imposed by colonialism. These relations demanded that the individual, torn from the context to which he owed his identity, should replace his habits of feeling, thinking, and acting by another set of habits which belonged to the strangers who dominated him. He cited the example of certain natives of the Belgian Congo, who, *accablé des complexes*, wished for an assimilation so complete that they would no longer be distinguishable from white men. This, said Diop, indicated the blind horror which the spiritual heritage of Africa inspired in their breasts.

The question of assimilation could not, however, be posed this way. It was not a question, on the one hand, of simply being swallowed up, of disappearing in the maw of Western culture, nor was it, on the other hand, a question of rejecting assimilation in order to be isolated within African culture. Neither was it a question of deciding which African values were to be retained and which European values were to be adopted. Life was not that simple.

It was due to the crisis which their cultures were now undergoing that black intellectuals had come together. They were here to define and accept their responsibilities, to assess the riches and the promise of their cultures, and to open, in effect, a dialogue with Europe. He ended with a brief and rather moving reference to the fifteen-year struggle of himself and his confreres to bring about this day.

His speech won a great deal of applause. Yet, I felt that among the dark people in the hall there was, perhaps, some disappointment that he had not been more specific, more bitter, in a word, more demagogical; whereas, among the whites in the hall, there was certainly expressed in their applause a somewhat shamefaced and uneasy relief. And, indeed, the atmosphere was strange. No one, black or white, seemed quite to believe what was happening and everyone was tense with the question of which direction the conference would take. Hanging in the air, as real as the heat from which we suffered, were the great specters of America and Russia, of the battle going on between them for the domination of the world. The resolution of this battle might very well depend on the earth's non-European population, a population vastly outnumbering Europe's, and which had suffered such injustices at European hands. With the best will in the world, no one now living could undo what past generations had accomplished. The great question was what, exactly, *had* they accomplished: whether the evil, of which there had been so much, alone lived after them, whether the good, and there had been some, had been interred with their bones.

Of the messages from well-wishers which were read immediately after Diop's speech, the one which caused the greatest stir came from America's W. E. B. Du Bois. "I am not present at your meeting," he began, "because the U.S. government will not give me a passport." The reading was interrupted at this point by great waves of laughter, by no means good-natured, and by a roar of applause, which, as it clearly could not have been intended for the State Department, was intended to express admiration for Du Bois' plain speaking. "Any American Negro traveling abroad today must either not care about Negroes or say what the State Department wishes him to say." This, of course, drew more applause. It also very neatly compromised whatever effectiveness the five-man American delegation then sitting in the hall might have hoped to have. It was less Du Bois' extremely ill-considered communication which did this than the incontestable fact that he had not been allowed to leave his country. It was a fact which could scarcely be explained or defended, particularly as one would have also had to explain just how the reasons for Du Bois' absence differed from those which had prevented the arrival of the delegation from South Africa. The very attempt at such an explanation, especially for people whose distrust of the West, however richly justified, also tends to make them dangerously blind and hasty, was to be suspected of "caring nothing about Negroes," of saying what the State Department "wished" you to say. It was a fact which increased and seemed to justify the distrust with which all Americans are regarded abroad, and it made yet deeper, for the five American Negroes present, that gulf which yawns between the American Negro and all other men of color. This is a very sad and dangerous state of affairs, for the American Negro is possibly the only man of color who can speak of the West with real authority, whose experience, painful as it is, also proves the vitality of the so transgressed Western ideals. The fact that Du Bois was not there and could not, therefore, be engaged in debate, naturally made the more seductive his closing argument: which was that, the future of Africa being socialist, African writers should take the road taken by Russia, Poland, China, etc., and not be "betrayed backward by the U.S. into colonialism."

When the morning session ended and I was spewed forth with the mob into the bright courtyard, Richard Wright introduced me to the American delegation. And it seemed quite unbelievable for a moment that the five men standing with Wright (and Wright and myself) were defined, and had been brought together in this courtyard by our relation to the African continent. The chief of the delegation, John Davis, was to be asked just *why* he considered himself a Negro—he was to be told that he certainly did not look like one. He *is* a Negro, of course, from the remarkable legal point of view which obtains in the United States, but, more importantly, as he tried to make clear to his interlocutor, he was a Negro by choice and by depth of involvement—by experience, in fact. But the question of choice in such a context can scarcely be coherent for an African and the experience referred to, which produces a John Davis, remains a closed book for him. Mr. Davis might have been rather darker, as were the others—Mercer Cook, William Fontaine, Horace Bond, and James Ivy—and it would not have helped matters very much.

For what, at bottom, distinguished the Americans from the Negroes who surrounded us, men from Nigeria, Senegal, Barbados, Martinique—so many names for so many disciplines—was the banal and abruptly quite overwhelming fact that we had been born in a society, which, in a way quite inconceivable for Africans, and no longer real for Europeans, was open, and, in a sense which has nothing to do with justice or injustice, was free. It was a society, in short, in which nothing was fixed and we had therefore been born to a greater number of possibilities, wretched as these possibilities seemed at the instant of our birth. Moreover, the land of our forefathers' exile had been made, by that travail, our home. It may have been the popular impulse to keep us at the bottom of the perpetually shifting and bewildered populace; but we were, on the other hand, almost personally indispensable to each of them, simply because, without us, they could never have been certain, in such a confusion, where the bottom was; and nothing, in any case, could take away our title to the land which we, too, had purchased with our blood. This results in a psychology very different—at its best and at its worst—from the psychology which is produced by a sense of having been invaded and overrun, the sense of having no recourse whatever against oppression other than overthrowing the machinery of the oppressor. We had been dealing with, had been made and mangled by, another machinery altogether. It had never been in our interest to overthrow it. It had been necessary to make the machinery work for our benefit and the possibility of its doing so had been, so to speak, built in.

We could, therefore, in a way, be considered the connecting link between Africa and the West, the most real and certainly the most shocking of all African contributions to Western cultural life. The articulation of this reality, however, was another matter. But it was clear that our relation to the mysterious continent of Africa would not be clarified until we had found some means of saying, to ourselves and to the world, more about the mysterious American continent than had ever been said before.

M. Lasebikan, from Nigeria, spoke that afternoon on the tonal strucure of Youriba poetry, a language spoken by five million people in his country. Lasebikan was a very winning and unassuming personality, dressed in a most arresting costume. What looked like a white lace poncho covered him from head to foot; beneath this he was wearing a very subdued but very ornately figured silk robe, which looked Chinese, and he wore a red velvet toque, a sign, someone told me, that he was a Mohammedan.

The Youriba language, he told us, had only become a written language in the middle of the last century and this had been done by missionaries. His face expressed some sorrow at this point, due, it developed, to the fact that this had not already been accomplished by the Youriba people. However—and his face brightened again—he lived in the hope that one day an excavation would bring to light a great literature written by the Youriba people. In the meantime, with great good nature, he resigned himself to sharing with us that literature which already existed. I doubt that I learned much about the tonal structure of Youriba poetry, but I found myself fascinated by the sensibility which had produced it. M. Lasebikan spoke first in Youriba and then in English. It was perhaps because he so clearly loved his subject that he not only succeeded in conveying the poetry of this extremely strange language, he also conveyed something of the style of life out of which it came. The poems quoted ranged from the devotional to a poem which described the pounding of yams. And one somehow felt the loneliness and the yearning of the first and the peaceful, rhythmic domesticity of the second. There was a poem about the memory of a battle, a poem about a faithless friend, and a poem celebrating the variety to be found in life, which conceived of this variety in rather startling terms: "Some would have been great eaters, but they haven't got the food; some, great drinkers, but they haven't got the wine." Some of the poetry demanded the use of a marvelously ornate drum, on which were many little bells. It was not the drum it once had been, he told us, but despite whatever mishap had befallen it, I could have listened to him play it for the rest of the afternoon.

He was followed by Leopold Senghor. Senghor is a very dark and impressive figure in a smooth, bespectacled kind of way, and he is very highly regarded as a poet. He was to speak on West African writers and artists.

He began by invoking what he called the "spirit of Bandung." In referring to Bandung, he was referring less, he said, to the liberation of black peoples than he was saluting the reality and the toughness of their culture, which, despite the vicissitudes of their history, had refused to perish. We were now witnessing, in fact, the beginning of its renaissance. This renaissance would owe less to politics than it would to black writers and artists. The "spirit of Bandung" had had the effect of "sending them to school to Africa."

One of the things, said Senghor—perhaps *the* thing—which

distinguishes Africans from Europeans is the comparative urgency of their ability to feel. "*Sentir c'est apercevoir*": it is perhaps a tribute to his personal force that this phrase then meant something which makes the literal English translation quite inadequate, seeming to leave too great a distance between the feeling and the perception. The feeling and the perception, for Africans, is one and the same thing. This is the difference between European and African reasoning: the reasoning of the African is not compartmentalized, and, to illustrate this, Senghor here used the image of the bloodstream in which all things mingle and flow to and through the heart. He told us that the difference between the function of the arts in Europe and their function in Africa lay in the fact that, in Africa, the function of the arts is more present and pervasive, is infinitely less special, "is done by all, for all." Thus, art for art's sake is not a concept which makes any sense in Africa. The division between art and life out of which such a concept comes does not exist there. Art itself is taken to be perishable, to be made again each time it disappears or is destroyed. What is clung to is the spirit which makes art possible. And the African idea of this spirit is very different from the European idea. European art attempts to imitate nature. African art is concerned with reaching beyond and beneath nature, to contact, and itself become a part of *la force vitale*. The artistic image is not intended to represent the thing itself, but, rather, the reality of the force the thing contains. Thus, the moon is fecundity, the elephant is force.

Much of this made great sense to me, even though Senghor was speaking of, and out of, a way of life which I could only very dimly and perhaps somewhat wistfully imagine. It was the esthetic which attracted me, the idea that the work of art expresses, contains, and is itself a part of that energy which is life. Yet, I was aware that Senghor's thought had come into my mind translated. What he had been speaking of was something more direct and less isolated than the line in which my imagination immediately began to move. The distortions used by African artists to create a work of art are not at all the same distortions which have become one of the principal aims of almost every artist in the West today. (They are not the same distortions even when they have been copied from Africa.) And this was due entirely to the different situations in which each had his being. Poems and stories, in the only situation I know anything about, were never told, except, rarely, to children, and, at the risk of mayhem, in bars. They were written to be read, alone, and by a handful of people at that—there was really beginning to be something suspect in being read by more than a handful. These creations no more insisted on the actual presence of other human beings than they demanded the collaboration of a dancer and a drum. They could not be said to celebrate the society any more than the homage which Western artists sometimes receive can be said to have anything to do with society's celebration of a work of art. The only thing in Western life which seemed even faintly to approximate Senghor's intense sketch of the creative interdependence, the active, actual, joyful intercourse obtaining among African artists and what only a Westerner would call their public, was the atmosphere sometimes created among jazz musicians and their fans during, say, a jam session. But the ghastly isolation of the jazz musician, the neurotic intensity of his listeners, was proof enough that what Senghor meant when he spoke of social art had no reality whatever in Western life. He was speaking out of his past, which had been lived where art was naturally and spontaneously social, where artistic creation did not presuppose divorce. (Yet he was not there. Here he was, in Paris, speaking the adopted language in which he also wrote his poetry.)

Just what the specific relation of an artist to his culture says about that culture is a very pretty question. The culture which had produced Senghor seemed, on the face of it, to have a greater coherence as regarded assumptions, traditions, customs, and beliefs than did the Western culture to which it stood in so problematical a relation. And this might very well mean that the culture represented by Senghor was healthier than the culture represented by the hall in which he spoke. But the leap to this conclusion, than which nothing would have seemed easier, was frustrated by the question of just what health is in relation to a culture. Senghor's culture, for example, did not seem to need the lonely activity of the singular intelligence on which the cultural life—the moral life—of the West depends. And a really cohesive society, one of the attributes, perhaps, of what is taken to be a "healthy" culture, has, generally, and, I suspect, necessarily, a much lower level of tolerance for the maverick, the dissenter, the man who steals the fire, than have societies in which, the common ground of belief having all but vanished, each man, in awful and brutal isolation, is for himself, to flower or to perish. Or, not impossibly, to make real and fruitful again that vanished common ground, which, as I take it, is nothing more or less than the culture itself, endangered and rendered nearly inaccessible by the complexities it has, itself, inevitably created.

Nothing is more undeniable than the fact that cultures vanish, undergo crises; are, in any case, in a perpetual state of change and fermentation, being perpetually driven, God knows where, by forces within and without. And one of the results, surely, of the present tension between the society represented by Senghor and the society represented by the Salle Descartes was just this perceptible drop, during the last decade, of the Western level of tolerance. I wondered what this would mean—for Africa, for us. I wondered just what effect the concept of art expressed by Senghor would have on that renaissance he had predicted and just what transformations this concept itself would undergo as it encountered the complexities of the century into which it was moving with such speed.

The evening debate rang perpetual changes on two questions. These questions—each of which splintered, each time it was asked, into a thousand more—were, first: What *is* a culture? This is a difficult question under the most serene circumstances—under which circumstances, incidentally, it mostly fails to present itself. (This implies, perhaps, one of the possible definitions of a culture, at least at a certain stage of its development.) In the context of the conference, it was a question which was helplessly at the mercy of another one. And the second question was this: Is it possible to describe as a culture what may simply be, after all, a history of oppression? That is, is this history and these present facts, which involve so many millions of people who are divided from each other by so many miles of the globe, which operates, and has operated, under such very different conditions, to such different effects, and which has produced so many different subhistories, problems, traditions, possibilities, aspirations, assumptions, languages, hybrids—is this history enough to have made of the earth's black populations anything that can legitimately be described as a culture? For what, beyond the fact that all black men at one time or another left Africa, or have remained there, do they really have in common?

And yet, it became clear as the debate wore on, that there *was* something which all black men held in common, something which cut across opposing points of view, and placed in the same context their widely dissimiliar experience. What they held in common was their precarious, their unutterably painful relation to the white world. What they held in common was the necessity to remake the world in their own image, to impose this image on the world, and no longer be controlled by the vision of the world, and of themselves, held by other people. What, in sum, black men held in common was their ache to come into the world as men. And this ache united people who might otherwise have been divided as to what a man should be.

Yet, whether or not this could properly be described as a *cultural* reality remained another question. Haiti's Jacques Alexis made the rather desperate observation that a cultural survey must have *something* to survey; but then seemed confounded, as, indeed, we all were, by the dimensions of the particular cultural survey in progress. It was necessary, for example, before one could relate the culture of Haiti to that of Africa, to know what the Haitian culture was. Within Haiti there were a great many cultures. Frenchmen, Negroes, and Indians had bequeathed it quite dissimilar ways of life; Catholics, voodooists, and animists cut across class and color lines. Alexis described as "pockets" of culture those related and yet quite specific and dissimilar ways of life to be found within the borders of any country in the world and wished to know by what alchemy these opposing ways of life became a national culture. And he wished to know, too, what relation national culture bore to national independence—was it possible, really, to speak of a national culture when speaking of nations which were not free?

Senghor remarked, apropos of this question, that one of the great difficulties posed by this problem of cultures within cultures, particularly within the borders of Africa herself, was the difficulty of establishing and maintaining contact with the people if one's language had been formed in Europe. And he went on, somewhat later, to make the point that the heritage of the American Negro was an African heritage. He used, as proof of this, a poem of Richard Wright's which was, he said, involved with African tensions and symbols, even though Wright himself had not been aware of this. He suggested that the study of African sources might prove extremely illuminating for American Negroes. For, he suggested, in the same way that white classics exist—classic here taken to mean an enduring revelation and statement of a specific, peculiar, cultural sensibility—black classics must also exist. This raised in my mind the question of whether or not white classics *did* exist, and, with this question, I began to see the implications of Senghor's claim.

For, if white classics existed, in distinction, that is, to merely French or English classics, these could only be the classics produced by Greece and Rome. If *Black Boy*, said Senghor, were to be analyzed, it would undoubtedly reveal the African heritage to which it owed its existence; in the same way, I supposed, that Dickens' *A Tale of Two Cities*, would, upon analysis, reveal its debt to Aeschylus. It did not seem very important.

And yet, I realized, the question had simply never come up in relation to European literature. It was not, now, the European necessity to go rummaging in the past, and through all the countries of the world, bitterly staking out claims to its cultural possessions.

Yet *Black Boy* owed its existence to a great many other factors, by no means so tenuous or so problematical; in so handsomely presenting Wright with his African heritage, Senghor rather seemed to be taking away his identity. *Black Boy* is the study of the growing up of a Negro boy in the Deep South, and is one of the major American autobiographies. I had never thought of it, as Senghor clearly did, as one of the major *African* autobiographies, only one more document, in fact, like one more book in the Bible, speaking of the African's long persecution and exile.

Senghor chose to overlook several gaps in his argument, not the least of which was the fact that Wright had not been in a position, as Europeans had been, to remain in contact with his hypothetical African heritage. The Greco-Roman tradition had, after all, been *written down*; it was by this means that it had kept itself alive. Granted that there was something African in *Black Boy*, as there was undoubtedly something African in all American Negroes, the great question of what this was, and how it had survived, remained wide open. Moreover, *Black Boy* had been written in the English language which Americans had inherited from England, that is, if you like, from Greece and Rome; its form, psychology, moral attitude, preoccupations, in short, its cultural validity, were all due to forces which had nothing to do with Africa. Or was it simply that we had been rendered unable to recognize Africa in it?—for, it seemed that, in Senghor's vast re-creation of the world, the footfall of the African would prove to have covered more territory than the footfall of the Roman.

Thursday's great event was Aimé Cesaire's speech in the afternoon, dealing with the relation between colonization and culture. Cesaire is a caramel-colored man from Martinique, probably around forty, with a great tendency to roundness and smoothness, physically speaking, and with the rather vaguely benign air of a schoolteacher. All this changes the moment he begins to speak. It becomes at once apparent that his curious, slow-moving blandness is related to the grace and patience of a jungle cat and that the intelligence behind those spectacles is of a very penetrating and demagogic order.

The cultural crisis through which we are passing today can be summed up thus, said Cesaire: that culture which is strongest from the material and technological point of view threatens to crush all weaker cultures, particularly in a world in which, distance counting for nothing, the technologically weaker cultures have no means of protecting themselves. All cultures have, furthermore, an economic, social, and political base, and no culture can continue to live if its political destiny is not in its own hands. "Any political and social regime which destroys the self-determination of a people also destroys the creative power of that people." When this has happened the culture of that people has been destroyed. And it is simply not true that the colonizers bring to the colonized a new culture to replace the old one, a culture not being something given to a people, but, on the contrary and by definition, something that they make themselves. Nor is it, in any case, in the nature of colonialism to wish or to permit such a degree of well-being among the colonized. The well-being of the colonized is desirable only insofar as this well-being enriches the dominant country, the necessity of which is simply to remain dominant. Now the civilizations of Europe, said Cesaire, speaking very clearly and intensely to a packed and attentive hall, evolved an economy based on capital and the capital was based on black labor; and thus, regardless of whatever arguments Europeans use to defend themselves, and in spite of the absurd palliatives with which they have sometimes tried to soften the blow, the fact, of their domination, in order to accomplish and maintain this domination—in order, in fact, to make money—they destroyed, with utter ruthlessness, everything that stood in their way, languages, customs, tribes, lives; and not only put nothing in its place, but erected, on the contrary, the most tremendous barriers between themselves and the people they ruled. Europeans never had the remotest intention of raising Africans to the Western level, of sharing with them the instruments of physical, political or economic power. It was precisely their intention, their necessity, to keep the people they ruled in a state of cultural anarchy, that is, simply in a barbaric state. "The famous inferiority complex one is pleased to observe as a characteristic of the colonized is no accident but something very definitely desired and deliberately inculcated by the colonizer." He was interrupted at this point—not for the first time—by long and prolonged applause.

"The situation, therefore, in the colonial countries, is

tragic," Cesaire continued. "Wherever colonization is a fact the indigenous culture begins to rot. And, among these ruins, something begins to be born which is not a culture but a kind of subculture, a subculture which is condemned to exist on the margin allowed it by European culture. This then becomes the province of a few men, the elite, who find themselves placed in the most artificial conditions, deprived of any revivifying contact with the masses of the people. Under such conditions, this subculture has no chance whatever of growing into an active, living culture." And what, he asked, before this situation, can be done?

The answer would not be simple. "In every society there is always a delicate balance between the old and the new, a balance which is perpetually being re-established, which is re-established by each generation. Black societies, cultures, civilizations, will not escape this law." Cesaire spoke of the energy already proved by black cultures in the past, and, declining to believe that this energy no longer existed, declined also to believe that the total obliteration of the existing culture was a condition for the renaissance of black people. "In the culture to be born there will no doubt be old and new elements. How these elements will be mixed is not a question to which any individual can respond. The response must be given by the community. But we can say this: that the response will be given, and not verbally, but in tangible facts, and by action."

He was interrupted by applause again. He paused, faintly smiling, and reached his peroration: "We find ourselves today in a cultural chaos. And this is our role: to liberate the forces which, alone, can organize from this chaos a new synthesis, a synthesis which will deserve the name of a culture, a synthesis which will be the reconciliation—*et dépassement*—of the old and the new. We are here to proclaim the right of our people to speak, to let our people, black people, make their entrance on the great stage of history."

This speech, which was very brilliantly delivered, and which had the further advantage of being, in the main, unanswerable (and the advantage, also, of being very little concerned, at bottom, with culture) wrung from the audience which heard it the most violent reaction of joy. Cesaire had spoken for those who could not speak and those who could not speak thronged around the table to shake his hand, and kiss him. I myself felt stirred in a very strange and disagreeable way. For Cesaire's case against Europe, which was watertight, was also a very easy case to make. The anatomizing of the great injustice which is the irreducible fact of colonialism was yet not enough to give the victims of that injustice a new sense of themselves. One may say, of course, that the very fact that Cesaire had spoken so thrillingly, and in one of the great institutions of Western learning, invested them with this new sense, but I do not think this is so. He had certainly played very skillfully on their emotions and their hopes, but he had not raised the central, tremendous question, which was, simply: What *had* this colonial experience made of them and what were they now to do with it? For they were all, now, whether they liked it or not, related to Europe, stained by European visions and standards, and their relation to themselves, and to each other, and to their past had changed. Their relation to their poets had also changed, as had the relation of their poets to them. Cesaire's speech left out of account one of the great effects of the colonial experience: its creation, precisely, of men like himself. His real relation to the people who thronged about him now had been changed, by this experience, into something very different from what it once had been. What made him so attractive now was the fact that he, without having ceased to be one of them, yet seemed to move with the European authority. He had penetrated into the heart of the great wilderness which was Europe and stolen the sacred fire. And this, which was the promise of their freedom, was also the assurance of his power.

Friday's session began in a rather tense atmosphere and this tension continued throughout the day. Diop opened the session by pointing out that each speaker spoke only for himself and could not be considered as speaking for the conference. I imagined that this had something to with Cesaire's speech of the day before and with some of its effects, among which, apparently, had been a rather sharp exchange between Cesaire and the American delegation.

This was the session during which it became apparent that there was a religious war going on at the conference, a war which suggested, in miniature, some of the tensions dividing Africa. A Protestant minister from the Cameroons, Pastor T. Ekollo, had been forced by the hostility of the audience the day before to abandon a dissertation in defense of Christianity in Africa. He was visibly upset still. "There will be Christians in Africa, even when there is not a white man there," he said, with a tense defiance, and added, with an unconsciously despairing irony to which, however, no one reacted, "supposing that to be possible." He had been asked how he could defend Christianity in view of what Christians had done in his country. To which his answer was that the doctrine of Christianity was of more moment than the crimes committed by Christians. The necessity which confronted Africans was to make Christianity real in their own lives, without reference to the crimes committed by others. The audience was extremely cold and hostile, forcing him again, in effect, from the floor. But I felt that this also had something to do with Pastor Ekollo's rather petulant and not notably Christian attitude toward them.

Dr. Marcus James, a priest of the Anglican church from Jamaica, picked up where Ekollo left off. Dr. James is a round, very pleasant-looking, chocolate-colored man, with spectacles. He began with a quotation to the effect that, when the Christian arrived in Africa, he had the Bible and the African had the land; but that, before long, the African had the Bible and the Christian had the land. There was a great deal of laughter at this, in which Dr. James joined. But the postscript to be added today, he said, is that the African not only has the Bible but has found in it a potential weapon for the recovery of his land. The Christians in the hall, who seemed to be in the minority, applauded and stomped their feet at this, but many others now rose and left.

Dr. James did not seem to be distressed and went on to discuss the relationship between Christianity and democracy. In

Africa, he said, there was none whatever. Africans do not, in fact, believe that Christianity is any longer real for Europeans, due to the immense scaffolding with which they have covered it, and the fact that this religion has no effect whatever on their conduct. There are, nevertheless, more than twenty million Christians in Africa, and Dr. James believed that the future of their country was very largely up to them. The task of making Christianity real in Africa was made the more difficult in that they could expect no help whatever from Europe: "Christianity, as practiced by Europeans in Africa, is a cruel travesty."

This bitter observation, which was uttered in sorrow, gained a great deal of force from the fact that so genial a man had felt compelled to make it. It made vivid, unanswerable, in a way which rage could not have done, how little the West has respected its own ideals in dealing with subject peoples, and suggested that there was a price we would pay for this. He speculated a little on what African Christianity might become, and how it might contribute to the rebirth of Christianity everywhere; and left his audience to chew on this momentous speculation: Considering, he said, that what Africa wishes to wrest from Europe is power, will it be necessary for Africa to take the same bloody road which Europe has followed? Or will it be possible for her to work out some means of avoiding this?

M. Wahal, from the Sudan, spoke in the afternoon on the role of the law in culture, using as an illustration the role the law had played in the history of the American Negro. He spoke at length on the role of French law in Africa, pointing out that French law is simply not equipped to deal with the complexity of the African situation. And what is even worse, of course, is that it makes virtually no attempt to do so. The result is that French law, in Africa, is simply a legal means of administering injustice. It is not a solution, either, simply to revert to African tribal custom, which is also helpless before the complexities of present-day African life. Wahal spoke with a quiet matter-of-factness, which lent great force to the ugly story he was telling, and he concluded by saying that the question was ultimately a political one and that there was no hope of solving it within the framework of the present colonial system.

He was followed by George Lamming. Lamming is tall, raw-boned, untidy, and intense, and one of his real distinctions is his refusal to be intimidated by the fact that he is a genuine writer. He proposed to raise certain questions pertaining to the quality of life to be lived by black people in that hypothetical tomorrow when they would no longer be ruled by whites. "The profession of letters is an untidy one," he began, looking as though he had dressed to prove it. He directed his speech to Aimé Cesaire and Jacques Alexis in particular, and quoted Djuna Barnes: "Too great a sense of identity makes a man feel he can do no wrong. And too little does the same." He suggested that it was important to bear in mind that the word Negro meant black—and meant nothing more than that; and commented on the great variety of heritages, experiences, and points of view which the conference had brought together under the heading of this single noun. He wished to suggest that the nature of power was unrelated to pigmentation, that bad faith was a phenomenon which was independent of race. He found—from the point of view of an untidy man of letters—something crippling in the obsession from which Negroes suffered as regards the existence and the attitudes of the Other—this Other being everyone who was not Negro. That black people faced great problems was surely not to be denied and yet the greatest problem facing us was what *we*, Negroes, would do among ourselves "when there was no longer any colonial horse to ride." He pointed out that this was the horse on which a great many Negroes, who were in what he called "the skin trade," hoped to ride to power, power which would be in no way distinguishable from the power they sought to overthrow.

Lamming was insisting on the respect which is due the private life. I respected him very much, not only because he raised this question, but because he knew what he was doing. He was concerned with the immensity and the variety of the experience called Negro; he was concerned that one should recognize this variety as wealth. He cited the case of Amos Tutuola's *The Palm-Wine Drinkard*, which he described as a fantasy, made up of legends, anecdotes, episodes, the product, in fact, of an oral story-telling tradition which disappeared from Western life generations ago. Yet "Tutuola really *does* speak English. It is *not* his second language." The English did not find the book strange. On the contrary, they were astonished by how truthfully it seemed to speak to them of their own experience. They felt that Tutuola was closer to the English than he could possibly be to his equivalent in Nigeria; and yet Tutuola's work could elicit this reaction only because, in a way which could never really be understood, but which Tutuola had accepted, he was closer to his equivalent in Nigeria than he would ever be to the English. It seemed to me that Lamming was suggesting to the conference a subtle and difficult idea, the idea that part of the great wealth of the Negro experience lay precisely in its double-edgedness. He was suggesting that all Negroes were held in a state of supreme tension between the difficult, dangerous relationship in which they stood to the white world and the relationship, not a whit less painful or dangerous, in which they stood to each other. He was suggesting that in the acceptance of this duality lay their strength, that in this, precisely, lay their means of defining and controlling the world in which they lived.

Lamming was interrupted at about this point, however, for it had lately been decided, in view of the great number of reports still to be read, to limit everyone to twenty minutes. This quite unrealistic rule was not to be observed very closely, especially as regarded the French-speaking delegates. But Lamming put his notes in his pocket and ended by saying that if, as someone had remarked, silence was the only common language, politics, for Negroes, was the only common ground.

The evening session began with a film, which I missed, and was followed by a speech from Cheik Anta Diop, which, in sum, claimed the ancient Egyptian empire as part of the Negro past. I can only say that this question has never greatly exercised my mind, nor did M. Diop succeed in doing so—at least not in the direction he intended. He quite refused to remain within the twenty-minute limit and, while his claims of the deliberate dishonesty of all Egyptian scholars may be quite well founded for all I know, I cannot say that he convinced me. He was, however, a great success in the hall, second only, in fact, to Aimé Cesaire.

He was followed by Richard Wright. Wright had been acting as liaison man between the American delegation and the Africans and this had placed him in rather a difficult position, since both factions tended to claim him as their spokesman. It had not, of course, occurred to the Americans that he could be anything less, whereas the Africans automatically claimed him because of his great prestige as a novelist and his reputation for calling a spade a spade—particularly if the spade were white. The consciousness of his peculiar and certainly rather grueling position weighed on him, I think, rather heavily.

He began by confessing that the paper he had written, while on his farm in Normandy, impressed him as being, after the events of the last few days, inadequate. Some of the things he had observed during the course of the conference had raised questions in him which his paper could not have foreseen. He had not, however, rewritten his paper, but would read it now, exactly as it had been written, interrupting himself whenever what he had written and what he had since been made to feel seemed to be at variance. He was exposing, in short, his conscience to the conference and asking help of them in his confusion.

There was, first of all, he said, a painful contradiction in being at once a Westerner and a black man. "I see both worlds from another, and third, point of view." This fact had nothing to do with his will, his desire, or his choice. It was simply that he had been born in the West and the West had formed him.

As a black Westerner, it was difficult to know what one's attitude should be toward three realities which were inextricably woven together in the Western fabric. These were religion, tradition, and imperialism, and in none of these realities had the lives of black men been taken into account: their advent dated back to 1455, when the church had determined to rule all infidels. And it just so happened, said Wright, ironically, that a vast proportion of these infidels were black. Nevertheless, this decision on the part of the church had not been, despite the church's intentions, entirely oppressive, for one of the results of 1455 had, at length, been Calvin and Luther, who shook the authority of the church in insisting on the authority of the individual conscience. This might not, he said accurately, have been precisely their intention, but it had certainly been one of their effects. For, with the authority of the church shaken, men were left prey to many strange and new ideas, ideas which led, finally, to the discrediting of the racial dogma. Neither had this been foreseen, but what men imagine they are doing and what they are doing in fact are rarely the same thing. This was a perfectly valid observation which would, I felt, have been just as valid without the remarkable capsule history with which Wright imagined he supported it.

Wright then went on to speak of the effects of European colonialism in the African colonies. He confessed—bearing in mind always the great gap between human intentions and human effects—that he thought of it as having been, in many ways, liberating, since it smashed old traditions and destroyed old gods. One of the things that surprised him in the last few days had been the realization that most of the delegates to the conference did not feel as he did. He felt, nevertheless, that, though Europeans had not realized what they were doing in freeing Africans from the "rot" of their past, they had been accomplishing a good. And yet—he was not certain that he had the right to say that, having forgotten that Africans are not American Negroes and were not, therefore, as he somewhat mysteriously considered American Negroes to be, free from their "irrational" past.

In sum, Wright said, he felt that Europe had brought the Enlightenment to Africa and that "what was good for Europe was good for all mankind." I felt that this was, perhaps, a tactless way of phrasing a debatable idea, but Wright went on to express a notion which I found even stranger. And this was that the West, having created an African and Asian elite, should now "give them their heads" and "refuse to be shocked" at the "methods they will feel compelled to use" in unifying their countries. We had not, ourselves, used very pretty methods.

Presumably, this left us in no position to throw stones at Nehru, Nasser, Sukarno, etc., should they decide, as they almost surely would, to use dictatorial methods in order to hasten the "social evolution." In any case, Wright said, these men, the leaders of their countries, once the new social order was established, would voluntarily surrender the "personal power." He did not say what would happen then, but I supposed it would be the second coming.

Saturday was the last day of the conference, which was scheduled to end with the invitation to the audience to engage with the delegates in the Euro-African dialogue. It was a day marked by much confusion and excitement and discontent—this last on the part of people who felt that the conference had been badly run, or who had not been allowed to read their reports. (They were often the same people.) It was marked, too, by rather a great deal of plain speaking, both on and off, but mostly off, the record. The hall was even more hot and crowded than it had been the first day and the photographers were back.

The entire morning was taken up in an attempt to agree on a "cultural inventory." This had to be done before the conference could draft those resolutions which they were, today, to present to the world. This task would have been extremely difficult even had there obtained in the black world a greater unity—geographical, spiritual, and historical—than is actually the case. Under the circumstances, it was an endeavor complicated by the nearly indefinable complexities of the word *culture*, by the fact that no coherent statement had yet been made concerning the relationship of black cultures to each other, and, finally, by the necessity, which had obtained throughout the conference, of avoiding the political issues.

The inability to discuss politics had certainly handicapped the conference, but it could scarcely have been run otherwise. The political question would have caused the conference to lose itself in a war of political ideologies. Moreover, the conference *was* being held in Paris, many of the delegates represented areas which belonged to France, most of them represented areas which were not free. There was also to be considered the delicate position of the American delegation, which had sat throughout the conference uncomfortably aware that they might at any moment be forced to rise and leave the hall.

The declaration of political points of view being thus prohibited, the "cultural" debate which raged in the hall that morning was in perpetual danger of drowning in the sea of the unstated. For, according to his political position, each delegate had a different interpretation of his culture, and a different idea of its future, as well as the means to be used to make that future a reality. A solution of a kind was offered by Senghor's suggestion that two committees be formed, one to take an inventory of the past, and one to deal with present prospects. There was some feeling that two committees were scarcely necessary. Diop suggested that one committee be formed, which, if necessary, could divide itself into two. Then the question arose as to just how the committee should be appointed, whether by countries or by cultural areas. It was decided, at length, that the committee should be set up on the latter basis, and should have resolutions drafted by noon. "It is by these resolutions," protested Mercer Cook, "that we shall make ourselves known. It cannot be done in an hour."

He was entirely right. At eleven-twenty a committee of eighteen members had been formed. At four o'clock in the afternoon they were still invisible. By this time, too, the most tremendous impatience reigned in the crowded hall, in which, today, Negroes by far outnumbered whites. At four-twenty-five the impatience of the audience erupted in whistles, catcalls, and stamping of feet. At four-thirty, Alioune Diop arrived and officially opened the meeting. He tried to explain some of the difficulties such a conference inevitably encountered and assured the audience that the committee on resolutions would not be absent much longer. In the meantime, in their absence, and in the absence of Dr. Price-Mars, he proposed to read a few messages from well-wishers. But the audience was not really interested in these messages and was manifesting a very definite tendency to get out of hand again when, at four-fifty-five, Dr.

Price-Mars entered. His arrival had the effect of calming the audience somewhat and, luckily, the committee on resolutions came in very shortly afterwards. At five-seven, Diop rose to read the document which had come one vote short of being unanimously approved.

As is the way with documents of this kind, it was carefully worded and slightly repetitious. This did not make its meaning less clear or diminish its importance.

It spoke first of the great importance of the cultural inventory here begun in relation to the various black cultures which had been "systematically misunderstood, underestimated, sometimes destroyed." This inventory had confirmed the pressing need for a re-examination of the history of these cultures ("*la verité historique*") with a view to their re-evaluation. The ignorance concerning them, the errors, and the willful distortions, were among the great contributing factors to the crisis through which they now were passing, in relation to themselves and to human culture in general. The active aid of writers, artists, theologians, thinkers, scientists, and technicians was necessary for the revival, the rehabilitation, and the development of these cultures as the first step toward their integration in the active cultural life of the world. Black men, whatever their political and religious beliefs, were united in believing that the health and growth of these cultures could not possibly come about until colonialism, the exploitation of undeveloped peoples, and racial discrimination had come to an end. (At this point the conference expressed its regret at the involuntary absence of the South African delegation and the reading was interrupted by prolonged and violent applause.) All people, the document continued, had the right to be able to place themselves in fruitful contact with their national cultural values and to benefit from the instruction and education which could be afforded them within this framework. It spoke of the progress which had taken place in the world in the last few years and stated that this progress permitted one to hope for the general abolition of the colonial system and the total and universal end of racial discrimination, and ended: "Our conference, which respects the cultures of all countries and appreciates their contributions to the progress of civilization, engages all black men in the defense, the illustration, and the dissemination throughout the world of the national values of their people. We, black writers and artists, proclaim our brotherhood toward all men and expect of them ('*nous attendons d'eux*') the manifestation of this same brotherhood toward our people."

When the applause in which the last words of this document were very nearly drowned had ended, Diop pointed out that this was not a declaration of war; it was, rather, he said, a declaration of love—for the culture, European, which had been of such importance in the history of mankind. But it had been very keenly felt that it was now necessary for black men to make the effort to define themselves *au lieu d'être toujours defini par les autres*. Black men had resolved "to take their destinies into their own hands." He spoke of plans for the setting up of an international association for the dissemination of black culture and, at five-twenty-two, Dr. Price-Mars officially closed the conference and opened the floor to the audience for the Euro-African dialogue.

Someone, a European, addressed this question to Aimé Cesaire: How, he asked, do you explain the fact that many Europeans—as well as many Africans, *bien entendu*—reject what is referred to as European culture? A European himself, he was far from certain that such a thing as a European culture existed. It was possible to be a European without accepting the Greco-Roman tradition. Neither did he believe in race. He wanted to know in what, exactly, this Negro-African culture consisted and, more, why it was judged necessary to save it. He ended, somewhat vaguely, by saying that, in his opinion, it was human values which had to be preserved, human needs which had to be respected and expressed.

This admirable but quite inadequate psychologist precipitated something of a storm. Diop tried to answer the first part of his question by pointing out that, in their attitudes toward their cultures, a great diversity of viewpoints also obtained among black men. Then an enormous, handsome, extremely impressive black man whom I had not remarked before, who was also named Cesaire, stated that the contemporary crisis of black cultures had been brought about by Europe's nineteenth- and twentieth-century attempts to impose their culture on other peoples. They did this without any recognition of the cultural validity of these peoples and thus aroused their resistance. In the case of Africa, where culture was fluid and largely unwritten, resistance had been most difficult. "Which is why," he said, "we are here. We are the most characteristic products of this crisis." And then a rage seemed to shake him, and he continued in a voice thick with fury, "Nothing will ever make us believe that our beliefs . . . are merely frivolous superstitions. No power will ever cause us to admit that we are lower than any other people." He then made a reference to the present Arab struggle against the French which I did not understand, and ended, "What we are doing is holding on to what is ours. Little," he added, sardonically, "but it belongs to us."

Aimé Cesaire, to whom the question had been addressed, was finally able to answer it. He pointed out, with a deliberate, mocking logic, that the rejection by a European of European culture was of the utmost unimportance. "Reject it or not, he is still a European, even his rejection is a European rejection. We do not choose our cultures, we belong to them." As to the speaker's implied idea of cultural relativity, and the progressive role this idea can sometimes play, he cited the French objection to this idea. It is an idea which, by making all cultures, as such, equal, undermines French justification for its presence in Africa. He also suggested that the speaker had implied that this conference was primarily interested in an idealistic reconstruction of the past. "But our attitude," said Cesaire, "toward colonialism and racial discrimination is very concrete. Our aims cannot be realized without this concreteness." And as for the question of race: "No one is suggesting that there is such a thing as a pure race, or that culture is a racial product. We are not Negroes by our own desire, but, in effect, because of Europe. What unites all Negroes is the injustices they have suffered at European hands."

The moment Cesaire finished, Cheik Anta Diop passionately demanded if it were a heresy from a Marxist point of view to try to hang onto a national culture. "Where," he asked, "is the European nation which, in order to progress, surrendered its past?"

There was no answer to this question, nor were there any further questions from the audience. Richard Wright spoke briefly, saying that this conference marked a turning point in the history of Euro-African relations: it marked, in fact, the beginning of the end of the European domination. He spoke of the great diversity of techniques and approaches now at the command of black people, with particular emphasis on the role the American Negro could be expected to play. Among black people, the American Negro was in the technological vanguard and this could prove of inestimable value to the developing African sovereignties. And the dialogue ended immediately afterward, at six-fifty-five, with Senghor's statement that this was the first of many such conferences, the first of many dialogues. As night was falling we poured into the Paris streets. Boys and girls, old men and women, bicycles, terraces, all were there, and the people were queueing up before the bakeries for bread.

3.

FIFTH AVENUE, UPTOWN:

A LETTER FROM HARLEM

THERE IS A housing project standing now where the house in which we grew up once stood, and one of those stunted city trees is snarling where our doorway used to be. This is on the rehabilitated side of the avenue. The other side of the avenue—for progress takes time—has not been rehabilitated yet and it looks exactly as it looked in the days when we sat with our noses pressed against the windowpane, longing to be allowed to go "across the street." The grocery store which gave us credit is still there, and there can be no doubt that it is still giving credit. The people in the project certainly need it—far more, indeed, than they ever needed the project. The last time I passed by, the Jewish proprietor was still standing among his shelves, looking sadder and heavier but scarcely any older. Farther down the block stands the shoe-repair store in which our shoes were repaired until reparation became impossible and in which, then, we bought all our "new" ones. The Negro proprietor is still in the window, head down, working at the leather.

These two, I imagine, could tell a long tale if they would (perhaps they would be glad to if they could), having watched so many, for so long, struggling in the fishhooks, the barbed wire, of this avenue.

The avenue is elsewhere the renowned and elegant Fifth. The area I am describing, which, in today's gang parlance, would be called "the turf," is bounded by Lenox Avenue on the west, the Harlem River on the east, 135th Street on the north, and 130th Street on the south. We never lived beyond these boundaries; this is where we grew up. Walking along 145th Street—for example—familiar as it is, and similar, does not have the same impact because I do not know any of the people on the block. But when I turn east on 131st Street and Lenox Avenue, there is first a soda-pop joint, then a shoeshine "parlor," then a grocery store, then a dry cleaners', then the houses. All along the street there are people who watched me grow up, people who grew up with me, people I watched grow up along with my brothers and sisters; and, sometimes in my arms, sometimes underfoot, sometimes at my shoulder—or on it—their children, a riot, a forest of children, who include my nieces and nephews.

When we reach the end of this long block, we find ourselves on wide, filthy, hostile Fifth Avenue, facing that project which hangs over the avenue like a monument to the folly, and the cowardice, of good intentions. All along the block, for anyone who knows it, are immense human gaps, like craters. These gaps are not created merely by those who have moved away, inevitably into some other ghetto; or by those who have risen, almost always into a greater capacity for self-loathing and self-delusion; or yet by those who, by whatever means—War II, the Korean war, a policeman's gun or billy, a gang war, a brawl, madness, an overdose of heroin, or, simply, unnatural exhaustion—are dead. I am talking about those who are left, and I am talking principally about the young. What are they doing? Well, some, a minority, are fanatical churchgoers, members of the more extreme of the Holy Roller sects. Many, many more are "moslems," by affiliation or sympathy, that is to say that they are united by nothing more—and nothing less—than a hatred of the white world and all its works. They are present, for example, at every Buy Black street-corner meeting—meetings in which the speaker urges his hearers to cease trading with white men and establish a separate economy. Neither the speaker nor his hearers can possibly do this, of course, since Negroes do not own General Motors or RCA or the A & P, nor, indeed, do they own more than a wholly insufficient fraction of anything else in Harlem (those who *do* own anything are more interested in their profits than in their fellows). But these meetings nevertheless keep alive in the participators a certain pride of bitterness without which, however futile this bitterness may be, they could scarcely remain alive at all. Many have given up. They stay home and watch the TV screen, living on the earnings of their parents, cousins, brothers, or uncles, and only leave the house to go to the movies or to the nearest bar. "How're you making it?" one may ask, running into them along the block, or in the bar. "Oh, I'm TV-ing it"; with the saddest, sweetest, most shamefaced of smiles, and from a great distance. This distance one is compelled to respect; anyone who has traveled so far will not easily be dragged again into the world. There are further retreats, of course, than the TV screen or the bar. There are those who are simply sitting on their stoops, "stoned," animated for a moment only, and hideously, by the approach of someone who may lend them the money for a "fix." Or by the approach of someone from whom they can purchase it, one of the shrewd ones, on the way to prison or just coming out.

And the others, who have avoided all of these deaths, get up in the morning and go downtown to meet "the man." They work in the white man's world all day and come home in the evening to this fetid block. They struggle to instill in their children some private sense of honor or dignity which will help the child to survive. This means, of course, that they must struggle, stolidly, incessantly, to keep this sense alive in themselves, in spite of the insults, the indifference, and the cruelty they are certain to encounter in their working day. They patiently browbeat the landlord into fixing the heat, the plaster, the plumbing; this demands prodigious patience; nor is patience usually enough. In trying to make their hovels habitable, they are perpetually throwing good money after bad. Such frustration, so long endured, is driving many strong, admirable men and women whose only crime is color to the very gates of paranoia.

One remembers them from another time—playing handball in the playground, going to church, wondering if they were going to be promoted at school. One remembers them going off to war—gladly, to escape this block. One remembers their return. Perhaps one remembers their wedding day. And one sees where the girl is now—vainly looking for salvation from some other embittered, trussed, and struggling boy—and sees the all-but-abandoned children in the streets.

Now I am perfectly aware that there are other slums in

which white men are fighting for their lives, and mainly losing. I know that blood is also flowing through those streets and that the human damage there is incalculable. People are continually pointing out to me the wretchedness of white people in order to console me for the wretchedness of blacks. But an itemized account of the American failure does not console me and it should not console anyone else. That hundreds of thousands of white people are living, in effect, no better than the "niggers" is not a fact to be regarded with complacency. The social and moral bankruptcy suggested by this fact is of the bitterest, most terrifying kind.

The people, however, who believe that this democratic anguish has some consoling value are always pointing out that So-and-So, white, and So-and-So, black, rose from the slums into the big time. The existence—the public existence—of, say, Frank Sinatra and Sammy Davis, Jr. proves to them that America is still the land of opportunity and that inequalities vanish before the determined will. It proves nothing of the sort. The determined will is rare—at the moment, in this country, it is unspeakably rare—and the inequalities suffered by the many are in no way justified by the rise of a few. A few have always risen—in every country, every era, and in the teeth of regimes which can by no stretch of the imagination be thought of as free. Not all of these people, it is worth remembering, left the world better than they found it. The determined will is rare, but it is not invariably benevolent. Furthermore, the American equation of success with the big times reveals an awful disrespect for human life and human achievement. This equation has placed our cities among the most dangerous in the world and has placed our youth among the most empty and most bewildered. The situation of our youth is not mysterious. Children have never been very good at listening to their elders, but they have never failed to imitate them. They must, they have no other models. That is exactly what our children are doing. They are imitating our immorality, our disrespect for the pain of others.

All other slum dwellers, when the bank account permits it, can move out of the slum and vanish altogether from the eye of persecution. No Negro in this country has ever made that much money and it will be a long time before any Negro does. The Negroes in Harlem, who have no money, spend what they have on such gimcracks as they are sold. These include "wider" TV screens, more "faithful" hi-fi sets, more "powerful" cars, all of which, of course, are obsolete long before they are paid for. Anyone who has ever struggled with poverty knows how extremely expensive it is to be poor; and if one is a member of a captive population, economically speaking, one's feet have simply been placed on the treadmill forever. One is victimized, economically, in a thousand ways—rent, for example, or car insurance. Go shopping one day in Harlem—for anything—and compare Harlem prices and quality with those downtown.

The people who have managed to get off this block have only got as far as a more respectable ghetto. This respectable ghetto does not even have the advantages of the disreputable one—friends, neighbors, a familiar church, and friendly tradesmen; and it is not, moreover, in the nature of any ghetto to remain respectable long. Every Sunday, people who have left the block take the lonely ride back, dragging their increasingly discontented children with them. They spend the day talking, not always with words, about the trouble they've seen and the trouble—one must watch their eyes as they watch their children—they are only too likely to see. For children do not like ghettos. It takes them nearly no time to discover exactly why they are there.

The projects in Harlem are hated. They are hated almost as much as policemen, and this is saying a great deal. And they are hated for the same reason: both reveal, unbearably, the real attitude of the white world, no matter how many liberal speeches are made, no matter how many lofty editorials are written, no matter how many civil-rights commissions are set up.

The projects are hideous, of course, there being a law, apparently respected throughout the world, that popular housing shall be as cheerless as a prison. They are lumped all over Harlem, colorless, bleak, high, and revolting. The wide windows look out on Harlem's invincible and indescribable squalor: the Park Avenue railroad tracks, around which, about forty years ago, the present dark community began; the unrehabilitated houses, bowed down, it would seem, under the great weight of frustration and bitterness they contain; the dark, the ominous schoolhouses from which the child may emerge maimed, blinded, hooked, or enraged for life; and the churches, churches, block upon block of churches, niched in the walls like cannon in the walls of a fortress. Even if the administration of the projects were not so insanely humiliating (for example: one must report raises in salary to the management, which will then eat up the profit by raising one's rent; the management has the right to know who is staying in your apartment; the management can ask you to leave, at their discretion), the projects would still be hated because they are an insult to the meanest intelligence.

Harlem got its first private project, Riverton*—which is now, naturally, a slum—about twelve years ago because at that time Negroes were not allowed to live in Stuyvesant Town. Harlem watched Riverton go up, therefore, in the most violent bitterness of spirit, and hated it long before the builders arrived. They began hating it at about the time people began moving out of their condemned houses to make room for this additional proof of how thoroughly the white world despised them. And they had scarcely moved in, naturally, before they began smashing windows, defacing walls, urinating in the elevators, and fornicating in the playgrounds. Liberals, both white and black, were appalled at the spectacle. I was appalled by the liberal innocence—or cynicism, which comes out in practice as much the same thing. Other people were delighted to be

---

* The inhabitants of Riverton were much embittered by this description; they have, apparently, forgotten how their project came into being; and have repeatedly informed me that I cannot possibly be referring to Riverton, but to another housing project which is directly across the street. It is quite clear, I think, that I have no interest in accusing any individuals or families of the depredations herein described: but neither can I deny the evidence of my own eyes. Nor do I blame anyone in Harlem for making the best of a dreadful bargain. But anyone who lives in Harlem and imagines that he has *not* struck this bargain, or that what he takes to be his status (in whose eyes?) protects him against the common pain, demoralization, and danger, is simply self deluded.

able to point to proof positive that nothing could be done to better the lot of the colored people. They were, and are, right in one respect: that nothing can be done as long as they are treated like colored people. The people in Harlem know they are living there because white people do not think they are good enough to live anywhere else. No amount of "improvement" can sweeten this fact. Whatever money is now being earmarked to improve this, or any other ghetto, might as well be burnt. A ghetto can be improved in one way only: out of existence.

Similarly, the only way to police a ghetto is to be oppressive. None of the Police Commissioner's men, even with the best will in the world, have any way of understanding the lives led by the people they swagger about in twos and threes controlling. Their very presence is an insult, and it would be, even if they spent their entire day feeding gumdrops to children. They represent the force of the white world, and that world's real intentions are, simply, for that world's criminal profit and ease, to keep the black man corraled up here, in his place. The badge, the gun in the holster, and the swinging club make vivid what will happen should his rebellion become overt. Rare, indeed, is the Harlem citizen, from the most circumspect church member to the most shiftless adolescent, who does not have a long tale to tell of police incompetence, injustice, or brutality. I myself have witnessed and endured it more than once. The businessmen and racketeers also have a story. And so do the prostitutes. (And this is not, perhaps, the place to discuss Harlem's very complex attitude toward black policemen, nor the reasons, according to Harlem, that they are nearly all downtown.)

It is hard, on the other hand, to blame the policeman, blank, good-natured, thoughtless, and insuperably innocent, for being such a perfect representative of the people he serves. He, too, believes in good intentions and is astounded and offended when they are not taken for the deed. He has never, himself, done anything for which to be hated—which of us has?—and yet he is facing, daily and nightly, people who would gladly see him dead, and he knows it. There is no way for him not to know it: there are few things under heaven more unnerving than the silent, accumulating contempt and hatred of a people.

He moves through Harlem, therefore, like an occupying soldier in a bitterly hostile country; which is precisely what, and where, he is, and is the reason he walks in twos and threes. And he is not the only one who knows why he is always in company: the people who are watching him know why, too. Any street meeting, sacred or secular, which he and his colleagues uneasily cover has as its explicit or implicit burden the cruelty and injustice of the white domination. And these days, of course, in terms increasingly vivid and jubilant, it speaks of the end of that domination. The white policeman standing on a Harlem street corner finds himself at the very center of the revolution now occurring in the world. He is not prepared for it—naturally, nobody is—and, what is possibly much more to the point, he is exposed, as few white people are, to the anguish of the black people around him. Even if he is gifted with the merest mustard grain of imagination, something must seep in. He cannot avoid observing that some of the children, in spite of their color, remind him of children he has known and loved, perhaps even of his own children. He knows that he certainly does not want *his* children living this way. He can retreat from his uneasiness in only one direction: into a callousness which very shortly becomes second nature. He becomes more callous, the population becomes more hostile, the situation grows more tense, and the police force is increased. One day, to everyone's astonishment, someone drops a match in the powder keg and everything blows up. Before the dust has settled or the blood congealed, editorials, speeches, and civil-rights commissions are loud in the land, demanding to know what happened. What happened is that Negroes want to be treated like men.

Negroes want to be treated like men: a perfectly straightforward statement, containing only seven words. People who have mastered Kant, Hegel, Shakespeare, Marx, Freud, and the Bible find this statement utterly impenetrable. The idea seems to threaten profound, barely conscious assumptions. A kind of panic paralyzes their features, as though they found themselves trapped on the edge of a steep place. I once tried to describe to a very well-known American intellectual the conditions among Negroes in the South. My recital disturbed him and made him indignant; and he asked me in perfect innocence, "Why don't all the Negroes in the South move North?" I tried to explain what *has* happened, unfailingly, whenever a significant body of Negroes move North. They do not escape Jim Crow: they merely encounter another, not-less-deadly variety. They do not move to Chicago, they move to the South Side; they do not move to New York, they move to Harlem. The pressure within the ghetto causes the ghetto walls to expand, and this expansion is always violent. White people hold the line as long as they can, and in as many ways as they can, from verbal intimidation to physical violence. But inevitably the border which has divided the ghetto from the rest of the world falls into the hands of the ghetto. The white people fall back bitterly before the black horde; the landlords make a tidy profit by raising the rent, chopping up the rooms, and all but dispensing with the upkeep; and what has once been a neighborhood turns into a "turf." This is precisely what happened when the Puerto Ricans arrived in their thousands—and the bitterness thus caused is, as I write, being fought out all up and down those streets.

Northerners indulge in an extremely dangerous luxury. They seem to feel that because they fought on the right side during the Civil War, and won, they have earned the right merely to deplore what is going on in the South, without taking any responsibility for it; and that they can ignore what is happening in Northern cities because what is happening in Little Rock or Birmingham is worse. Well, in the first place, it is not possible for anyone who has not endured both to know which is "worse." I know Negroes who prefer the South and white Southerners, because "At least there, you haven't got to play any guessing games!" The guessing games referred to have driven more than one Negro into the narcotics ward, the madhouse, or the river. I know another Negro, a man very dear to me, who says, with conviction and with truth, "The spirit of the South is the spirit of America." He was born in the North and did his military training in the South. He did not, as far as I can gather, find the South "worse"; he found it, if anything, all too familiar. In the second place, though, even if Birmingham *is* worse, no doubt Johannesburg, South Africa, beats it by several miles, and Buchenwald was one of the worst things that ever happened in the entire history of the world. The world has never lacked for horrifying examples; but I do not believe that these examples are meant to be used as justification for our own crimes. This perpetual justification empties the heart of all human feeling. The emptier our hearts become, the greater will be our crimes. Thirdly, the South is not merely an embarrassingly backward region, but a part of this country, and what happens there concerns every one of us.

As far as the color problem is concerned, there is but one great difference between the Southern white and the Northerner: the Southerner remembers, historically and in his own psyche, a kind of Eden in which he loved black people and they loved him. Historically, the flaming sword laid across this Eden is the Civil War. Personally, it is the Southerner's sexual coming of age, when, without any warning, unbreakable taboos are set up between himself and his past. Everything, thereafter, is permitted him except the love he remembers and has never ceased to need. The resulting, indescribable torment affects every Southern mind and is the basis of the Southern hysteria.

None of this is true for the Northerner. Negroes represent nothing to him personally, except, perhaps, the dangers of carnality. He never sees Negroes. Southerners see them all the time. Northerners never think about them whereas Southerners are never really thinking of anything else. Negroes are, therefore, ignored in the North and are under surveillance in the South, and suffer hideously in both places. Neither the Southerner nor the Northerner is able to look on the Negro simply as a man. It seems to be indispensable to the national self-esteem that the Negro be considered either as a kind of ward (in which case we are told how many Negroes, comparatively, bought Cadillacs last year and how few, comparatively, were lynched), or as a victim (in which case we are promised that he will never vote in our assemblies or go to school with our kids). They are two sides of the same coin and the South will not change—*cannot* change—until the North changes. The country will not change until it re-examines itself and discovers what it really means by freedom. In the meantime, generations keep being born, bitterness is increased by incompetence, pride, and folly, and the world shrinks around us.

It is a terrible, an inexorable, law that one cannot deny the humanity of another without diminishing one's own: in the face of one's victim, one sees oneself. Walk through the streets of Harlem and see what we, this nation, have become.

4.

EAST RIVER, DOWNTOWN:
POSTSCRIPT TO A LETTER FROM HARLEM

THE FACT THAT American Negroes rioted in the U.N. while Adlai Stevenson was addressing the Assembly shocked and baffled most white Americans. Stevenson's speech, and the spectacular disturbance in the gallery, were both touched off by the death, in Katanga, the day before, of Patrice Lumumba. Stevenson stated, in the course of his address, that the United States was "against" colonialism. God knows what the African nations, who hold 25 per cent of the voting stock in the U.N. were thinking—they may, for example, have been thinking of the U.S. abstention when the vote on Algerian freedom was before the Assembly—but I think I have a fairly accurate notion of what the Negroes in the gallery were thinking. I had intended to be there myself. It was my first reaction upon hearing of Lumumba's death. I was curious about the impact of this political assassination on Negroes in Harlem, for Lumumba had—has—captured the popular imagination there. I was curious to know if Lumumba's death, which is surely among the most sinister of recent events, would elicit from "our" side anything more than the usual, well-meaning rhetoric. And I was curious about the African reaction.

However, the chaos on my desk prevented my being in the U.N. gallery. Had I been there, I, too, in the eyes of most Americans, would have been merely a pawn in the hands of the Communists. The climate and the events of the last decade, and the steady pressure of the "cold" war, have given Americans yet another means of avoiding self-examination, and so it has been decided that the riots were "Communist" inspired. Nor was it long, naturally, before prominent Negroes rushed forward to assure the republic that the U.N. rioters do not represent the real feeling of the Negro community.

According, then, to what I take to be the prevailing view, these rioters were merely a handful of irresponsible, Stalinist-corrupted *provocateurs*.

I find this view amazing. It is a view which even a minimal effort at observation would immediately contradict. One has only, for example, to walk through Harlem and ask oneself two questions. The first question is: Would *I* like to live here? And the second question is: Why don't those who now live here move out? The answer to both questions is immediately obvious. Unless one takes refuge in the theory—however disguised—that Negroes are, somehow, different from white people, I do not see how one can escape the conclusion that the Negro's status in this country is not only a cruel injustice but a grave national liability.

Now, I do not doubt that, among the people at the U.N. that day, there were Stalinist and professional revolutionists acting out of the most cynical motives. Wherever there is great social discontent, these people are, sooner or later, to be found. Their presence is not as frightening as the discontent which creates their opportunity. What I find appalling—and really dangerous—is the American assumption that the Negro is so contented with his lot here that only the cynical agents of a foreign power can rouse him to protest. It is a notion which contains a gratuitous insult, implying, as it does, that Negroes can make no move unless they are manipulated. It forcibly suggests that the Southern attitude toward the Negro is also, essentially, the national attitude. When the South has trouble with its Negroes—when the Negroes refuse to remain in their "place"—it blames "outside" agitators and "Northern interference." When the nation has trouble with the Northern Negro, it blames the Kremlin. And this, by no means incidentally, is a very dangerous thing to do. We thus give credit to the Communists for attitudes and victories which are not theirs. We make of them the champions of the oppressed, and they could not, of course, be more delighted.

If, as is only too likely, one prefers not to visit Harlem and expose oneself to the anguish there, one has only to consider the two most powerful movements among Negroes in this country today. At one pole, there is the Negro student movement. This movement, I believe, will prove to be the very last attempt made by American Negroes to achieve acceptance in the republic, to force the country to honor its own ideals. The movement does not have as its goal the consumption of over-cooked hamburgers and tasteless coffee at various sleazy lunch counters. Neither do Negroes, who have, largely, been produced by miscegenation, share the white man's helplessly hypocritical attitudes toward the time-honored and universal mingling. The goal of the student movement is nothing less than the liberation of the entire country from its most crippling attitudes and habits. The reason that it is important—of the utmost importance—for white people, here, to see the Negroes as people like themselves is that white people will not, otherwise, be able to see themselves as they are.

At the other pole is the Muslim movement, which daily becomes more powerful. The Muslims do not expect anything at all from the white people of this country. They do not believe that the American professions of democracy or equality have ever been even remotely sincere. They insist on the total separation of the races. This is to be achieved by the acquisition of land from the United States—land which is owed the Negroes as "back wages" for the labor wrested from them when they were slaves, and for their unrecognized and unhonored contributions to the wealth and power of this country. The student movement depends, at bottom, on an act of faith, an ability to see, beneath the cruelty and hysteria and apathy of white people, their bafflement and pain and essential decency. This is superbly difficult. It demands a perpetually cultivated spiritual resilience, for the bulk of the evidence contradicts the vision. But the Muslim movement has all the evidence on its side. Unless one supposes that the idea of black supremacy has virtues denied to the idea of white supremacy, one cannot possibly accept the deadly conclusions a Muslim draws from this evidence. On the other hand, it is quite impossible to argue with a Muslim concerning the actual state of Negroes in this country—the truth, after all, is the truth.

This is the great power a Muslim speaker has over his

audience. His audience has not heard this truth—the truth about their daily lives—honored by anyone else. Almost anyone else, black or white, prefers to soften this truth, and point to a new day which is coming in America. But this day has been coming for nearly one hundred years. Viewed solely in the light of this country's moral professions, this lapse is inexcusable. Even more important, however, is the fact that there is desperately little in the record to indicate that white America ever seriously desired—or desires—to see this day arrive.

Usually, for example, those white people who are in favor of integration prove to be in favor of it later, in some other city, some other town, some other building, some other school. The arguments, or rationalizations, with which they attempt to disguise their panic cannot be respected. Northerners proffer their indignation about the South as a kind of badge, as proof of good intentions; never suspecting that they thus increase, in the heart of the Negro they are speaking to, a kind of helpless pain and rage—and pity. Negroes know how little most white people are prepared to implement their words with deeds, how little, when the chips are down, they are prepared to risk. And this long history of moral evasion has had an unhealthy effect on the total life of the country, and has eroded whatever respect Negroes may once have felt for white people.

We are beginning, therefore, to witness in this country a new thing. "I am not at all sure," states one prominent Negro, who is *not* a Muslim, "that I *want* to be integrated into a burning house." "I might," says another, "consider being integrated into something else, an American society more real and more honest—but *this*? No, thank you, man, who *needs* it?" And this searching disaffection has everything to do with the emergence of Africa: "At the rate things are going here, all of Africa will be free before we can get a lousy cup of coffee."

Now, of course, it is easy to say—and it is true enough, as far as it goes—that the American Negro deludes himself if he imagines himself capable of any loyalty other than his loyalty to the United States. He is an American, too, and he will survive or perish with the country. This seems an unanswerable argument. But, while I have no wish whatever to question the loyalty of American Negroes, I think this argument may be examined with some profit. The argument is used, I think, too often and too glibly. It obscures the effects of the passage of time, and the great changes that have taken place in the world.

In the first place, as the homeless wanderers of the twentieth century prove, the question of nationality no longer necessarily involves the question of allegiance. Allegiance, after all, has to work two ways; and one can grow weary of an allegiance which is not reciprocal. I have the right and the duty, for example, in my country, to vote; but it is my country's responsibility to protect my right to vote. People now approaching, or past, middle age, who have spent their lives in such struggles, have thereby acquired an understanding of America, and a belief in her potential which cannot now be shaken. (There are exceptions to this, however, W. E. B. Du Bois, for example. It is easy to dismiss him as a Stalinist; but it is more interesting to consider just why so intelligent a man became so disillusioned.) But I very strongly doubt that any Negro youth, now approaching maturity, and with the whole, vast world before him, is willing, say, to settle for Jim Crow in Miami, when he can—or, before the travel ban, *could*—feast at the welcome table in Havana. And he need not, to prefer Havana, have any pro-Communist, or, for that matter, pro-Cuban, or pro-Castro sympathies: he need merely prefer not to be treated as a second-class citizen.

These are extremely unattractive facts, but they *are* facts, and no purpose is served by denying them. Neither, as I have already tried to indicate, is any purpose served by pretending that Negroes who refuse to be bound by this country's peculiar attitudes are subversive. They have every right to refuse to be bound by a set of attitudes as useless now and as obsolete as the pillory. Finally, the time is forever behind us when Negroes could be expected to "wait." What is demanded now, and at once, is not that Negroes continue to adjust themselves to the cruel racial pressures of life in the United States but that the United States readjust itself to the facts of life in the present world.

One of these facts is that the American Negro can no longer, nor will he ever again, be controlled by white America's image of him. This fact has everything to do with the rise of Africa in world affairs. At the time that I was growing up, Negroes in this country were taught to be ashamed of Africa. They were taught it bluntly, as I was, for example, by being told that Africa had never contributed "anything" to civilization. Or one was taught the same lesson more obliquely, and even more effectively, by watching nearly naked, dancing, comic-opera, cannibalistic savages in the movies. They were nearly always all bad, sometimes funny, sometimes both. If one of them was good, his goodness was proved by his loyalty to the white man. A baffling sort of goodness, particularly as one's father, who certainly wanted one to be "good," was more than likely to come home cursing—cursing the white man. One's hair was always being attacked with hard brushes and combs and Vaseline: it was shameful to have "nappy" hair. One's legs and arms and face were always being greased, so that one would not look "ashy" in the wintertime. One was always being mercilessly scrubbed and polished, as though in the hope that a stain could thus be washed away—I hazard that the Negro children of my generation, anyway, had an earlier and more painful acquaintance with soap than any other children anywhere. The women were forever straightening and curling their hair, and using bleaching creams. And yet it was clear that none of this effort would release one from the stigma and danger of being a Negro; this effort merely increased the shame and rage. There was not, no matter where one turned, any acceptable image of oneself, no proof of one's existence. One had the choice, either of "acting just like a nigger" or of *not* acting just like a nigger—and only those who have tried it know how impossible it is to tell the difference.

My first hero was Joe Louis. I was ashamed of Father Divine. Haile Selassie was the first black emperor I ever saw—in a newsreel; he was pleading vainly with the West to prevent the rape of his country. And the extraordinary complex of tensions thus set up in the breast, between hatred of whites and contempt for blacks, is very hard to describe. Some of the most energetic people of my generation were destroyed by this interior warfare.

But none of this is so for those who are young now. The

power of the white world to control their identities was crumbling as they were born; and by the time they were able to react to the world, Africa was on the stage of history. This could not but have an extraordinary effect on their own morale, for it meant that they were not merely the descendants of slaves in a white, Protestant, and puritan country: they were also related to kings and princes in an ancestral homeland, far away. And this has proved to be a great antidote to the poison of self-hatred.

It also signals, at last, the end of the Negro situation in this country, as we have so far known it. Any effort, from here on out, to keep the Negro in his "place" can only have the most extreme and unlucky repercussions. This being so, it would seem to me that the most intelligent effort we can now make is to give up this doomed endeavor and study how we can most quickly end this division in our house. The Negroes who rioted in the U.N. are but a very small echo of the black discontent now abroad in the world. If we are not able, and quickly, to face and begin to eliminate the sources of this discontent in our own country, we will never be able to do it on the great stage of the world.

5.
A FLY IN BUTTERMILK

"YOU CAN TAKE the child out of the country," my elders were fond of saying, "but you can't take the country out of the child." They were speaking of their own antecedents, I supposed; it didn't, anyway, seem possible that they could be warning me; I took myself out of the country and went to Paris. It was there I discovered that the old folks knew what they had been talking about: I found myself, willy-nilly, alchemized into an American the moment I touched French soil.

Now, back again after nearly nine years, it was ironical to reflect that if I had not lived in France for so long I would never have found it necessary—or possible—to visit the American South. The South had always frightened me. How deeply it had frightened me—though I had never seen it—and how soon, was one of the things my dreams revealed to me while I was there. And this made me think of the privacy and mystery of childhood all over again, in a new way. I wondered where children got their strength—the strength, in this case, to walk through mobs to get to school.

"You've got to remember," said an older Negro friend to me, in Washington, "that no matter what you see or how it makes you feel, it can't be compared to twenty-five, thirty years ago—you remember those photographs of Negroes hanging from trees?" I looked at him differently. *I* had seen the photographs—but *he* might have been one of them. "I remember," he said, "when conductors on streetcars wore pistols and had police powers." And he remembered a great deal more. He remembered, for example, hearing Booker T. Washington speak, and the day-to-day progress of the Scottsboro case, and the rise and bloody fall of Bessie Smith. These had been books and headlines and music for me but it now developed that they were also a part of my identity.

"You're just one generation away from the South, you know.

You'll find," he added, kindly, "that people will be willing to talk to you . . . if they don't feel that you look down on them just because you're from the North."

The first Negro I encountered, an educator, didn't give me any opportunity to look down. He forced me to admit, at once, that I had never been to college; that Northern Negroes lived herded together, like pigs in a pen; that the campus on which we met was a tribute to the industry and determination of Southern Negroes. "Negroes in the South form a *community*." My humiliation was complete with his discovery that I couldn't even drive a car. I couldn't ask him anything. He made me feel so hopeless an example of the general Northern spinelessness that it would have seemed a spiteful counterattack to have asked him to discuss the integration problem which had placed his city in the headlines.

At the same time, I felt that there was nothing which bothered him more; but perhaps he did not really know what he thought about it; or thought too many things at once. His campus risked being very different twenty years from now. Its special function would be gone—and so would his position, arrived at with such pain. The new day a-coming was not for him. I don't think this fact made him bitter but I think it frightened him and made him sad; for the future is like heaven—everyone exalts it but no one wants to go there now. And I imagine that he shared the attitude, which I was to encounter so often later, toward the children who were helping to bring this future about: admiration before the general spectacle and skepticism before the individual case.

That evening I went to visit G., one of the "integrated" children, a boy of about fifteen. I had already heard something of his first day in school, the peculiar problems his presence caused, and his own extraordinary bearing.

He seemed extraordinary at first mainly by his silence. He was tall for his age and, typically, seemed to be constructed mainly of sharp angles, such as elbows and knees. Dark gingerbread sort of coloring, with ordinary hair, and a face disquietingly impassive, save for his very dark, very large eyes. I got the impression, each time that he raised them, not so much that they spoke but that they registered volumes; each time he dropped them it was as though he had retired into the library.

We sat in the living room, his mother, younger brother and sister, and I, while G. sat on the sofa, doing his homework. The father was at work and the older sister had not yet come home. The boy had looked up once, as I came in, to say, "Good evening, sir," and then left all the rest to his mother.

Mrs. R. was a very strong-willed woman, handsome, quiet-looking, dressed in black. Nothing, she told me, beyond name-calling, had marked G.'s first day at school; but on the second day she received the last of several threatening phone calls. She was told that if she didn't want her son "cut to ribbons" she had better keep him at home. She heeded this warning to the extent of calling the chief of police.

"He told me to go on and send him. He said he'd be there when the cutting started. So I sent him." Even more remarkably perhaps, G. went.

No one cut him, in fact no one touched him. The students formed a wall between G. and the entrances, saying only enough, apparently, to make their intention clearly understood, watching him, and keeping him outside. (I asked him, "What did you feel when they blocked your way?" G. looked up at me, very briefly, with no expression on his face, and told me, "Nothing, sir.") At last the principal appeared and took him by the hand and they entered the school, while the children shouted behind them, "Nigger-lover!"

G. was alone all day at school.

"But I thought you already knew some of the kids there," I said. I had been told that he had friends among the white students because of their previous competition in a Soapbox Derby.

"Well, none of them are in his classes," his mother told me—a shade too quickly, as though she did not want to dwell on the idea of G.'s daily isolation.

"We don't have the same schedule," G. said. It was as though he were coming to his mother's rescue. Then, unwillingly, with a kind of interior shrug, "Some of the guys had lunch with me but then the other kids called them names." He went back to his homework.

I began to realize that there were not only a great many things G. would not tell me, there was much that he would never tell his mother.

"But nobody bothers you, anyway?"

"No," he said. "They just—call names. I don't let it bother me."

Nevertheless, the principal frequently escorts him through the halls. One day, when G. was alone, a boy tripped him and knocked him down and G. reported this to the principal. The white boy denied it but a few days later, while G. and the principal were together, he came over and said, "I'm sorry I tripped you; I won't do it again," and they shook hands. But it doesn't seem that this boy has as yet developed into a friend. And it is clear that G. will not allow himself to expect this.

I asked Mrs. R. what had prompted her to have her son reassigned to a previously all-white high school. She sighed, paused; then, sharply, "Well, it's not because I'm so anxious to have him around white people." Then she laughed. "I really don't know how I'd feel if I was to carry a white baby around who was calling me Grandma." G. laughed, too, for the first time. "White people say," the mother went on, "that that's all a Negro wants. I don't think they believe that themselves."

Then we switched from the mysterious question of what white folks believe to the relatively solid ground of what she, herself, knows and fears.

"You see that boy? Well, he's always been a straight-A student. He didn't hardly have to work at it. You see the way he's so quiet now on the sofa, with his books? Well, when he was going to ———— High School, he didn't have no homework or if he did, he could get it done in five minutes. Then, there he was, out in the streets, getting into mischief, and all he did all day in school was just keep clowning to make the other boys laugh. He wasn't learning nothing and didn't nobody care if he *never* learned nothing and I could just see what was going to happen to him if he kept on like that."

The boy was very quiet.

"What were you learning in ———— High?" I asked him.

"Nothing!" he exploded, with a very un-boyish laugh. I asked him to tell me about it.

"Well, the teacher comes in," he said, "and she gives you something to read and she goes out. She leaves some other student in charge . . ." ("You can just imagine how much reading gets done," Mrs. R. interposed.) "At the end of the period," G. continued, "she comes back and tells you something to read for the next day."

So, having nothing else to do, G. began amusing his classmates and his mother began to be afraid. G. is just about at the age when boys begin dropping out of school. Perhaps they get a girl into trouble; she also drops out; the boy gets work for a time or gets into trouble for a long time. I was told that forty-five girls had left school for the maternity ward the year before. A week or ten days before I arrived in the city eighteen boys from G.'s former high school had been sentenced to the chain gang.

"My boy's a good boy," said Mrs. R., "and I wanted to see him have a chance."

"Don't the teachers care about the students?" I asked. This brought forth more laughter. How could they care? How much could they do if they *did* care? There were too many children, from shaky homes and worn-out parents, in aging, inadequate plants. They could be considered, most of them, as already doomed. Besides, the teachers' jobs were safe. They were responsible only to the principal, an appointed official, whose judgment, apparently, was never questioned by his (white) superiors or confreres.

The principal of G.'s former high school was about seventy-five when he was finally retired and his idea of discipline was to have two boys beat each other—"under his supervision"—with leather belts. This once happened with G., with no other results than that his parents gave the principal a tongue-lashing. It happened with two boys of G.'s acquaintance with the result that, after school, one boy beat the other so badly that he had to be sent to the hospital. The teachers have themselves arrived at a dead end, for in a segregated school system they cannot rise any higher, and the students are aware of this. Both students and teachers soon cease to struggle.

"If a boy can wash a blackboard," a teacher was heard to say, "I'll promote him."

I asked Mrs. R. how other Negroes felt about her having had G. reassigned.

"Well, a lot of them don't like it," she said—though I gathered that they did not say so to her. As school time approached, more and more people asked her, "Are you going to send him?" "Well," she told them, "the man says the door is open and I feel like, yes, I'm going to go on and send him."

Out of a population of some fifty thousand Negroes, there had been only forty-five applications. People had said that they would send their children, had talked about it, had made plans; but, as the time drew near, when the application blanks were actually in their hands, they said, "I don't believe I'll sign this right now. I'll sign it later." Or, "I been thinking about this. I don't believe I'll send him right now."

"Why?" I asked. But to this she couldn't, or wouldn't, give me any answer.

I asked if there had been any reprisals taken against herself or her husband, if she was worried while G. was at school all day. She said that, no, there had been no reprisals, though some white people, under the pretext of giving her good advice, had expressed disapproval of her action. But she herself doesn't have a job and so doesn't risk losing one. Nor, she told me, had anyone said anything to her husband, who, however, by her own proud suggestion, is extremely closemouthed. And it developed later that he was not working at his regular trade but at something else.

As to whether she was worried, "No," she told me; in much the same way that G., when asked about the blockade, had said, "Nothing, sir." In her case it was easier to see what she meant: she hoped for the best and would not allow herself, in the meantime, to lose her head. "I don't feel like nothing's going to happen," she said, soberly. "I *hope* not. But I know if anybody tries to harm me or any one of my children, I'm going to strike back with all my strength. I'm going to strike them in God's name."

G., in the meantime, on the sofa with his books, was preparing himself for the next school day. His face was as impassive as ever and I found myself wondering—again—how he managed to face what must surely have been the worst moment of his day—the morning, when he opened his eyes and realized that it was all to be gone through again. Insults, and incipient violence, teachers, and—exams.

"One among so many," his mother said, "that's kind of rough."

"Do you think you'll make it?" I asked him. "Would you rather go back to ——— High?"

"No," he said, "I'll make it. I ain't going back."

"He ain't thinking about going back," said his mother—proudly and sadly. I began to suspect that the boy managed to support the extreme tension of his situation by means of a nearly fanatical concentration on his schoolwork; by holding in the center of his mind the issue on which, when the deal went down, others would be *forced* to judge him. Pride and silence were his weapons. Pride comes naturally, and soon, to a Negro, but even his mother, I felt, was worried about G.'s silence, though she was too wise to break it. For what was all this doing to him really?

"It's hard enough," the boy said later, still in control but with flashing eyes, "to keep quiet and keep walking when they call you nigger. But if anybody ever spits on me, I *know* I'll have to fight."

His mother laughs, laughs to ease them both, then looks at me and says, "I wonder sometimes what makes white folks so mean."

This is a recurring question among Negroes, even among the most "liberated"—which epithet is meant, of course, to describe the writer. The next day, with this question (more elegantly phrased) still beating in my mind, I visited the principal of G.'s new high school. But he didn't look "mean" and he wasn't "mean": he was a thin, young man of about my age, bewildered and in trouble. I asked him how things were working out, what he thought about it, what he thought would happen—in the long run, or the short.

"Well, I've got a job to do," he told me, "and I'm going to do it." He said that there hadn't been any trouble and that he didn't expect any. "Many students, after all, never see G. at all." None of the children have harmed him and the teachers are, apparently, carrying out their rather tall orders, which are to be kind to G. and, at the same time, to treat him like any other student.

I asked him to describe to me the incident, on the second day of school, when G.'s entrance had been blocked by the students. He told me that it was nothing at all—"It was a gesture more than anything else." He had simply walked out and spoken to the students and brought G. inside. "I've seen them do the same thing to other kids when they were kidding," he said. I imagine that he would like to be able to place this incident in the same cheerful if rowdy category, despite the shouts (which he does not mention) of "nigger-lover!"

Which epithet does not, in any case, describe him at all.

"Why," I asked, "is G. the only Negro student here?" According to this city's pupil-assignment plan, a plan designed to allow the least possible integration over the longest possible period of time, G. was the only Negro student who qualified.

"And, anyway," he said, "I don't think it's right for colored children to come to white schools just *because* they're white."

"Well," I began, "even if you don't like it . . ."

"Oh," he said quickly, raising his head and looking at me sideways, "I never said I didn't like it."

And then he explained to me, with difficulty, that it was simply contrary to everything he'd ever seen or believed. He'd never dreamed of a mingling of the races; had never lived that way himself and didn't suppose that he ever would; in the same way, he added, perhaps a trifle defensively, that he only associated with a certain stratum of white people. But, "I've never seen a colored person toward whom I had any hatred or ill-will."

His eyes searched mine as he said this and I knew that he was wondering if I believed him.

I certainly did believe him; he impressed me as being a very gentle and honorable man. But I could not avoid wondering if he had ever really *looked* at a Negro and wondered about the life, the aspirations, the universal humanity hidden behind the dark skin. As I wondered, when he told me that race relations in his city were "excellent" and had not been strained by recent developments, how on earth he managed to hold on to this delusion.

I later got back to my interrupted question, which I phrased more tactfully.

"Even though it's very difficult for all concerned—this situation—doesn't it occur to you that the reason colored children wish to come to white schools isn't because they want to be with white people but simply because they want a better education?"

"Oh, I don't know," he replied, "it seems to me that colored schools are just as good as white schools." I wanted to ask him on what evidence he had arrived at this conclusion and also how they could possibly be "as good" in view of the kind of life they came out of, and perpetuated, and the dim prospects faced by all but the most exceptional or ruthless Negro students. But I only suggested that G. and his family, who certainly should have known, so thoroughly disagreed with him that they had been willing to risk G.'s present well-being and his future psychological and mental health in order to bring about a change in his environment. Nor did I mention the lack of enthusiasm evinced by G.'s mother when musing on the prospect of a fair grandchild. There seemed no point in making this man any more a victim of his heritage than he so gallantly was already.

"Still," I said at last, after a rather painful pause, "I should think that the trouble in this situation is that it's very hard for *you* to face a child and treat him unjustly because of something for which he is no more responsible than—than *you* are."

The eyes came to life then, or a veil fell, and I found myself staring at a man in anguish. The eyes were full of pain and bewilderment and he nodded his head. This was the impossibility which he faced every day. And I imagined that his tribe would increase, in sudden leaps and bounds was already increasing.

For segregation has worked brilliantly in the South, and, in fact, in the nation, to this extent: it has allowed white people, with scarcely any pangs of conscience whatever, to *create*, in every generation, only the Negro they wished to see. As the walls come down they will be forced to take another, harder look at the shiftless and the menial and will be forced into a wonder concerning them which cannot fail to be agonizing. It is not an easy thing to be forced to re-examine a way of life and to speculate, in a personal way, on the general injustice.

"What do you think," I asked him, "will happen? What do you think the future holds?"

He gave a strained laugh and said he didn't know. "I don't want to think about it." Then, "I'm a religious man," he said, "and I believe the Creator will always help us find a way to solve our problems. If a man loses that, he's lost everything he had." I agreed, struck by the look in his eyes.

"You're from the North?" he asked me, abruptly.

"Yes," I said.

"Well," he said, "you've got your troubles too."

"Ah, yes, we certainly do," I admitted, and shook hands and left him. I did not say what I was thinking, that our troubles were the same trouble and that, unless we were very swift and honest, what is happening in the South today will be happening in the North tomorrow.

6.
NOBODY KNOWS MY NAME:
A LETTER FROM THE SOUTH

> I walked down the street,
> didn't have on no hat,
> Asking everybody I meet,
> Where's my man at?
>
> —MA RAINEY

NEGROES IN THE north are right when they refer to the South as the Old Country. A Negro born in the North who finds himself in the South is in a position similar to that of the son of the Italian emigrant who finds himself in Italy, near the village where his father first saw the light of day. Both are in countries they have never seen, but which they cannot fail to recognize. The landscape has always been familiar; the speech is archaic, but it rings a bell; and so do the ways of the people, though their ways are not his ways. Everywhere he turns, the revenant finds himself reflected. He sees himself as he was before he was born, perhaps; or as the man he would have become, had he actually been born in this place. He sees the world, from an angle odd indeed, in which his fathers awaited his arrival, perhaps in the very house in which he narrowly avoided being born. He sees, in effect, his ancestors, who, in everything they do and are, proclaim his inescapable identity. And the Northern Negro in the South sees, whatever he or anyone else may wish to believe, that his ancestors are both white and black. The white men, flesh of his flesh, hate him for that very reason. On the other hand, there is scarcely any way for him to join the black community in the South: for both he and this community are in the grip of the immense illusion that their state is more miserable than his own.

This illusion owes everything to the great American illusion that our state is a state to be envied by other people: we are powerful, and we are rich. But our power makes us uncomfortable and we handle it very ineptly. The principal effect of our material well-being has been to set the children's teeth on edge. If we ourselves were not so fond of this illusion, we might understand ourselves and other peoples better than we do, and be enabled to help them understand us. I am very often tempted to believe that this illusion is all that is left of the great dream that was to have become America; whether this is so or not, this illusion certainly prevents us from making America what we say we want it to be.

But let us put aside, for the moment, these subversive speculations. In the fall of last year, my plane hovered over the rust-red earth of Georgia. I was past thirty, and I had never seen this land before. I pressed my face against the window, watching the earth come closer; soon we were just above the tops of trees. I could not suppress the thought that this earth had acquired its color from the blood that had dripped down from these trees. My mind was filled with the image of a black man, younger than I, perhaps, or my own age, hanging from a tree, while white men watched him and cut his sex from him with a knife.

My father must have seen such sights—he was very old when he died—or heard of them, or had this danger touch him. The Negro poet I talked to in Washington, much younger than my father, perhaps twenty years older than myself, remembered such things very vividly, had a long tale to tell, and counseled me to think back on those days as a means of steadying the soul. I was to remember that time, whatever else it had failed to do, nevertheless had passed, that the situation, whether or not it was better, was certainly no longer the same. I was to remember that Southern Negroes had endured things I could not imagine; but this did not really place me at such a great disadvantage, since they clearly had been unable to imagine what awaited them in Harlem. I remembered the Scottsboro case, which I had followed as a child. I remembered Angelo Herndon and wondered, again, whatever had become of him. I remembered the soldier in uniform blinded by an enraged white man, just after the Second World War. There had been many such incidents after the First War, which was one of the reasons I had been born in Harlem. I remembered Willie McGhee, Emmett Till, and the others. My younger brothers had visited Atlanta some years before. I remembered what they had told me about it. One of my brothers, in uniform, had had his front teeth kicked out by a white officer. I remembered my mother telling us how she had wept and prayed and tried to kiss the venom out of her suicidally embittered son. (She managed to do it, too; heaven only knows what she herself was feeling, whose father and brothers had lived and died down here.) I remembered myself as a very small boy, already so bitter about the pledge of allegiance that I could scarcely bring myself to say it, and never, never believed it.

I was, in short, but one generation removed from the South, which was now undergoing a new convulsion over whether black children had the same rights, or capacities, for education as did the children of white people. This is a criminally frivolous dispute, absolutely unworthy of this nation; and it is being carried on, in complete bad faith, by completely uneducated people. (We do not trust educated people and rarely, alas, produce them, for we do not trust the independence of mind which alone makes a genuine education possible.) Educated people, of any color, are so extremely rare that it is unquestionably one of the first tasks of a nation to open all of its schools to all of its citizens. But the dispute has actually nothing to do with education, as some among the eminently uneducated know. It has to do with political power and it has to do with sex. And this is a nation which, most unluckily, knows very little about either.

The city of Atlanta, according to my notes, is "big, wholly segregated, sprawling; population variously given as six hundred thousand or one million, depending on whether one goes beyond or remains within the city limits. Negroes 25 to 30 per cent of the population. Racial relations, on the record, can be described as fair, considering that this is the state of Georgia. Growing industrial town. Racial relations manipulated by the mayor and a fairly strong Negro middle class. This works mainly in the areas of compromise and concession and has very little effect on the bulk of the Negro population and none whatever on the rest of the state. No integration, pending or actual." Also, it seemed to me that the Negroes in Atlanta were "very vividly *city* Negroes"—they seemed less patient than their rural brethren, more dangerous, or at least more unpredictable. And: "Have seen one wealthy Negro section, very pretty, but with an unpaved road. . . . The section in which I am living is composed of frame houses in various stages of disrepair and neglect, in which two and three families live, often sharing a single toilet. This is the other side of the tracks; literally, I mean. It is located, as I am told is the case in many Southern cities, just beyond the underpass." Atlanta contains a high proportion of Negroes who own their own homes and exist, visibly anyway, independently of the white world. Southern towns distrust this class and do everything in their power to prevent its appearance. But it is a class which has a certain usefulness in Southern cities. There is an incipient war, in fact, between Southern cities and Southern towns—between the city, that is, and the state—which we will discuss later. Little Rock is an ominous example of this and it is likely—indeed, it is certain—that we will see many more such examples before the present crisis is over.

Before arriving in Atlanta I had spent several days in Charlotte, North Carolina. This is a bourgeois town, Presbyterian, pretty—if you like towns—and socially so hermetic that it contains scarcely a single decent restaurant. I was told that Negroes there are not even licensed to become electricians or plumbers. I was also told, several times, by white people, that "race relations" there were excellent. I failed to find a single Negro who agreed with this, which is the usual story of "race relations" in this country. Charlotte, a town of 165,000, was in a ferment when I was there because, of its 50,000 Negroes, four had been assigned to previously all-white schools, one to each school. In fact, by the time I got there, there were only three. Dorothy Counts, the daughter of a Presbyterian minister, after several days of being stoned and spat on by the mob—"spit," a woman told me, "was hanging from the hem of Dorothy's dress"—had withdrawn from Harding High. Several white students, I was told, had called—not called *on*—Miss Counts, to beg her to stick it out. Harry Golden, editor of *The Carolina Israelite*, suggested that the "hoodlum element" might not so have shamed the town and the nation if several of the town's leading businessmen had personally escorted Miss Counts to school.

I saw the Negro schools in Charlotte, saw, on street corners, several of their alumnae, and read about others who had been sentenced to the chain gang. This solved the mystery of just what made Negro parents send their children out to face mobs. White people do not understand this because they do not know, and do not want to know, that the alternative to this ordeal is nothing less than a lifelong ordeal. Those Negro parents who spend their days trembling for their children and the rest of their time praying that their children have not been too badly damaged inside, are not doing this out of "ideals" or "convictions" or because they are in the grip of a perverse desire to send their children where "they are not wanted." They are doing it because they want the child to receive the education which will allow him to defeat, possibly escape, and not impossibly help one day abolish the stifling environment in which they see, daily, so many children perish.

This is certainly not the purpose, still less the effect, of most Negro schools. It is hard enough, God knows, under the best of circumstances, to get an education in this country. White children are graduated yearly who can neither read, write, nor think, and who are in a state of the most abysmal ignorance concerning the world around them. But at least they are white. They are under the illusion—which, since they are so badly educated, sometimes has a fatal tenacity—that they can do whatever they want to do. Perhaps that is exactly what they *are* doing, in which case we had best all go down in prayer.

The level of Negro education, obviously, is even lower than the general level. The general level is low because, as I have said, Americans have so little respect for genuine intellectual effort. The Negro level is low because the education of Negroes occurs in, and is designed to perpetuate, a segregated society. This, in the first place, and no matter how much money the South boasts of spending on Negro schools, is utterly demoralizing. It creates a situation in which the Negro teacher is soon as powerless as his students. (There are exceptions among the teachers as there are among the students, but, in this country surely, schools have not been built for the exceptional. And, though white people often seem to expect Negroes to produce nothing but exceptions, the fact is that Negroes are really just like everybody else. Some of them are exceptional and most of them are not.)

The teachers are answerable to the Negro principal, whose power over the teachers is absolute but whose power with the school board is slight. As for this principal, he has arrived at the summit of his career; rarely indeed can he go any higher. He has his pension to look forward to, and he consoles himself, meanwhile, with his status among the "better class of Negroes." This class includes few, if any, of his students and by no means all of his teachers. The teachers, as long as they remain in this school system, and they certainly do not have much choice, can only aspire to become the principal one day. Since not all of them will make it, a great deal of the energy which ought to go into their vocation goes into the usual bitter, purposeless rivalry. They are underpaid and ill treated by the white world and rubbed raw by it every day; and it is altogether understandable that they, very shortly, cannot bear the sight of their students. The children know this; it is hard to fool young people. They also know why they are going to an overcrowded, outmoded plant, in classes so large that even the most strictly attentive student, the most gifted teacher cannot but feel himself slowly drowning in the sea of general helplessness.

It is not to be wondered at, therefore, that the violent distractions of puberty, occurring in such a cage, annually take their toll, sending female children into the maternity wards and male children into the streets. It is not to be wondered at that a boy, one day, decides that if all this studying is going to prepare him only to be a porter or an elevator boy—or his teacher—well, then, the hell with it. And there they go, with an overwhelming bitterness which they will dissemble all their lives, an unceasing effort which completes their ruin. They become the menial or the criminal or the shiftless, the Negroes whom segregation has produced and whom the South uses to prove that segregation is right.

In Charlotte, too, I received some notion of what the South means by "time to adjust." The NAACP there had been trying for six years before Black Monday to make the city fathers honor the "separate but equal" statute and do something about the situation in Negro schools. Nothing whatever was done. After Black Monday, Charlotte begged for "time": and what she did with this time was work out legal stratagems designed to get the least possible integration over the longest possible period. In August of 1955, Governor Hodges, a moderate, went on the air with the suggestion that Negroes segregate themselves voluntarily—for the good, as he put it, of both races. Negroes seeming to be unmoved by this moderate proposal, the Klan reappeared in the counties and was still active there when I left. So, no doubt, are the boys on the chain gang.

But "Charlotte," I was told, "is not the South." I was told, "You haven't seen the South yet." Charlotte seemed quite Southern enough for me, but, in fact, the people in Charlotte were right. One of the reasons for this is that the South is not the monolithic structure which, from the North, it appears to be, but a most various and divided region. It clings to the myth of its past but it is being inexorably changed, meanwhile, by an entirely unmythical present: its habits and its self-interest are at war. Everyone in the South feels this and this is why there is such panic on the bottom and such impotence on the top.

It must also be said that the racial setup in the South is not, for a Negro, very different from the racial setup in the North. It is the etiquette which is baffling, not the spirit. Segregation is unofficial in the North and official in the South, a crucial difference that does nothing, nevertheless, to alleviate the lot of most Northern Negroes. But we will return to this question when we discuss the relationship between the Southern cities and states.

Atlanta, however, *is* the South. It is the South in this respect, that it has a very bitter interracial history. This is written in the faces of the people and one feels it in the air. It was on the outskirts of Atlanta that I first felt how the Southern landscape—the trees, the silence, the liquid heat, and the fact that one always seems to be traveling great distances—seems designed for violence, seems, almost, to demand it. What passions cannot be unleashed on a dark road in a Southern night! Everything seems so sensual, so languid, and so private. Desire can be acted out here; over this fence, behind that tree, in the darkness, there; and no one will see, no one will ever know. Only the night is watching and the night was made for desire. Protestantism is the wrong religion for people in such climates; America is perhaps the last nation in which such a climate belongs. In the Southern night everything seems possible, the most private, unspeakable longings; but then arrives the Southern day, as hard and brazen as the night was soft and dark. It brings what was done in the dark to light. It must have seemed something like this for those people who made the region what it is today. It must have caused them great pain. Perhaps the master who had coupled with his slave saw his guilt in his wife's pale eyes in the morning. And the wife saw his children in the slave quarters, saw the way his concubine, the sensual-looking black girl, looked at her—a woman, after all, and scarcely less sensual, but white. The youth, nursed and raised by the black Mammy whose arms had then held all that there was of warmth and love and desire, and still confounded by the dreadful taboos set up between himself and her progeny, must have wondered, after his first experiment with black flesh, where, under the blazing heavens, he could hide. And the white man must have seen his guilt written somewhere else, seen it all the time, even if his sin was merely lust, even if his sin lay in nothing but his power: in the eyes of the black man. He may not have stolen his woman, but he had certainly stolen his freedom—this black man, who had a body like his, and passions like his, and a ruder, more erotic beauty. How many times has the Southern day come up to find that black man, sexless, hanging from a tree!

It was an old black man in Atlanta who looked into my eyes and directed me into my first segregated bus. I have spent a long time thinking about that man. I never saw him again. I cannot describe the look which passed between us, as I asked him for directions, but it made me think, at once, of Shakespeare's "the oldest have borne most." It made me think of the blues: *Now, when a woman gets the blues, Lord, she hangs her head and cries. But when a man gets the blues, Lord, he grabs a train and rides.* It was borne in on me, suddenly, just why these men had so often been grabbing freight trains as the evening sun went down. And it was, perhaps, because I was getting on a segregated bus, and wondering how Negroes had borne this and other indignities for so long, that this man so struck me. He seemed to know what I was feeling. His eyes seemed to say that what I was feeling he had been feeling, at much higher pressure, all his life. But my eyes would never see the hell his eyes had seen. And this hell was, simply, that he had never in his life owned anything, not his wife, not his house, not his child, which could not, at any instant, be taken from him by the power of white people. This is what paternalism means. And for the rest of the time that I was in the South I watched the eyes of old black men.

Atlanta's well-to-do Negroes never take buses, for they all have cars. The section in which they live is quite far away from the poor Negro section. They own, or at least are paying for, their own homes. They drive to work and back, and have cocktails and dinner with each other. They see very little of the white world; but they are cut off from the black world, too.

Now, of course, this last statement is not literally true. The teachers teach Negroes, the lawyers defend them. The ministers preach to them and bury them, and others insure their lives, pull their teeth, and cure their ailments. Some of the lawyers work with the NAACP and help push test cases through the courts. (If anything, by the way, disproves the charge of "extremism" which has so often been made against this organization, it is the fantastic care and patience such legal efforts demand.) Many of the teachers work very hard to bolster the morale of their students and prepare them for their new responsibilities; nor did those I met fool themselves about the hideous system under which they work. So when I say that they are cut off from the black world, I am not sneering, which, indeed, I scarcely have any right to do. I am talking about their position as a class—*if* they are a class—and their role in a very complex and shaky social structure.

The wealthier Negroes are, at the moment, very useful for the administration of the city of Atlanta, for they represent there the potential, at least, of interracial communication. That this phrase is a euphemism, in Atlanta as elsewhere, becomes clear when one considers how astonishingly little has been communicated in all these generations. What the phrase almost always has reference to is the fact that, in a given time and place, the Negro vote is of sufficient value to force politicians to bargain for it. What interracial communication also refers to is that Atlanta is really growing and thriving, and because it wants to make even more money, it would like to prevent incidents that disturb the peace, discourage investments, and permit test cases, which the city of Atlanta would certainly lose, to come to the courts. Once this happens, as it certainly will one day, the state of Georgia will be up in arms and the present administration of the city will be out of power. I did not meet a soul in Atlanta (I naturally did not meet any members of the White Citizen's Council, not, anyway, to talk to) who did not pray that the present mayor would be re-elected. Not that they loved him particularly, but it is his administration which holds off the holocaust.

Now this places Atlanta's wealthy Negroes in a really quite sinister position. Though both they and the mayor are devoted to keeping the peace, their aims and his are not, and cannot be, the same. Many of those lawyers are working day and night on test cases which the mayor is doing his best to keep out of court. The teachers spend their working day attempting to destroy in their students—and it is not too much to say, in themselves—those habits of inferiority which form one of the principal cornerstones of segregation as it is practiced in the South. Many of the parents listen to speeches by people like Senator Russell and find themselves unable to sleep at night. They are in the extraordinary position of being compelled to work for the destruction of all they have bought so dearly—their homes, their comfort, the safety of their children. But the safety of their children is merely comparative; it is all that their comparative strength as a class has bought them so far; and they are not safe, really, as long as the bulk of Atlanta's Negroes live in such darkness. On any night, in that other part of town, a policeman may beat up one Negro too many, or some Negro or some white man may simply go berserk. This is all it takes to drive so delicately balanced a city mad. And the island on which these Negroes have built their handsome houses will simply disappear.

This is not at all in the interests of Atlanta, and almost everyone there knows it. Left to itself, the city might grudgingly work out compromises designed to reduce the tension and raise the level of Negro life. But it is not left to itself; it belongs to the state of Georgia. The Negro vote has no power in the state, and the governor of Georgia—that "third-rate man," Atlantans call him—makes great political capital out of keeping the Negroes in their place. When six Negro ministers attempted to create a test case by ignoring the segregation ordinance on the buses, the governor was ready to declare martial law and hold the ministers incommunicado. It was the mayor who prevented this, who somehow squashed all publicity, treated the ministers with every outward sign of respect, and it is his office which is preventing the case from coming into court. And remember that it was the governor of Arkansas, in an insane bid for political power, who created the present crisis in Little Rock—against the will of most of its citizens and against the will of the mayor.

This war between the Southern cities and states is of the utmost importance, not only for the South, but for the nation. The Southern states are still very largely governed by people whose political lives, insofar, at least, as they are able to conceive of life or politics, are dependent on the people in the rural regions. It might, indeed, be more honorable to try to guide these people out of their pain and ignorance instead of locking them within it, and battening on it; but it is, admittedly, a difficult task to try to tell people the truth and it is clear that most Southern politicians have no intention of attempting it. The attitude of these people can only have the effect of stiffening the already implacable Negro resistance, and this attitude is absolutely certain, sooner or later, to create great trouble in the cities. When a race riot occurs in Atlanta, it will not spread merely to Birmingham, for example. (Birmingham is a doomed city.) The trouble will spread to every metropolitan center in the nation which has a significant Negro population. And this is not only because the ties between Northern and Southern Negroes are still very close. It is because the nation, the entire nation, has spent a hundred years avoiding the question of the place of the black man in it.

That this has done terrible things to black men is not even a question. "Integration," said a very light Negro to me in Alabama, "has always worked very well in the South, after the sun goes down." "It's not miscegenation," said another Negro to me, "unless a black man's involved." Now, I talked to many Southern liberals who were doing their best to bring integration about in the South, but met scarcely a single Southerner who did not weep for the passing of the old order. They were perfectly sincere, too, and, within their limits, they were right. They pointed out how Negroes and whites in the South had loved each other, they recounted to me tales of devotion and heroism which the old order had produced, and which, now, would never come again. But the old black men I looked at down there—those same black men that the Southern liberal had loved; for whom, until now, the Southern liberal—and not only the liberal—has been willing to undergo great inconvenience and danger—they were not weeping. Men do not like to be protected, it emasculates them. This is what black men know, it is the reality they have lived with; it is what white men do not want to know. It is not a pretty thing to be a father and be ultimately dependent on the power and kindness of some other man for the well-being of your house.

But what this evasion of the Negro's humanity has done to the nation is not so well known. The really striking thing, for me, in the South was this dreadful paradox, that the black men were stronger than the white. I do not know how they did it, but it certainly has something to do with that as yet unwritten history of the Negro woman. What it comes to, finally, is that the nation has spent a large part of its time and energy looking away from one of the principal facts of its life. This failure to look reality in the face diminishes a nation as it diminishes a person, and it can only be described as unmanly. And in exactly the same way that the South imagines that it "knows" the Negro, the North imagines that it has set him free. Both camps are deluded. Human freedom is a complex, difficult—and private—thing. If we can liken life, for a moment, to a furnace, then freedom is the fire which burns away illusion. Any honest examination of the national life proves how far we are from the standard of human freedom with which we began. The recovery of this standard demands of everyone who loves this country a hard look at himself, for the greatest achievements must begin somewhere, and they always begin with the person. If we are not capable of this examination, we may yet become one of the most distinguished and monumental failures in the history of nations.

7.
FAULKNER AND DESEGREGATION

ANY REAL CHANGE implies the breakup of the world as one has always known it, the loss of all that gave one an identity, the end of safety. And at such a moment, unable to see and not daring to imagine what the future will now bring forth, one clings to what one knew, or thought one knew; to what one possessed or dreamed that one possessed. Yet, it is only when a man is able, without bitterness or self-pity, to surrender a dream he has long cherished or a privilege he has long possessed that he is set free—he has set himself free—for higher dreams, for greater privileges. All men have gone through this, go through it, each according to his degree, throughout their lives. It is one of the irreducible facts of life. And remembering this, especially since I am a Negro, affords me almost my only means of understanding what is happening in the minds and hearts of white Southerners today.

For the arguments with which the bulk of relatively articulate white Southerners of good will have met the necessity of desegregation have no value whatever as arguments, being almost entirely and helplessly dishonest, when not, indeed, insane. After more than two hundred years in slavery and ninety years of quasi-freedom, it is hard to think very highly of William Faulkner's advice to "go slow." "They don't mean go slow," Thurgood Marshall is reported to have said, "they mean don't go." Nor is the squire of Oxford very persuasive when he suggests that white Southerners, left to their own devices, will realize that their own social structure looks silly to the rest of the world and correct it of their own accord. It has looked silly, to use Faulkner's rather strange adjective, for a long time; so far from trying to correct it, Southerners, who seem to be characterized by a species of defiance most perverse when it is most despairing, have clung to it, at incalculable cost to themselves, as the only conceivable and as an absolutely sacrosanct way of life. They have never seriously conceded that their social structure was mad. They have insisted, on the contrary, that everyone who criticized it was mad.

Faulkner goes further. He concedes the madness and moral wrongness of the South but at the same time he raises it to the level of a mystique which makes it somehow unjust to discuss Southern society in the same terms in which one would discuss any other society. "Our position is wrong and untenable," says Faulkner, "but it is not wise to keep an emotional people off balance." This, if it means anything, can only mean that this "emotional people" have been swept "off balance" by the pressure of recent events, that is, the Supreme Court decision outlawing segregation. When the pressure is taken off—and not an instant before—this "emotional people" will presumably find themselves once again on balance and will then be able to free themselves of an "obsolescence in [their] own land" in their own way and, of course, in their own time. The question left begging is what, in their history to date, affords any evidence that they have any desire or capacity to do this. And it is, I suppose, impertinent to ask just what Negroes are supposed to do while the South works out what, in Faulkner's rhetoric, becomes something very closely resembling a high and noble tragedy.

The sad truth is that whatever modifications have been effected in the social structure of the South since the Reconstruction, and any alleviations of the Negro's lot within it, are due to great and incessant pressure, very little of it indeed from within the South. That the North has been guilty of Pharisaism in its dealing with the South does not negate the fact that much of this pressure has come from the North. That some—not nearly as many as Faulkner would like to believe—Southern Negroes prefer, or are afraid of changing, the status quo does not negate the fact that it is the Southern Negro himself who, year upon year, and generation upon generation, has kept the Southern waters troubled. As far as the Negro's life in the South is concerned, the NAACP is the only organization which has struggled, with admirable single-mindedness and skill, to raise him to the level of a citizen. For this reason alone, and quite apart from the individual heroism of many of its Southern members, it cannot be equated, as Faulkner equates it, with the pathological Citizen's Council. One organization is working within the law and the other is working against and outside it. Faulkner's threat to leave the "middle of the road" where he has, presumably, all these years, been working for the benefit of Negroes, reduces itself to a more or less up-to-date version of the Southern threat to secede from the Union.

Faulkner—among so many others!—is so plaintive concerning this "middle of the road" from which "extremist" elements of both races are driving him that it does not seem unfair to ask just what he has been doing there until now. Where is the evidence of the struggle he has been carrying on there on behalf of the Negro? Why, if he and his enlightened confreres in the South have been boring from within to destroy segregation, do they react with such panic when the walls show any signs of falling? Why—and how—does one move from the middle of the road where one was aiding Negroes into the streets—to shoot them?

Now it is easy enough to state flatly that Faulkner's middle of the road does not—cannot—exist and that he is guilty of great emotional and intellectual dishonesty in pretending that it does. I think this is why he clings to his fantasy. It is easy enough to accuse him of hypocrisy when he speaks of man being "indestructible because of his simple will to freedom." But he is not being hypocritical; he means it. It is only that Man is one thing—a rather unlucky abstraction in this case—and the Negroes he has always known, so fatally tied up in his mind with his grandfather's slaves, are quite another. He is at his best, and is perfectly sincere, when he declares, in *Harpers*, "To live anywhere in the world today and be against equality because of race or color is like living in Alaska and being against snow. We have already got snow. And as with the Alaskan, merely to live in armistice with it is not enough. Like the Alaskan, we had better use it." And though this seems to be flatly opposed to his statement (in an interview printed in *The Reporter*) that, if it came to a contest between the federal government and Mississippi, he would fight for Mississippi, "even if it meant going out into the streets and shooting Negroes," he means that, too. Faulkner means everything he says, means them all at once, and with very nearly the same intensity. This is why his statements demand our attention. He has perhaps never before more concretely expressed what it means to be a Southerner.

What seems to define the Southerner, in his own mind at any rate, is his relationship to the North, that is to the rest of the Republic, a relationship which can at the very best be described as uneasy. It is apparently very difficult to be at once a Southerner and an American; so difficult that many of the South's most independent minds are forced into the American exile; which is not, of course, without its aggravating, circular effect on the interior and public life of the South. A Bostonian, say, who leaves Boston is not regarded by the citizenry he has abandoned with the same venomous distrust as is the Southerner who leaves the South. The citizenry of Boston do not consider that they have been abandoned, much less betrayed. It is only the American Southerner who seems to be fighting, in his own entrails, a peculiar, ghastly, and perpetual war with all the rest of the country. ("Didn't you say," demanded a Southern woman of Robert Penn Warren, "that you was born down here, used to live right near here?" And when he agreed that this was so: "Yes . . . but you never said where you living now!")

The difficulty, perhaps, is that the Southerner clings to two entirely antithetical doctrines, two legends, two histories. Like all other Americans, he must subscribe, and is to some extent controlled by the beliefs and the principles expressed in the Constitution; at the same time, these beliefs and principles seem determined to destroy the South. He is, on the one hand, the proud citizen of a free society and, on the other, is committed to a society which has not yet dared to free itself of the necessity of naked and brutal oppression. He is part of a country which boasts that it has never lost a war; but he is also the representative of a conquered nation. I have not seen a single statement of Faulkner's concerning desegregation which does not inform us that his family has lived in the same part of Mississippi for generations, that his great-grandfather owned slaves, and that his ancestors fought and died in the Civil War. And so compelling is the image of ruin, gallantry and death thus evoked that it demands a positive effort of the imagination to remember that slaveholding Southerners were not the only people who perished in that war. Negroes and Northerners were also blown to bits. American history, as opposed to Southern history, proves that Southerners were not the only slaveholders, Negroes were not even the only slaves. And the segregation which Faulkner sanctifies by references to Shiloh, Chickamauga, and Gettysburg does not extend back that far, is in fact scarcely as old as the century. The "racial condition" which Faulkner will not have changed by "mere force of law or economic threat" was imposed by precisely these means. The Southern tradition, which is, after all, all that Faulkner is talking about, is not a tradition at all: when Faulkner evokes it, he is simply evoking a legend which contains an accusation. And that accusation, stated far more simply than it should be, is that the North, in winning the war, left the South only one means of asserting its identity and that means was the Negro.

"My people owned slaves," says Faulkner, "and the very obligation we have to take care of these people is morally bad." "This problem is . . . far beyond the moral one it is and still was a hundred years ago, in 1860, when many Southerners, including Robert Lee, recognized it as a moral one at the very instant they in turn elected to champion the underdog because that underdog was blood and kin and home." But the North escaped scot-free. For one thing, in freeing the slave, it established a moral superiority over the South which the South has not learned to live with until today; and this despite—or possibly because of—the fact that this moral superiority was bought, after all, rather cheaply. The North was no better prepared than the South, as it turned out, to make citizens of former slaves, but it was able, as the South was not, to wash its hands of the matter. Men who knew that slavery was wrong were forced, nevertheless, to fight to perpetuate it because they were unable to turn against "blood and kin and home." And when blood and kin and home were defeated, they found themselves, more than ever, committed: committed, in effect, to a way of life which was as unjust and crippling as it was inescapable. In sum, the North, by freeing the slaves of their masters, robbed the masters of any possibility of freeing themselves of the slaves.

When Faulkner speaks, then, of the "middle of the road," he is simply speaking of the hope—which was always unrealistic and is now all but smashed—that the white Southerner, with no coercion from the rest of the nation, will lift himself above his ancient, crippling bitterness and refuse to add to his already intolerable burden of blood-guiltiness. But this hope would seem to be absolutely dependent on a social and psychological stasis which simply does not exist. "Things have been getting better," Faulkner tells us, "for a long time. Only six Negroes were killed by whites in Mississippi last year, according to police figures." Faulkner surely knows how little consolation this offers a Negro and he also knows something about "police figures" in the Deep South. And he knows, too, that murder is not the worst thing that can happen to a man, black or white. But murder may be the worst thing a man can do. Faulkner is not trying to save Negroes, who are, in his view, already saved; who, having refused to be destroyed by terror, are far stronger than the terrified white populace; and who have, moreover, fatally, from his point of view, the weight of the federal government behind them. He is trying to save "whatever good remains in those white people." The time he pleads for is the time in which the Southerner will come to terms with himself, will cease fleeing from his conscience, and achieve, in the words of Robert Penn Warren, "moral identity." And he surely believes, with Warren, that "Then in a country where moral identity is hard to come by, the South, because it has had to deal concretely with a moral problem, may offer some leadership. And we need any we can get. If we are to break out of the national rhythm, the rhythm between complacency and panic."

But the time Faulkner asks for does not exist—and he is not the only Southerner who knows it. There is never time in the future in which we will work out our salvation. The challenge is in the moment, the time is always now.

8.

IN SEARCH OF A MAJORITY:
AN ADDRESS

I AM SUPPOSED to speak this evening on the goals of American society as they involve minority rights, but what I am really going to do is to invite you to join me in a series of speculations. Some of them are dangerous, some of them painful, all of them are reckless. It seems to me that before we can begin to speak of minority rights in this country, we've got to make some attempt to isolate or to define the majority.

Presumably the society in which we live is an expression—in some way—of the majority will. But it is not so easy to locate this majority. The moment one attempts to define this majority one is faced with several conundrums. Majority is not an expression of numbers, of numerical strength, for example. You may far outnumber your opposition and not be able to impose your will on them or even to modify the rigor with which they impose their will on you, i.e., the Negroes in South Africa or in some counties, some sections, of the American South. You may have beneath your hand all the apparatus of power, political, military, state, and still be unable to use these things to achieve your ends, which is the problem faced by de Gaulle in Algeria and the problem which faced Eisenhower when, largely because of his own inaction, he was forced to send paratroopers into Little Rock. Again, the most trenchant observers of the scene in the South, those who are embattled there, feel that the Southern mobs are not an expression of the Southern majority will. Their impression is that these mobs fill, so to speak, a moral vacuum and that the people who form these mobs would be very happy to be released from their pain, and their ignorance, if someone arrived to show them the way. I would be inclined to agree with this, simply from what we know of human nature. It is not my impression that people wish to become worse; they really wish to become better but very often do not know how. Most people assume the position, in a way, of the Jews in Egypt, who really wished to get to the Promised Land but were afraid of the rigors of the journey; and, of course, before you embark on a journey the terrors of whatever may overtake you on that journey live in the imagination and paralyze you. It was through Moses, according to legend, that they discovered, by undertaking this journey, how much they could endure.

These speculations have led me a little bit ahead of myself. I suppose it can be said that there was a time in this country when an entity existed which could be called the majority, let's say a class, for the lack of a better word, which created the standards by which the country lived or which created the standards to which the country aspired. I am referring or have in mind, perhaps somewhat arbitrarily, the aristocracies of Virginia and New England. These were mainly of Anglo-Saxon stock and they created what Henry James was to refer to, not very much later, as our Anglo-American heritage, or Anglo-American connections. Now at no time did these men ever form anything resembling a popular majority. Their importance was that they kept alive and they bore witness to two elements of a man's life which are not greatly respected among us now: (1) the social forms, called manners, which prevent us from rubbing too abrasively against one another and (2) the interior life, or the life of the mind. These things were important; these things were realities for them and no matter how rough-hewn or dark the country was then, it is important to remember that this was also the time when people sat up in log cabins studying very hard by lamplight or candlelight. That they were better educated than we are now can be proved by comparing the political speeches of that time with those of our own day.

Now, what I have been trying to suggest in all this is that the only useful definition of the word "majority" does not refer to numbers, and it does not refer to power. It refers to influence. Someone said, and said it very accurately, that what is honored in a country is cultivated there. If we apply this touchstone to American life we can scarcely fail to arrive at a very grim view of it. But I think we have to look grim facts in the face because if we don't, we can never hope to change them.

These vanished aristocracies, these vanished standard bearers, had several limitations, and not the least of these limitations was the fact that their standards were essentially nostalgic. They referred to a past condition; they referred to the achievements, the laborious achievements, of a stratified society; and what was evolving in America had nothing to do with the past. So inevitably what happened, putting it far too simply, was that the old forms gave way before the European tidal wave, gave way before the rush of Italians, Greeks, Spaniards, Irishmen, Poles, Persians, Norwegians, Swedes, Danes, wandering Jews from every nation under heaven, Turks, Armenians, Lithuanians, Japanese, Chinese, and Indians. Everybody was here suddenly in the melting pot, as we like to say, but without any intention of being melted. They were here because they had wanted to leave wherever they had been and they were here to make their lives, and achieve their futures, and to establish a new identity. I doubt if history has ever seen such a spectacle, such a conglomeration of hopes, fears, and desires. I suggest, also, that they presented a problem for the Puritan God, who had never heard of them and of whom they had never heard. Almost always as they arrived, they took their places as a minority, a minority because their influence was so slight and because it was their necessity to make themselves over in the image of their new and unformed country. There were no longer any universally accepted forms or standards, and since all the roads to the achievement of an identity had vanished, the problem of status in American life became and it remains today acute. In a way, status became a kind of substitute for identity, and because money and the things money can buy is the universally accepted symbol here of status, we are often condemned as materialists. In fact, we are much closer to being metaphysical because nobody has ever expected from things the miracles that we expect.

Now I think it will be taken for granted that the Irish, the Swedes, the Danes, etc., who came here can no longer be considered in any serious way as minorities; and the question of anti-Semitism presents too many special features to be profitably discussed here tonight. The American minorities can be placed on a kind of color wheel. For example, when we think of the American boy, we don't usually think of a Spanish, Turkish, a Greek, or a Mexican type, still less of an Oriental type. We usually think of someone who is kind of a cross between the Teuton and the Celt, and I think it is interesting to consider what this image suggests. Outrageous as this image is, in most cases, it is the national self-image. It is an image which suggests hard work and good clean fun and chastity and piety and success. It leaves out of account, of course, most of the people in the country, and most of the facts of life, and there is not much point in discussing those virtues it suggests, which are mainly honored in the breach. The point is that it has almost nothing to do with what or who an American really is. It has nothing to do with what life is. Beneath this bland, this conqueror-image, a great many unadmitted despairs and confusions, and anguish and unadmitted crimes and failures hide. To speak in my own person, as a member of the nation's most oppressed minority, the oldest oppressed minority, I want to suggest most seriously that before we can do very much in the way of clear thinking or clear doing as relates to the minorities in this country, we must first crack the American image and find out and deal with what it hides. We cannot discuss the state of our minorities until we first have some sense of what we are, who we are, what our goals are, and what we take life to be. The question is not what we can do now for the hypothetical Mexican, the hypothetical Negro. The question is what we really want out of life, for ourselves, what we think is real.

Now I think there is a very good reason why the Negro in this country has been treated for such a long time in such a cruel way, and some of the reasons are economic and some of them are political. We have discussed these reasons without ever coming to any kind of resolution for a very long time. Some of them are social, and these reasons are somewhat more important because they have to do with our social panic, with our fear of losing status. This really amounts sometimes to a kind of social paranoia. One cannot afford to lose status on this peculiar ladder, for the prevailing notion of American life seems to involve a kind of rung-by-rung ascension to some hideously desirable state. If this is one's concept of life, obviously one cannot afford to slip back one rung. When one slips, one slips back not a rung but back into chaos and no longer knows who he is. And this reason, this fear, suggests to me one of the real reasons for the status of the Negro in this country. In a way, the Negro tells us where the bottom is: *because he is there*, and *where* he is, beneath us, we know where the limits are and how far we must not fall. We must not fall beneath him. We must never allow ourselves to fall that low, and I am not trying to be cynical or sardonic. I think if one examines the myths which have proliferated in this country concerning the Negro, one discovers beneath these myths a kind of sleeping terror of some condition which we refuse to imagine. In a way, if the Negro were not here, we might be forced to deal within ourselves and our own personalities, with all those vices, all those conundrums, and all those mysteries with which we have invested the Negro race. Uncle Tom is, for example, if he is called uncle, a kind of saint. He is there, he endures, he will forgive us, and this is a key to that image. But if he is not uncle, if he is merely Tom, he is a danger to everybody. He will wreak havoc on the countryside. When he is Uncle Tom he has no sex—when he is Tom, he does—and this obviously says much more about the people who invented this myth than it does about the people who are the object of it.

If you have been watching television lately, I think this is unendurably clear in the faces of those screaming people in the South, who are quite incapable of telling you what it is they are afraid of. They do not really know what it is they are afraid of, but they know they are afraid of something, and they are so frightened that they are nearly out of their minds. And this same fear obtains on one level or another, to varying degrees, throughout the entire country. We would never, never allow Negroes to starve, to grow bitter, and to die in ghettos all over the country if we were not driven by some nameless fear that has nothing to do with Negroes. We would never victimize, as we do, children whose only crime is color and keep them, as we put it, in their place. We wouldn't drive Negroes mad as we do by accepting them in ball parks, and on concert stages, but not in our homes and not in our neighborhoods, and not in our churches. It is only too clear that even with the most malevolent will in the world Negroes can never manage to achieve one-tenth of the harm which we fear. No, it has everything to do with ourselves and this is one of the reasons that for all these generations we have disguised this problem in the most incredible jargon. One of the reasons we are so fond of sociological reports and research and investigational committees is because they hide something. As long as we can deal with the Negro as a kind of statistic, as something to be manipulated, something to be fled from, or something to be given something to, there is something we can avoid, and what we can avoid is what he really, really means to us. The question that still ends these discussions is an extraordinary question: Would you let your sister marry one? The question, by the way, depends on several extraordinary assumptions. First of all it assumes, if I may say so, that I *want* to marry your sister and it also assumes that if I asked your sister to marry me, she would immediately say yes. There is no reason to make either of these assumptions, which are clearly irrational, and the key to why these assumptions are held is not to be found by asking Negroes. The key to why these assumptions are held has something to do with some insecurity in the people who hold them. It is only, after all, too clear that everyone born is going to have a rather difficult time getting through his life. It is only too clear that people fall in love according to some principle that we have not as yet been able to define, to discover or to isolate, and that marriage depends entirely on the two people involved; so that this objection does not hold water. It certainly is not justification for segregated schools or for ghettos or for mobs. I suggest that the role of the Negro in American life has something to do with our concept of what God is, and from my point of view, this concept is not big enough. It has got to be made much bigger than it is because God is, after all, not anybody's toy. To be with God is really to be involved with some enormous, overwhelming desire, and joy, and power which you cannot control, which controls you.

I conceive of my own life as a journey toward something I do not understand, which in the going toward, makes me better. I conceive of God, in fact, as a means of liberation and not a means to control others. Love does not begin and end the way we seem to think it does. Love is a battle, love is a war; love is a growing up. No one in the world—in the entire world—knows more—knows Americans better or, odd as this may sound, loves them more than the American Negro. This is because he has had to watch you, outwit you, deal with you, and bear you, and sometimes even bleed and die with you, ever since we got here, that is, since both of us, black and white, got here—and this is a wedding. Whether I like it or not, or whether you like it or not, we are bound together forever. We are part of each other. What is happening to every Negro in the country at any time is also happening to you. There is no way around this. I am suggesting that these walls—these artificial walls—which have been up so long to protect us from something we fear, must come down. I think that what we really have to do is to create a country in which there are no minorities—for the first time in the history of the world. The one thing that all Americans have in common is that they have no other identity apart from the identity which is being achieved on this continent. This is not the English necessity, or the Chinese necessity, or the French necessity, but they are born into a framework which allows them their identity. The necessity of Americans to achieve an identity is a historical and a present personal fact and this is the connection between you and me.

This brings me back, in a way, to where I started. I said that we couldn't talk about minorities until we had talked about majorities, and I also said that majorities had nothing to do with numbers or with power, but with influence, with moral influence, and I want to suggest this: that the majority for which everyone is seeking which must reassess and release us from our past and deal with the present and create standards worthy of what a man may be—this majority is you. No one else can do it. The world is before you and you need not take it or leave it as it was when you came in.

PART TWO
. . . WITH EVERYTHING ON MY MIND

9.
NOTES FOR A HYPOTHETICAL NOVEL:
AN ADDRESS

WE'VE BEEN TALKING about writing for the last two days, which is a very reckless thing to do, so that I shall be absolutely reckless tonight and pretend that I'm writing a novel in your presence. I'm going to ramble on a little tonight about my own past, not as though it were my own past exactly, but as a subject for fiction. I'm doing this in a kind of halting attempt to relate the terms of my experience to yours; and to find out what specific principle, if any, unites us in spite of all the obvious disparities, some of which are superficial and some of which are profound, and most of which are entirely misunderstood. We'll come back to that, in any case, this misunderstanding, I mean, in a minute, but I want to warn you that I'm not pretending to be unbiased. I'm certain that there is something which unites all the Americans in this room, though I can't say what it is. But if I were to meet any one of you in some other country, England, Italy, France, or Spain, it would be at once apparent to everybody else, though it might not be to us, that we had something in common which scarcely any other people, or no other people could really share.

Let's pretend that I want to write a novel concerning the people or some of the people with whom I grew up, and since we are only playing let us pretend it's a very long novel. I want to follow a group of lives almost from the time they open their eyes on the world until some point of resolution, say, marriage, or childbirth, or death. And I want to impose myself on these people as little as possible. That means that I do not want to tell them or the reader what principle their lives illustrate, or what principle is activating their lives, but by examining their lives I hope to be able to make them convey to me and to the reader what their lives mean.

Now I know that this is not altogether possible. I mean that

I know that my people are controlled by my point of view and that by the time I begin the novel I have some idea of what I want the novel to do, or to say, or to be. But just the same, whatever my point of view is and whatever my intentions, because I am an American writer my subject and my material inevitably has to be a handful of incoherent people in an incoherent country. And I don't mean incoherent in any light sense, and later on we'll talk about what I mean when I use that word.

Well, who are these people who fill my past and seem to clamor to be expressed? I was born on a very wide avenue in Harlem, and in those days that part of town was called The Hollow and now it's called Junkie's Hollow. The time was the 1920's, and as I was coming into the world there was something going on called The Negro Renaissance; and the most distinguished survivor of that time is Mr. Langston Hughes. This Negro Renaissance is an elegant term which means that white people had then discovered that Negroes could act and write as well as sing and dance and this Renaissance was not destined to last very long. Very shortly there was to be a depression and the artistic Negro, or the noble savage, was to give way to the militant or the new Negro; and I want to point out something in passing which I think is worth our time to look at, which is this: that the country's image of the Negro, which hasn't very much to do with the Negro, has never failed to reflect with a kind of frightening accuracy the state of mind of the country. This was the Jazz Age you will remember. It was the epoch of F. Scott Fitzgerald, Josephine Baker had just gone to France, Mussolini had just come to power in Italy, there was a peculiar man in Germany who was plotting and writing, and the lord knows what Lumumba's mother was thinking. And all of these things and a million more which are now known to the novelist, but not to his people, are to have a terrible effect on their lives.

There's a figure I carry in my mind's eye to this day and I don't know why. He can't really be the first person I remember, but he seems to be, apart from my mother and my father, and this is a man about as old perhaps as I am now who's coming up our street, very drunk, falling-down drunk, and it must have been a Saturday and I was sitting in the window. It must have been winter because I remember he had a black overcoat on—because his overcoat was open—and he's stumbling past one of those high, iron railings with spikes on top, and he falls and he bumps his head against one of these railings, and blood comes down his face, and there are kids behind him and they're tormenting him and laughing at him. And that's all I remember and I don't know why. But I only throw him in to dramatize this fact, that however solemn we writers, or myself, I, may sometimes sound, or how pontifical I may sometimes seem to be, on that level from which any genuine work of the imagination springs, I'm really, and we all are, absolutely helpless and ignorant. But this figure is important because he's going to appear in my novel. He can't be kept out of it. He occupies too large a place in my imagination.

And then, of course, I remember the church people because I was practically born in the church, and I seem to have spent most of the time that I was helpless sitting on someone's lap in the church and being beaten over the head whenever I fell asleep, which was usually. I was frightened of all those brothers and sisters of the church because they were all powerful, I thought they were. And I had one ally, my brother, who was a very undependable ally because sometimes I got beaten for things he did and sometimes he got beaten for things I did. But we were united in our hatred for the deacons and the deaconesses and the shouting sisters and of our father. And one of the reasons for this is that we were always hungry and he was always inviting those people over to the house on Sunday for an enormous banquet and we sat next to the icebox in the kitchen watching all those hams, and chickens, and biscuits go down those righteous bellies, which had no bottom.

Now so far, in this hypothetical sketch of an unwritten and probably unwritable novel, so good. From what we've already sketched we can begin to anticipate one of those long, warm, toasty novels. You know, those novels in which the novelist is looking back on himself, absolutely infatuated with himself as a child and everything is in sentimentality. But I think we ought to bring ourselves up short because we don't need another version of *A Tree Grows in Brooklyn* and we can do without another version of *The Heart Is a Lonely Hunter*. This hypothetical book is aiming at something more implacable than that. Because no matter how ridiculous this may sound, that unseen prisoner in Germany is going to have an effect on the lives of these people. Two Italians are going to be executed presently in Boston, there's going to be something called the Scottsboro case which will give the Communist party hideous opportunities. In short, the social realities with which these people, the people I remember, whether they knew it or not, were really contending can't be left out of the novel without falsifying their experience. And—this is very important—this all has something to do with the sight of that tormented, falling down, drunken, bleeding man I mentioned at the beginning. Who is he and what does he mean?

Well, then I remember, principally I remember, the boys and girls in the streets. The boys and girls on the streets, at school, in the church. I remember in the beginning I only knew Negroes except for one Jewish boy, the only white boy in an all-Negro elementary school, a kind of survivor of another day in Harlem, and there was an Italian fruit vendor who lived next door to us who had a son with whom I fought every campaign of the Italian-Ethiopian war. Because, remember that we're projecting a novel, and Harlem is in the course of changing all the time, very soon there won't be any white people there, and this is also going to have some effect on the people in my story.

Well, more people now. There was a boy, a member of our church, and he backslid, which means he achieved a sex life and started smoking cigarettes, and he was therefore rejected from the community in which he had been brought up, because Harlem is also reduced to communities. And I've always believed that one of the reasons he died was because of this rejection. In any case, eighteen months after he was thrown out of the church he was dead of tuberculosis.

And there was a girl, who was a nice girl. She was a niece of one of the deaconesses. In fact, she was my girl. We were very young then, we were going to get married and we were always singing, praying and shouting, and we thought we'd live that way forever. But one day she was picked up in a nightgown on Lenox Avenue screaming and cursing and they carried her away to an institution where she still may be.

And by this time I was a big boy, and there were the friends of my brothers, my younger brothers and sisters. And I had danced to Duke Ellington, but they were dancing to Charlie Parker; and I had learned how to drink gin and whisky, but they were involved with marijuana and the needle. I will not really insist upon continuing this roster. I have not known many survivors. I know mainly about disaster, but then I want to remind you again of that man I mentioned in the beginning, who haunts the imagination of this novelist. The imagination of a novelist has everything to do with what happens to his material.

Now, we're a little beyond the territory of Betty Smith and Carson McCullers, but we are not quite beyond the territory of James T. Farrell or Richard Wright. Let's go a little bit farther. By and by I left Harlem. I left all those deaconesses, all those sisters, and all those churches, and all those tambourines, and I entered or anyway I encountered the white world. Now this white world which I was just encountering was, just the same, one of the forces that had been controlling me from the time I opened my eyes on the world. For it is important to ask, I think, where did these people I'm talking about come from and where did they get their peculiar school of ethics? What was its origin? What did it mean to them? What did it come out of? What function did it serve and why was it happening here? And why were they living where they were and what was it doing to them? All these things which sociologists think they can find out and haven't managed to do, which no chart can tell us. People are not, though in our age we seem to think so, endlessly manipulable. We think that once one has discovered that thirty thousand, let us say, Negroes, Chinese or Puerto Ricans or whatever have syphilis or don't, or are unemployed or not, that we've discovered something about the Negroes, Chinese or Puerto Ricans. But in fact, this is not so. In fact, we've discovered nothing very useful because people cannot be handled in that way.

Anyway, in the beginning I thought that the white world

was very different from the world I was moving out of and I turned out to be entirely wrong. It seemed different. It seemed safer, at least the white people seemed safer. It seemed cleaner, it seemed more polite, and, of course, it seemed much richer from the material point of view. But I didn't meet anyone in that world who didn't suffer from the very same affliction that all the people I had fled from suffered from and that was that they didn't know who they were. They wanted to be something that they were not. And very shortly I didn't know who I was, either. I could not be certain whether I was really rich or really poor, really black or really white, really male or really female, really talented or a fraud, really strong or merely stubborn. In short, I had become an American. I had stepped into, I had walked right into, as I inevitably had to do, the bottomless confusion which is both public and private, of the American republic.

Now we've brought this hypothetical hero to this place, now what are we going to do with him, what does all of this mean, what can we make it mean? What's the thread that unites all these peculiar and disparate lives, whether it's from Idaho to San Francisco, from Idaho to New York, from Boston to Birmingham? Because there is something that unites all of these people and places. What does it mean to be an American? What nerve is pressed in you or me when we hear this word?

Earlier I spoke about the disparities and I said I was going to try and give an example of what I meant. Now the most obvious thing that would seem to divide me from the rest of my countrymen is the fact of color. The fact of color has a relevance objectively and some relevance in some other way, some emotional relevance and not only for the South. I mean that it persists as a problem in American life because it means something, it fulfills something in the American personality. It is here because the Americans in some peculiar way believe or think they need it. Maybe we can find out what it is that this problem fulfills in the American personality, what it corroborates and in what way this peculiar thing, until today, helps Americans to feel safe.

When I spoke about incoherence I said I'd try to tell you

what I meant by that word. It's a kind of incoherence that occurs, let us say, when I am frightened, I am absolutely frightened to death, and there's something which is happening or about to happen that I don't want to face, or, let us say, which is an even better example, that I have a friend who has just murdered his mother and put her in the closet and I know it, but we're not going to talk about it. Now this means very shortly since, after all, I know the corpse is in the closet, and he knows I know it, and we're sitting around having a few drinks and trying to be buddy-buddy together, that very shortly, we can't talk about anything because we can't talk about that. No matter what I say I may inadvertently stumble on this corpse. And this incoherence which seems to afflict this country is analogous to that. I mean that in order to have a conversation with someone you have to reveal yourself. In order to have a real relationship with somebody you have got to take the risk of being thought, God forbid, "an oddball." You know, you have to take a chance which in some peculiar way we don't seem willing to take. And this is very serious in that it is not so much a writer's problem, that is to say, I don't want to talk about it from the point of view of a writer's problem, because, after all, you didn't ask me to become a writer, but it seems to me that the situation of the writer in this country is symptomatic and reveals, says something, very terrifying about this country. If I were writing hypothetically about a Frenchman I would have in a way a frame of reference and a point of view and in fact it is easier to write about Frenchmen, comparatively speaking, because they interest me so much less. But to try to deal with the American experience, that is to say to deal with this enormous incoherence, these enormous puddings, this shapeless thing, to try and make an American, well listen to them, and try to put that on a page. The truth about dialogue, for example, or the technical side of it, is that you try and make people say what they would say if they could and then you sort of dress it up to look like speech. That is to say that it's really an absolute height, people don't ever talk the way they talk in novels, but I've got to make you believe they do because I can't possibly do a tape recording.

But to try and find out what Americans mean is almost

impossible because there are so many things they do not want to face. And not only the Negro thing which is simply the most obvious and perhaps the simplest example, but on the level of private life which is after all where we have to get to in order to write about anything and also the level we have to get to in order to live, it seems to me that the myth, the illusion, that this is a free country, for example, is disastrous. Let me point out to you that freedom is not something that anybody can be given; freedom is something people take and people are as free as they want to be. One hasn't got to have an enormous military machine in order to be unfree when it's simpler to be asleep, when it's simpler to be apathetic, when it's simpler, in fact, not to want to be free, to think that something else is more important. And I'm not using freedom now so much in a political sense as I'm using it in a personal sense. It seems to me that the confusion is revealed, for example, in those dreadful speeches by Eisenhower, those incredible speeches by Nixon, they sound very much, after all, like the jargon of the Beat generation, that is, in terms of clarity. Not a pin to be chosen between them, both levels, that is, the highest level presumably, the administration in Washington, and the lowest level in our national life, the people who are called "beatniks" are both involved in saying that something which is really on their heels does not exist. Jack Kerouac says "Holy, holy" and we say Red China does not exist. But it really does. I'm simply trying to point out that it's the symptom of the same madness.

Now, in some way, somehow, the problem the writer has which is, after all, his problem and perhaps not yours is somehow to unite these things, to find the terms of our connection, without which we will perish. The importance of a writer is continuous; I think it's socially debatable and usually socially not terribly rewarding, but that's not the point; his importance, I think, is that he is here to describe things which other people are too busy to describe. It is a function, let's face it, it's a special function. There is no democracy on this level. It's a very difficult thing to do, it's a very special thing to do and people who do it cannot by that token do many other things. But their importance is, and the importance of writers in this country now is this, that this country is yet to be discovered in any real sense. There is an illusion about America, a myth about America to which we are clinging which has nothing to do with the lives we lead and I don't believe that anybody in this country who has really thought about it or really almost anybody who has been brought up against it—and almost all of us have one way or another—this collision between one's image of oneself and what one actually is is always very painful and there are two things you can do about it, you can meet the collision head-on and try and become what you really are or you can retreat and try to remain what you thought you were, which is a fantasy, in which you will certainly perish. Now, I don't want to keep you any longer. But I'd like to leave you with this, I think we have some idea about reality which is not quite true. Without having anything whatever against Cadillacs, refrigerators or all the paraphernalia of American life, I yet suspect that there is something much more important and much more real which produces the Cadillac, refrigerator, atom bomb, and what produces it, after all, is something which we don't seem to want to look at, and that is the person. A country is only as good—I don't care now about the Constitution and the laws, at the moment let us leave these things aside—a country is only as strong as the people who make it up and the country turns into what the people want it to become. Now, this country is going to be transformed. It will not be transformed by an act of God, but by all of us, by you and me. I don't believe any longer that we can afford to say that it is entirely out of our hands. We made the world we're living in and we have to make it over.

10.

THE MALE PRISON

THERE IS SOMETHING immensely humbling in this last document [*Madeleine* by André Gide] from the hand of a writer whose elaborately graceful fiction very often impressed me as simply cold, solemn and irritatingly pious, and whose precise memoirs made me accuse him of the most exasperating egocentricity. He does not, to be sure, emerge in *Madeleine* as being less egocentric; but one is compelled to see this egocentricity as one of the conditions of his life and one of the elements of his pain. Nor can I claim that reading *Madeleine* has caused me to re-evaluate his fiction (though I care more now for *The Immoralist* than I did when I read it several years ago); it has only made me feel that such a re-evaluation must be made. For, whatever Gide's shortcomings may have been, few writers of our time can equal his devotion to a very high ideal.

It seems to me now that the two things which contributed most heavily to my dislike of Gide—or, rather, to the discomfort he caused me to feel—were his Protestantism and his homosexuality. It was clear to me that he had not got over his Protestantism and that he had not come to terms with his nature. (For I believed at one time—rather oddly, considering the examples by which I was surrounded, to say nothing of the spectacle I myself presented—that people *did* "get over" their earliest impressions and that "coming to terms" with oneself simply demanded a slightly more protracted stiffening of the will.) It was his Protestantism, I felt, which made him so pious, which invested all of his work with the air of an endless winter, and which made it so difficult for me to care what happened to any of his people.

And his homosexuality, I felt, was his own affair which he ought to have kept hidden from us, or, if he needed to be so explicit, he ought at least to have managed to be a little more scientific—whatever, in the domain of morals, that word may mean—less illogical, less romantic. He ought to have leaned less heavily on the examples of dead, great men, of vanished cultures, and he ought certainly to have known that the examples provided by natural history do not go far toward illuminating the physical, psychological and moral complexities faced by men. If he were going to talk about homosexuality at all, he ought, in a word, to have sounded a little less *disturbed*.

This is not the place and I am certainly not the man to assess the work of André Gide. Moreover, I confess that a great deal of what I felt concerning his work I still feel. And that argument, for example, as to whether or not homosexuality is natural seems to me completely pointless—pointless because I really do not see what difference the answer makes. It seems clear, in any case, at least in the world we know, that no matter what encyclopedias of physiological and scientific knowledge are brought to bear the answer never can be Yes. And one of the reasons for this is that it would rob the normal—who are simply the many—of their very necessary sense of security and order, of their sense, perhaps, that the race is and should be devoted to outwitting oblivion—and will surely manage to do so.

But there are a great many ways of outwitting oblivion, and to ask whether or not homosexuality is natural is really like asking whether or not it was natural for Socrates to swallow hemlock, whether or not it was natural for St. Paul to suffer for the Gospel, whether or not it was natural for the Germans to send upwards of six million people to an extremely twentieth-century death. It does not seem to me that nature helps us very much when we need illumination in human affairs. I am certainly convinced that it is one of the greatest impulses of mankind to arrive at something higher than a natural state. How to be natural does not seem to me to be a problem—quite the contrary. The great problem is how to be—in the best sense of that kaleidoscopic word—a man.

This problem was at the heart of all Gide's anguish, and it proved itself, like most real problems, to be insoluble. He died, as it were, with the teeth of this problem still buried in his throat. What one learns from *Madeleine* is what it cost him, in terms of unceasing agony, to live with this problem at all. Of what it cost her, his wife, it is scarcely possible to conjecture. But she was not so much a victim of Gide's sexual nature—homosexuals do not choose women for their victims, nor is the difficulty of becoming a victim so great for a woman that she is compelled to turn to homosexuals for this—as she was a victim of his overwhelming guilt, which connected, it would seem, and most unluckily, with her own guilt and shame.

If this meant, as Gide says, that "the spiritual force of my love [for Madeleine] inhibited all carnal desire," it also meant that some corresponding inhibition in her prevented her from seeking carnal satisfaction elsewhere. And if there is scarcely any suggestion throughout this appalling letter that Gide ever really understood that he had married a woman or that he had any apprehension of what a woman was, neither is there any suggestion that she ever, in any way, insisted on or was able to believe in her womanhood and its right to flower.

Her most definite and also most desperate act is the burning of his letters—and the anguish this cost her, and the fact that in this burning she expressed what surely must have seemed to her life's monumental failure and waste, Gide characteristically (indeed, one may say, necessarily) cannot enter into and cannot understand. "They were my most precious belongings," she tells him, and perhaps he cannot be blamed for protecting himself against the knife of this dreadful conjugal confession. But: "It is the best of me that disappears," he tells us, "*and it will no longer counterbalance the worst.*" (Italics mine.) He had entrusted, as it were, to her his purity, that part of him that was not carnal; and it is quite clear that, though he suspected it, he could not face the fact that it was only when her purity ended that her life could begin, that the key to her liberation was in his hands.

But if he had ever turned that key madness and despair would have followed for him, his world would have turned completely dark, the string connecting him to heaven would have been cut. And this is because then he could no longer have loved Madeleine as an ideal, as Emanuele, God-with-us, but would have been compelled to love her as a woman, which he could not have done except physically. And then he would have had to hate her, and at that moment those gates which, as it seemed to him, held him back from utter corruption would have been opened. He loved her as a woman, indeed, only in the sense that no man could have held the place in Gide's dark sky which was held by Madeleine. She was his Heaven who would forgive him for his Hell and help him to endure it. As indeed she was and, in the strangest way possible, did—by allowing him to feel guilty about *her* instead of the boys on the *Piazza d'Espagne*—with the result that, in Gide's work, both his Heaven and his Hell suffer from a certain lack of urgency.

Gide's relations with Madeleine place his relations with men in rather a bleak light. Since he clearly could not forgive himself for his anomaly, he must certainly have despised them—which almost certainly explains the fascination felt by Gide and so many of his heroes for countries like North Africa. It is not necessary to despise people who are one's inferiors—whose inferiority, by the way, is amply demonstrated by the fact that they appear to relish, without guilt, their sensuality.

It is possible, as it were, to have one's pleasure without paying for it. But to have one's pleasure without paying for it is precisely the way to find oneself reduced to a search for pleasure which grows steadily more desperate and more grotesque. It does not take long, after all, to discover that sex is only sex, that there are few things on earth more futile or more deadening than a meaningless round of conquests. The really horrible thing about the phenomenon of present-day homosexuality, the horrible thing which lies curled like a worm at the heart of Gide's trouble and his work and the reason that he so clung to Madeleine, is that today's unlucky deviate can only save himself by the most tremendous exertion of all his forces from falling into an underworld in which he never meets either men or women, where it is impossible to have either a lover or a friend, where the possibility of genuine human involvement has altogether ceased. When this possibility has ceased, so has the possibility of growth.

And, again: It is one of the facts of life that there are two sexes, which fact has given the world most of its beauty, cost it not a little of its anguish, and contains the hope and glory of the world. And it is with this fact, which might better perhaps be called a mystery, that every human being born must find some way to live. For, no matter what demons drive them, men cannot live without women and women cannot live without men. And this is what is most clearly conveyed in the agony of Gide's last journal. However little he was able to understand it, or, more important perhaps, take upon himself the responsibility for it, Madeleine kept open for him a kind of door of hope, of possibility, the possibility of entering into communion with another sex. This door, which is the door to life and air and freedom from the tyranny of one's own personality, *must* be kept open, and none feel this more keenly than those on whom the door is perpetually threatening or has already seemed to close.

Gide's dilemma, his wrestling, his peculiar, notable and extremely valuable failure testify—which should not seem odd—to a powerful masculinity and also to the fact that he found no way to escape the prison of that masculinity. And the fact that he endured this prison with such dignity is precisely what ought to humble us all, living as we do in a time and country where communion between the sexes has become so sorely threatened that we depend more and more on the strident exploitation of externals, as, for example, the breasts of Hollywood glamour girls and the mindless grunting and swaggering of Hollywood he-men.

It is important to remember that the prison in which Gide struggled is not really so unique as it would certainly comfort us to believe, is not very different from the prison inhabited by, say, the heroes of Mickey Spillane. Neither can they get through to women, which is the only reason their muscles, their fists and their tommy guns have acquired such fantastic importance. It is worth observing, too, that when men can no longer love women they also cease to love or respect or trust each other, which makes their isolation complete. Nothing is more dangerous than this isolation, for men will commit any crimes whatever rather than endure it. We ought, for our own sakes, to be humbled by Gide's confession as he was humbled by his pain and make the generous effort to understand that his sorrow was not different from the sorrow of all men born. For, if we do not learn this humility, we may very well be strangled by a most petulant and unmasculine pride.

11.
THE NORTHERN PROTESTANT

I ALREADY KNEW that Bergman had just completed one movie, was mixing the sound for it, and was scheduled to begin another almost at once. When I called the Filmstaden, he himself, incredibly enough, came to the phone. He sounded tired but very pleasant, and told me he could see me if I came at once.

The Filmstaden is in a suburb of Stockholm called Rasunda, and is the headquarters of the Svensk Filmindustri, which is one of the oldest movie companies in the world. It was here that Victor Sjöström made those remarkable movies which, eventually (under the name of Victor Seastrom) carried him—briefly—to the arid plains of Hollywood. Here Mauritz Stiller directed *The Legend of Gösta Berling*, after which he and the star thus discovered, Garbo, also took themselves west—a disastrous move for Stiller and not, as it was to turn out, altogether the most fruitful move, artistically anyway, that Garbo could have made. Ingrid Bergman left here in 1939. (She is not related to Ingmar Bergman.) The Svensk Filmindustri is proud of these alumni, but they are prouder of no one, at the moment, than they are of Ingmar Bergman, whose films have placed the Swedish film industry back on the international map. And yet, on the whole, they take a remarkably steady view of the Bergman vogue. They realize that it *is* a vogue, they are bracing themselves for the inevitable reaction, and they hope that Bergman is doing the same. He is neither as great nor as limited as the current hue and cry suggests. But he is one of the very few genuine artists now working in films.

He is also, beyond doubt, the freest. Not for him the necessity of working on a shoestring, with unpaid performers, as has been the case with many of the younger French directors. He is backed by a film company; Swedish film companies usually own their laboratories, studios, rental distribution services, and theaters. If they did not they could scarcely afford to make movies at all, movies being more highly taxed in this tiny country than anywhere else in the world—except Denmark—and 60 per cent of the playing time in these company-owned theaters being taken up by foreign films. Nor can the Swedish film industry possibly support anything resembling the American star system. This is healthy for the performers, who never have to sit idly by for a couple of years, waiting for a fat part, and who are able to develop a range and flexibility rarely permitted even to the most gifted of our stars. And, of course, it's fine for Bergman because he is absolutely free to choose his own performers: if he wishes to work, say, with Geraldine Page, studio pressure will not force him into extracting a performance from Kim Novak. If it were not for this freedom we would almost certainly never have heard of Ingmar Bergman. Most of his twenty-odd movies were not successful when they were made, nor are they today his company's biggest money-makers. (His vogue has changed this somewhat, but, as I say, no one expects this vogue to last.) "He wins the prizes and brings us the prestige," was the comment of one of his co-workers, "but it's So-and-So and So-and-So—" and here he named two very popular Swedish directors—"who can be counted on to bring in the money."

I arrived at the Filmstaden a little early; Bergman was still busy and would be a little late in meeting me, I was told. I was taken into his office to wait for him. I welcomed the opportunity of seeing the office without the man.

It is a very small office, most of it taken up by a desk. The desk is placed smack in front of the window—not that it could have been placed anywhere else; this window looks out on the daylight landscape of Bergman's movies. It was gray and glaring the first day I was there, dry and fiery. Leaves kept falling from the trees, each silent descent bringing a little closer the long, dark, Swedish winter. The forest Bergman's characters are always traversing is outside this window and the ominous carriage from which they have yet to escape is still among the properties. I realized, with a small shock, that the landscape of Bergman's mind was simply the landscape in which he had grown up.

On the desk were papers, folders, a few books, all very neatly arranged. Squeezed between the desk and the wall was a spartan cot; a brown leather jacket and a brown knitted cap were lying on it. The visitor's chair in which I sat was placed at an angle to the door, which proximity, each time that I was there, led to much bumping and scraping and smiling exchanges in Esperanto. On the wall were three photographs of Charlie Chaplin and one of Victor Sjöström.

Eventually, he came in, bareheaded, wearing a sweater, a tall man, economically, intimidatingly lean. He must have been the gawkiest of adolescents, his arms and legs still seeming to be very loosely anchored; something in his good-natured, self-possessed directness suggests that he would also have been among the most belligerently opinionated: by no means an easy man to deal with, in any sense, any relationship whatever, there being about him the evangelical distance of someone possessed by a vision. This extremely dangerous quality—authority—has never failed to incite the hostility of the many. And I got the impression that Bergman was in the habit of saying what he felt because he knew that scarcely anyone was listening.

He suggested tea, partly, I think, to give both of us time to become easier with each other, but also because he really needed a cup of tea before going back to work. We walked out of the office and down the road to the canteen.

I had arrived in Stockholm with what turned out to be the "flu" and I kept coughing and sneezing and wiping my eyes. After a while Bergman began to look at me worriedly and said that I sounded very ill.

I hadn't come there to talk about my health and I tried to change the subject. But I was shortly to learn that any subject changing to be done around Bergman is done by Bergman. He was not to be sidetracked.

"Can I do anything for you?" he persisted; and when I did not answer, being both touched and irritated by his question, he smiled and said, "You haven't to be shy. I know what it is like to be ill and alone in a strange city."

It was a hideously, an inevitably self-conscious gesture and yet it touched and disarmed me. I know that his concern, at bottom, had very little to do with me. It had to do with his memories of himself and it expressed his determination never to be guilty of the world's indifference.

He turned and looked out of the canteen window, at the brilliant October trees and the glaring sky, for a few seconds and then turned back to me.

"Well," he asked me, with a small laugh, "are you for me or against me?"

I did not know how to answer this question right away and he continued, "I don't care if you are or not. Well, that's not true. Naturally, I prefer—I would be happier—if you were *for* me. But I have to know."

I told him I was for him, which might, indeed, turn out to be my principal difficulty in writing about him. I had seen many of his movies—but did not intend to try to see them all—and I felt identified, in some way, with what I felt he was trying to do. What he saw when he looked at the world did not seem very different from what *I* saw. Some of his films seemed rather cold to me, somewhat too deliberate. For example, I had possibly heard too much about *The Seventh Seal* before seeing it, but it had impressed me less than some of the others.

"I cannot discuss that film," he said abruptly, and again turned to look out of the window. "I had to do it. I had to be free of that argument, those questions." He looked at me. "It's the same for you when you write a book? You just do it because you must and then, when you have done it, you are relieved, no?"

He laughed and poured some tea. He had made it sound as though we were two urchins playing a deadly and delightful game which must be kept a secret from our elders.

"Those questions?"

"Oh. God and the Devil. Life and Death. Good and Evil." He smiled. "*Those* questions."

I wanted to suggest that his being a pastor's son contributed not a little to his dark preoccupations. But I did not quite know how to go about digging into his private life. I hoped that we would be able to do it by way of the movies.

I began with: "The question of love seems to occupy you a great deal, too."

I don't doubt that it occupies you, too, was what he seemed to be thinking, but he only said, mildly, "Yes." Then, before I could put it another way, "You may find it a bit hard to talk to me. I really do not see much point in talking about my past work. And I cannot talk about work I haven't done yet."

I mentioned his great preoccupation with egotism, so many of his people being centered on themselves, necessarily, and disastrously: Vogler in *The Magician*, Isak Borg in *Wild Strawberries*, the ballerina in *Summer Interlude*.

"I am very fond of *Summer Interlude*," he said. "It is my favorite movie.

"I don't mean," he added, "that it's my best. I don't know which movie is my best."

Summer Interlude was made in 1950. It is probably not Bergman's best movie—I would give that place to the movie which has been shown in the States as *The Naked Night*—but it is certainly among the most moving. Its strength lies in its portrait of the ballerina, uncannily precise and truthful, and in its perception of the nature of first love, which first seems to open the universe to us and then seems to lock us out of it. It is one of the group of films—including *The Waiting Women*, *Smiles of a Summer Night*, and *Brink of Life*—which have a woman, or women, at their center and in which the men, generally, are rather shadowy. But all the Bergman themes are in it: his preoccupation with time and the inevitability of death, the comedy of human entanglements, the nature of illusion, the nature of egotism, the price of art. These themes also run through the movies which have at their center a man: *The Naked Night* (which should really be called *The Clown's Evening*), *Wild Strawberries*, *The Face*, *The Seventh Seal*. In only one of these movies—*The Face*—is the male-female relation affirmed from the male point of view; as being, that is, a source of strength for the man. In the movies concerned with women, the male-female relation succeeds only through the passion, wit, or patience of the woman and depends on how astutely she is able to manipulate the male conceit. *The Naked Night* is the most blackly ambivalent of Bergman's films—and surely one of the most brutally erotic movies ever made—but it is essentially a study of the masculine helplessness before the female force. *Wild Strawberries* is inferior to it, I think, being afflicted with a verbal and visual rhetoric which is Bergman's most annoying characteristic. But the terrible assessments that the old Professor is forced to make in it prove that he is not merely the victim of his women: he is responsible for what his women have become.

We soon switched from Bergman's movies to the subject of Stockholm.

"It is not a city at all," he said, with intensity. "It is ridiculous of it to think of itself as a city. It is simply a rather larger village, set in the middle of some forests and some lakes. You wonder what it thinks it is doing there, looking so important."

I was to encounter in many other people this curious resistance to the idea that Stockholm could possibly become a city. It certainly seemed to be trying to become a city as fast as it knew how, which is, indeed, the natural and inevitable fate of any nation's principal commercial and cultural clearing house. But for Bergman, who is forty-one, and for people who are considerably younger, Stockholm seems always to have had the aspect of a village. They do not look forward to seeing it change. Here, as in other European towns and cities, people can be heard bitterly complaining about the "Americanization" which is taking place.

This "Americanization," so far as I could learn, refers largely to the fact that more and more people are leaving the countryside and moving into Stockholm. Stockholm is not prepared to receive these people, and the inevitable social tensions result, from housing problems to juvenile delinquency. Of course, there are juke boxes grinding out the inevitable rock-and-roll tunes, and there are, too, a few jazz joints which fail, quite, to remind one of anything in the States. And the ghost—one is tempted to call it the effigy—of the late James Dean, complete with uniform, masochistic girl friend, motorcycle, or (hideously painted) car, has made its appearance on the streets of

Stockholm. These do not frighten me nearly as much as do the originals in New York, since they have yet to achieve the authentic American bewilderment or the inimitable American snarl. I ought to add, perhaps, that the American Negro remains, for them, a kind of *monstre sacré*, which proves, if anything does, how little they know of the phenomena which they feel compelled to imitate. They are unlike their American models in many ways: for example, they are not suffering from a lack of order but from an excess of it. Sexually, they are not drowning in taboos; they are anxious, on the contrary, to establish one or two.

 But the people in Stockholm are right to be frightened. It is not Stockholm's becoming a city which frightens them. What frightens them is that the pressures under which everyone in this century lives are destroying the old simplicities. This is almost always what people really mean when they speak of Americanization. It is an epithet which is used to mask the fact that the entire social and moral structure that they have built is proving to be absolutely inadequate to the demands now being placed on it. The old cannot imagine a new one, or create it. The young have no confidence in the old; lacking which, they cannot find any standards in themselves by which to live. The most serious result of such a chaos, though it may not seem to be, is the death of love. I do not mean merely the bankruptcy of the concept of romantic love—it is entirely possible that this concept has had its day—but the breakdown of communication between the sexes.

Bergman talked a little about the early stages of his career. He came to the Filmstaden in 1944, when he wrote the script for *Torment*. This was a very promising beginning. But promising beginnings do not mean much, especially in the movies. Promise, anyway, was never what Bergman lacked. He lacked flexibility. Neither he nor anyone else I talked to suggested that he has since acquired much of this quality; and since he was young and profoundly ambitious and thoroughly untried, he lacked confidence. This lack he disguised by tantrums so violent that they are still talked about at the Filmstaden today. His exasperating allergies extended to such things as refusing to work with a carpenter, say, to whom he had never spoken but whose face he disliked. He has been known, upon finding guests at his home, to hide himself in the bathroom until they left. Many of these people never returned and it is hard, of course, to blame them. Nor was he, at this time in his life, particularly respectful of the feelings of his friends.

"He's improved," said a woman who has been working with him for the last several years, "but he was impossible. He could say the most terrible things, he could make you wish you were dead. Especially if you were a woman."

She reflected. "Then, later, he would come and apologize. One just had to accept it, that's all."

He was referred to in those days, without affection as "the young one" or "the kid" or "the demon director." An American property whose movies, in spite of all this temperament, made no money at the box office, would have suffered, at best, the fate of Orson Welles. But Bergman went on working, as screen writer and director in films and as a director on the stage.

"I was an actor for a while," he says, "a terribly bad actor. But it taught me much."

It probably taught him a great deal about how to handle actors, which is one of his great gifts.

He directed plays for the municipal theaters of Hälsingborg, Göteborg, and Malmö, and is now working—or will be as soon as he completes his present film schedule—for the Royal Dramatic Theatre of Stockholm.

Some of the people I met told me that his work on stage is even more exciting than his work in films. They were the same people, usually, who were most concerned for Bergman's future when his present vogue ends. It was as though they were giving him an ace in the hole.

I did not interrogate Bergman on this point, but his record suggests that he is more attracted to films than to the theater. It would seem, too, that the theater very often operates for him as a kind of prolonged rehearsal or preparation for a film already embryonic in his consciousness. This is almost certainly the case with at least two of his theatrical productions. In 1954, he directed, for the municipal theater of Malmö, Franz Lehár's *The Merry Widow*. The next year he wrote and directed the elaborate period comedy, *Smiles of a Summer Night*, which beautifully utilizes—for Bergman's rather savage purposes—the atmosphere of romantic light opera. In 1956, he published his play *A Medieval Fresco*. This play was not produced, but it forms the basis for *The Seventh Seal*, which he wrote and directed the same year. It is safe, I think, to assume that the play will now never be produced, at least not by Bergman.

He has had many offers, of course, to work in other countries. I asked him if he had considered taking any of them.

He looked out of the window again. "I am home here," he said. "It took me a long time, but now I have all my instruments—everything—where I want them. I know my crew, my crew knows me, I know my actors."

I watched him. Something in me, inevitably, envied him for being able to love his home so directly and for being able to stay at home and work. And, in another way, rather to my surprise, I envied him not at all. Everything in a life depends on how that life accepts its limits: it would have been like envying him his language.

"If I were a violinist," he said after a while, "and I were invited to play in Paris—well, if the condition was that I could not bring my own violin but would have to play a French one—well, then, I could not go." He made a quick gesture toward the window. "This is my violin."

It was getting late. I had the feeling that I should be leaving, though he had not made any such suggestion. We got around to talking about *The Magician*.

"It doesn't have anything to do with hypnotism, does it?" I asked him.

"No. No, of course not."

"Then it's a joke. A long, elaborate metaphor for the condition of the artist—I mean, any time, anywhere, all the time—"

He laughed in much the same conspiratorial way he had laughed when talking about his reasons for doing *The Seventh Seal*. "Well, yes. He is always on the very edge of disaster, he is always on the very edge of great things. Always. Isn't it so? It is his element, like water is the element for the fish."

People had been interrupting us from the moment we sat down, and now someone arrived who clearly intended to take Bergman away with him. We made a date to meet early in the coming week. Bergman stood with me until my cab came and told the driver where I lived. I watched him, tall, bare-headed, and fearfully determined, as he walked away. I thought how there was something in the weird, mad, Northern Protestantism which reminded me of the visions of the black preachers of my childhood.

One of the movies which has made the most profound impression on Bergman is Victor Sjöström's *The Phantom Carriage*. It is based on a novel by Selma Lagerlöf which I have not read—and which, as a novel, I cannot imagine. But it makes great sense as a Northern fable; it has the atmosphere of a tale which has been handed down, for generations, from father to son. The premise of the movie is that whoever dies, in his sins, on New Year's Eve must drive Death's chariot throughout the coming year. The story that the movie tells is how a sinner—beautifully played by Sjöström himself—outwits Death. He outwits Death by virtue, virtue in the biblical, or, rather, in the New Testament sense: he outwits Death by opposing to this anonymous force his weak and ineradicable humanity.

Now this is, of course, precisely the story that Bergman is telling in *The Seventh Seal*. He has managed to utilize the old framework, the old saga, to speak of our condition in the world today and the way in which this loveless and ominous condition can be transcended. This ancient saga is part of his personal past and one of the keys to the people who produced him.

Since I had been so struck by what seemed to be our similarities, I amused myself, on the ride back into town, by projecting a movie, which, if I were a movie-maker, would occupy, among my own productions, the place *The Seventh Seal* holds among Bergman's. I did not have, to hold my films together, the Northern sagas; but I had the Southern music. From the African tom-toms, to Congo Square, to New Orleans, to Harlem—and, finally, all the way to Stockholm, and the European sectors of African towns. My film would begin with slaves, boarding the good ship *Jesus:* a white ship, on a dark sea, with masters as white as the sails of their ships, and slaves as black as the ocean. There would be one intransigent slave, an eternal figure, destined to appear, and to be put to death in every generation. In the hold of the slave ship, he would be a witch-doctor or a chief or a prince or a singer; and he would die, be hurled into the ocean, for protecting a black woman. Who would bear his child, however, and this child would lead a slave insurrection; and be hanged. During the Reconstruction, he would be murdered upon leaving Congress. He would be a returning soldier during the first World War, and be buried alive; and then, during the Depression, he would become a jazz musician, and go mad. Which would bring him up to our own day—what would his fate be now? What would I entitle this grim and vengeful fantasy? What would be happening, during all this time, to the descendants of the masters? It did not seem likely, after all, that I would ever be able to make of my past, on film, what Bergman had been able to make of his. In some ways, his past is easier to deal with: it was, at once, more remote and more present. Perhaps what divided the black Protestant from the white one was the nature of my still unwieldy, unaccepted bitterness. My hero, now, my tragic hero, would probably be a junkie—which, certainly, in one way, suggested the distance covered by America's dark generations. But it was in only one way, it was not the whole story; and it then occurred to me that my bitterness might be turned to good account if I should dare to envision the tragic hero for whom I was searching—as myself. All art is a kind of confession, more or less oblique. All artists, if they are to survive, are forced, at last, to tell the whole story, to vomit the anguish up. All of it, the literal and the fanciful. Bergman's authority seemed, then, to come from the fact that he was reconciled to this arduous, delicate, and disciplined self-exposure.

Bergman and his father had not got on well when Bergman was young.

"But how do you get along now?" I had asked him.

"Oh, now," he said, "we get on very well. I go to see him often."

I told him that I envied him. He smiled and said, "Oh, it is always like that—when such a battle is over, fathers and sons can be friends."

I did not say that such a reconciliation had probably a great deal to do with one's attitude toward one's past, and the uses to which one could put it. But I now began to feel, as I saw my hotel glaring up out of the Stockholm gloom, that what was lacking in my movie was the American despair, the search, in our country, for authority. The blue-jeaned boys on the Stockholm streets were really imitations, so far; but the streets of my native city were filled with youngsters searching desperately for the limits which would tell them who they were, and create for them a challenge to which they could rise. What would a Bergman make of the American confusion? How would he handle a love story occurring in New York?

12.
ALAS, POOR RICHARD

I. Eight Men

UNLESS A WRITER is extremely old when he dies, in which case he has probably become a neglected institution, his death must always seem untimely. This is because a real writer is always shifting and changing and searching. The world has many labels for him, of which the most treacherous is the label of Success. But the man behind the label knows defeat far more intimately than he knows triumph. He can never be absolutely certain that he has achieved his intention.

This tension and authority—the authority of the frequently defeated—are in the writer's work, and cause one to feel that, at the moment of his death, he was approaching his greatest achievements. I should think that guilt plays some part in this reaction, as well as a certain unadmitted relief. Guilt, because of our failure in a relationship, because it is extremely difficult to deal with writers as people. Writers are said to be extremely egotistical and demanding, and they are indeed, but that does not distinguish them from anyone else. What distinguishes them is what James once described as a kind of "holy stupidity." The writer's greed is appalling. He wants, or seems to want, everything and practically everybody; in another sense, and at the same time, he needs no one at all; and families, friends, and lovers find this extremely hard to take. While he is alive, his work is fatally entangled with his personal fortunes and misfortunes, his personality, and the social facts and attitudes of his time. The unadmitted relief, then, of which I spoke has to do with a certain drop in the intensity of our bewilderment, for the baffling creator no longer stands between us and his works.

He does not, but many other things do, above all our own preoccupations. In the case of Richard Wright, dead in Paris at fifty-two, the fact that he worked during a bewildering and demoralizing era in Western history makes a proper assessment of his work more difficult. In *Eight Men*, the earliest story, "The Man Who Saw the Flood," takes place in the deep South and was first published in 1937. One of the two previously unpublished stories in the book, "Man, God Ain't Like That," begins in Africa, achieves its hideous resolution in Paris, and brings us, with an ironical and fitting grimness, to the threshold of the 1960's. It is because of this story, which is remarkable, and "Man of All Work," which is a masterpiece, that I cannot avoid feeling that Wright, as he died, was acquiring a new tone, and a less uncertain esthetic distance, and a new depth.

Shortly after we learned of Richard Wright's death, a Negro woman who was re-reading *Native Son* told me that it meant more to her now than it had when she had first read it. This, she said, was because the specific social climate which had produced it, or with which it was identified, seemed archaic now, was fading from our memories. Now, there was only the book itself to deal with, for it could no longer be read, as it had been read in 1940, as a militant racial manifesto. Today's racial manifestoes were being written very differently, and in many different languages; what mattered about the book now was how accurately or deeply the life of Chicago's South Side had been conveyed.

I think that my friend may prove to be right. Certainly, the two oldest stories in this book, "The Man Who Was Almost a Man," and "The Man Who Saw the Flood," both Depression stories, both occurring in the South, and both, of course, about Negroes, do not seem dated. Perhaps it is odd, but they did not make me think of the 1930's, or even, particularly, of Negroes. They made me think of human loss and helplessness. There is a dry, savage, folkloric humor in "The Man Who Was Almost a Man." It tells the story of a boy who wants a gun, finally manages to get one, and, by a hideous error, shoots a white man's mule. He then takes to the rails, for he would have needed two years to pay for the mule. There is nothing funny about "The Man Who Saw the Flood," which is as spare and moving an account as that delivered by Bessie Smith in "Backwater Blues."

*

It is strange to begin to suspect, now, that Richard Wright was never, really, the social and polemical writer he took himself to be. In my own relations with him, I was always exasperated by his notions of society, politics, and history, for they seemed to me utterly fanciful. I never believed that he had any real sense of how a society is put together. It had not occurred to me, and perhaps it had not occurred to him, that his major interests as well as his power lay elsewhere. Or perhaps it *had* occurred to me, for I distrusted his association with the French intellectuals, Sartre, de Beauvoir, and company. I am not being vindictive toward them or condescending toward Richard Wright when I say that it seemed to me that there was very little they could give him which he could use. It has always seemed to me that ideas were somewhat more real to them than people; but anyway, and this is a statement made with the very greatest love and respect, I always sensed in Richard Wright a Mississippi pickaninny, mischievous, cunning, and tough. This always seemed to be at the bottom of everything he said and did, like some fantastic jewel buried in high grass. And it was painful to feel that the people of his adopted country were no more capable of seeing this jewel than were the people of his native land, and were in their own way as intimidated by it.

Even more painful was the suspicion that Wright did not want to know this. The meaning of Europe for an American Negro was one of the things about which Richard Wright and I disagreed most vehemently. He was fond of referring to Paris as the "city of refuge"—which it certainly was, God knows, for the likes of us. But it was not a city of refuge for the French, still less for anyone belonging to France; and it would not have been a city of refuge for us if we had not been armed with American passports. It did not seem worthwhile to me to have fled the native fantasy only to embrace a foreign one. (Someone, some day, should do a study in depth of the role of the American Negro in the mind and life of Europe, and the extraordinary perils, different from those of America but not less grave, which the American Negro encounters in the Old World.)

*

But now that the storm of Wright's life is over, and politics is ended forever for him, along with the Negro problem and the fearful conundrum of Africa, it seems to have been the tough and intuitive, the genuine Richard Wright, who was being recorded all along. It now begins to seem, for example, that Wright's unrelentingly bleak landscape was not merely that of the Deep South, or of Chicago, but that of the world, of the human heart. The landscape does not change in any of these stories. Even the most good-natured performance this book contains, good-natured by comparison only, "Big Black Good Man," takes place in Copenhagen in the winter, and in the vastly more chilling confines of a Danish hotel-keeper's fears.

In "Man of All Work," a tight, raging, diamond-hard exercise in irony, a Negro male who cannot find a job dresses himself up in his wife's clothes and hires himself out as a cook. ("Who," he demands of his horrified, bedridden wife, "ever looks at us colored folks anyhow?") He gets the job, and Wright uses this incredible situation to reveal, with beautiful spite and accuracy, the private lives of the master race. The story is told entirely in dialogue, which perfectly accomplishes what it sets out to do, racing along like a locomotive and suggesting far more than it states.

The story, without seeming to, goes very deeply into the demoralization of the Negro male and the resulting fragmentization of the Negro family which occurs when the female is forced to play the male role of breadwinner. It is also a maliciously funny indictment of the sexual terror and hostility of American whites: and the horror of the story is increased by its humor.

"Man, God Ain't Like That," is a fable of an African's discovery of God. It is a far more horrible story than "Man of All Work," but it too manages its effects by a kind of Grand Guignol humor, and it too is an unsparing indictment of the frivolity, egotism, and wrong-headedness of white people—in this case, a French artist and his mistress. It too is told entirely in dialogue and recounts how a French artist traveling through Africa picks up an African servant, uses him as a model, and, in order to shock and titillate his jaded European friends, brings the African back to Paris with him.

Whether or not Wright's vision of the African sensibility will be recognized by Africans, I do not know. But certainly he has managed a frightening and truthful comment on the inexorably mysterious and dangerous relationships between ways of life, which are also ways of thought. This story and "Man of All Work" left me wondering how much richer our extremely poor theater might now be if Wright had chosen to work in it.

But "The Man Who Killed a Shadow" is something else again; it is Wright at the mercy of his subject. His great forte, it now seems to me, was an ability to convey inward states by means of externals: "The Man Who Lived Underground," for example, conveys the spiritual horror of a man and a city by a relentless accumulation of details, and by a series of brief, sharply cut-off tableaus, seen through chinks and cracks and keyholes. The specifically sexual horror faced by a Negro cannot be dealt with in this way. "The Man Who Killed a Shadow" is a story of rape and murder, and neither the murderer nor his victim ever comes alive. The entire story seems to be occurring, somehow, beneath cotton. There are many reasons for this. In most of the novels written by Negroes until today (with the exception of Chester Himes's *If He Hollers Let Him Go*) there is a great space where sex ought to be; and what usually fills this space is violence.

This violence, as in so much of Wright's work, is gratuitous and compulsive. It is one of the severest criticisms that can be leveled against his work. The violence is gratuitous and compulsive because the root of the violence is never examined. The root is rage. It is the rage, almost literally the howl, of a man who is being castrated. I do not think that I am the first person to notice this, but there is probably no greater (or more misleading) body of sexual myths in the world today than those which have proliferated around the figure of the American Negro. This means that he is penalized for the guilty imagination of the white people who invest him with their hates and longings, and is the principal target of their sexual paranoia. Thus, when in Wright's pages a Negro male is found hacking a white woman to death, the very gusto with which this is done, and the great attention paid to the details of physical destruction reveal a terrible attempt to break out of the cage in which the American imagination has imprisoned him for so long.

In the meantime, the man I fought so hard and who meant so much to me, is gone. First America, then Europe, then Africa failed him. He lived long enough to find all of the terms on which he had been born become obsolete; presently, all of his attitudes seemed to be historical. But as his life ended, he seems to me to have been approaching a new beginning. He had survived, as it were, his own obsolescence, and his imagination was beginning to grapple with that darkest of all dark strangers for him, the African. The depth thus touched in him brought him a new power and a new tone. He had survived exile on three continents and lived long enough to begin to tell the tale.

II. The Exile

I WAS FAR from imagining, when I agreed to write this memoir, that it would prove to be such a painful and difficult task. What, after all, can I really say about Richard . . . ? Everything founders in the sea of what might have been. We might have been friends, for example, but I cannot honestly say that we were. There might have been some way of avoiding our quarrel, our rupture; I can only say that I failed to find it. The quarrel having occurred, perhaps there might have been a way to have become reconciled. I think, in fact, that I counted on this coming about in some mysterious, irrevocable way, the way a child dreams of winning, by means of some dazzling exploit, the love of his parents.

However, he is dead now, and so we never shall be reconciled. The debt I owe him can now never be discharged, at least not in the way I hoped to be able to discharge it. In fact, the saddest thing about our relationship is that my only means of discharging my debt to Richard was to become a writer; and this effort revealed, more and more clearly as the years went on, the deep and irreconcilable differences between our points of view.

This might not have been so serious if I had been older when we met.... If I had been, that is, less uncertain of myself, and less monstrously egotistical. But when we met, I was twenty, a carnivorous age; he was then as old as I am now, thirty-six; he had been my idol since high school, and I, as the fledgling Negro writer, was very shortly in the position of his protégé. This position was not really fair to either of us. As writers we were about as unlike as any two writers could possibly be. But no one can read the future, and neither of us knew this then. We were linked together, really, because both of us were black. I had made my pilgrimage to meet him because he was the greatest black writer in the world for me. In *Uncle Tom's Children*, in *Native Son*, and, above all, in *Black Boy*, I found expressed, for the first time in my life, the sorrow, the rage, and the murderous bitterness which was eating up my life and the lives of those around me. His work was an immense liberation and revelation for me. He became my ally and my witness, and alas! my father.

I remember our first meeting very well. It was in Brooklyn; it was winter, I was broke, naturally, shabby, hungry, and scared. He appeared from the depths of what I remember as an extremely long apartment. Now his face, voice, manner, figure are all very sadly familiar to me. But they were a great shock to me then. It is always a shock to meet famous men. There is always an irreducible injustice in the encounter, for the famous man cannot possibly fit the image which one has evolved of him. My own image of Richard was almost certainly based on Canada Lee's terrifying stage portrait of Bigger Thomas. Richard was not like that at all. His voice was light and even rather sweet, with a Southern melody in it; his body was more round than square, more square than tall; and his grin was more boyish than I had expected, and more diffident. He had a trick, when he greeted me, of saying, "Hey, boy!" with a kind of pleased, surprised expression on his face. It was very friendly, and it was also, faintly, mockingly conspiratorial—as though we were two black boys, in league against the world, and had just managed to spirit away several loads of watermelon.

We sat in the living room and Richard brought out a bottle of bourbon and ice and glasses. Ellen Wright was somewhere in the back with the baby, and made only one brief appearance near the end of the evening. I did not drink in those days, did not know how to drink, and I was terrified that the liquor, on my empty stomach, would have the most disastrous consequences. Richard talked to me or, rather, drew me out on the subject of the novel I was working on then. I was so afraid of falling off my chair and so anxious for him to be interested in me, that I told him far more about the novel than I, in fact, knew about it, madly improvising, one jump ahead of the bourbon, on all the themes which cluttered up my mind. I am sure that Richard realized this, for he seemed to be amused by me. But I think he liked me. I know that I liked him, then, and later, and all the time. But I also know that, later on, he did not believe this.

He agreed, that night, to read the sixty or seventy pages I had done on my novel as soon as I could send them to him. I didn't dawdle, naturally, about getting the pages in the mail, and Richard commented very kindly and favorably on them, and his support helped me to win the Eugene F. Saxton Fellowship. He was very proud of me then, and I was puffed up with pleasure that he was proud, and was determined to make him prouder still.

But this was not to be, for, as so often happens, my first real triumph turned out to be the herald of my first real defeat. There is very little point, I think, in regretting anything, and yet I do, nevertheless, rather regret that Richard and I had not become friends by this time, for it might have made a great deal of difference. We might at least have caught a glimpse of the difference between my mind and his; and if we could have argued about it then, our quarrel might not have been so painful later. But we had not become friends mainly, indeed, I suppose, because of this very difference, and also because I really was too young to be his friend and adored him too much and was too afraid of him. And this meant that when my first wintry exposure to the publishing world had resulted in the irreparable ruin—carried out by me—of my first novel, I scarcely knew how to face anyone, let alone Richard. I was too ashamed of myself and I was sure that he was ashamed of me, too. This was utter foolishness on my part, for Richard knew far more about first novels and fledgling novelists than that; but I had been out for his approval. It simply had not occurred to me in those days that anyone *could* approve of me if I had tried for something and failed. The young think that failure is the Siberian end of the line, banishment from all the living, and tend to do what I then did—which was to hide.

I, nevertheless, did see him a few days before he went to Paris in 1946. It was a strange meeting, melancholy in the way a theater is melancholy when the run of the play is ended and the cast and crew are about to be dispersed. All the relationships so laboriously created now no longer exist, seem never to have existed; and the future looks gray and problematical indeed. Richard's apartment—by this time, he lived in the Village, on Charles Street—seemed rather like that, dismantled, everything teetering on the edge of oblivion; people rushing in and out, friends, as I supposed, but alas, most of them were merely admirers; and Richard and I seemed really to be at the end of *our* rope, for he had done what he could for me, and it had not worked out, and now he was going away. It seemed to me that he was sailing into the most splendid of futures, for he was going, of all places! to France, and he had been invited there by the French government. But Richard did not seem, though he was jaunty, to be overjoyed. There was a striking sobriety in his face that day. He talked a great deal about a friend of his, who was in trouble with the U.S. Immigration authorities, and was about to be, or already had been, deported. Richard was not being deported, of course, he was traveling to a foreign country as an honored guest; and he was vain enough and young enough and vivid enough to find this very pleasing and exciting. Yet he knew a great deal about exile, all artists do, especially American artists, especially American Negro artists. He had endured already, liberals and literary critics to the contrary, a long exile in his own country. He must have wondered what the real thing would be like. And he must have wondered, too, what would be the unimaginable effect on his daughter, who could now be raised in a country which would not penalize her on account of her color.

And that day was very nearly the last time Richard and I spoke to each other without the later, terrible warfare. Two years later, I, too, quit America, never intending to return. The day I got to Paris, before I even checked in at a hotel, I was carried to the Deux Magots, where Richard sat, with the editors of *Zero* magazine. "Hey, boy!" he cried, looking more surprised and pleased and conspiratorial than ever, and younger and happier. I took this meeting as a good omen, and I could not possibly have been more wrong.

I later became rather closely associated with *Zero* magazine, and wrote for them the essay called "Everybody's Protest Novel." On the day the magazine was published, and before I had seen it, I walked into the Brasserie Lipp. Richard was there, and he called me over. I will never forget that interview, but I doubt that I will ever be able to re-create it.

Richard accused me of having betrayed him, and not only him but all American Negroes by attacking the idea of protest literature. It simply had not occurred to me that the essay could be interpreted in that way. I was still in that stage when I imagined that whatever was clear to me had only to be pointed out to become immediately clear to everyone. I was young enough to be proud of the essay and, sad and incomprehensible as it now sounds, I really think that I had rather expected to be patted on the head for my original point of view. It had not occurred to me that this point of view, which I had come to, after all, with some effort and some pain, could be looked on as treacherous or subversive. Again, I had mentioned Richard's *Native Son* at the end of the essay because it was the most important and most celebrated novel of Negro life to have appeared in America. Richard thought that I had attacked it, whereas, as far as I was concerned, I had scarcely even criticized it. And Richard thought that I was trying to destroy his novel and his reputation; but it had not entered my mind that either of these *could* be destroyed, and certainly not by me. And yet, what made the interview so ghastly was not merely the foregoing or the fact that I could find no words with which to defend myself. What made it most painful was that Richard was right to be hurt, I was wrong to have hurt him. He saw clearly enough, far more clearly than I had dared to allow myself to see, what I had done: I had used his work as a kind of springboard into my own. His work was a road-block in my road, the sphinx, really, whose riddles I had to answer before I could become myself. I thought confusedly then, and feel very definitely now, that this was the greatest tribute I could have paid him. But it is not an easy tribute to bear and I do not know how I will take it when my time comes. For, finally, Richard was hurt because I had not given him credit for any human feelings or failings. And indeed I had not, he had never really been a human being for me, he had been an idol. And idols are created in order to be destroyed.

This quarrel was never really patched up, though it must be said that, over a period of years, we tried. "What do you mean, *protest!*" Richard cried. "*All* literature is protest. You can't name a single novel that isn't protest." To this I could only weakly counter that all literature might be protest but all protest was not literature. "Oh," he would say then, looking, as he so often did, bewilderingly juvenile, "here you come again with all that art for art's sake crap." This never failed to make me furious, and my anger, for some reason, always seemed to amuse him. Our rare, best times came when we managed to exasperate each other to the point of helpless hilarity. "Roots," Richard would snort, when I had finally worked my way around to this dreary subject, "what——roots! Next thing you'll be telling me is that all colored folks have rhythm." Once, one evening, we managed to throw the whole terrifying subject to the winds, and Richard, Chester Himes, and myself went out and got drunk. It was a good night, perhaps the best I remember in all the time I knew Richard. For he and Chester were friends, they brought out the best in each other, and the atmosphere they created brought out the best in me. Three absolutely tense, unrelentingly egotistical, and driven people, free in Paris but far from home, with so much to be said and so little time in which to say it!

And time was flying. Part of the trouble between Richard and myself, after all, was that I was nearly twenty years younger and had never seen the South. Perhaps I can now imagine Richard's odyssey better than I could then, but it is only imagination. I have not, in my own flesh, traveled, and paid the price of such a journey, from the Deep South to Chicago to New York to Paris; and the world which produced Richard Wright has vanished and will never be seen again. Now, it seems almost in the twinkling of an eye, nearly twenty years have passed since Richard and I sat nervously over bourbon in his Brooklyn living room. These years have seen nearly all of the props of the Western reality knocked out from under it, all of the world's capitals have changed, the Deep South has changed, and Africa has changed.

For a long time, it seems to me, Richard was cruelly caught in this high wind. His ears, I think, were nearly deafened by the roar, all about him, not only of falling idols but of falling enemies. Strange people indeed crossed oceans, from Africa and America, to come to his door; and he really did not know who these people were, and they very quickly sensed this. Not until the very end of his life, judging by some of the stories in his last book, *Eight Men*, did his imagination really begin to assess the century's new and terrible dark stranger. Well, he worked up until the end, died, as I hope to do, in the middle of a sentence, and his work is now an irreducible part of the history of our swift and terrible time. Whoever He may be, and wherever you may be, may God be with you, Richard, and may He help me not to fail that argument which you began in me.

III. Alas, Poor Richard

AND MY RECORD'S clear today, the church brothers and sisters used to sing, *for He washed my sins away, And that old account was settled long ago!* Well, so, perhaps it was, for them; they were under the illusion that they could read their records right.

I am far from certain that I am able to read my own record at all, I would certainly hesitate to say that I am able to read it right. And, as for accounts, it is doubtful that I have ever really "settled" an account in my life.

Not that I haven't tried. In my relations with Richard, I was always trying to set the record "straight," to "settle" the account. This is but another way of saying that I wanted Richard to see me, not as the youth I had been when he met me, but as a man. I wanted to feel that he had accepted me, had accepted my right to my own vision, my right, as his equal, to disagree with him. I nourished for a long time the illusion that this day was coming. One day, Richard would turn to me, with the light of sudden understanding on his face, and say, "Oh, *that's* what you mean." And then, so ran the dream, a great and invaluable dialogue would have begun. And the great value of this dialogue would have been not only in its power to instruct all of you, and the ages. Its great value would have been in its power to instruct me, its power to instruct Richard: for it would have been nothing less than that so universally desired, so rarely achieved reconciliation between spiritual father and spiritual son.

Now, of course, it is not Richard's fault that I felt this way. But there is not much point, on the other hand, in dismissing it as simply my fault, or my illusion. I had identified myself with him long before we met: in a sense by no means metaphysical, his example had helped me to survive. He was black, he was young, he had come out of the Mississippi nightmare and the Chicago slums, and he was a writer. He proved it could be done—proved it to me, and gave me an arm against all those others who assured me it could *not* be done. And I think I had expected Richard, on the day we met, somehow, miraculously, to understand this, and to rejoice in it. Perhaps that sounds foolish, but I cannot honestly say, not even now, that I really think it is foolish. Richard Wright had a tremendous effect on countless numbers of people whom he never met, multitudes whom he now will never meet. This means that his responsibilities and his hazards were great. I don't think that Richard ever thought of me as one of his responsibilities—*bien au contraire!*—but he certainly seemed, often enough, to wonder just what he had done to deserve me.

Our reconciliation, anyway, never took place. This was a great loss for me. But many of our losses have a compensating gain. In my efforts to get through to Richard, I was forced to begin to wonder exactly why he held himself so rigidly against me. I could not believe—especially if one grants *my* reading of our relationship—that it could be due only to my criticism of his work. It seemed to me then, and it seems to me now, that one really needs those few people who take oneself and one's work seriously enough to be unimpressed by the public hullabaloo surrounding the former or the uncritical solemnity which menaces the latter from the instant that, for whatever reason, it finds itself in vogue.

No, it had to be more than that—the more especially as his attitude toward me had not, it turned out, been evolved for my particular benefit. It seemed to apply, with equal rigor, against a great many others. It applied against old friends, incontestably his equals, who had offended him, always, it turned out, in the same way: by failing to take his word for all the things he imagined, or had been led to believe, his word could cover. It applied against younger American Negroes who felt that Joyce, for example, not he, was the master; and also against younger American Negroes who felt that Richard did not know anything about jazz, or who insisted that the Mississippi and the Chicago he remembered were not precisely the Mississippi and the Chicago that they knew. It applied against Africans who refused to take Richard's word for Africa, and it applied against Algerians who did not feel that Paris was all that Richard had it cracked up to be. It applied, in short, against anyone who seemed to threaten Richard's system of reality. As time went on, it seemed to me that these people became more numerous and that Richard had fewer and fewer friends. At least, most of those people whom I had known to be friends of Richard's seemed to be saddened by him, and, reluctantly, to drift away. He's been away too long, some of them said. He's cut himself off from his roots. I resisted this judgment with all my might, more for my own sake than for Richard's, for it was far too easy to find this judgment used against myself. For the same reason I defended Richard when an African told me, with a small, mocking laugh, *I believe he thinks he's white.* I did *not* think I had been away too long: but I could not fail to begin, however unwillingly, to wonder about the uses and hazards of expatriation. I did not think I was white, either, or I did not *think* I thought so. But the Africans might think I did, and who could blame them? In their eyes, and in terms of my history, I could scarcely be considered the purest or most dependable of black men.

And I think that it was at about this point that I began to watch Richard as though he were a kind of object lesson. I could not help wondering if he, when facing an African, felt the same awful tension between envy and despair, attraction and revulsion. I had always been considered very dark, both Negroes and whites had despised me for it, and I had despised myself. But the Africans were much darker than I; I was a paleface among them, and so was Richard. And the disturbance thus created caused all of my extreme ambivalence about color to come floating to the surface of my mind. The Africans seemed at once simpler and more devious, more directly erotic and at the same time more subtle, and they were proud. If they had ever despised themselves for their color, it did not show, as far as I could tell. I envied them and feared them—feared that they had good reason to despise me. What did Richard feel? And what did Richard feel about other American Negroes abroad?

For example: one of my dearest friends, a Negro writer now living in Spain, circled around me and I around him for months before we spoke. One Negro meeting another at an all-white cocktail party, or at that larger cocktail party which is the American colony in Europe, cannot but wonder how the other got there. The question is: Is he for real? or is he kissing ass? Almost all Negroes, as Richard once pointed out, are almost always acting, but before a white audience—which is quite incapable of judging their performance: and even a "bad nigger" is, inevitably, giving something of a performance, even if the entire purpose of his performance is to terrify or blackmail white people.

Negroes know about each other what can here be called family secrets, and this means that one Negro, if he wishes, can "knock" the other's "hustle"—can give his game away. It is still not possible to overstate the price a Negro pays to climb out of obscurity—for it is a *particular* price, involved with being a Negro; and the great wounds, gouges, amputations, losses, scars, endured in such a journey cannot be calculated. But even this is not the worst of it, since he is really dealing with two hierarchies, one white and one black, the latter modeled on the former. The higher he rises, the less is his journey worth, since (unless he is extremely energetic and anarchic, a genuinely "bad nigger" in the most positive sense of the term) all he can possibly find himself exposed to is the grim emptiness of the white world—which does not live by the standards it uses to victimize him—and the even more ghastly emptiness of black people who wish they were white. Therefore, one "exceptional" Negro watches another "exceptional" Negro in order to find out if he knows how vastly successful and bitterly funny the hoax has been. Alliances, in the great cocktail party of the white man's world, are formed, almost purely, on this basis, for if both of you can laugh, you have a lot to laugh about. On the other hand, if only one of you can laugh, one of you, inevitably, is laughing at the other.

In the case of my new-found friend, Andy, and I, we were able, luckily, to laugh together. We were both baffled by Richard, but still respectful and fond of him—we accepted from Richard pronouncements and attitudes which we would certainly never have accepted from each other, or from anyone else—at the time Richard returned from wherever he had been to film *Native Son*. (In which, to our horror, later abundantly justified, he himself played Bigger Thomas.) He returned with a brainstorm, which he outlined to me one bright, sunny afternoon, on the terrace of the Royal St. Germain. He wanted to do something to protect the rights of American Negroes in Paris; to form, in effect, a kind of pressure group which would force American businesses in Paris, and American government offices, to hire Negroes on a proportional basis.

This seemed unrealistic to me. How, I asked him, in the

first place, could one find out how many American Negroes there were in Paris? Richard quoted an approximate, semi-official figure, which I do not remember, but I was still not satisfied. Of this number, how many were looking for jobs? Richard seemed to feel that they spent most of their time being turned down by American bigots, but this was not really my impression. I am not sure I said this, though, for Richard often made me feel that the word "frivolous" had been coined to describe me. Nevertheless, my objections made him more and more impatient with me, and I began to wonder if I were not guilty of great disloyalty and indifference concerning the lot of American Negroes abroad. (I find that there is something helplessly sardonic in my tone now, as I write this, which also handicapped me on that distant afternoon. Richard, more than anyone I have ever known, brought this tendency to the fore in me. I always wanted to kick him, and say, "Oh, come off it, baby, ain't no white folks around now, let's tell it like it *is*.")

Still, most of the Negroes I knew had *not* come to Paris to look for work. They were writers or dancers or composers, they were on the G.I. Bill, or fellowships, or more mysterious shoestrings, or they worked as jazz musicians. I did not know anyone who doubted that the American hiring system remained in Paris exactly what it had been at home—but how was one to prove this, with a handful, at best, of problematical Negroes, scattered throughout Paris? Unlike Richard, I had no reason to suppose that any of them even *wanted* to work for Americans—my evidence, in fact, suggested that this was just about the last thing they wanted to do. But, even if they did, and even if they were qualified, how could one *prove* that So-and-So had not been hired by TWA *because* he was a Negro? I had found this almost impossible to do at home. Isn't this, I suggested, the kind of thing which ought to be done from Washington? Richard, however, was not to be put off, and he had made me feel so guilty that I agreed to find out how many Negroes were then working for the ECA.

There turned out to be two or three or four, I forget how many. In any case, we were dead, there being no way on earth to prove that there should have been six or seven. But we were all in too deep to be able to turn back now, and, accordingly, there was a pilot meeting of this extraordinary organization, quite late, as I remember, one evening, in a private room over a bistro. It was in some extremely inconvenient part of town, and we all arrived separately or by twos. (There was some vague notion, I think, of defeating the ever-present agents of the CIA, who certainly ought to have had better things to do, but who, quite probably, on the other hand, didn't.) We may have defeated pursuit on our way there, but there was certainly no way of defeating detection as we arrived: slinking casually past the gaping mouths and astounded eyes of a workingman's bistro, like a disorganized parade, some thirty or forty of us, through a back door, and up the stairs. My friend and I arrived a little late, perhaps a little drunk, and certainly on a laughing jag, for we felt that we had been trapped in one of the most improbable and old-fashioned of English melodramas.

But Richard was in his glory. He was on the platform above us, I think he was alone there; there were only Negroes in the room. The results of the investigations of others had proved no more conclusive than my own—one could certainly not, on the basis of our findings, attack a policy or evolve a strategy—but this did not seem to surprise Richard or, even, to disturb him. It was decided, since we could not be a pressure group, to form a fellowship club, the purpose of which would be to get to know the French, and help the French to get to know us. Given our temperaments, neither Andy nor myself felt any need to join a club for this, we were getting along just fine on our own; but, somewhat to my surprise, we did not know many of the other people in the room, and so we listened. If it were only going to be a social club, then, obviously, the problem, as far as we were concerned, was over.

Richard's speech, that evening, made a great impact on me. It frightened me. I felt, but suppressed the feeling, that he was being mightily condescending toward the people in the room. I suppressed the feeling because most of them did not, in fact, interest me very much; but I was still in that stage when I felt guilty about not loving every Negro that I met. Still, perhaps for this very reason, I could not help resenting Richard's aspect and Richard's tone. I do not remember how his speech began, but I will never forget how it ended. News of this get-together, he told us, had caused a great stir in Parisian intellectual circles. Everyone was filled with wonder (as well they might be) concerning the future of such a group. A great many white people had wished to be present, Sartre, de Beauvoir, Camus—"and," said Richard, "*my own wife*. But I told them, before I can allow you to come, we've got to prepare the Negroes to receive you!"

This revelation, which was uttered with a smile, produced the most strained, stunned, uneasy silence. I looked at Andy, and Andy looked at me. There was something terribly funny about it, and there was something not funny at all. I rather wondered what the probable response would have been had Richard dared make such a statement in, say, a Negro barber shop; rather wondered, in fact, what the probable response would have been had anyone else dared make such a statement to anyone in the room, under different circumstances. ("Nigger, I been receiving white folks all my life—prepare *who?* Who you think you going to *prepare?*") It seemed to me, in any case, that the preparation ought, at least, to be conceived of as mutual: there was no reason to suppose that Parisian intellectuals were more "prepared" to "receive" American Negroes than American Negroes were to receive them—rather, all things considered, the contrary.

This was the extent of my connection with the Franco-American Fellowship Club, though the club itself, rather anemically, seemed to drag on for some time. I do not know what it accomplished—very little, I should imagine; but it soon ceased to exist because it had never had any reason to come into existence. To judge from complaints I heard, Richard's interest in it, once it was—roughly speaking—launched, was minimal. He told me once that it had cost him a great deal of money—this referred, I think, to some disastrous project, involving a printer's bill, which the club had undertaken. It seemed, indeed, that Richard felt that, with the establishment of this club, he had paid his dues to American Negroes abroad, and at home, and forever; had paid his dues, and was off the hook, since they had once more proved themselves incapable of following where he led. For yet one or two years to come, young Negroes would cross the ocean and come to Richard's door, wanting his sympathy, his help, his time, his money. God knows it must have been trying. And yet, they could not possibly have taken up more of his time than did the dreary sycophants by whom, as far as I could tell, he was more and more surrounded. Richard and I, of course, drifted farther and farther apart—our dialogues became too frustrating and too acrid—but, from my helplessly sardonic distance, I could only make out, looming above what seemed to be an indescribably cacophonous parade of mediocrities, and a couple of the world's most empty and pompous black writers, the tough and loyal figure of Chester Himes. There was a noticeable chill in the love affair which had been going on between Richard and the French intellectuals. He had always made American intellectuals uneasy, and now they were relieved to discover that he bored them, and even more relieved to say so. By this time he had managed to estrange himself from almost all of the younger American Negro writers in Paris. They were often to be found in the same café, Richard compulsively playing the pin-ball machine, while they, spitefully and deliberately, refused to acknowledge his presence. Gone were the days when he had only to enter a café to be greeted with the American Negro equivalent of *"cher maître"* ("Hey, Richard, how you making it, my man? Sit down and tell me something"), to be seated at a table, while all the bright faces turned toward him. The brightest faces were now turned from him, and among these faces were the faces of the Africans and the Algerians. They did not trust him—and their distrust was venomous because they felt that he had promised them so much. When the African said to me *I believe he thinks he's white*, he meant that Richard cared more about his safety and comfort than he cared about the black condition. But it was to this condition, at least in part, that he owed his safety and comfort and power and fame. If one-tenth of the suffering which obtained (and obtains) among Africans and Algerians in Paris had been occurring in Chicago, one could not help feeling that Richard would have raised the roof. He never ceased to raise the roof, in fact, as far as the American color problem was concerned. But time passes quickly. The American Negroes had discovered that Richard did not really know much about the present dimensions and complexity of the Negro problem here, and, profoundly, did not want to know. And one of the reasons that he did not want to know was that his real impulse toward American Negroes, individually, was to despise them. They, therefore, dismissed his rage and his public pronouncements as an unmanly reflex; as for the Africans, at least the younger ones, they knew he did not know them and did not want to know them, and they despised *him*. It must have been extremely hard to bear, and it was certainly very frightening to watch. I could not help feeling: *Be careful. Time is passing for you, too, and this may be happening to you one day.*

For who has not hated his black brother? Simply *because* he is black, *because* he is brother. And who has not dreamed of violence? That fantastical violence which will drown in blood, wash away in blood, not only generation upon generation of horror, but which will also release one from the individual horror, carried everywhere in the heart. Which of us has overcome his past? And the past of a Negro is blood dripping down through leaves, gouged-out eyeballs, the sex torn from its socket and severed with a knife. But this past is not special to the Negro. This horror is also the past, and the everlasting potential, or temptation, of the human race. If we do not know this, it seems to me, we know nothing about ourselves, nothing about each other; to have accepted this is also to have found a source of strength—source of all our power. But one must first accept this paradox, with joy.

The American Negro has paid a hidden, terrible price for his slow climbing to the light; so that, for example, Richard was able, at last, to live in Paris exactly as he would have lived, had he been a white man, here, in America. This may seem desirable, but I wonder if it is. Richard paid the price such an illusion of safety demands. The price is a turning away from, an ignorance of, all of the powers of darkness. This sounds mystical, but it is not; it is a hidden fact. It is the failure of the moral imagination of Europe which has created the forces now determined to overthrow it. No European dreamed, during

Europe's heyday, that they were sowing, in a dark continent, far away, the seeds of a whirlwind. It was not dreamed, during the Second World War, that Churchill's ringing words to the English were overheard by English slaves—who, now, coming in their thousands to the mainland, menace the English sleep. It is only now, in America, and it may easily be too late, that any of the anguish, to say nothing of the rage, with which the American Negro has lived so long begins, dimly, to trouble the public mind. The suspicion has been planted—and the principal effect, so far, here, has been panic—that perhaps the world is darker and therefore more real than we have allowed ourselves to believe.

Time brought Richard, as it has brought the American Negro, to an extraordinarily baffling and dangerous place. An American Negro, however deep his sympathies, or however bright his rage, ceases to be simply a black man when he faces a black man from Africa. When I say simply a black man, I do not mean that being a black man is simple, anywhere. But I am suggesting that one of the prices an American Negro pays—or can pay—for what is called his "acceptance" is a profound, almost ineradicable self-hatred. This corrupts every aspect of his living, he is never at peace again, he is out of touch with himself forever. And, when he faces an African, he is facing the unspeakably dark, guilty, erotic past which the Protestant fathers made him bury—for their peace of mind, and for their power—but which lives in his personality and haunts the universe yet. What an African, facing an American Negro sees, I really do not yet know; and it is too early to tell with what scars and complexes the African has come up from the fire. But the war in the breast between blackness and whiteness, which caused Richard such pain, need not be a war. It is a war which just as it denies both the heights and the depths of our natures, takes, and has taken, visibly and invisibly, as many white lives as black ones. And, as I see it, Richard was among the most illustrious victims of this war. This is why, it seems to me, he eventually found himself wandering in a no-man's land between the black world and the white. It is no longer important to be white—thank heaven—the white face is no longer invested with the power of this world; and it is devoutly to be hoped that it will soon no longer be important to be black. The experience of the American Negro, if it is ever faced and assessed, makes it possible to hope for such a reconciliation. The hope and the effect of this fusion in the breast of the American Negro is one of the few hopes we have of surviving the wilderness which lies before us now.

13.

THE BLACK BOY LOOKS AT THE WHITE BOY

> I walked and I walked
> Till I wore out my shoes.
> I can't walk so far, but
> Yonder come the blues.
>
> —MA RAINEY

I FIRST MET Norman Mailer about five years ago, in Paris, at the home of Jean Malaquais. Let me bring in at once the theme that will repeat itself over and over throughout this love letter: I was then (and I have not changed much) a very tight, tense, lean, abnormally ambitious, abnormally intelligent, and hungry black cat. It is important that I admit that, at the time I met Norman, I was extremely worried about my career; and a writer who is worried about his career is also fighting for his life. I was approaching the end of a love affair, and I was not taking it very well. Norman and I are alike in this, that we both tend to suspect others of putting us down, and we strike before we're struck. Only, our styles are very different: I am a black boy from the Harlem streets, and Norman is a middle-class Jew. I am not dragging my personal history into this gratuitously, and I hope I do not need to say that no sneer is implied in the above description of Norman. But these are the facts and in my own relationship to Norman they are crucial facts.

Also, I have no right to talk about Norman without risking a distinctly chilling self-exposure. I take him very seriously, he is very dear to me. And I think I know something about his journey from my black boy's point of view because my own journey is not really so very different, and also because I have spent most of my life, after all, watching white people and outwitting them, so that I might survive. I think that I know something about the American masculinity which most men of my generation do not know because they have not been menaced by it in the way that I have been. It is still true, alas, that to be an American Negro male is also to be a kind of walking phallic symbol: which means that one pays, in one's own personality, for the sexual insecurity of others. The relationship, therefore, of a black boy to a white boy is a very complex thing.

There is a difference, though, between Norman and myself in that I think he still imagines that he has something to save, whereas I have never had anything to lose. Or, perhaps I ought to put it another way: the thing that most white people imagine that they can salvage from the storm of life is really, in sum, their innocence. It was this commodity precisely which I had to get rid of at once, literally, on pain of death. I am afraid that most of the white people I have ever known impressed me as being in the grip of a weird nostalgia, dreaming of a vanished state of security and order, against which dream, unfailingly and unconsciously, they tested and very often lost their lives. It is a terrible thing to say, but I am afraid that for a very long time the troubles of white people failed to impress me as being real trouble. They put me in mind of children crying because the breast has been taken away. Time and love have modified my tough-boy lack of charity, but the attitude sketched above was my first attitude and I am sure that there is a great deal of it left.

To proceed: two lean cats, one white and one black, met in a French living room. I had heard of him, he had heard of me. And here we were, suddenly, circling around each other. We liked each other at once, but each was frightened that the other would pull rank. He could have pulled rank on me because he was more famous and had more money and also because he was white; but I could have pulled rank on him precisely because I was black and knew more about that periphery he so helplessly maligns in *The White Negro* than he could ever hope to know. Already, you see, we were trapped in our roles and our attitudes: the toughest kid on the block was meeting the toughest kid on the block. I think that both of us were pretty weary of this grueling and thankless role, I know that

I am; but the roles that we construct are constructed because we feel that they will help us to survive and also, of course, because they fulfill something in our personalities; and one does not, therefore, cease playing a role simply because one has begun to understand it. All roles are dangerous. The world tends to trap and immobilize you in the role you play; and it is not always easy—in fact, it is always extremely hard—to maintain a kind of watchful, mocking distance between oneself as one appears to be and oneself as one actually is.

I think that Norman was working on *The Deer Park* at that time, or had just finished it, and Malaquais, who had translated *The Naked and the Dead* into French, did not like *The Deer Park*. I had not then read the book; if I had, I would have been astonished that Norman could have expected Malaquais to like it. What Norman was trying to do in *The Deer Park*, and quite apart, now, from whether or not he succeeded, could only—it seems to me—baffle and annoy a French intellectual who seemed to me essentially rationalistic. Norman has many qualities and faults, but I have never heard anyone accuse him of possessing this particular one. But Malaquais' opinion seemed to mean a great deal to him—this astonished me, too; and there was a running, good-natured but astringent argument between them, with Malaquais playing the role of the old lion and Norman playing the role of the powerful but clumsy cub. And, I must say, I think that each of them got a great deal of pleasure out of the other's performance. The night we met, we stayed up very late, and did a great deal of drinking and shouting. But beneath all the shouting and the posing and the mutual showing off, something very wonderful was happening. I was aware of a new and warm presence in my life, for I had met someone I wanted to know, who wanted to know me.

Norman and his wife, Adele, along with a Negro jazz musician friend, and myself, met fairly often during the few weeks that found us all in the same city. I think that Norman had come in from Spain, and he was shortly to return to the States; and it was not long after Norman's departure that I left Paris for Corsica. My memory of that time is both blurred and sharp, and, oddly enough, is principally of Norman—confident, boastful, exuberant, and loving—striding through the soft Paris nights like a gladiator. And I think, alas, that I envied him: his success, and his youth, and his love. And this meant that though Norman really wanted to know me, and though I really wanted to know him, I hung back, held fire, danced, and lied. I was not going to come crawling out of my ruined house, all bloody, no, baby, sing no sad songs for *me*. And the great gap between Norman's state and my own had a terrible effect on our relationship, for it inevitably connected, not to say collided, with that myth of the sexuality of Negroes which Norman, like so many others, refuses to give up. The sexual battleground, if I may call it that, is really the same for everyone; and I, at this point, was just about to be carried off the battleground on my shield, if anyone could find it; so how could I play, in any way whatever, the noble savage?

At the same time, my temperament and my experience in this country had led me to expect very little from most American whites, especially, horribly enough, my friends: so it did not seem worthwhile to challenge, in any real way, Norman's views of life on the periphery, or to put him down for them. I was weary, to tell the truth. I had tried, in the States, to convey something of what it felt like to be a Negro and no one had been able to listen: they wanted their romance. And, anyway, the really ghastly thing about trying to convey to a white man the reality of the Negro experience has nothing whatever to do with the fact of color, but has to do with this man's relationship to his own life. He will face in your life only what he is willing to face in his. Well, this means that one finds oneself tampering with the insides of a stranger, to no purpose, which one probably has no right to do, and I chickened out. And matters were not helped at all by the fact that the Negro jazz musicians, among whom we sometimes found ourselves, who really liked Norman, did not for an instant consider him as being even remotely "hip" and Norman did not know this and I could not tell him. He never broke through to them, at least not as far I know; and they were far too "hip," if that is the word I want, even to consider breaking through to him. They thought he was a real sweet ofay cat, but a little frantic.

But we were far more cheerful than anything I've said might indicate and none of the above seemed to matter very much at the time. Other things mattered, like walking and talking and drinking and eating, and the way Adele laughed, and the way Norman argued. He argued like a young man, he argued to win: and while I found him charming, he may have found me exasperating, for I kept moving back before that short, prodding forefinger. I couldn't submit my arguments, or my real questions, for I had too much to hide. Or so it seemed to me then. I submit, though I may be wrong, that I was then at the beginning of a terrifying adventure, not too unlike the conundrum which seems to menace Norman now:

"I had done a few things and earned a few pence"; but the things I had written were behind me, could not be written again, could not be repeated. I was also realizing that all that the world could give me as an artist, it had, in effect, already given. In the years that stretched before me, all that I could look forward to, in that way, were a few more prizes, or a lot more, and a little more, or a lot more money. And my private life had failed—had failed, had failed. One of the reasons I had fought so hard, after all, was to wrest from the world fame and money and love. And here I was, at thirty-two, finding my notoriety hard to bear, since its principal effect was to make me more lonely; money, it turned out, was exactly like sex, you thought of nothing else if you didn't have it and thought of other things if you did; and love, as far as I could see, was over. Love seemed to be over not merely because an affair was ending; it would have seemed to be over under any circumstances; for it was the dream of love which was ending. I was beginning to realize, most unwillingly, all the things love could not do. It could not make me over, for example. It could not undo the journey which had made of me such a strange man and brought me to such a strange place.

But at that time it seemed only too clear that love had gone out of the world, and not, as I had thought once, because I was poor and ugly and obscure, but precisely because I was no longer any of these things. What point, then, was there in working if the best I could hope for was the Nobel Prize? And *how*, indeed, would I be able to keep on working if I could never be released from the prison of my egocentricity? By what act could I escape this horror? For horror it was, let us make no mistake about that.

And, beneath all this, which simplified nothing, was that sense, that suspicion—which is the glory and torment of every writer—that what was happening to me might be turned to good account, that I was trembling on the edge of great revelations, was being prepared for a very long journey, and might now begin, having survived my apprenticeship (but had I survived it?), a great work. I might really become a great writer. But in order to do this I would have to sit down at the typewriter again, alone—I would have to accept my despair: and I could not do it. It really does not help to be a strong-willed person or, anyway, I think it is a great error to misunderstand the nature of the will. In the most important areas of anybody's life, the will usually operates as a traitor. My own will was busily pointing out to me the most fantastically unreal alternatives to my pain, all of which I tried, all of which—luckily—failed. When, late in the evening or early in the morning, Norman and Adele returned to their hotel on the Quai Voltaire, I wandered through Paris, the underside of Paris, drinking, screwing, fighting—it's a wonder I wasn't killed. And then it was morning, I would somehow be home—usually, anyway—and the typewriter would be there, staring at me; and the manuscript of the new novel, which it seemed I would never be able to achieve, and from which clearly I was never going to be released, was scattered all over the floor.

That's the way it is. I think it is the most dangerous point in the life of any artist, his longest, most hideous turning; and especially for a man, an American man, whose principle is action and whose jewel is optimism, who must now accept what certainly then seems to be a gray passivity and an endless despair. It is the point at which many artists lose their minds, or commit suicide, or throw themselves into good works, or try to enter politics. For all of this is happening not only in the wilderness of the soul, but in the real world which accomplishes its seductions not by offering you opportunities to be wicked but by offering opportunities to be good, to be active and effective, to be admired and central and apparently loved.

Norman came on to America, and I went to Corsica. We wrote each other a few times. I confided to Norman that I was very apprehensive about the reception of *Giovanni's Room*, and he was good enough to write some very encouraging things about it when it came out. The critics had jumped on him with both their left feet when he published *The Deer Park*—which I still had not read—and this created a kind of bond, or strengthened the bond already existing between us. About a year and several overflowing wastebaskets later, I, too, returned to America, not vastly improved by having been out of it, but not knowing where else to go; and one day, while I was sitting dully in my house, Norman called me from Connecticut. A few people were going to be there—for the weekend—and he wanted me to come, too. We had not seen each other since Paris.

Well, I wanted to go, that is, I wanted to see Norman; but I did not want to see any people, and so the tone of my acceptance was not very enthusiastic. I realized that he felt this, but I did not know what to do about it. He gave me train schedules and hung up.

Getting to Connecticut would have been no hassle if I could have pulled myself together to get to the train. And I was sorry, as I meandered around my house and time flew and trains left, that I had not been more honest with Norman and told him exactly how I felt. But I had not known how to do this, or it had not really occurred to me to do it, especially not over the phone.

So there was another phone call, I forget who called whom, which went something like this:

N: Don't feel you have to. I'm not trying to bug you.

J: It's not that. It's just—

N: You don't really want to come, do you?

J: I don't really feel up to it.

N: I understand. I guess you just don't like the Connecticut gentry.

J: Well—don't you ever come to the city?
N: Sure. We'll see each other.
J: I hope so. I'd like to see you.
N: Okay, till then.

And he hung up. I thought, I ought to write him a letter, but of course I did nothing of the sort. It was around this time I went South, I think; anyway, we did not see each other for a long time.

But I thought about him a great deal. The grapevine keeps all of us advised of the others' movements, so I knew when Norman left Connecticut for New York, heard that he had been present at this or that party and what he had said: usually something rude, often something penetrating, sometimes something so hilariously silly that it was difficult to believe he had been serious. (This was my reaction when I first heard his famous running-for-President remark. I dismissed it. I was wrong.) Or he had been seen in this or that Village spot, in which unfailingly there would be someone—out of spite, idleness, envy, exasperation, out of the bottomless, eerie, aimless hostility which characterizes almost every bar in New York, to speak only of bars—to put him down. I heard of a couple of fist-fights, and, of course, I was always encountering people who hated his guts. These people always mildly surprised me, and so did the news of his fights: it was hard for me to imagine that anyone could really dislike Norman, anyone, that is, who had encountered him personally. I knew of one fight he had had, forced on him, apparently, by a blow-hard Village type whom I considered rather pathetic. I didn't blame Norman for this fight, but I couldn't help wondering why he bothered to rise to such a shapeless challenge. It seemed simpler, as I was always telling myself, just to stay out of Village bars.

And people talked about Norman with a kind of avid glee, which I found very ugly. Pleasure made their saliva flow, they sprayed and all but drooled, and their eyes shone with that blood-lust which is the only real tribute the mediocre are capable of bringing to the extraordinary. Many of the people who claimed to be seeing Norman all the time impressed me as being, to tell the truth, pitifully far beneath him. But this is also true, alas, of much of my own entourage. The people who are in one's life or merely continually in one's presence reveal a great deal about one's needs and terrors. Also, one's hopes.

I was not, however, on the scene. I was on the road—not quite, I trust, in the sense that Kerouac's boys are; but I presented, certainly, a moving target. And I was reading Norman Mailer. Before I had met him, I had only read *The Naked and the Dead*, *The White Negro*, and *Barbary Shore*—I think this is right, though it may be that I only read *The White Negro* later and confuse my reading of that piece with some of my discussions with Norman. Anyway, I could not, with the best will in the world, make any sense out of *The White Negro* and, in fact, it was hard for me to imagine that this essay had been written by the same man who wrote the novels. Both *The Naked and the Dead* and (for the most part) *Barbary Shore* are written in a lean, spare, muscular prose which accomplishes almost exactly what it sets out to do. Even *Barbary Shore*, which loses itself in its last half (and which deserves, by the way, far more serious treatment than it has received) never becomes as downright impenetrable as *The White Negro* does.

Now, much of this, I told myself, had to do with my resistance to the title, and with a kind of fury that so antique a vision of the blacks should, at this late hour, and in so many borrowed heirlooms, be stepping off the A train. But I was also baffled by the passion with which Norman appeared to be imitating so many people inferior to himself, i.e., Kerouac, and all the other Suzuki rhythm boys. From them, indeed, I expected nothing more than their pablum-clogged cries of *Kicks!* and *Holy!* It seemed very clear to me that their glorification of the orgasm was but a way of avoiding all of the terrors of life and love. But Norman knew better, had to know better. *The Naked and the Dead*, *Barbary Shore*, and *The Deer Park* proved it. In each of these novels, there is a toughness and subtlety of conception, and a sense of the danger and complexity of human relationships which one will search for in vain, not only in the work produced by the aforementioned coterie, but in most of the novels produced by Norman's contemporaries. What in the world, then, was he doing, slumming so outrageously, in such a dreary crowd?

For, exactly because he knew better, and in exactly the same way that no one can become more lewdly vicious than an imitation libertine, Norman felt compelled to carry their *mystique* further than they had, to be more "hip," or more "beat," to dominate, in fact, their dreaming field; and since this *mystique* depended on a total rejection of life, and insisted on the fulfillment of an infantile dream of love, the *mystique* could only be extended into violence. No one is more dangerous than he who imagines himself pure in heart: for his purity, by definition, is unassailable.

But *why* should it be necessary to borrow the Depression language of deprived Negroes, which eventually evolved into jive and bop talk, in order to justify such a grim system of delusions? Why malign the sorely menaced sexuality of Negroes in order to justify the white man's own sexual panic? Especially as, in Norman's case, and as indicated by his work, he has a very real sense of sexual responsibility, and, even, odd as it may sound to some, of sexual morality, and a genuine commitment to life. None of his people, I beg you to notice, spend their lives on the road. They really become entangled with each other, and with life. They really suffer, they spill real blood, they have real lives to lose. This is no small achievement; in fact, it is absolutely rare. No matter how uneven one judges Norman's work to be, all of it is genuine work. No matter how harshly one judges it, it is the work of a genuine novelist, and an absolutely first-rate talent.

Which makes the questions I have tried to raise—or, rather, the questions which Norman Mailer irresistibly represents—all the more troubling and terrible. I certainly do not know the answers, and even if I did, this is probably not the place to state them.

But I have a few ideas. Here is Kerouac, ruminating on what I take to be the loss of the garden of Eden:

> At lilac evening I walked with every muscle aching among the lights of 27th and Welton in the Denver colored section, wishing I were a Negro, feeling that the

best the white world had offered was not enough ecstasy for me, not enough life, joy, kicks, darkness, music, not enough night. I wished I were a Denver Mexican, or even a poor overworked Jap, anything but what I so drearily was, a "white man" disillusioned. All my life I'd had white ambitions. . . . I passed the dark porches of Mexican and Negro homes; soft voices were there, occasionally the dusky knee of some mysterious sensuous gal; and dark faces of the men behind rose arbors. Little children sat like sages in ancient rocking chairs.

Now, this is absolute nonsense, of course, objectively considered, and offensive nonsense at that: I would hate to be in Kerouac's shoes if he should ever be mad enough to read this aloud from the stage of Harlem's Apollo Theater.

And yet there is real pain in it, and real loss, however thin; and it is thin, like soup too long diluted; thin because it does not refer to reality, but to a dream. Compare it, at random, with any old blues:

> Backwater blues done caused me
> To pack my things and go.
> 'Cause my house fell down
> And I can't live there no mo'.

"Man," said a Negro musician to me once, talking about Norman, "the only trouble with that cat is that he's white." This does not mean exactly what it says—or, rather, it *does* mean exactly what it says, and not what it might be taken to mean—and it is a very shrewd observation. What my friend meant was that to become a Negro man, let alone a Negro artist, one had to make oneself up as one went along. This had to be done in the not-at-all-metaphorical teeth of the world's determination to destroy you. The world had prepared no place for you, and if the world had its way, no place would ever exist. Now, this is true for everyone, but, in the case of a Negro, this truth is absolutely naked: if he deludes himself about it, he will die. This is not the way this truth presents itself to white men, who believe the world is theirs and who, albeit unconsciously, expect the world to help them in the achievement of their identity. But the world does not do this—for anyone; the world is not interested in anyone's identity. And, therefore, the anguish which can overtake a white man comes in the middle of his life, when he must make the almost inconceivable effort to divest himself of everything he has ever expected or believed, when he must take himself apart and put himself together again, walking out of the world, into limbo, or into what certainly looks like limbo. This cannot yet happen to any Negro of Norman's age, for the reason that his delusions and defenses are either absolutely impenetrable by this time, or he has failed to survive them. "I want to know how power works," Norman once said to me, "how it really works, in detail." Well, I know how power works, it has worked on me, and if I didn't know how power worked, I would be dead. And it goes without saying, perhaps, that I have simply never been able to afford myself any illusions concerning the manipulation of that power. My revenge, I decided very early, would be to achieve a power which outlasts kingdoms.

II

When I finally saw Norman again, I was beginning to suspect daylight at the end of my long tunnel, it was a summer day, I was on my way back to Paris, and I was very cheerful. We were at an afternoon party, Norman was standing in the kitchen, a drink in his hand, holding forth for the benefit of a small group of people. There seemed something different about him, it was the belligerence of his stance, and the really rather pontifical tone of his voice. I had only seen him, remember, in Malaquais' living room, which Malaquais indefatigably dominates, and on various terraces and in various dives in Paris. I do not mean that there was anything unfriendly about him. On the contrary, he was smiling and having a ball. And yet—he was leaning against the refrigerator, rather as though he had his back to the wall, ready to take on all comers.

Norman has a trick, at least with me, of watching, somewhat ironically, as you stand on the edge of the crowd around him, waiting for his attention. I suppose this ought to be exasperating, but in fact I find it rather endearing, because it is so transparent and because he gets such a bang out of being the center of attention. So do I, of course, at least some of the time.

We talked, bantered, a little tensely, made the usual, doomed effort to bring each other up to date on what we had been doing. I did not want to talk about my novel, which was only just beginning to seem to take shape, and, therefore, did not dare ask him if he were working on a novel. He seemed very pleased to see me, and I was pleased to see him, but I also had the feeling that he had made up his mind about me, adversely, in some way. It was as though he were saying, Okay, so now I know who *you* are, baby.

I was taking a boat in a few days, and I asked him to call me.

"Oh, no," he said, grinning, and thrusting that forefinger at me, "*you* call me."

"That's fair enough," I said, and I left the party and went on back to Paris. While I was out of the country, Norman published *Advertisements for Myself*, which presently crossed the ocean to the apartment of James Jones. Bill Styron was also in Paris at that time, and one evening the three of us sat in Jim's living room, reading aloud, in a kind of drunken, masochistic fascination, Norman's judgment of our personalities and our work. Actually, I came off best, I suppose; there was less about me, and it was less venomous. But the condescenion infuriated me; also, to tell the truth, my feelings were hurt. I felt that if that was the way Norman felt about me, he should have told me so. He had said that I was incapable of saying "F--- you" to the reader. My first temptation was to send him a cablegram which would disabuse him of that notion, at least insofar as one reader was concerned. But then I thought, No, I would be cool about it, and fail to react as he so clearly wanted me to. Also, I must say, his judgment of myself seemed so wide of the mark and so childish that it was hard to stay angry. I wondered what in the world was going on in his mind. Did he really suppose that he had now become the builder and destroyer of reputations.

And of *my* reputation?

We met in the Actors' Studio one afternoon, after a performance of *The Deer Park*—which I deliberately arrived too late to see, since I really did not know how I was going to react to Norman, and didn't want to betray myself by clobbering his play. When the discussion ended, I stood, again on the edge of the crowd around him, waiting. Over someone's shoulder, our eyes met, and Norman smiled.

"We've got something to talk about," I told him.

"I figured that," he said, smiling.

We went to a bar, and sat opposite each other. I was relieved to discover that I was not angry, not even (as far as I could tell) at the bottom of my heart. But, "Why did you write those things about me?"

"Well, I'll tell you about that," he said—Norman has several accents, and I think this was his Texas one—"I sort of figured you had it coming to you."

"Why?"

"Well, I think there's some truth in it."

"Well, if you felt that way, why didn't you ever say so—to me?"

"Well, I figured if this was going to break up our friendship, something else would come along to break it up just as fast."

I couldn't disagree with that.

"You're the only one I kind of regret hitting so hard," he said, with a grin. "I think I—probably—wouldn't say it quite that way now."

With this, I had to be content. We sat for perhaps an hour, talking of other things and, again, I was struck by his stance: leaning on the table, shoulders hunched, seeming, really, to roll like a boxer's, and his hands moving as though he were dealing with a sparring partner. And we were talking of physical courage, and the necessity of never letting another guy get the better of you.

I laughed. "Norman, I can't go through the world the way you do because I haven't got your shoulders."

He grinned, as though I were his pupil. "But you're a pretty tough little mother, too," he said, and referred to one of the grimmer of my Village misadventures, a misadventure which certainly proved that I had a dangerously sharp tongue, but which didn't really prove anything about my courage. Which, anyway, I had long ago given up trying to prove.

I did not see Norman again until Provincetown, just after his celebrated brush with the police there, which resulted, according to Norman, in making the climate of Provincetown as "mellow as Jello." The climate didn't seem very different to me—dull natives, dull tourists, malevolent policemen; I certainly, in any case, would never have dreamed of testing Norman's sanguine conclusion. But we had a great time, lying around the beach, and driving about, and we began to be closer than we had been for a long time.

It was during this Provincetown visit that I realized, for the first time, during a long exchange Norman and I had, in a kitchen, at someone else's party, that Norman was really fascinated by the nature of political power. But, though he said so, I did not really believe that he was fascinated by it as a possibility for himself. He was then doing the great piece on the Democratic convention which was published in *Esquire*, and I put his fascination down to that. I tend not to worry about writers as long as they are working—which is not as romantic as it may sound—and he seemed quite happy with his wife, his family, himself. I declined, naturally, to rise at dawn, as he apparently often did, to go running or swimming or boxing, but Norman seemed to get a great charge out of these admirable pursuits and didn't put me down too hard for my comparative decadence.

He and Adele and the two children took me to the plane one afternoon, the tiny plane which shuttles from Provincetown to Boston. It was a great day, clear and sunny, and that was the way I felt: for it seemed to me that we had all, at last, re-established our old connection.

And then I heard that Norman was running for mayor, which I dismissed as a joke and refused to believe until it became hideously clear that it was not a joke at all. I was furious. I thought, You son of a bitch, you're copping out. You're one of the very few writers around who might really become a great writer, who might help to excavate the buried consciousness of this country, and you want to settle for being the lousy mayor of New York. *It's not your job.* And I don't at all mean to suggest that writers are not responsible to and for—in any case, always for—the social order. I don't, for that matter, even mean to suggest that Norman would have made a particularly bad Mayor, though I confess that I simply cannot see him in this role. And there is probably some truth in the suggestion, put forward by Norman and others, that the shock value of having such a man in such an office, or merely running for such an office, would have had a salutary effect on the life of this city—particularly, I must say, as relates to our young people, who are certainly in desperate need of adults who love them and take them seriously, and whom they can respect. (Serious citizens may not respect Norman, but young people do, and do not respect the serious citizens; and their instincts are quite sound.)

But I do not feel that a writer's responsibility can be discharged in this way. I do not think, if one is a writer, that one escapes it by trying to become something else. One does *not* become something else: one becomes nothing. And what is crucial here is that the writer, however unwillingly, always, somewhere, knows this. There is no structure he can build strong enough to keep out this self-knowledge. What *has* happened, however, time and time again, is that the fantasy structure the writer builds in order to escape his central responsibility operates not as his fortress, but his prison, and he perishes within it. Or: the structure he has built becomes so stifling, so lonely, so false, and acquires such a violent and dangerous life of its own, that he can break out of it only by bringing the entire structure down. With a great crash, inevitably, and on his own head, and on the heads of those closest to him. It is like smashing the windows one second before one asphyxiates; it is like burning down the house in order, at last, to be free of it. And this, I think, really, to touch upon it lightly, is the key to the events at that monstrous, baffling, and so publicized party. Nearly everyone in the world—or nearly everyone, at least, in this extraordinary city—was there: policemen, Mafia types, the people whom we quaintly refer to as "beatniks," writers, actors, editors, politicians, and gossip columnists. It must be admitted that it was a considerable achievement to have brought so many unlikely types together under one roof; and, in spite of everything, I can't help wishing that I had been there to witness the mutual bewilderment. But the point is that no politician would have dreamed of giving such a party in order to launch his mayoralty campaign. Such an imaginative route is not usually an attribute of politicians. In addition, the price one pays for pursuing any profession, or calling, is an intimate knowledge of its ugly side. It is scarcely worth observing that political activity is often, to put it mildly, pungent, and I think that Norman, perhaps for the first time, really doubted his ability to deal with such a world, and blindly struck his way out of it. We do not, in this country now, have much taste for, or any real sense of, the extremes human beings can reach; time will improve us in this regard; but in the meantime the general fear of experience is one of the reasons that the American writer has so peculiarly difficult and dangerous a time.

One can never really see into the heart, the mind, the soul of another. Norman is my very good friend, but perhaps I do not really understand him at all, and perhaps everything I have tried to suggest in the foregoing is false. I do not think so, but it may be. One thing, however, I am certain is *not* false, and that is simply the fact of his being a writer, and the incalculable potential he as a writer contains. His work, after all, is all that will be left when the newspapers are yellowed, all the gossip columnists silenced, and all the cocktail parties over, and when Norman and you and I are dead. I know that this point of view is not terribly fashionable these days, but I think we *do* have a responsibility, not only to ourselves and to our own time, but to those who are coming after us. (I refuse to believe that no one is coming after us.) And I suppose that this responsibility can only be discharged by dealing as truthfully as we know how with our present fortunes, these present days. So that my concern with Norman, finally, has to do with how deeply he has understood these last sad and stormy events. If he has understood them, then he is richer and we are richer, too; if he has not understood them, we are all much poorer. For, though it clearly needs to be brought into focus, he has a real vision of ourselves as we are, and it cannot be too often repeated in this country now, that, where there is no vision, the people perish.

NO NAME
IN THE STREET

for Berdis Baldwin
and
Beauford DeLaney
and
Rudy Lombard
and
Jerome

His remembrance shall perish from the earth
and He shall have no name in the street.
He shall be driven from light into darkness,
and chased out of the world.

JOB 18:17–18

TAKE ME TO
THE WATER

If I had-a- my way
I'd tear this building down.
Great God, then, if I had-a- my way
If I had-a- my way, little children,
I'd tear this building down.
—SLAVE SONG

Just a little while to stay here,
Just a little while to stay.
—TRADITIONAL

"THAT *IS* A GOOD IDEA," I heard my mother say. She was staring at a wad of black velvet, which she held in her hand, and she carefully placed this bit of cloth in a closet. We can guess how old I must have been from the fact that for years afterward I thought that an "idea" was a piece of black velvet.

Much, much, much has been blotted out, coming back only lately in bewildering and untrustworthy flashes. I must have been about five, I should think, when I made my connection between ideas and velvet, but I may have been younger; this may have been the same year that my father had me circumcised, a terrifying event which I scarcely remember at all; or I may think I was five because I remember tugging at my mother's skirts once and watching her face while she was telling someone else that she was twenty-seven. This meant, for me, that she was virtually in the grave already, and I tugged a little harder at her skirts. I already knew, for some reason, or had given myself some reason to believe, that she had been twenty-two when I was born. And, though I can't count today, I could count when I was little.

I was the only child in the house—or houses—for a while, a halcyon period which memory has quite repudiated; and if I remember myself as tugging at my mother's skirts and staring up into her face, it was because I was so terrified of the man we called my father; who did not arrive on *my* scene, really, until I was more than two years old. I have written both too much and too little about this man, whom I did not understand till he was past understanding. In my first memory of him, he is standing in the kitchen, drying the dishes. My mother had dressed me to go out, she is taking me someplace, and it must be winter, because I am wearing, in my memory, one of those cloth hats with a kind of visor, which button under the chin—a Lindbergh hat, I think. I am apparently in my mother's arms, for I am staring at my father over my mother's shoulder, we are near the door; and my father smiles. This may be a memory, I think it is, but it may be a fantasy. One of the very last times I saw my father on his feet, I was staring at him over my mother's shoulder—she had come rushing into the room to separate us—and my father was not smiling and neither was I.

His mother, Barbara, lived in our house, and she had been born in slavery. She was so old that she never moved from her bed. I remember her as pale and gaunt and she must have worn a kerchief because I don't remember her hair. I remember that she loved me; she used to scold her son about the way he treated me; and he was a little afraid of her. When she died, she called me into the room to give me a present—one of those old, round, metal boxes, usually with a floral design, used for candy. *She* thought it was full of candy and *I* thought it was full of candy, but it wasn't. After she died, I opened it and it was full of needles and thread.

This broke my heart, of course, but her going broke it more because I had loved her and depended on her. I knew—children *must* know—that she would always protect me with all her strength. So would my mother, too, I knew that, but my mother's strength was only to be called on in a desperate emergency. It did not take me long, nor did the children, as they came tumbling into this world, take long to discover that our mother paid an immense price for standing between us and our father. He had ways of making her suffer quite beyond our ken, and so we soon learned to depend on each other and became a kind of wordless conspiracy to protect *her*. (We were all, absolutely and mercilessly, united against our father.) We soon realized, anyway, that she scarcely belonged to us: she was always in the hospital, having another baby. Between his merciless children, who were terrified of him, the pregnancies, the births, the rats, the murders on Lenox Avenue, the whores who lived downstairs, his job on Long Island—to which he went every morning, wearing a Derby or a Homburg, in a black suit, white shirt, dark tie, looking like the preacher he was, and with his black lunch-box in his hand—and his unreciprocated love for the Great God Almighty, it is no wonder our father went mad. We, on the other hand, luckily, on the whole, for our father, and luckily indeed for our mother, simply took over each new child and made it ours. I want to avoid generalities as far as possible; it will, I hope, become clear presently that what I am now attempting dictates this avoidance; and so I will not say that children love miracles, but I will say that I think we did. A newborn baby is an extraordinary event; and I have never seen two babies who looked or even sounded remotely alike. Here it is, this breathing miracle who could not live an instant without you, with a skull more fragile than an egg, a miracle of eyes, legs, toenails, and (especially) lungs. It gropes in the light like a blind thing—it *is*, for the moment, blind—what can it make of what it sees? It's got a little hair, which it's going to lose, it's got no teeth, it pees all over you, it belches, and when it's frightened or hungry, quite without knowing what a miracle it's accomplishing, it exercises its lungs. You watch it discover it has a hand; then it discovers it has toes. Presently, it discovers it has *you*, and since it has already decided it wants to live, it gives you a toothless smile when you come near it, gurgles or giggles when you pick it up, holds you tight by the thumb or the eyeball or the hair, and, having already opted against solitude, howls when you put it down. You begin the extraordinary journey of beginning to know and to control this creature. You know the sound—the meaning—of one cry from another; without knowing that you know it. You know when it's hungry—that's one sound. You know when it's wet—that's another sound. You know when it's angry. You know when it's bored. You know when it's frightened. You know when it's suffering. You come or you go or you sit still according to the sound the baby makes. And you watch over it where I was born, even in your sleep, because rats love the odor of newborn babies and are much, much bigger.

By the time it has managed to crawl under every bed, nearly suffocate itself in every drawer, nearly strangle itself with string, somehow, God knows how, trapped itself behind the radiator, been pulled back, by one leg, from its suicidal investigation of the staircase, and nearly poisoned itself with everything—*its* hand being quicker than *your* eye—it can possibly get into its mouth, you have either grown to love it or you have left home.

I, James, in August. George, in January. Barbara, in August. Wilmer, in October, David, in December. Gloria, Ruth, Elizabeth, and (when we thought it was over!) Paula Maria, named by me, born on the day our father died, all in the summertime.

The youngest son of the New Orleans branch of the family—family, here, is used loosely and has to be; we knew almost nothing about this branch, which knew nothing about us; Daddy, the great good friend of the Great God Almighty, had simply fled the South, leaving a branch behind. As I have said, he was the son of a slave, and his youngest daughter, by his first marriage, is my mother's age and his youngest son is nine years older than I. This boy, who did not get along with his father, was my elder brother, as far as I then knew, and he sometimes took me with him here and there. He took me into the Coney Island breakers on his back one day, teaching me to swim, and somehow ducked beneath me, playing, or was carried away from me for a moment, terrified, caught me and brought me above the waves. In the time that his body vanished beneath me and the waters rolled over my head, I still remember the slimy sea water and the blinding green—it was not green; it was all the world's snot and vomit; it entered into me; when my head was abruptly lifted out of the water, when I felt my brother's arms and saw his worried face—his eyes looking steadily into mine with the intense and yet impersonal anxiety of a surgeon, the sky above me not yet in focus, my lungs failing to deliver the mighty scream I had nearly burst with in the depths, my four- or five- or six-year-old legs kicking—and my brother slung me over his shoulder like a piece of meat, or a much beloved child, and strode up out of the sea with me, with me! he had saved me, after all, I learned something about the terror and the loneliness and the depth and the height of love.

Not so very much later, this brother, who was in his teens, fooling around with girls or shooting dice with his friends, who knows, came home late, which was forbidden in our Baptist house, and had a terrible fight with his Daddy and left the house and never came back. He swore that he never would come back, that his Daddy would never see him again. And he never did come back, not while Daddy was still alive. Daddy wrote, but his son never answered. When I became a young minister, I was asked to write him, and I did—sometimes, my father dictated the letters to me. And the boy answered me, sometimes, but he never answered his father and never mentioned him. Daddy slowly began to realize that he was never going to see that son, who was his darling, the apple of his eye, anymore, and this broke his heart and destroyed his will and helped him into the madhouse and the grave—my only intimation, perhaps, during all those years, that he was human. The son came home, when his father died, to help me bury him. Then he went away again, and I didn't see him until I had to go to California on a Civil Rights gig, and he met me at the airport. By then, I was thirty-nine and he was nearly fifty, I had made his disowned father's name famous, and I had left home in exactly the same way he did, for more or less the same reasons, and when I was seventeen.

Since Martin's death, in Memphis, and that tremendous day in Atlanta, something has altered in me, something has gone away. Perhaps even more than the death itself, the manner of his death has forced me into a judgment concerning human life and human beings which I have always been reluctant to make—indeed, I can see that a great deal of what the knowledgeable would call my life-style is dictated by this reluctance. Incontestably, alas, most people are not, in action, worth very much; and yet, every human being is an unprecedented miracle. One tries to treat them as the miracles they are, while trying to protect oneself against the disasters they've become. This is not very different from the act of faith demanded by all those marches and petitions while Martin was still alive. One could scarcely be deluded by Americans anymore, one scarcely dared expect anything from the great, vast, blank generality; and yet one was compelled to demand of Americans—and for their sakes, after all—a generosity, a clarity, and a nobility which they did not dream of demanding of themselves. Part of the error was irreducible, in that the marchers and petitioners were forced to suppose the existence of an entity which, when the chips were down, could not be located—*i.e.*, there *are* no American people yet: but to this speculation (or desperate hope) we shall presently return. Perhaps, however, the moral of the story (and the hope of the world) lies in what one demands, not of others, but of oneself. However that may be, the failure and the betrayal are in the record book forever, and sum up, and condemn, forever, those descendants of a barbarous Europe who arbitrarily and arrogantly reserve the right to call themselves Americans.

The mind is a strange and terrible vehicle, moving according to rigorous rules of its own; and my own mind, after I had left Atlanta, began to move backward in time, to places, people, and events I thought I had forgotten. Sorrow drove it there, I think, sorrow, and a certain kind of bewilderment, triggered, perhaps, by something which happened to me in connection with Martin's funeral.

When Martin was murdered, I was based in Hollywood, working—working, in fact, on the screen version of *The Autobiography of Malcolm X*. This was a difficult assignment, since I had known Malcolm, after all, crossed swords with him, worked with him, and held him in that great esteem which is not easily distinguishable, if it is distinguishable at all, from love. (The Hollywood gig did not work out because I did not wish to be a party to a second assassination: but we will also return to Hollywood, presently.)

Very shortly before his death, I had to appear with Martin at Carnegie Hall, in New York. Having been on the Coast so long, I had nothing suitable to wear for my Carnegie Hall gig, and so I rushed out, got a dark suit, got it fitted, and made my appearance. Something like two weeks later, I wore this same suit to Martin's funeral; returned to Hollywood; presently, had to come East again, on business. I ran into Leonard Lyons one night, and I told him that I would never be able to wear that suit again. Leonard put this in his column. I went back to Hollywood.

Weeks later, either because of a Civil Rights obligation, or because of Columbia Pictures, I was back in New York. On my desk in New York were various messages—and it must be said that my sister, Gloria, who worked for me then, is extremely selective, not to say brutal, about the messages she leaves on my desk. I don't see, simply, most of the messages I get. I couldn't conceivably live with them. No one could—as Gloria knows. However, my best friend, black, when I had been in junior high school, when I was twelve or thirteen, had been calling and calling and calling. The guilt of the survivor is a real guilt—as I was now to discover. In a way that I may never be able to make real for my countrymen, or myself, the fact that I had "made it"—that is, had been seen on television, and at Sardi's, could (presumably!) sign a check anywhere in the world, could, in short, for the length of an entrance, a dinner, or a drink, intimidate headwaiters by the use of a name which had not been mine when I was born and which love had compelled me to make my own—meant that I had betrayed the people who had produced me. Nothing could be more unutterably paradoxical: to have thrown in your lap what you never dreamed of getting, and, in sober, bitter truth, could never have dreamed of having, and that at the price of an assumed betrayal of your brothers and your sisters! One is always disproving the accusation in action as futile as it is inevitable.

I had not seen this friend—who could scarcely, any longer, be called a friend—in many years. I was brighter, or more driven than he—not my fault!—and, though neither of us knew it then, our friendship really ended during my ministry and was deader than my hope of heaven by the time I left the pulpit, the church, and home. Hindsight indicates, obviously, that this particular rupture, which was, of necessity, exceedingly brutal and which involved, after all, the deliberate repudiation of everything and everyone that had given me an identity until that moment, must have left some scars. The current of my life meant that I did not see this person very often, but I was always terribly guilty when I did. I was guilty because I had nothing to say to him, and at one time I had told him everything, or nearly everything. I was guilty because he was just another post-office worker, and we had dreamed such tremendous futures for ourselves. I was guilty because he and his family had been very nice to me during an awful time in my life and now none of that meant anything to me. I was guilty because I knew, at the bottom of my heart, that I judged this unremarkable colored man very harshly, far more harshly than I would have done if he were white, and I knew this to be unjust as well as sinister. I was furious because he thought my life was easy and I thought my life was hard, and I yet had to see that by his lights, certainly, and by any ordinary yardstick, my life was enviable compared to his. And if, as I kept saying, it was not my fault, it was not *his* fault, either. You can certainly see why I tended to avoid my old school chum.

But I called him, of course. I thought that he probably needed money, because that was the only thing, by now, that I could possibly hope to give him. But, no. He, or his wife, or a relative, had read the Leonard Lyons column and knew that I had a suit I wasn't wearing, and—as he remembered in one way and I in quite another—he was just my size.

Now, for me, that suit was drenched in the blood of all the crimes of my country. If I had said to Leonard, somewhat melodramatically, no doubt, that I could never wear it again, I was, just the same, being honest. I simply could not put it on, or look at it, without thinking of Martin, and Martin's end, of what he had meant to me, and to so many. I could not put it on without a bleak, pale, cold wonder about the future. I could not, in short, live with it, it was too heavy a garment. Yet—it was only a suit, worn, at most, three times. It was not a very expensive suit, but it was still more expensive than any my friend could buy. He could not afford to have suits in his closet which he didn't wear, he couldn't afford to throw suits away—he couldn't, in short, afford my elegant despair. Martin was dead, but *he* was living, he needed a suit, and—I was just his size. He invited me for dinner that evening, and I said that I would bring him the suit.

The American situation being what it is, and American taxi drivers being what they mostly are, I have, in effect, been forbidden to expose myself to the quite tremendous hazards of getting a cab to stop for me in New York, and have been forced to hire cars. Naturally, the car which picked me up on that particular guilty evening was a Cadillac limousine about seventy-three blocks long, and, naturally, the chauffeur was white. Neither did he want to drive a black man through Harlem to the Bronx, but American democracy has always been at the mercy of the dollar: the chauffeur may not have liked the gig, but he certainly wasn't about to lose the bread. Here we were, then, this terrified white man and myself, trapped in this leviathan, eyed bitterly, as it passed, by a totally hostile population. But it was not the chauffeur which the population looked on with such wry contempt: I held the suit over my arm, and was tempted to wave it: *I'm only taking a suit to a friend!*

I knew how they felt about black men in limousines—unless they were popular idols—and I couldn't blame them, and I knew that I could never explain. We found the house, and, with the suit over my arm, I mounted the familiar stairs.

I was no longer the person my friend and his family had known and loved—I was a stranger now, and keenly aware of it, and trying hard to act, as it were, normal. But nothing *can* be normal in such a situation. They *had* known me, and they *had* loved me; but now they couldn't be blamed for feeling *He thinks he's too good for us now*. I certainly didn't feel that, but I had no conceivable relationship to them anymore—that shy, pop-eyed thirteen year old my friend's mother had scolded and loved was no more. *I* was not the same, but *they* were, as though they had been trapped, preserved, in that moment in time. They seemed scarcely to have grown any older, my friend and his mother, and they greeted me as they had greeted me years ago, though I was now well past forty and felt every hour of it. My friend and I remained alike only in that neither of us had gained any weight. His face was as boyish as ever, and his voice; only a touch of grey in his hair proved that we were no longer at

P.S. 139. And my life came with me into their small, dark, unspeakably respectable, incredibly hard-won rooms like the roar of champagne and the odor of brimstone. They still believed in the Lord, but I had quarreled with Him, and offended Him, and walked out of His house. They didn't smoke, but they knew (from seeing me on television) that I did, and they had placed about the room, in deference to me, those hideous little ash trays which can hold exactly one cigarette butt. And there was a bottle of whiskey, too, and they asked me if I wanted steak or chicken; for, in my travels, I might have learned not to like fried chicken anymore. I said, much relieved to be able to tell the truth, that I preferred chicken. I gave my friend the suit.

My friend's stepdaughter is young, considers herself a militant, and we had a brief argument concerning Bill Styron's *Nat Turner,* which I suggested that she read before condemning. This rather shocked the child, whose militancy, like that of many, tends to be a matter of indigestible fury and slogans and quotations. It rather checked the company, which had not imagined that I and a black militant could possibly disagree about anything. But what was most striking about our brief exchange was that it obliquely revealed how little the girl respected her stepfather. She appeared not to respect him at all. This was not revealed by anything she said to him, but by the fact that she said nothing to him. She barely looked at him. He didn't count.

I always think that this is a terrible thing to happen to a man, especially in his own house, and I am always terribly humiliated for the man to whom it happens. Then, of course, you get angry at the man for allowing it to happen.

And *how* had it happened? He had never been the brightest boy in the world, nobody is, but he had been energetic, active, funny, wrestling, playing handball, cheerfully submitting to being tyrannized by me, even to the extent of kneeling before the altar and having his soul saved—my insistence had accomplished that. I looked at him and remembered his sweating and beautiful face that night as he wrestled on the church floor and we prayed him through. I remembered his older brother, who had died in Sicily, in battle for the free world—he had barely had time to see Sicily before he died and had assuredly never seen the free world. I remembered the day he came to see me to tell me that his sister, who had been very ill, had died. We sat on the steps of the tenement, he was looking down as he told me, one finger making a circle on the step, and his tears splashed on the wood. We were children then, his sister had not been much older, and he was the youngest and now the only boy. But this was not *how* it had happened, although I thought I could see, watching his widowed mother's still very handsome face watching him, how her human need might have held and trapped and frozen him. She had been sewing in the garment center all the years I knew them, rushing home to get supper on the table before her husband got home from *his* job; at night, and on Sundays, he was a deacon; and God knows, or should, where his energy came from. When I began working for the garment center, I used to see her, from time to time, rushing to catch the bus, in a crowd of black and Puerto Rican ladies.

And, yes, we had all loved each other then, and I had had great respect for my friend, who was handsomer than I, and more athletic, and more popular, and who beat me in every game I was foolish enough to play with him. I had gone my way and life had accomplished its inexorable mathematic—and what in the world was I by now but an aging, lonely, sexually dubious, politically outrageous, unspeakably erratic freak? his old friend. And what was *he* now? he worked for the post office and was building a house next door to his mother, in, I think, Long Island. They, too, then, had made it. But what I could not understand was how nothing seemed to have touched this man. We are living through what our church described as "these last and evil days," through wars and rumors of wars, to say the least. He could, for example, have known something about the anti-poverty program if only because his wife was more or less involved in it. He should have known something about the then raging school battle, if only because his stepdaughter was a student; and she, whether or not she had thought her position through, was certainly involved. She may have hoped, at one time, anyway, for his clarity and his help. But, no. He seemed as little touched by the cataclysm in his house and all around him as he was by the mail he handled every day. I found this unbelievable, and, given my temperament and our old connection, maddening. We got into a battle about the war in Vietnam. I probably really should not have allowed this to happen, but it was partly the stepdaughter's prodding. And I was astounded that my friend would defend this particular racist folly. What for? for his job at the post office? And the answer came back at once, alas—yes. For his job at the post office. I told him that Americans had no business at all in Vietnam; and that black people certainly had no business there, aiding the slave master to enslave yet more millions of dark people, and also identifying themselves with the white American crimes: we, the blacks, are going to need our allies, for the Americans, odd as it may sound at the moment, will presently have none. It wasn't, I said, hard to understand why a black boy, standing, futureless, on the corner, would decide to join the Army, nor was it hard to decipher the slave master's reasons for hoping that he wouldn't live to come home, with a gun; but it wasn't necessary, after all, to defend it: to defend, that is, one's murder and one's murderers. "Wait a minute," he said, "let me stand up and tell you what I think we're trying to do there." "*We?*" I cried, "what motherfucking *we?* You stand up, motherfucker, and I'll kick you in the ass!"

He looked at me. His mother conveyed—but the good Lord knows I had hurt her—that she didn't want that language in her house, and that I had never talked that way before. And I love the lady. I had meant no disrespect. I stared at my friend, my old friend, and felt millions of people staring at us both. I tried to make a kind of joke out of it all. But it was too late. The way they looked at me proved that I had tipped my hand. And *this* hurt *me*. They should have known me better, or at least enough, to have known that I meant what I said. But the general reaction to famous people who hold difficult opinions is that they can't really mean it. It's considered, generally, to be merely an astute way of attracting public attention, a way of making oneself interesting: one marches in Montgomery, for example, merely (in my own case) to sell one's books. Well. There is nothing, then, to be said. There went the friendly fried chicken dinner. There went the loving past. I watched the mother watching me, wondering what had happened to her beloved Jimmy, and giving me up: her sourest suspicions confirmed. In great weariness I poured myself yet another stiff drink, by now definitively condemned, and lit another cigarette, they watching me all the while for symptoms of cancer, and with a precipice at my feet.

For that bloody suit was *their* suit, after all, it had been bought *for* them, it had even been bought *by* them: *they* had created Martin, he had not created them, and the blood in which the fabric of that suit was stiffening was theirs. The distance between us, and I had never thought of this before, was that they did not know this, and I now dared to realize that I loved them more than they loved me. And I do not mean that my love was greater: who dares judge the inexpressible expense another pays for his life? who knows how much one is loved, by whom, or what that love may be called on to do? No, the way the cards had fallen meant that I had to face more about them than they could know about me, knew their rent, whereas they did not know mine, and was condemned to make them uncomfortable. For, on the other hand, they certainly wanted that freedom which they thought was mine—that frightening limousine, for example, or the power to give away a suit, or my increasingly terrifying trans-Atlantic journeys. How can one say that freedom is taken, not given, and that no one is free until all are free? and that the price is high.

My friend tried on the suit, a perfect fit, and they all admired him in it, and I went home.

Well. Time passes and passes. It passes backward and it passes forward and it carries you along, and no one in the whole wide world knows more about time than this: it is carrying you through an element you do not understand into an element you will not remember. Yet, *something* remembers—it can even be said that something avenges: the trap of our century, and the subject now before us.

I left home—Harlem—in 1942. I returned, in 1946, to do, with a white photographer, one of several unpublished efforts; had planned to marry, then realized that I couldn't—or shouldn't, which comes to the same thing—threw my wedding rings into the Hudson River, and left New York for Paris, in 1948. By this time, of course, I was mad, as mad as my dead father. If I had not gone mad, I could not have left.

I starved in Paris for a while, but I learned something: for one thing, I fell in love. Or, more accurately, I realized, and accepted for the first time that love was not merely a general, human possibility, nor merely the disaster it had so often, by then, been for me—according to me—nor was it something that happened to other people, like death, nor was it merely a mortal danger: it was among *my* possibilities, for here it was, breathing and belching beside me, and it was the key to life. Not merely the key to *my* life, but to life itself. My falling in love is in no way the subject of this book, and yet honesty compels me to place it among the details, for I think—I know—that my story would be a very different one if love had not forced me to attempt to deal with myself. It began to pry open for me the trap of color, for people do not fall in love according to their color—this may come as news to noble pioneers and eloquent astronauts, to say nothing of most of the representatives of most of the American states—and when lovers quarrel, as indeed they inevitably do, it is not the degree of their pigmentation that they are quarreling about, nor can lovers, on any level whatever, use color as a weapon. This means that one must accept one's nakedness. And nakedness has no color: this can come as news only to those who have never covered, or been covered by, another naked human being.

In any case, the world changes then, and it changes forever. Because you love one human being, you see everyone else very differently than you saw them before—perhaps I only mean to say that you begin to *see*—and you are both stronger and more vulnerable, both free and bound. Free, paradoxically, because, now, you have a home—your lover's arms. And bound: to that mystery, precisely, a bondage which liberates you into something of the glory and suffering of the world.

I had come to Paris with no money and this meant that in those early years I lived mainly among *les misérables*—and, in Paris, *les misérables* are Algerian. They slept four or five or six to a room, and they slept in shifts, they were treated like dirt, and they scraped such sustenance as they could off the filthy, unyielding Paris stones. The French called them lazy because they appeared to spend most of their time sitting around, drinking tea, in their cafés. But they were not lazy. They were mostly unable to find work, and their rooms were freezing. (French students spent most of their time in cafés, too, for the same reason, but no one called them lazy.) The Arab cafés were warm and cheap, and they were together there. They could not, in the main, afford the French cafés, nor in the main, were they welcome there. And, though they spoke French, and had been, in a sense, produced by France, they were not at home in Paris, no more at home than I, though for a different reason. They remembered, as it were, an opulence, opulence of taste, touch, water, sun, which I had barely dreamed of, and they had not come to France to stay. One day they were going home, and they knew exactly where home was. They, thus, held something within them which they would never surrender to France. But on my side of the ocean, or so it seemed to me then, we had surrendered everything, or had had everything taken away, and there was no place for us to go: we *were* home. The Arabs were together in Paris, but the American blacks were alone. The Algerian poverty was absolute, their stratagems grim, their personalities, for me, unreadable, their present bloody and their future certain to be more so: and yet, after all, their situation was far more coherent than mine. I will not say that I envied them, for I didn't, and the directness of their hunger, or hungers, intimidated me; but I respected them, and as I began to discern what their history had made of them, I began to suspect, somewhat painfully, what my history had made of me.

The French were still hopelessly slugging it out in Indo-China when I first arrived in France, and I was living in Paris when Dien Bien Phu fell. The Algerian rug-sellers and peanut vendors on the streets of Paris then had obviously not the remotest connection with this most crucial of the French reverses; and yet the attitude of the police, which had always been menacing, began to be yet more snide and vindictive. This puzzled me at first, but it shouldn't have. This is the way people react to the loss of empire—for the loss of an empire also implies a radical revision of the individual identity—and I was to see this over and over again, not only in France. The Arabs were not a part of Indo-China, but they *were* part of an empire visibly and swiftly crumbling, and part of a history which was achieving, in the most literal and frightening sense, its *dénouement*—was revealing itself, that is, as being not at all the myth which the French had made of it—and the French authority to rule over them was being more hotly contested with every hour. The challenged authority, unable to justify itself and not dreaming indeed of even attempting to do so, simply increased its force. This had the interesting result of revealing how frightened the French authority had become, and many a North African then resolved, *coûte que coûte*, to bring the French to another Dien Bien Phu.

Something else struck me, which I was to watch more closely in my own country. The French were hurt and furious that their stewardship should be questioned, especially by those they ruled, and if, in this, they were not very original, they were exceedingly intense. After all, as they continually pointed out, there had been nothing in those colonies before they got there, nothing at all; or what meagre resources of mineral or oil there might have been weren't doing the natives any good because the natives didn't even know that they were there, or what they were there for. Thus, the exploitation of the colony's resources was done for the good of the natives; and so vocal could the French become as concerns what they had brought into their colonies that it would have been the height of bad manners to have asked what they had brought out. (I was later to see something of how this fair exchange worked when I visited Senegal and Guinea.)

It was strange to find oneself, in another language, in

another country, listening to the same old song and hearing oneself condemned in the same old way. The French (for example) had always had excellent relations with their natives, and they had a treasurehouse of anecdotes to prove it. (I never found any natives to corroborate the anecdotes, but, then, I have never met an African who did not loathe Dr. Schweitzer.) They cited the hospitals built, and the schools—I was to see some of these later, too. Every once in a while someone might be made uneasy by the color of my skin, or an expression on my face, or I might say something to make him uneasy, or I might, arbitrarily (there was no reason to suppose that they wanted me), claim kinship with the Arabs. Then, I was told, with a generous smile, that I was different: *le noir Americain est très évolué, voyons!* But the Arabs were not like me, they were not "civilized" like me. It was something of a shock to hear myself described as civilized, but the accolade thirsted for so long had, alas, been delivered too late, and I was fascinated by one of several inconsistencies. I have never heard a Frenchman describe the United States as civilized, not even those Frenchmen who like the States. Of course, I think the truth is that the French do not consider that the world contains any nation as civilized as France. But, leaving that aside, if so crude a nation as the United States could produce so gloriously civilized a creature as myself, how was it that the French, armed with centuries of civilized grace, had been unable to civilize the Arab? I thought that this was a very cunning question, but I was wrong, because the answer was so simple: the Arabs did not wish to be civilized. Oh, it was not possible for an American to understand these people as the French did; after all, they had got on well together for nearly one hundred and thirty years. But they had, the Arabs, their customs, their dialects, languages, tribes, regions, another religion, or, perhaps, many religions—and the French were not *raciste*, like the Americans, they did not believe in destroying indigenous cultures. And then, too, the Arab was always hiding something; you couldn't guess what he was thinking and couldn't trust what he was saying. And they had a different attitude toward women, they were very brutal with them, in a word they were rapists, and they stole, and they carried knives. But the French had endured this for more than a hundred years and were willing to endure it for a hundred years more, in spite of the fact that Algeria was a great drain on the national pocketbook and the fact that any Algerian—due to the fact that Algeria was French, was, in fact, a French *département*, and was damn well going to stay that way—was free to come to Paris at any time and jeopardize the economy and prowl the streets and prey on French women. In short, the record of French generosity was so exemplary that it was impossible to believe that the children could seriously be bent on revolution.

Impossible for a Frenchman, perhaps, but not for me. I had watched the police, one sunny afternoon, beat an old, one-armed Arab peanut vendor senseless in the streets, and I had watched the unconcerned faces of the French on the café terraces, and the congested faces of the Arabs. Yes, I could believe it: and here it came.

Not without warning, and not without precedent: but only poets, since they must excavate and re-create history, have ever learned anything from it.

I returned to New York in 1952, after four years away, at the height of the national convulsion called McCarthyism. This convulsion did not surprise me, for I don't think that it was possible for Americans to surprise me anymore; but it was very frightening, in many ways, and for many reasons. I realized, for one thing, that I was saved from direct—or, more accurately, public—exposure to the American Inquisitors only by my color, my obscurity, and my comparative youth: or, in other words, by the lack, on their parts, of any imagination. I was just a shade too young to have had any legally recognizable political history. A boy of thirteen is a minor, and, in the eyes of the Republic, if he is black, and lives in a black ghetto, he was born to carry packages; but, in fact, at thirteen, I had been a convinced fellow traveler. I marched in one May Day parade, carrying banners, shouting, *East Side, West Side, all around the town, We want the landlords to tear the slums down!* I didn't know anything about Communism, but I knew a lot about slums. By the time I was nineteen, I was a Trotskyite, having learned a great deal by then, if not about Communism, at least about Stalinists. The convulsion was the more ironical for me in that I had been an anti-Communist when America and Russia were allies. I had nearly been murdered on 14th Street, one evening, for putting down too loudly, in the presence of patriots, that memorable contribution to the War effort, the Warner Brothers production of *Mission to Moscow*. The very same patriots now wanted to burn the film and hang the filmmakers, and Warners, during the McCarthy era, went to no little trouble to explain their film away. Warners was abject, and so was nearly everybody else, it was a foul, ignoble time: and my contempt for most American intellectuals, and/or liberals dates from what I observed of their manhood then. I say most, not all, but the exceptions constitute a remarkable pantheon, even, or, rather, especially those who did not survive the flames into which their lives and their reputations were hurled. I had come home to a city in which nearly everyone was gracelessly scurrying for shelter, in which friends were throwing their friends to the wolves, and justifying their treachery by learned discourses (and tremendous tomes) on the treachery of the Comintern. Some of the things written during those years, justifying, for example, the execution of the Rosenbergs, or the crucifixion of Alger Hiss (and the beatification of Whittaker Chambers) taught me something about the irresponsibility and cowardice of the liberal community which I will never forget. Their performance, then, yet more than the combination of ignorance and arrogance with which this community has always protected itself against the deepest implications of black suffering, persuaded me that brilliance without passion is nothing more than sterility. It must be remembered, after all, that I did not begin meeting these people at the point that they began to meet *me:* I had been delivering their packages and emptying their garbage and taking their tips for years. (And they don't tip well.) And what I watched them do to each other during the McCarthy era was, in some ways, worse than anything they had ever done to me, for I, at least, had never been mad enough to depend on their devotion. It seemed very clear to me that they were lying about their motives and were being blackmailed by their guilt; were, in fact, at bottom, nothing more than the respectable issue of various immigrants, struggling to hold on to what they had acquired. For, intellectual activity, according to me, is, and must be, disinterested—the truth *is* a two-edged sword—and if one is not willing to be pierced by that sword, even to the extreme of dying on it, then all of one's intellectual activity is a masturbatory delusion and a wicked and dangerous fraud.

I made such motions as I could to understand what was happening, and to keep myself afloat. But I had been away too long. It was not only that I *could* not readjust myself to life in New York—it was also that I *would* not: I was never going to be anybody's nigger again. But I was now to discover that the world has more than one way of keeping you a nigger, has evolved more than one way of skinning the cat; if the hand slips here, it tightens there, and now I was offered, gracefully indeed: membership in the club. I had lunch at some elegant bistros, dinner at some exclusive clubs. I tried to be understanding about my countrymen's concern for difficult me, and unruly mine—and I really *was* trying to be understanding, though not without some bewilderment, and, eventually, some malice. I began to be profoundly uncomfortable. It was a strange kind of discomfort, a terrified apprehension that I had lost my bearings. I did not altogether understand what I was hearing. I did not trust what I heard myself saying. In very little that I heard did I hear anything that reflected anything which *I* knew, or had endured, of life. My mother and my father, my brothers and my sisters were not present at the tables at which I sat down, and no one in the company had ever heard of them. My own beginnings, or instincts, began to shift as nervously as the cigarette smoke that wavered around my head. I was not trying to hold on to my wretchedness. On the contrary, if my poverty was coming, at last, to an end, so much the better, and it wasn't happening a moment too soon—and yet, I felt an increasing chill, as though the rest of my life would have to be lived in silence.

I think it may have been my own obsession with the McCarthy phenomenon which caused me to suspect the impotence and narcissism of so many of the people whose names I had respected. I had never had any occasion to judge them, as it were, intimately. For me, simply, McCarthy was a coward and a bully, with no claim to honor, nor any claim to honorable attention. For me, emphatically, there were *not* two sides to this dubious coin, and, as to his baleful and dangerous effect, there could be no *question* at all. Yet, they spent hours debating whether or not McCarthy was an enemy of domestic liberties. I couldn't but wonder what conceivable further proof they were awaiting: I thought of German Jews sitting around debating whether or not Hitler was a threat to their lives until the debate was summarily resolved for them by a knocking at the door. Nevertheless, this learned, civilized, intellectual-liberal debate cheerfully raged in its vacuum, while every hour brought more distress and confusion—and dishonor—to the country they claimed to love. The pretext for all this, of course, was the necessity of "containing" Communism, which, they unblushingly informed me, was a threat to the "free" world. I did not say to what extent this free world menaced me, and millions like me. But I wondered how the justification of blatant and mindless tyranny, on any level, could operate in the interests of liberty, and I wondered what interior, unspoken urgencies of these people made necessary so thoroughly unattractive a delusion. I wondered what they really felt about human life, for they were so choked and cloaked with formulas that they no longer seemed to have any connection with it. They were all, for a while anyway, very proud of me, of course, proud that I had been able to crawl up to their level and been "accepted." What *I* might think of *their* level, how *I* might react to this "acceptance," or what this acceptance might cost me, were not among the questions which racked them in the midnight hour. One wondered, indeed, if anything could ever disturb their sleep. They walked the same streets I walked, after all, rode the same subways, must have seen the same increasingly desperate and hostile boys and girls, must, at least occasionally, have passed through the garment center. It is true that even those who taught at Columbia never saw Harlem, but, on the other hand, everything that New York has become, in 1971, was visibly and swiftly beginning to happen in 1952: one had only to take a bus from the top of the city and ride through it to see how it was darkening and deteriorating, how human bewilderment and hostility rose, how human contact was endangered and dying. Of course, these liberals were not, as I was, forever being found by the police in the "wrong" neighborhood, and so could not have had first-hand knowledge of how gleefully a policeman translates his orders from above. But they had no right not to know that; if they did not know that, they knew nothing and had no right to speak as though they were responsible actors in their society; for their complicity with the patriots of that hour meant that the policeman was acting on *their* orders, too.

No, I couldn't hack it. When my first novel was finally sold, I picked up my advance and walked straight to the steamship office and booked passage back to France.

I place it here, though it occurred during a later visit: I found myself in a room one night, with my liberal friends, after a private showing of the French film, *The Wages of Fear*. The question on the floor was whether or not this film should be shown in the United States. The reason for the question was that the film contained unflattering references to American oil companies. I do not know if I said anything, or not; I rather doubt that I could have said much. I felt as paralyzed, fascinated, as a rabbit before a snake. I had, in fact, already seen the film in France. It had not occurred to me, or to anyone I knew, that the film was even remotely anti-American: by no stretch of the imagination could this be considered the film's *motif*. Yet, here were the autumn patriots, hotly discussing the dangers of a film which dared to suggest that American oil interests didn't give a shit about human life. There was a French woman in the room, tight-mouthed, bitter, far from young. She may or may not have been the widow of a Vichyite General, but her sympathies were in that region: and I will never forget her saying, looking straight at me, "We always knew that you, the Americans, would realize, one day, that you fought on the wrong side!"

I was ashamed of myself for being in that room: but, I must say, too, that I was glad, glad to have been a witness, glad to have come far enough to have heard the devil speak. That woman gave me something, I will never forget her, and I walked away from the welcome table.

Yet, hope—the hope that we, human beings, can be better than we are—dies hard; perhaps one can no longer live if one allows that hope to die. But it is also hard to see what one sees. One sees that most human beings are wretched, and, in one way or another, become wicked: because they are so wretched. And one's turning away, then, from what I have called the welcome table is dictated by some mysterious vow one scarcely knows one's taken—never to allow oneself to fall so low. Lower, perhaps, much lower, to the very dregs: but never there.

When I came back to Paris at the end of the summer, most of the Arab cafés I knew had been closed. My favorite money-changer and low-life guide, a beautiful stone hustler, had disappeared, no one knew—or no one said—where. Another cat had had his eyes put out—some said by the police, some said by his brothers, because he was a police informer. In a sense, that beautiful, blinded boy who had been punished either as a traitor to France or as a traitor to Algeria, sums up the Paris climate in the years immediately preceding the revolution. One was either French, or Algerian; one could not be both.

There began, now, a time of rumor unlike anything I had ever been through before. In a way, I was somewhat insulated against what was happening to the Algerians, or was aware of it from a certain distance, because what was happening to the Algerians did not appear to be happening to the blacks. I was still operating, unconsciously, within the American framework, and, in that framework, since Arabs are paler than blacks, it is the blacks who would have suffered most. But the blacks, from Martinique and Senegal, and so on, were as visible and vivid as they had always been, and no one appeared to molest them or to pay them any particular attention at all. Not only was I operating within the American frame of reference, I was also a member of the American colony, and we were, in general, slow to pick up on what was going on around us.

Nevertheless, I began to realize that I could not find *any* of the Algerians I knew, not one; and since I could not find one, there was no way to ask about the others. They were in none of the dives we had frequented, they had apparently abandoned their rooms, their cafés, as I have said, were closed, and they were no longer to be seen on the Paris sidewalks, changing money, or selling their rugs, their peanuts, or themselves. We heard that they had been placed in camps around Paris, that they were being tortured there, that they were being murdered. No one wished to believe any of this, it made us exceedingly uncomfortable, and we felt that we should do something, but there was nothing we could do. We began to realize that there *had* to be some truth to these pale and cloudy rumors: one woman told me of seeing an Algerian hurled by the proprietor of a café in Pigalle *through* the café's *closed* plate-glass door. If she had not witnessed a murder, she had certainly witnessed a murder attempt. And, in fact, Algerians *were* being murdered in the streets, and corraled into prisons, and being dropped into the Seine, like flies.

Not only Algerians. Everyone in Paris, in those years, who was not, resoundingly, from the north of Europe was suspected of being Algerian; and the police were on every street corner, sometimes armed with machine guns. Turks, Greeks, Spaniards, Jews, Italians, American blacks, and Frenchmen from Marseilles, or Nice, were all under constant harassment, and we will never know how many people having not the remotest connection with Algeria were thrown into prison, or murdered, as it were, by accident. The son of a world-famous actor, and an actor himself, swarthy, and speaking no French—rendered speechless indeed by the fact that the policeman had a gun leveled at him—was saved only by the fact that he was close enough to his hotel to shout for the night porter, who came rushing out and identified him. Two young Italians, on holiday, did not fare so well: speeding merrily along on their Vespa, they failed to respond to a policeman's order to halt, whereupon the policeman fired, and the holiday came to a bloody end. Everyone one knew was full of stories like these, which eventually began to appear in the press, and one had to be careful how one moved about in the fabulous city of light.

I had never, thank God—and certainly not once I found myself living there—been even remotely romantic about Paris. I may have been romantic about London—because of Charles Dickens—but the romance lasted for exactly as long as it took me to carry my bags out of Victoria Station. My journey, or my flight, had not been *to* Paris, but simply *away* from America. For example, I had seriously considered going to work on a kibbutz in Israel, and I ended up in Paris almost literally by closing my eyes and putting my finger on a map. So I was not as demoralized by all of this as I would certainly have been if I had ever made the error of considering Paris the most civilized of cities and the French as the least primitive of peoples. I knew too much about the French Revolution for that. I had read too much Balzac for that. Whenever I crossed la place de la Concorde, I heard the tumbrils arriving, and the roar of the mob, and where the obelisk now towers, I saw—and see—*la guillotine*. Anyone who has ever been at the mercy of the people, then, knows something awful about us, will forever distrust the popular patriotism, and avoids even the most convivial of mobs.

Still, my flight had been dictated by my hope that I could find myself in a place where I would be treated more humanely than my society had treated me at home, where my risks would be more personal, and my fate less austerely sealed. And Paris had done this for me: by leaving me completely alone. I lived in Paris for a long time without making a single French friend, and even longer before I saw the inside of a French home. This did not really upset me, either, for Henry James had been here before me and had had the generosity to clue me in. Furthermore, for a black boy who had grown up on Welfare and the chicken-shit goodwill of American liberals, this total indifference came as a great relief and, even, as a mark of respect. If I could make it, I could make it; so much the better. And if

I couldn't, I couldn't—so much the worse. I didn't want any help, and the French certainly didn't give me any—they let me do it myself; and for that reason, even knowing what I know, and unromantic as I am, there will always be a kind of love story between myself and that odd, unpredictable collection of bourgeois chauvinists who call themselves *la France*.

Or, in other words, my reasons for coming to France, and the comparative freedom of my life in Paris, meant that my attitude toward France was very different from that of any Algerian. He, and his brothers, were, in fact, being murdered by my hosts. And Algeria, after all, is a part of Africa, and France, after all, is a part of Europe: that Europe which invaded and raped the African continent and slaughtered those Africans whom they could not enslave—that Europe from which, in sober truth, Africa has yet to liberate herself. The fact that I had never seen the Algerian casbah was of no more relevance before this unanswerable panorama than the fact that the Algerians had never seen Harlem. The Algerian and I were both, alike, victims of this history, and I was still a part of Africa, even though I had been carried out of it nearly four hundred years before.

The question of my identity had never before been so crucially allied with the reality—the doom—of the moral choice. The irreducible inconvenience of the moral choice is that it is, by definition, arbitrary—through it sounds so grandiose—and, on the surface, unreasonable, and has no justification but (or in) itself. My reaction, in the present instance, was unreasonable on its face, not only because of my ignorance of the Arab world, but also because I could not affect their destiny in any degree. And yet, their destiny was somehow tied to mine, their battle was not theirs alone but was my battle also, and it began to be a matter of my honor not to attempt to avoid this loaded fact.

And, furthermore—though this was truer in principle than it was in fact, as I had had occasion to learn—my life in Paris was to some extent protected by the fact that I carried a green passport. This passport proclaimed that I was a free citizen of a free country, and was not, therefore, to be treated as one of Europe's uncivilized, black possessions. This same passport, on the other side of the ocean, underwent a sea change and proclaimed that I was not an African prince, but a domestic nigger and that no foreign government would be offended if my corpse were to be found clogging up the sewers. I had never had occasion to reflect before on the brilliance of the white strategy: blacks didn't know each other, could barely speak to each other, and, therefore, could scarcely trust each other—and therefore, wherever we turned, we found ourselves in the white man's territory, and at the white man's mercy. Four hundred years in the West had certainly turned me into a Westerner—there was no way around that. But four hundred years in the West had also failed to bleach me—there was no way around *that*, either—and my history in the West had, for its daily effect, placed me in such mortal danger that I had fled, all the way around the corner, to France. And if I had fled, to Israel, a state created for the purpose of protecting Western interests, I would have been in yet a tighter bind: on which side of Jerusalem would I have decided to live? In 1948, no African nation, as such, existed, and could certainly neither have needed, nor welcomed, a penniless black American, with the possible exception of Liberia. But, even with black overseers, I would not have lasted long on the Firestone rubber plantation.

I have said that I was almost entirely ignorant of the details of the Algerian-French complexity, but I was endeavoring to correct this ignorance; and one of the ways in which I was going about it compelled me to keep a file of the editorial pronouncements made by M. Albert Camus in the pages of the French political newspaper, *Combat*. Camus had been born in Oran, which is the scene of his first novel, *The Stranger*. He could be described, perhaps, as a radical humanist; he was young, he was lucid, and it was not illogical to assume that he would bring—along with the authority of knowing the land of his birth—some of these qualities to bear on his apprehension of the nature of the French-Algerian conflict.

I have never esteemed this writer as highly as do so many

others. I was struck by the fact that, for Camus, the European humanism appeared to expire at the European gates: so that Camus, who was dedicated to liberty, in the case of Europeans, could only speak of "justice" in the case of Algeria. And yet, he must surely have known, must have seen with his own eyes, some of the results of French "justice" in Algeria. ("A legal means," said an African recipient, "of administering injustice.") Given the precepts upon which he based his eloquent discourses concerning the problems of individual liberty, he must have seen that what the battle of Algiers was really about was the fact that the French refused to give the Algerians the right to be wrong; refused to allow them, so to speak, that "existentialist" situation, of which the French, for a season, were so enamored; or, more accurately, did not even dare imagine that the Algerian situation could be "existentialist"; precisely because the French situation was so extreme. There was no way for him not to have known that Algeria was French only insofar as French power had decreed it to be French. It existed on the European map only insofar as European power had placed it there. It is power, not justice, which keeps rearranging the map, and the Algerians were not fighting the French for justice (of which, indeed, they must have had their fill by that time) but for the power to determine their own destinies.

It was during this time that Camus translated and directed, for the Mathurin Theatre, in Paris, William Faulkner's *Requiem for a Nun*, and an American magazine asked me to review it. I would almost certainly not have seen this production otherwise, for I had seen the play in New York, and I had read the book, and had found Faulkner's fable to be a preposterous bore. But I trotted off to the Mathurin Theatre to see it, taking along a gallant lady friend. And we suffered through this odd and interminable account of the sins of a white Southern lady, and her cardboard husband, and the nigger-whore-dope fiend maid, Nancy. Nancy, in order to arrest her mistress's headlong flight to self-destruction—to bring her to her senses—murders the white lady's infant. This may seem an odd way of healing the sick, but Nancy is, in fact, the Christ figure, and has taken her mistress's sins on herself.

Why? Nancy has enough sins of her own, which on the whole would seem to be rather more interesting, and the lady she takes such drastic means of saving is too dull, and much, much too talkative—in a word, too unreal—to warrant such concern.

The key to a tale is to be found in who tells it; and so I thought I could see why Faulkner may have needed to believe in a black forgiveness, furthermore, which, if one stands aside from what Faulkner wishes us to make of it, can scarcely be distinguished from the bloodiest, most classical Old Testament revenge. What Faulkner wishes us to believe, and what he wishes to believe, is at war with what he, fatally, suspects. He suspects that black Nancy may have murdered white Temple's white baby out of pure, exasperated hatred. In life, in any case, it would scarcely matter: Nancy's forgiveness, or Nancy's revenge, result, anyway, in infanticide; and it is this tension between hope and terror, this panic-stricken inability to read the meaning of the event, which condemns the play to an insupportable turgidity. I could see why Faulkner needed Nancy: but why did Camus need Faulkner? On what ground did they meet, the mind of the great, aging, Mississippi novelist, and the mind of the young writer from Oran?

Neither of them could accurately, or usefully, be described as racists, in spite of Faulkner's declared intention of shooting Negroes in the streets if he found this necessary for the salvation of the state of Mississippi. This statement had to be read as an excess of patriotism, unlikely, in Faulkner's case, to lead to any further action. The mischief of the remark lay in the fact that it certainly encouraged others to such action. And Faulkner's portraits of Negroes, which lack a system of nuances that, perhaps, only a black writer can see in black life—for Faulkner could see Negroes only as they related to him, not as they related to each other—are nevertheless made vivid by the torment of their creator. He is seeking to exorcise a history which is also a curse. He wants the old order, which came into existence through unchecked greed and wanton murder, to redeem itself without further bloodshed—without, that is, any further menacing itself—and without coercion. This, old orders never do, less because they would not than because they cannot. They cannot because they have always existed in relation to a force which they have had to subdue. This subjugation is the key to their identity and the triumph and justification of their history, and it is also on this continued subjugation that their material well-being depends. One may see that the history, which is now indivisible from oneself, has been full of errors and excesses; but this is not the same thing as seeing that, for millions of people, this history—oneself—has been nothing but an intolerable yoke, a stinking prison, a shrieking grave. It is not so easy to see that, for millions of people, life itself depends on the speediest possible demolition of this history, even if this means the leveling, or the destruction of its heirs. And whatever this history may have given to the subjugated is of absolutely no value, since they have never been free to reject it; they will never even be able to assess it until they are free to take from it what they need, and to add to history the monumental fact of their presence. The South African coal miner, or the African digging for roots in the bush, or the Algerian mason working in Paris, not only have no reason to bow down before Shakespeare, or Descartes, or Westminster Abbey, or the cathedral at Chartres: they have, once these monuments intrude on their attention, no honorable access to them. Their apprehension of this history cannot fail to reveal to them that they have been robbed, maligned, and rejected: to bow down before that history is to accept that history's arrogant and unjust judgment.

This is why, ultimately, all attempts at dialogue between the subdued and subduer, between those placed within history and those dispersed outside, break down. One may say, indeed, that until this hour such a dialogue has scarcely been attempted: the subdued and the subduer do not speak the same language. What has passed for dialogue has usually involved one of "our" niggers, or, say, an *évolué* from Dakar. The "evolved," or civilized one is almost always someone educated by, and for, France, and some of "our" niggers, proving how well they have been educated, become spokesmen for "black" capitalism—a concept demanding yet more faith and infinitely more in schizophrenia than the concept of the Virgin Birth. Dakar is a French city on the West African coast, and a representative from Dakar is not necessarily a man from Senegal. He is much more likely to be a spiritual citizen of France, in which event he cannot possibly convey the actual needs of his part of Africa, or of Africa. And when such a dialogue truly erupts, it cannot avoid the root question of the possession of the land, and the exploitation of the land's resources. At that point, the cultural pretensions of history are revealed as nothing less than a mask for power, and thus it happens that, in order to be rid of Shell, Texaco, Coca-Cola, the Sixth Fleet, and the friendly American soldier whose mission it is to protect these investments, one finally throws Balzac and Shakespeare—and Faulkner and Camus—out with them. Later, of course, one may welcome them back, but on one's own terms, and, absolutely, on one's own land.

When the pagan and the slave spit on the cross and pick up the gun, it means that the halls of history are about to be invaded once again, destroying and dispersing the present occupants. These, then, can call only on their history to save them—that same history which, in the eyes of the subjugated, has already condemned them. Therefore, Faulkner hoped that American blacks would have the generosity to "go slow"—would allow white people, that is, the time to save themselves, as though they had not had more than enough time already, and as though their victims still believed in white miracles—and Camus repeated the word "justice" as though it were a magical incantation to which all of Africa would immediately respond. American blacks could not "go slow" because they had made a rendezvous with history for the purpose of taking their children out of history's hands. And Camus' "justice" was a concept forged and betrayed in Europe, in exactly the same way as the Christian church has betrayed and dishonored and blasphemed that Saviour in whose name they have slaughtered millions and millions and millions of people. And if this mighty objection seems trivial, it can only be because of the total hardening of the heart and the coarsening of the conscience among those people who believed that their power has given them the exclusive right to history. If the Christians do not believe in their Saviour (who has certainly, furthermore, failed to save them) why, then, wonder the unredeemed, should I abandon my gods for yours? For I *know* my gods are real: they have enabled me to withstand you.

In the fall of 1956, I was covering, for *Encounter* (or for the CIA) the first International Conference of Black Writers and Artists, at the Sorbonne, in Paris. One bright afternoon, several of us, including the late Richard Wright, were meandering up the Boulevard St.-Germain, on the way to lunch. Much, if not most of the group was African, and all of us (though some only legally) were black. Facing us, on every newspaper kiosk on that wide, tree-shaded boulevard, were photographs of fifteen-year-old Dorothy Counts being reviled and spat upon by the mob as she was making her way to school in Charlotte, North Carolina. There was unutterable pride, tension, and anguish in that girl's face as she approached the halls of learning, with history, jeering, at her back.

It made me furious, it filled me with both hatred and pity, and it made me ashamed. Some one of us should have been there with her! I dawdled in Europe for nearly yet another year, held by my private life and my attempt to finish a novel, but it was on that bright afternoon that I knew I was leaving France. I could, simply, no longer sit around in Paris discussing the Algerian and the black American problem. Everybody else was paying their dues, and it was time I went home and paid mine.

I took a boat home in the summer of 1957, intending to go South as soon as I could get the bread together. This meant, in my case, as soon as I could get an assignment. This was not so easy in 1957, and I was stuck in New York for a discouragingly long time. And now I had to begin to arrive at some kind of *modus vivendi* with New York—for here I was, home again, for the first time in nine years—to stay. *To stay:* if this thought chilled me, it also relieved me. It was only here, after all, that I would be able to find out what my journey had meant to me, or what it had made of me.

And I began to see New York in a different way, seeing beneath the formlessness, in the detail of a cornice, the shape of a window, the movement of stone steps—*stoep*, say the Dutch, and we say, *stoop*—beneath the nearly invincible and despairing noise, the sound of many tongues, all struggling for dominance. Since I was here to stay, I had to examine it, learn it all over again, and try to find out if I had ever loved it. But the question contained, or so I suspected, its own melancholy answer. If I had ever loved New York, that love had, literally, been beaten out of me; if I had ever loved it, my life could never have depended on so long an absence and so deep a divorce; or, if I had ever loved it, I would have been glad, not frightened, to be back in my home town. No, I didn't love it, at least not any more, but I was going to have to survive it. In order to survive it, I would have to watch it. And, though I had nightmares about that Southland which I had never seen, I was terribly anxious to get there, perhaps to corroborate the nightmare, but certainly to get out of what was once described to me as "the great unfinished city."

Finally, I got my assignment, and I went South. Something began, for me, tremendous. I met some of the noblest, most beautiful people a man can hope to meet, and I saw some beautiful and some terrible things. I was old enough to recognize how deep and strangling were my fears, how manifold and mighty my limits: but no one can demand more of life than that life do him the honor to demand that he learn to live with his fears, and learn to live, every day, both within his limits and beyond them.

I must add, for the benefit of my so innocent and criminal countrymen, that, today, fifteen years later, the photograph of Angela Davis has replaced the photograph of Dorothy Counts. These two photographs would appear to sum up the will of the Americans—heirs of all the ages—in relation to the blacks.

There comes floating up to me, out of a life I lived long ago—during the cybernetics craze, the Wilhelm Reich misapprehension, the Karen Horney precisions, that time, pre-dating

Sartre, when many of my friends vanished into the hills, or into anarchies called communes, or into orgone boxes, never to be seen, and certainly never to make love again—the memory of a young white man, beautiful, Jewish, American, who ate his wife's afterbirth, frying it in a frying pan. He did this because—who knows?—Wilhelm Reich, according to him, had ordered it. He comes floating up to me because, though he never knew it, I loved him, and the silence between us was the precise indication of how deeply something in me responded to, and is still bewildered by, his trouble. I remember his face when he told me about it, long after his courageous culinary effort. By this effort, he made his wife and child a part of himself. The question which has remained in my mind, no doubt, is why so extreme an effort should have been needed to prove a fact which should have been so obvious and so joyous. By the time he told me, he had lost both the wife and the child, was virtually adopting another one, black, this time, and, though he was younger than I, and I am speaking of a long time ago, had, emotionally, it seemed to me, ceased to exist. I got the impression that he had hurried himself through a late and tormented adolescence into an early middle age, with an almost audible sigh of relief, having encountered only theorems along the way: and, though he did not know it, was now helplessly and hopelessly in love with a small black boy, not more than ten. I do not mean to suggest that he had sexual designs on the boy. It might, indeed, have been better for him if he had, however outrageous that may sound—it would, at least, have landed him in deep emotional trouble and brought to the fore the question of his honor: I mean that he appeared to be able to love only the helpless. I have not seen this man in many years, and I hope that everything I say here has since been proven false. I hope, in short, that he has been able to live. But I have always been struck, in America, by an emotional poverty so bottomless, and a terror of human life, of human touch, so deep, that virtually no American appears able to achieve any viable, organic connection between his public stance and his private life. This is what makes them so baffling, so moving, so exasperating, and so untrustworthy. "Only connect," Henry

James has said. Perhaps only an American writer would have been driven to say it, his very existence being so threatened by the failure, in most American lives, of the most elementary and crucial connections.

This failure of the private life has always had the most devastating effect on American public conduct, and on black-white relations. If Americans were not so terrified of their private selves, they would never have needed to invent and could never have become so dependent on what they still call "the Negro problem." This problem, which they invented in order to safeguard their purity, has made of them criminals and monsters, and it is destroying them; and this not from anything blacks may or may not be doing but because of the role a guilty and constricted white imagination has assigned to the blacks. That the scapegoat pays for the sins of others is well known, but this is only legend, and a revealing one at that. In fact, however the scapegoat may be made to suffer, his suffering cannot purify the sinner; it merely incriminates him the more, and it seals his damnation. The scapegoat, eventually, is released, to death: his murderer continues to live. The suffering of the scapegoat has resulted in seas of blood, and yet not one sinner has been saved, or changed, by this despairing ritual. Sin has merely been added to sin, and guilt piled upon guilt. In the private chambers of the soul, the guilty party is identified, and the accusing finger, there, is not legend, but consequence, not fantasy, but the truth. People pay for what they do, and, still more, for what they have allowed themselves to become. And they pay for it very simply: by the lives they lead. The crucial thing, here, is that the sum of these individual abdications menaces life all over the world. For, in the generality, as social and moral and political and sexual entities, white Americans are probably the sickest and certainly the most dangerous people, of any color, to be found in the world today. I may not have realized this before my first journey South. But, once I found myself there, I recognized that the South was a riddle which could be read only in the light, or the darkness, of the unbelievable disasters which had overtaken the private life.

I say, "riddle": not the riddle of what this unhappy people

claim, madly enough, as their "folk" ways. I had been a nigger for a long time. I was not struck by their wickedness, for that wickedness was but the spirit and the history of America. What struck me was the unbelievable dimension of their sorrow. I felt as though I had wandered into hell. But, it must also be said that, if they were in hell, some among them were beginning to recognize what fuel, in themselves, fed the flames. Their sorrow placed them far beyond, exactly, as at that hour, it seemed to have placed them far beneath, their compatriots—who did not yet know that sorrow existed, and who imagined that hell was a condition to which others were sentenced. For this reason, and I am not the only black man who will say this, I have more faith in Southerners than I will ever have in Northerners: the mighty and pious North could never, after all, have acquired its wealth without utilizing, brutally, and consciously, those "folk" ways, and locking the South within them. And when this country's absolutely inescapable disaster levels it, it is in the South and not in the North that the rebirth will begin.

I went, first, if memory serves, to Charlotte, North Carolina, where I met, among others, *The Carolina Israelite*. I went to Little Rock, where I met, among others, Mr. and Mrs. Bates. I went to Atlanta, where I met, among others, Reverend Martin Luther King, Jr. I went to Birmingham. I went to Montgomery. I went to Tuskegee. I don't know how long I was on the road. The canvas suitcase I had carried down was so full of contraband by the time I lugged it, on one shoulder, up, that it burst in the middle of Grand Central Station, scattering underground secrets all over the floor: no one, luckily, exhibited the remotest curiosity. I managed to get it all together, tied the suitcase together with the belt from my trousers, and got up the stairs, into the city. I collapsed in the home of a friend who lived in what was not yet known as the East Village—when I had been a tenant, it was known as the Lower East Side—and, re-living my trip, surrendered to my nightmares, and, as far as the city was concerned, vanished. I could not take it on, I could not move out of that cold-water flat. I kept meaning to, I kept putting it off: for five days. I had called my sister, Gloria, from the station, so she knew that I was back in New York, but she did not know where. Therefore, my family and friends were searching for me in every Village street and bar and were considering the dubious and desperate extreme of calling the police. But, finally, I surfaced, fully conscious of how irresponsible I had been, and more than a little shaken by the realization that it had been a kind of retrospective terror which had paralyzed me so long. While in the South I had suppressed my terror well enough, in any case, to function; but when the pressure came off, a kind of wonder of terror overcame me, making me as useless as a snapped rubber band. This worried me exceedingly. I sensed in it a pattern which I was never, in fact, thoroughly to overcome. I will never forget the weary face of a black friend who had been searching for me for days, meeting me on Sixth Avenue as I was on my repentant way to the subway. He saw me as he turned from Waverly Place onto the avenue at the same time that I saw him. He stood stock-still as I was forced to walk toward him. A small, unwilling smile tugged at the corners of his lips. Then, I was in front of him and Lonnie said, "Well, *I'm* not going to curse you out. You've done it to yourself already." And he bought me a drink, and I went uptown to my sister's house, where I was sleeping on the couch in those days.

In the church, the preacher says, after an apparently meaningless anecdote, "I have said all that to say"—this: I doubt that I really knew much about terror before I went South. I do not mean, merely, though I very well might, that visceral reaction produced by the realization that one is facing one's own death. Then, as now, a Northern policeman, black or white, a white co-worker, or a black one, the colorless walls of precinct basements, the colorless handcuffs, the colorless future, are quite enough to introduce into one's life the stunning realization that that life can be ended at any moment. Furthermore, this terror can produce its own antidote: an overwhelming pride and rage, so that, whether or not one is ready to die, one gives every appearance of being willing to die. And at that moment, in fact, since retreat means accepting a death far worse, one *is* willing to die, hoping merely (God's last small mercy) to drag one's murderer along.

Not many among the redeemed have any sense of this passion, which they describe, without knowing how profoundly they are describing themselves, as suicidal. They mean that it is suicidal to contend with a force obviously, or apparently, greater than oneself and that they would never dream of doing such a thing. They also mean that they, by definition, by their numbers, are the greater force, and they never suspect to what merciless level of contempt this oblique and arrogant confession exposes them. A man who knows that he is facing death, or, more accurately, who knows that it is, after all, he, himself, who has insisted on and brought about this moment, may, involuntarily, helplessly, shout or weep, or even piss or shit in his pants, where he stands. But he will not turn back. To turn back is no longer among his possibilities: that is why he may shout or weep and his stink may then fill the air. He has brought himself to this moment, and this is *he*—if only for a moment—*he;* and the others are beneath him, and anonymous forever because they value their manhood less than he.

But the terror I am speaking of has little to do with one's specific fears for oneself: it relates to Dante's *I would not have believed that death had undone so many.*

I arrived in Little Rock, for example, during the famous—then famous, now all but forgotten—school convulsion. This convulsion, it is to be remembered, had apparently to do with the question of the integration or education of black children—integration and education are not synonyms, though Americans appear to think so. I am a city boy. My life began in the Big City, and had to be slugged out, toe to toe, on the city pavements. This meant that I was badly prepared for an entity like Little Rock, which, while it was certainly not yet a city, was, equally certainly, no longer a town. For that matter, it was not, geographically speaking, Southern. It was Southern only in truth, in terms of what its history had made of it, which is to say, ultimately, that it was Southern by choice. It was Southern, therefore, to put it brutally, because of the history of America—the United States of America: and small black boys and girls were now paying for this holocaust. They were attempting to go to school. They were attempting to get an education, in a country in which education is a synonym for indoctrination, if you are white, and subjugation, if you are black. It was rather as though small Jewish boys and girls, in Hitler's Germany, insisted on getting a German education in order to overthrow the Third Reich. Here they were, nevertheless, scrubbed and shining, in their never-to-be-forgotten stiff little dresses, in their never-to-be-forgotten little blue suits, facing an army, facing a citizenry, facing white fathers, facing white mothers, facing the progeny of these co-citizens, facing the white past, to say nothing of the white present: small soldiers, armed with stiff, white dresses, and long or short dark blue pants, entering a leper colony, and young enough to believe that the colony could be healed, and saved. They paid a dreadful price, those children, for their missionary work among the heathen.

My terror involved my realization of the nature of the heathen. I did not meet any of my official murderers, not during that first journey. I met the Negro's friends. Thus, I was forced to recognize that, so long as your friend thinks of you as a Negro, you do not have a friend, and neither does he—your friend. You have become accomplices. Everything between you depends on what he cannot say to you, and what you will not say to him. And one of you is listening. If one of you is listening, to all those things, precisely, which are not being said, the intensity of this attention can scarcely be described as the attention one friend brings to another. If one of you is listening, both of you are plotting, though, perhaps, only one of you knows it. Both of you may be plotting to escape, but, since very different avenues appear to be open to each of you, you are plotting your escape from each other.

I have written elsewhere about those early days in the South, but from a distance more or less impersonal. I have never, for example, written about my unbelieving shock when I realized that I was being groped by one of the most powerful men in one of the states I visited. He had got himself sweating drunk in order to arrive at this despairing titillation. With his wet eyes staring up at my face, and his wet hands groping for my cock, we were both, abruptly, in history's ass-pocket. It was very frightening—not the gesture itself, but the abjectness of it, and the assumption of a swift and grim complicity: as my identity was defined by his power, so was my humanity to be placed at the service of his fantasies. If the lives of those children were in those wet, despairing hands, if their future was to be read in those wet, blind eyes, there was reason to tremble. This man, with a phone call, could prevent or provoke a lynching. This was one of the men you called (or had a friend call) in order to get your brother off the prison farm. A phone call from him might prevent your brother from being dug up, later, during some random archaeological expedition. Therefore, one had to be friendly: but the price for this was your cock.

This will sound an exaggerated statement to Americans, who will suppose it to refer, merely, to sexual (or sectional) abnormality. This supposition misses the point: which is double-edged. The slave knows, however his master may be deluded on this point, that he is called a slave because his manhood has been, or can be, or will be taken from him. To be a slave means that one's manhood is engaged in a dubious battle indeed, and this stony fact is not altered by whatever devotion some masters and some slaves may have arrived at in relation to each other. In the case of American slavery, the black man's right to his women, as well as to his children, was simply taken from him, and whatever bastards the white man begat on the bodies of black women took their condition from the condition of their mother: blacks were not the only stallions on the slave-breeding farms! And one of the many results of this loveless, money-making conspiracy was that, in giving the masters every conceivable sexual and commercial license, it also emasculated them of any human responsibility—to their women, to their children, to their wives, or to themselves. The results of this blasphemy resound in this country, on every private and public level, until this hour. When the man grabbed my cock, I didn't think of him as a faggot, which, indeed, if having a wife and children, house, cars, and a respectable and powerful standing in the community, mean anything, he wasn't: I watched his eyes, thinking, with great sorrow, *The unexamined life is not worth living.* The despair among the loveless is that they must narcoticize themselves before they can touch any human being at all. They, then, fatally, touch the wrong person, not merely because they have gone blind, or have lost the sense of touch, but because they no longer have any way of knowing that any loveless touch is a violation, whether one is touching a woman or a man. When the loveless come to power, or when sexual despair comes to power, the sexuality of the object is either a threat or a fantasy. That most men will choose women to debase is not a matter of rejoicing either for the chosen women or anybody else; brutal truth, furthermore, forces the observation, particularly if one is a black man, that this choice is by no means certain. That men have an enormous need to debase other men—and only because they are *men*—is a truth which history forbids us to labor. And it is absolutely certain that white men, who invented the nigger's big black prick, are still at the mercy of this nightmare, and are still, for the most part, doomed, in one way or another, to attempt to make this prick their own: so much for the progress which the Christian world has made from that jungle in which it is their clear intention to keep black men treed forever.

Every black man walking in this country pays a tremendous price for walking: for men are not women, and a man's balance depends on the weight he carries between his legs. All men, however they may face or fail to face it, however they may handle, or be handled by it, know something about each other, which is simply that a man without balls is not a man; that the word *genesis* describes the male, involves the phallus, and refers to the seed which gives life. When one man can no longer honor this in another man—and this remains true even if that man is his lover—he has abdicated from a man's estate, and, hard upon the heels of that abdication, chaos arrives. It was something like this that I began to see, watching black men in the South and watching white men watching them. For that marvelously mocking, salty authority with which black men walked was dictated by the tacit and shared realization of the price each had paid to be able to walk at all. Their fights came out of that, their laughter came out of that, their curses, their tears, their decisions, their so menaced loves, their courage, and even their cowardice—and perhaps especially the stunning and unexpected changes they could play on these so related strings—their music, their dancing: it all came from the center. "No," said an elderly black man, standing in front of his barber shop, "I don't believe I'll join this voting registration drive. You see, I only cut the white folks' hair in here, and they'll close me up." He was very tall; as he said this, he seemed to be looking up at me, a physical impossibility; he had been bowing so long, my brother said, that his head would never be straight on his neck again. Yet, there he stood, a gnarled old tree, and the authority of his response made it impossible to question his decision: he may have been planning to cut a white man's throat one day. If I had been white, I certainly would never have allowed him anywhere near *me* with a razor in his hand. Most white men, by comparison, seemed to be barely shuffling along, and one always doubted whatever they said, because one realized that they doubted it themselves. As far as personal authority went, one could imagine that their shriveled faces were an exact indication of how matters were with them below the belt. And the women were worse—proof, if proof were needed: nowhere in the world have I encountered women so blighted, and blighted so soon. It began to seem to me, indeed, not entirely frivolously, that the only thing which prevented the South from being an absolutely homosexual community was, precisely, the reverbating absence of men.

One could not be in any Southern community for long and not be confronted with the question of what a man is, should do, or become. The world in which we live is, after all, a reflection of the desires and activities of men. We are responsible for the world in which we find ourselves, if only because we are the only sentient force which can change it. What brought this question to the front of my mind, of course, was the fact that so many of the black men I talked to in the South in those years were—I can find no other word for them—heroic. I don't want to be misunderstood as having fallen into an easy chauvinism when I say that: but I don't see how any observer of the Southern scene in those years can have arrived at any other judgment. Their heroism was to be found less in large things than in small ones, less in public than in private. Some of the men I am thinking of could be very impressive publicly, too, and responsible for large events; but it was not this which impressed me. What impressed me was how they went about their daily tasks, in the teeth of the Southern terror. The first time I saw Reverend Shuttlesworth, for example, he came strolling across the parking lot of the motel where I was staying, his hat perched precariously between the back of his skull and the nape of his neck, alone. It was late at night, and Shuttlesworth was a marked man in Birmingham. He came up into my room, and, while we talked, he kept walking back and forth to the window. I finally realized that he was keeping an eye on his car—making sure that no one put a bomb in it, perhaps. As he said nothing about this, however, naturally I could not. But I was worried about his driving home alone, and, as he was leaving, I could not resist saying something to this effect. And he smiled—smiled as though I were a novice, with much to learn, which was true, and as though he would be glad to give me a few pointers, which, indeed, not much later on, he did—and told me he'd be all right and went downstairs and got into his car, switched on the motor and drove off into the soft Alabama night. There was no hint of defiance or bravado in his manner. Only, when I made my halting observation concerning his safety, a shade of sorrow crossed his face, deep, impatient, dark; then it was gone. It was the most impersonal anguish I had ever seen on a man's face. It was as though he were wrestling with the mighty fact that the danger in which he stood was as nothing compared to the spiritual horror which drove those who were trying to destroy him. They endangered him, but they doomed themselves.

I had never seen this horror, this poverty, before, though I had worked among Southerners, years before, when I was working for the Army, during the war. It was very frightening, disagreeable, and dangerous, but I was not, after all, in their territory—in a sense, or at least as they resentfully supposed, they were in mine. Also, I could, in a sense, protect myself against their depredations and the fear that they inspired in me by considering them, quite honestly, as mad. And I was too young for the idea of my death or destruction really to have taken hold of my mind. It is hard for anyone under twenty to realize that death has already assigned him a number, which is going to come up one day.

But I was not in my territory now. I was in territory absolutely hostile and exceedingly strange, and I was old enough to realize that I could be destroyed. It was lucky, oddly enough, that I had been out of the country for so long and had come South from Paris, in effect, instead of from New York. If I had not come from Paris, I would certainly have attempted to draw on my considerable kit of New York survival tricks, with what results I cannot imagine, for they would certainly not have worked in the South. But I had so far forgotten all my New York tricks as to have been unable to use them in New York, and now I was simply, helplessly, nakedly, an odd kind of foreigner and could only look on the scene that way. And this meant that, exactly like a foreigner, I was more fascinated than frightened.

There was more than enough to fascinate. In the Deep South—Florida, Georgia, Alabama, Mississippi, for example—there is the great, vast, brooding, welcoming and bloodstained land, beautiful enough to astonish and break the heart. The land seems nearly to weep beneath the burden of this civilization's unnameable excrescences. The people and the children wander blindly through their forest of billboards, antennae, Coca-Cola bottles, gas stations, drive-ins, motels, beer cans, music of a strident and invincible melancholy, stilted wooden porches, snapping fans, aggressively blue-jeaned buttocks, strutting crotches, pint bottles, condoms, in the weeds, rotting automobile corpses, brown as beetles, earrings flashing in the gloom of bus stops: over all there seems to hang a miasma of lust and longing and rage. Every Southern city seemed to me to have been but lately rescued from the swamps, which were patiently waiting to reclaim it. The people all seemed to remember their time under water, and to be both dreading and anticipating their return to that freedom from responsibility. Every black man, whatever his style, had been scarred, as in some tribal rite; and every white man, though white men, mostly, had no style, had been maimed. And, everywhere, the women, the most fearfully mistreated creatures of this region, with narrowed eyes and pursed lips—lips turned inward on a foul aftertaste—watched and rocked and waited. Some of them reminded me of a moment in my adolescent life when a church sister, not much older than I, who had been my girl friend, went mad, and was incarcerated. I went to visit her, in the women's wing of the asylum, and, coming out into the courtyard, stood there for a moment to catch my breath. Something, eventually, made me turn my head. Then I realized that I was standing in the sight of hundreds of incarcerated women. Behind those bars and windows, I don't know how many pairs of female eyes were riveted on the one male in that courtyard. I could dimly see their faces at the windows all up and down that wall; and they did not make a sound. For a moment I thought that I would never be able to persuade my feet to carry me away from that unspeakable, despairing, captive avidity.

My first night in Montgomery, I, like a good reporter, decided to investigate the town a little. I had been warned to be very careful how I moved about in the South after dark—indeed, I had been told not to move at all; but it was a pleasant evening, night just beginning to fall: suppertime. I walked a ways, past dark porches which were mostly silent, yet one felt a presence, or presences, sitting deep in the dark, sometimes silhouetted—but rarely—in the light from an open door, or one saw the ember of a cigarette, or heard a child's voice. It was very peaceful, and, though it may sound odd, I was very glad that I had come South. In spite of all that could have divided us, and in spite of the fact that some of them looked on me with an inevitable suspicion, I felt very much at home among the dark people who lived where I, if so much had not been disrupted, would logically have been born. I felt, beneath everything, a profound acceptance, an unfamiliar peace, almost as though, after despairing and debilitating journeys, I had, at last, come home. If there was, in this, some illusion, there was also some truth. In the years in Paris, I had never been homesick for anything American—neither waffles, ice cream, hot dogs, baseball, majorettes, movies, nor the Empire State Building, nor Coney

Island, nor the Statue of Liberty, nor the *Daily News*, nor Times Square. All of these things had passed out of me as naturally and simply as taking a leak, and even less self-consciously. They might never have existed for me, and it made absolutely no difference to me if I never saw them again. But I had missed my brothers and my sisters, and my mother—they made a difference. I wanted to be able to see them, and to see their children. I hoped that they wouldn't forget me. I missed Harlem Sunday mornings and fried chicken and biscuits, I missed the music, I missed the style—that style possessed by no other people in this world. I missed the way the dark face closes, the way dark eyes watch, and the way, when a dark face opens, a light seems to go on everywhere. I missed my brothers especially—missed David's grin and George's solemnity and Wilmer's rages, missed, in short, my connections, missed the life which had produced me and nourished me and paid for me. Now, though I was a stranger, I was home.

The racial dividing lines of Southern towns are baffling and treacherous for a stranger, for they are not as clearly marked as in the North—or not as clearly marked for *him*. I passed a porch with dark people; on the corner about a block away there was a restaurant. When I reached the corner, I entered the restaurant.

I will never forget it. I don't know if I can describe it. Everything abruptly froze into what, even at that moment, struck me as a kind of Marx Brothers parody of horror. Every white face turned to stone: the arrival of the messenger of death could not have had a more devastating effect than the appearance in the restaurant doorway of a small, unarmed, utterly astounded black man. I had realized my error as soon as I opened the door: but the absolute terror on all these white faces—I swear that not a soul moved—paralyzed me. They stared at me, I stared at them.

The spell was broken by one of those women, produced, I hope, only in the South, with a face like a rusty hatchet, and eyes like two rusty nails—nails left over from the Crucifixion. She rushed at me as though to club me down, and she barked—for it was not a human sound: "What you want, boy? What you want in here?" And then, a decontaminating gesture, "Right around there, boy. Right around there."

I had no idea what she was talking about. I backed out the door.

"Right around there, boy," said a voice behind me.

A white man had appeared out of nowhere, on the sidewalk which had been empty not more than a second before. I stared at him blankly. He watched me steadily, with a kind of suspended menace.

My first shock had subsided. I really had not had time to feel either fear or anger. Now, both began to rise in me. I knew I had to get off this street.

He had pointed to a door, and I knew immediately that he was pointing to the colored entrance.

And this was a dreadful moment—as brief as lightning, and far more illuminating. I realized that this man thought that he was being kind; and he was, indeed, being as kind as can be expected from a guide in hell. I realized that I must not speak to him, must not involve myself with him in any way whatever. I wasn't hungry anymore, but I certainly couldn't say *that*. Not only because this would have forced both of us to go further, into what confrontation I dared not think, but because of my Northern accent. It was the first time I realized that this accent was going to be a very definite liability; since I certainly couldn't change it, I was going to have to find some way of turning it into some kind of asset. But not at this very flaming moment, on this dark and empty street.

I saved my honor, hopefully, by reflecting, *Well, this is what you came here for. Hit it*—and I tore my eyes from his face and walked through the door he had so kindly pointed out.

I found myself in a small cubicle, with one electric light, and a counter, with, perhaps, four or five stools. On one side of the cubicle was a window. This window more closely resembled a cage-wire mesh, and an opening in the mesh. I was, now, in the back of the restaurant, though no one in the restaurant could see me. I was behind the restaurant counter, behind the hatchet-faced woman, who had her back to me, serving the white customers at the counter. I was nearly close enough to touch them, certainly close enough to touch her, close enough to kill them all, but they couldn't see me, either.

Hatchet-Face now turned to me, and said, "What you want?" This time, she did not say, "boy": it was no longer necessary.

I told her I wanted a hamburger and a cup of coffee, which I didn't; but I wanted to see how those on my side of the mesh were served; and I wondered if she had to wash her hands each time, before she served the white folks again. Possibly not: for the hamburger came in paper, and the coffee in a paper cup.

I had all I could do to be silent as I paid her, and she turned away. I sat down on one of the stools, and a black man came in, grunted a greeting to me, went to the window, ordered, paid, sat down, and began to eat. I sat there for a while, thinking that I'd certainly asked for one hell of a gig. I wasn't sorry I'd come—I was never, in fact, ever to be sorry about that, and, until the day I die, I will always consider myself among the greatly privileged because, however inadequately, I was there. But I could see that the difficulties were not going to be where I had confidently placed them—in others—but in me. I was far from certain that I was equipped to get through a single day down here, and if I could not so equip myself then I would be a menace to all that others were trying to do, and a betrayal of their vast travail. They had been undergoing and overcoming for a very long time without me, after all, and they hadn't asked me to come: my role was to do a story and avoid becoming one. I watched the patient man as he ate, watched him with both wonder and respect. If he could do that, then the people on the other side of the mesh were right to be frightened—if he could do that, he could do anything and when he walked through the mesh there would be nothing to stop him. But *I* couldn't do it yet; my stomach was as tight as a black rubber ball. I took my hamburger and walked outside and dropped it into the weeds. The dark silence of the streets now frightened me a little, and I walked back to my hotel.

My hotel was a very funky black joint, so poverty stricken and for so long, that no one had anything to hide, or lose— not that they had stopped trying: they failed in the first endeavor as monotonously as they succeeded in the second.

Life still held out the hope of what Americans, helplessly and honestly enough, call a "killing" and what blacks, revealingly enough, call a "hit." There seemed to be music all the time, someone was dancing all the time. It would have seemed, from a casual view, that this hotel was the gathering place for all the dregs of the town and that was true enough. But, since these dregs included the entire black society, it was a very various and revealing truth. Lodging for transient blacks, or entertainment for the locals, is a severely circumscribed matter in the Deep South, so that, for example, if one is not staying with friends or relatives, one stays in a hotel like mine, or, if one's friends or relatives decide to buy you a drink, they will bring you to the bar of this hotel. I liked it very much. I liked watching staid Baptist ministers and their plump, starched wives seated but a table away from the town's loose and fallen ladies and their unstarched men. I thought it healthy, because it reduced the possibilities of self-delusion—especially in those years. The Man had everybody in the same bag, and for the same reason, no matter what kind of suit he was wearing, or what kind of car he drove. And the people treated each other, it seemed to me, with rather more respect than was typical of New York, where, of course, the opportunities for self-delusion were, comparatively, so much greater.

Where whiskey was against the law, you simply bought your whiskey from the law enforcers. I did it, many times, all over the South, at first simply to find out if what I had been told was true—to see it with my own eyes and to pay the man with my own hands—and then, later, because life on the road began to run me ragged. It was almost impossible to get anything but bourbon, and the very smell of bourbon is still associated in my mind with the mean little eyes of deputy sheriffs and the holster on the hip and the ominous trees which line the highways. Nor can you get a meal anywhere in the South without being confronted with "grits"; a pale, lumpy, tasteless kind of porridge which the Southerner insists is a delicacy but which I believe they ingest as punishment for their sins. "What? you don't want no grits?" asks the wide-eyed waitress; not hostile yet, merely baffled. She moves away and spreads the word all over the region: "You see that man there? Well, he don't *eat* no grits"—and you are, suddenly, a marked man.

It is not difficult to become a marked man in the South—all you have to do, in fact, is go there. The Montgomery airport, for example, was, in those years, a brave little shack, set down, defiantly, in limbo. It was being guarded, on the morning of my first arrival, by three more or less senior citizens, metallic of color and decidedly sparing of speech. I was the only thing, of any color, to descend from that plane that morning, and they stood at the gate and watched me as I crossed the field. I was carrying my typewriter, which suddenly seemed very heavy. I was frightened. The way they watched me frightened me. Their silence frightened me. Martin Luther King, Jr., had promised to have a car meet me at the airport. There was no car in sight, but I had the phone number of the Montgomery Improvement Association—if I could find a phone, if I could get past the men at the wire. It was eerie and instructive to realize that, though these were human beings like myself, I could not expect them to respond to any human request from me. There was nothing but space behind me, and those three men before me: I could do nothing but walk toward them. Three grown men: and what was the point of this pathetic, boys-together, John Wayne stance? Here I was, after all, having got on a plane with the intention of coming here. The plane had landed and here I was—and what did they suppose they could do about it now? short, of course, of murdering every black passenger who arrived, or bombing the airport. But these alternatives, however delectable, could not lightly be undertaken. I walked past them and into the first phone booth I saw, not checking to see, and not caring whether I had entered the white or the black waiting room. I had resolved to avoid incidents, if possible, but it was already clear that it wouldn't always be possible. By the time I got my number, they watching me all the while, the MIA car drove up. And if the eyes of those men had had the power to pulverize that car, it would have been done, exactly as, in the Bible, the wicked city is leveled—I had never in all my life seen such a concentrated, malevolent poverty of spirit.

The Montgomery blacks were marching then, remember,

and were in the process of bringing the bus company to its knees. What had begun in Montgomery was beginning to happen all over the South. The student sit-in movement has yet to begin. No one has yet heard of James Foreman or James Bevel. We have only begun to hear of Martin Luther King, Jr. Malcolm X has yet to be taken seriously. No one, except their parents, has ever heard of Huey Newton or Bobby Seale or Angela Davis. Emmett Till had been dead two years. Bobby Hutton and Jonathan Jackson have just mastered their first words, and, with someone holding them by the hand, are discovering how much fun it is to climb up and down the stairs. Oh, pioneers!—I got into the car, and we drove into town: the cradle of the Confederacy, the whitest town this side of Casablanca, and one of the most wretched on the face of the earth. And wretched because no one in authority in the town, the state, or the nation, had the force or the courage or the love to attempt to correct the manners or redeem the souls of those three desperate men, standing before that dismal airport, imagining that they were holding back a flood.

But how can I suggest any of the quality of some of those black men and women in the South then?—for it is important that I try. I can't name the names; sometimes because I can't remember them, or never knew them; and sometimes for other reasons. They were, the men, mostly preachers, or small tradesmen—this last word describes, or must be taken to suggest, a multitude of indescribable efforts—or professionals, such as teachers, or dentists, or lawyers. Because the South is, or certainly was then, so closed a community, their colors struck the light—the eye—far more vividly than these same colors strike one in the North: the prohibition, precisely, of the social mingling revealed the extent of the sexual amalgamation. Girls the color of honey, men nearly the color of chalk, hair like silk, hair like cotton, hair like wire, eyes blue, grey, green, hazel, black, like the gypsy's, brown like the Arab's, narrow nostrils, thin, wide lips, thin lips, every conceivable variation struck along incredible gamuts—it was not in the Southland that one could hope to keep a secret! And the niggers, of course, didn't try, though they knew their white brothers and sisters and papas, and watched them, daily, strutting around in their white skins. And sometimes shoveled garbage for their kith and kin, and sometimes went, hat in hand, looking for a job, or on more desperate errands. But: they could do it, knowing what they knew. And white men couldn't bear it—knowing that they knew: it is not only in the Orient that white is the color of death.

I remember the Reverend S., for example, a small, pale man, with hair resembling charred popcorn, and his tiny church, in a tiny town, where every black man was owned by a white man. In democratic parlance, of course, one says that every black man *worked* for a white man, and the democratic myth wishes us to believe that they worked together as men, and respected and honored and loved each other as men. But the democratic circumlocution pretends a level of liberty which does not exist and cannot exist until slavery in America comes to an end: in those towns, in those days, to speak only of the towns, and only of those days, a black man who displeased his employers was not going to eat for very long, which meant that neither he, nor his wife, nor children, were intended to live for very long. Yet, here he was, the Reverend S., every Sunday, in his pulpit, with his wife and children in the church, and bullet holes in the church basement, urging the people to move, to march, and to vote. For we believed, in those days, or made ourselves believe, that the black move to the registrar's office would be protected from Washington. I remember a Reverend D., who was also a grocer, and the night he described to me his conversion to nonviolence. A black grocer in the Deep South must also, like all grocers everywhere, purchase somewhere, somehow, the beans he places on his shelves to sell. This means that a black grocer who is one of the guiding spirits of a voting registration drive and who is also, virtually, a one-man car pool, can find remaining in business, to say nothing of his skin, an exceedingly strenuous matter. This was a big, cheerful man, as strong as an ox and stubborn as a mule, a fly not destined for the fly-paper, and he stayed in business. It cost him something. Bombing was not yet the great Southern sport which it was to become: they simply hurled bricks through his windows. He armed himself and his sons and they sat in the dark store night after night, waiting for their co-citizens—who, knowing they were armed, did not appear. And then, one morning, after the long night, the Reverend D. decided that this was no way for a man or a woman or a child to live. He may, of course, by this time, have been forced to change his mind again, but he was the first person to make the concept of nonviolence real to me: for it entered, then, precisely, the realm of individual and, above all, private choice and I saw, for the first time, how difficult a choice it could be.

TO BE BAPTIZED

I told Jesus it would be all right
If He changed my name.

—TRADITIONAL

ALL OF THE Western nations have been caught in a lie, the lie of their pretended humanism; this means that their history has no moral justification, and that the West has no moral authority. Malcolm, yet more concretely than Frantz Fanon—since Malcolm operated in the Afro-American idiom, and referred to the Afro-American situation—made the nature of this lie, and its implications, relevant and articulate to the people whom he served. He made increasingly articulate the ways in which this lie, given the history and the power of the Western nations, had become a global problem, menacing the lives of millions. "Vile as I am," states one of the characters in Dostoevski's *The Idiot*, "I don't believe in the wagons that bring bread to humanity. For the wagons that bring bread to humanity, without any moral basis for conduct, may coldly exclude a considerable part of humanity from enjoying what is brought; so it has been already." Indeed. And so it is now. Dostoevski's personage was speaking of the impending proliferation of railways, and the then prevalent optimism (which was perfectly natural) as to the uplifting effect this conquest of distance would have on the life of man. But Dostoevski saw that the rise of this power would "coldly exclude a considerable part of humanity." Indeed, it was on this exclusion that the rise of this power inexorably depended; and now the excluded—"so it has been already"—whose lands have been robbed of the minerals, for example, which go into the building of railways and telegraph wires and TV sets and jet airliners and guns and bombs and fleets, must attempt, at exorbitant cost, to buy their manufactured resources back—which is not even remotely possible, since they must attempt this purchase with money borrowed from their exploiters. If they attempt to work out their salvation—their autonomy—on terms dictated by those who have excluded them, they are in a delicate and dangerous position, and if they refuse, they are in a desperate one: it is hard to know which case is worse. In both cases, they are confronted with the relentless necessities of human life, and the rigors of human nature. Anyone, for example, who has worked in, or witnessed, any of the "anti-poverty" programs in the American ghetto has an instant understanding of "foreign aid" in the "underdeveloped" nations. In both locales, the most skillful adventurers improve their material lot; the most dedicated of the natives are driven mad or inactive—or underground—by frustration; while the misery of the hapless, voiceless millions is increased—and not only that: their reaction to their misery is described to the world as criminal. Nowhere is this grisly pattern clearer than it is in America today, but what America is doing within her borders, she is doing around the world. One has only to remember that American investments cannot be considered safe wherever the population cannot be considered tractable; with this in mind, consider the American reaction to the Jew who boasts of sending arms to Israel, and the probable fate of an American black who wishes to stage a rally for the purpose of sending arms to black South Africa.

America proves, certainly, if any nation ever has, that man cannot live by bread alone; on the other hand, men can scarcely begin to react to this principle until they—and, still more, their children—have enough bread to eat. Hunger has no principles, it simply makes men, at worst, wretched, and, at best, dangerous. Also, it must be remembered—it cannot be overstated—that those centuries of oppression are also the history of a system of thought, so that both the ex-man who considers himself master and the ex-man who is treated like a mule suffer from a particular species of schizophrenia, in which each contains the other, in which each longs to be the other: "What connects a slave to his master," observes David Caute, in his novel, *The Decline of the West*, "is more tragic than that which separates them."

It is true that political freedom is a matter of power and has nothing to do with morality; and if one had ever hoped to find a way around this principle, the performance of power at bay, which is the situation of the Western nations, and the very definition of the American crisis, has dashed this hope to pieces. Moreover, as habits of thought reinforce and sustain the habits of power, it is not even remotely possible for the excluded to become included, for this inclusion means, precisely, the end of the *status quo*—or would result, as so many of the wise and honored would put it, in a mongrelization of the races.

But for power truly to feel itself menaced, it must somehow sense itself in the presence of another power—or, more accurately, an energy—which it has not known how to define and therefore does not really know how to control. For a very long time, for example, America prospered—or seemed to prosper: this prosperity cost millions of people their lives. Now, not even the people who are the most spectacular recipients of the benefits of this prosperity are able to endure these benefits: they can neither understand them nor do without them, nor can they go beyond them. Above all, they cannot, or dare not, assess or imagine the price paid by their victims, or subjects, for this way of life, and so they cannot afford to know why the victims are revolting. They are forced, then, to the conclusion that the victims—the barbarians—are revolting against all established civilized values—which is both true and not true—and, in order to preserve these values, however stifling and joyless these values have caused their lives to be, the bulk of the people desperately seek out representatives who are prepared to make up in cruelty what both they and the people lack in conviction.

This is a formula for a nation's or a kingdom's decline, for no kingdom can maintain itself by force alone. Force does not work the way its advocates seem to think it does. It does not, for example, reveal to the victim the strength of his adversary. On the contrary, it reveals the weakness, even the panic of his adversary, and this revelation invests the victim with patience. Furthermore, it is ultimately fatal to create too many victims. The victor can do nothing with these victims, for they do not belong to him, but—to the victims. They belong to the people he is fighting. The people know this, and as inexorably as the roll call—the honor roll—of victims expands, so does their will become inexorable: they resolve that these dead, their brethren, shall not have died in vain. When this point is reached, however long the battle may go on, the victor can never be the victor: on the contrary, all his energies, his entire life, are bound up in a terror he cannot articulate, a mystery he cannot read, a battle he cannot win—he has simply become the prisoner of the people he thought to cow, chain, or murder into submission.

Power, then, which can have no morality in itself, is yet dependent on human energy, on the wills and desires of human beings. When power translates itself into tyranny, it means that the principles on which that power depended, and which were its justification, are bankrupt. When this happens, and it is happening now, power can only be defended by thugs and mediocrities—and seas of blood. The representatives of the *status quo* are sickened and divided, and dread looking into the eyes of their young; while the excluded begin to realize, having endured everything, that they *can* endure everything. They do not know the precise shape of the future, but they know that the future belongs to them. They realize this—paradoxically—by the failure of the moral energy of their oppressors and begin, almost instinctively, to forge a new morality, to create the principles on which a new world will be built.

My sister, Paula, and my brother, David, and I lived together in London for a while in 1968. London was very peaceful, partly because we hardly ever went out. The house was big, so that we were not on top of each other, and all of us could cook. Besides, going out was hazardous. London was reacting to its accelerating racial problem and compounding the disaster by denying that it had one. My famous face created a certain kind of hazard—or hazards: for example, I remember a girl sitting next to me in a cinema suddenly *seeing* me in the light from the match with which she was lighting her cigarette. She stared and shook—I could not tell whether she was about to cry *Rape!* or ask for an autograph. In the event, she moved away. My dusky tribe had the same troubles, without the tremendous pause.

Nevertheless, London was still far from being as hysterical and dangerous as New York. Eventually, of course, black Englishmen, Indians, students, conscientious objectors, and CIA infiltrators—no doubt—tracked me down, as we had known was inevitable. Dick Gregory came to town and we shared a platform before part of London's black community. A British columnist told his readers before or during this time that he wished I would either "drop dead or shut up"; and on King's Road, near our house, British hippies paraded one day, carrying banners, one of which read, "Keep Britain Black." I felt myself in London on borrowed time, for sometime before, the Home Office, as I learned when I landed at Heathrow Airport, had declared me *persona non grata* in Britain. They had let me land, finally, but it took awhile. (They had thrown Stokely out about a week before.) I thought of the late Lorraine Hansberry's statement (to me) concerning the solidarity of the Western powers, and the impossibility, for such as we, of hoping for political asylum anywhere in the West. I thought of Robert Williams, who had not intended and almost surely never desired, to go East. And I thought of Malcolm.

Alex Haley wrote *The Autobiography of Malcolm X*. Months before the foregoing, in New York, he and Elia Kazan and I had agreed to do it as a play—and I still wish we had. We were vaguely aware that Hollywood was nibbling for a book, but, as Hollywood is always nibbling, it occurred to no one, certainly not to me, to take these nibbles seriously. It simply was not a subject which Hollywood could manage, and I didn't see any point in talking to them about it. But the book was sold to an independent producer, named Marvin Worth, who would produce it for Columbia Pictures. By this time, I was already in London; and I was also on the spot. For, while I didn't believe Hollywood could do it, I didn't quite see, since they declared themselves sincerely and seriously willing to attempt it, how I could duck the challenge. What it came to, in fact, was an enormous question: to what extent was I prepared again to gamble on the good faith of my countrymen?

In that time, now so incredibly far behind us, when the Black Muslims meant to the American people exactly what the Black Panthers mean today, and when they were described in exactly the same terms by that High Priest, J. Edgar Hoover, and when many of us believed or made ourselves believe that the American state still contained within itself the power of self-confrontation, the power to change itself in the direction of honor and knowledge and freedom, or, as Malcolm put it, "to atone," I first met Malcolm X. Perhaps it says a great deal about the black American experience, both negatively and positively, that so many should have believed so hard, so long, and paid such a price for believing: but what this betrayed belief says about white Americans is very accurately and abjectly summed up by the present, so-called Nixon Administration.

I had heard a great deal about Malcolm, as had everyone else, and I was a little afraid of him, as was everyone else, and I was further handicapped by having been out of the country for so long. When I returned to America, I again went South, and thus, imperceptibly, found myself mainly on the road. I saw Malcolm before I met him. I had just returned from someplace like Savannah, I was giving a lecture somewhere in New York, and Malcolm was sitting in the first or second row of the hall, bending forward at such an angle that his long arms nearly caressed the ankles of his long legs, staring up at me. I very nearly panicked. I knew Malcolm only by legend, and this legend, since I was a Harlem street boy, I was sufficiently astute to distrust. I distrusted the legend because we, in Harlem, have been betrayed so often. Malcolm might be the torch white people claimed he was—though, in general, white America's evaluations of these matters would be laughable and even pathetic did not these evaluations have such wicked results—or he might be the hustler I remembered from my pavements. On the other hand, Malcolm had no reason to trust me, either—and so I stumbled through my lecture, with Malcolm never taking his eyes from my face.

It must be remembered that in those great days I was considered to be an "integrationist"—this was never, quite, my own idea of myself—and Malcolm was considered to be a "racist in reverse." This formulation, in terms of power—and power is the arena in which racism is acted out—means absolutely nothing: it may even be described as a cowardly formulation. The powerless, by definition, can never be "racists," for they can never make the world pay for what they feel or fear except by the suicidal endeavor which makes them fanatics or revolutionaries, or both; whereas, those in power can be urbane and charming and invite you to those which they know you will never own. The powerless must do their own dirty work. The powerful have it done for them.

Anyway: somewhat later, I was the host, or moderator, for a radio program starring Malcolm X and a sit-in student from the Deep South. I was the moderator because both the radio station and I were afraid that Malcolm would simply eat the boy alive. I didn't want to be there, but there was no way out of it. I had come prepared to throw various camp stools under the child, should he seem wobbly; to throw out the lifeline whenever Malcolm should seem to be carrying the child beyond his depth. Never has a moderator been less needed. Malcolm understood that child and talked to him as though he were talking to a younger brother, and with that same watchful attention. What most struck me was that he was not at all trying to proselytize the child: he was trying to make him think. He was trying to do for the child what he supposed, for too long a time, that the Honorable Elijah had done for him. But I did not think of that until much later. I will never forget Malcolm and that child facing each other, and Malcolm's extraordinary gentleness. And that's the truth about Malcolm: he was one of the gentlest people I have ever met. And I am sure that the child remembers him that way. That boy, by the way, battling so valiantly for civil rights, might have been, for all I can swear to, Stokely Carmichael or Huey Newton or Bobby Seale or Rap Brown or one of my nephews. That's how long or how short— *oh, pioneers!*—the apprehension of betrayal takes: "If you are an American citizen," Malcolm asked the boy, "why have you got to fight for your rights as a citizen? To be a citizen means that you have the rights of a citizen. If you haven't got the rights of a citizen, then you're not a citizen." "It's not as simple as that," the boy said. "Why not?" asked Malcolm.

I was, in some way, in those years, without entirely realizing it, the Great Black Hope of the Great White Father. I was *not* a racist—so I thought; Malcolm *was* a racist, so *he* thought. In fact, we were simply trapped in the same situation, as poor

Martin was later to discover (who, in those days, did not talk to Malcolm and was a little nervous with me). As the GBH of the GWF, anyway, I appeared on a television program, along with Malcolm and several other hopes, including Mr. George S. Schuyler. It was pretty awful. If I had ever hoped to become a racist, Mr. Schuyler dashed my hopes forever, then and there. I can scarcely discuss this program except to say that Malcolm and I very quickly dismissed Mr. Schuyler and virtually everyone else, and, as the old street rats and the heirs of Baptist ministers, played the program off each other.

Nothing could have been more familiar to me than Malcolm's style in debate. I had heard it all my life. It was vehemently non-stop and Malcolm was young and looked younger; this caused his opponents to suppose that Malcolm was reckless. Nothing could have been less reckless, more calculated, even to those loopholes he so often left dangling. These were not loopholes at all, but hangman's knots, as whoever rushed for the loophole immediately discovered. Whenever this happened, the strangling interlocutor invariably looked to me, as being the more "reasonable," to say something which would loosen the knot. Mr. Schuyler often *did* say something, but it was always the wrong thing, giving Malcolm yet another opportunity. All I could do was elaborate on some of Malcolm's points, or modify, or emphasize, or seem to try to clarify, but there was no way I could disagree with him. The others were discussing the past or the future, or a country which may once have existed, or one which may yet be brought into existence—Malcolm was speaking of the bitter and unanswerable present. And it was too important that this be heard for anyone to attempt to soften it. It was important, of course, for white people to hear it, if they were still able to hear; but it was of the utmost importance for black people to hear it, for the sake of their morale. It was important for them to know that there was someone like them, in public life, telling the truth about their condition. Malcolm considered himself to be the spiritual property of the people who produced him. He did not consider himself to be their saviour, he was far too modest for that, and gave that role to another; but he considered himself to be their servant and in order not to betray that trust, he was willing to die, and died. Malcolm was not a racist, not even when he thought he was. His intelligence was more complex than that; furthermore, if he had been a racist, not many in this racist country would have considered him dangerous. He would have sounded familiar and even comforting, his familiar rage confirming the reality of white power and sensuously inflaming a bizarre species of guilty eroticism without which, I am beginning to believe, most white Americans of the more or less liberal persuasion cannot draw a single breath. What made him unfamiliar and dangerous was not his hatred for white people but his love for blacks, his apprehension of the horror of the black condition, and the reasons for it, and his determination so to work on their hearts and minds that they would be enabled to see their condition and change it themselves.

For this, after all, not only were no white people needed; they posed, *en bloc*, the very greatest obstacle to black self-knowledge and had to be considered a menace. But white people have played so dominant a role in the world's history for so long that such an attitude toward them constitutes the most disagreeable of novelties; and it may be added that, though they have never learned how to live with the darker brother, they do not look forward to having to learn how to live without him. Malcolm, finally, was a genuine revolutionary, a virile impulse long since fled from the American way of life—in himself, indeed, he was a kind of revolution, both in the sense of a return to a former principle, and in the sense of an upheaval. It is pointless to speculate on his probable fate had he been legally white. Given the white man's options, it is probably just as well for all of us that he was legally black. In some church someday, so far unimagined and unimaginable, he will be hailed as a saint. Of course, this day waits on the workings of the temporal power which Malcolm understood, at last, so well. Rome, for example, has just desanctified some saints and invented, if one dares to use so utilitarian a word in relation to so divine an activity, others, and the Pope has been to Africa, driven there, no doubt, however belatedly, by his concern for the souls of black folk: who dares imagine the future of such a litany as *black like me!* Malcolm, anyway, had this much in common with all real saints and prophets, he had the power, if not to drive the money-changers from the temple, to tell the world what they were doing there.

For reasons I will never understand, on the day that I realized that a play based on *The Autobiography* was not going to be done, that sooner or later I would have to say yes or no to the idea of doing a movie, I flew to Geneva. I will never know why I flew to Geneva, which is far from being my favorite town. I will never know how it is that I arrived there with no toilet articles whatever, no toothbrush, no toothpaste, no razor, no hairbrush, no comb, and virtually no clothes. Furthermore, I have a brother-in-law and a sister-in-law living in Geneva of whom I'm very fond and it didn't even occur to me that they were there. All that I seem to have brought with me is *The Autobiography*. And I sat in the hotel bedroom all the weekend long, with the blinds drawn, reading and re-reading—or, rather, endlessly traversing—the great jungle of Malcolm's book.

The problems involved in a cinematic translation were clearly going to be formidable, and wisdom very strongly urged that I have nothing to do with it. It could not possibly bring me anything but grief. I still would have much preferred to have done it as a play, but that possibility was gone. I had grave doubts and fears about Hollywood. I had been there before, and I had not liked it. The idea of Hollywood doing a truthful job on Malcolm could not but seem preposterous. And yet—I didn't want to spend the rest of my life thinking: *It could have been done if you hadn't been chicken*. I felt that Malcolm would never have forgiven me for that. He had trusted me in life and I believed he trusted me in death, and that trust, as far as I was concerned, was my obligation.

From Geneva, I eventually went to London, to join my brother and sister. It was from London that I wired Kazan to say that the play was off, and I was doing the movie. This was only to take K. off the hook, for I wired no one else, had made no agreement to do the movie, and was very troubled and uncertain in my own mind.

*

Sometime during all this, through William Styron, I learned that a friend of mine, black, was in prison in Hamburg, Germany, charged with murder. This was William A. (Tony) Maynard, Jr., who had worked for me for some time, several years before, as bodyguard and chauffeur and man Friday. He had been arrested by Interpol and was being held in a Hamburg prison, from which he would probably be extradited to the States. The murder had been committed in New York's Greenwich Village in April of 1967. Tony knew Bill Styron because he had often driven me to Bill's house in Connecticut, and his letter to Bill, since he knew Bill to be rather more stationary than I, was a way of alerting me, and any other friends he had outside, of his desperate situation.

I did not doubt his innocence. Tony is a big man and can be very loud, is far from discreet, and has done his share of street fighting: but it is hard to imagine him killing anybody, especially, as was claimed, with a sawed-off shotgun. No one who knows Tony can believe that he would ever so lower himself as to be seen with so inelegant a weapon. For he has, in fact, a kind of pantherlike, street-boy elegance—he walks something like a cat—and a tricky, touchy, dangerous pride, which, in the years we worked together, kept him in all kinds of fruitless trouble; and he had a taste for white women (who had a taste for him) which made him, especially given his aggressively virile good looks, particularly unattractive to the NYPD. I had not seen Tony in some years. We had worked together in civil rights demonstrations and rallies, but, after the bombing of the Birmingham Sunday school—a much underrated event in this country's shameful history, and one which had a devastating effect on all black people—we had had a serious disagreement concerning the strategy needed to handle a rent strike, and had, thereafter, gone our separate ways. But I still considered him a friend. I wrote to him and I flew from London to Hamburg to visit him.

That winter, the beginning of 1968, London was cold, but damp and grey. Hamburg was frosty and dry as a bone, and blinding with ice and snow; and the sun, which never came to London, loitered in Hamburg all day long: *über alles*. Germans say that Hamburg is the German city which most resembles London. It is hard to know, from their tone, whether they are bragging or complaining, and it did not really remind me of London, lacking London's impressive sprawl; yet, it did confirm my ancient sense of the British and the Germans as cousins. Hamburg looks like a city built only for the purposes of affairs of state—an extraordinary sequence of stony façades. It makes one think of trumpets; there should be at least six trumpeters on every roof. The people are as friendly as people are in London, and in the same way: with a courtesy as final as the raised drawbridge and as unsettling as the deep moat at one's feet. Behind the façade, of course, lives the city, furtive, paranoiac, puritanical, obsessed and in love with what it imagines to be sin—and also with what it imagines to be joy, it being difficult in Western culture to distinguish between these two. The prison was not far from my hotel, and I eventually acquired enough of a sense of direction to be able to walk from one castle to another. All the time I spent in Hamburg was spent between these two fixed points. The hotel was called The Four Seasons; because of the Maynard case, I once called Senator Javits from there; and ran into Pierre Salinger in the lobby once, he on his way out, I on my way in. If he had not been rushing out and if I had known him better, I might have tried to discuss the case with him. I needed help and advice and I have always rather liked Mr. Salinger. But I am not very good at buttonholing people, and besides I have learned that it frightens them.

It is not an easy matter to be allowed to visit a prisoner. Without the really extraordinary cooperation of my German publishers, I could never have managed it at all. But manage it we did, and so the day came when I was deposited in the waiting room of the prison at Holstenglacis.

The prison is part of a complex of intimidating structures, scattered over quite a large area—a little like the complex on l'Ile de la Cité in Paris, or the complex on Center Street in New York—but it resembles neither of them. It is more medieval than either, and gives the impression of being far more isolated—though, as I say, I could walk to it from my exceedingly fashionable hotel. Yet, the streets were torn up all around it—men at work; I learned to walk from there because taxis seemed never to come anywhere near it; there was a tramline, but I did not know how to use it, and it also seemed to skirt the prison. The only people I ever saw around there were clearly connected with the prison, or were visitors; you could tell the lawyers by their briefcases and their slightly chastened air of self-importance. To visit the prisoner, one had, of course, to have a pass. I am not, legally, related to Tony by blood, and my only pretext to have the right to visit (a right later to be taken from me) was that I was the only friend he had in Germany, and I had traveled quite a long way to see him. This was all arranged between my publishers and the lawyer, and I will never quite know how it was done. But the lawyer rang the bell, anyway, one frosty afternoon, before the great door, which opened and let us in. Then, I was deposited in the waiting room, and before me, at the height of two or three steps, was the great barred door which led to the interior of the prison. There were two or three people in the room with me. One man silently offered me a cigarette and, silently, I took it. The smoke between us, then, was all that we could manage of communion.

    I was frightened in a way very hard to describe. The fact that this was the fabled Germany of the Third Reich, and this was a German prison, certainly had something to do with it. I was not so much afraid to see him as I was afraid of what might have happened to him—in him—the way one feels when about to see a loved one who has encountered great misfortune. One does not know what is left of the person. Human help often arrives too late, and if the person has really turned his face to the wall, no human being can help. The great barred door had opened often, letting people in or out; then, I was called or beckoned, and mounted the stone steps, standing before the bars; the turnkey smiled at me as he turned the key in the lock. Then I was led into another waiting room, narrow, two long benches on either side of a long table. The prisoners sat on one side, their visitors on the other. The guard stood at the door.

Tall, and thinner than I had ever seen him, his high cheekbones pushing out of his skin, his hair too long, wearing clothes he hated, and with his eyes both wet and blazing, Tony stood and smiled. We held each other a moment, and sat down, facing each other, and Tony grinned: I saw that he hadn't turned his face to the wall.

"Hey—!" he said, "how you doing?"

The room was very crowded, and I hardly knew what to say. It would be hard to discuss his case.

"Upon my soul," said Tony, "I didn't do it."

I was glad he said it, though he didn't have to say it.

"Upon my soul," I said, "we'll get you out."

Between the night and the morning of April 3–4, in 1967, a Marine, Michael E. Kroll, was murdered on West 3rd Street, in Greenwich Village. He was killed, according to the newspaper stories, as a result of his intervention in a heated argument which a young sailor, Michael Crist, was having with two men, one white and one black. The black man is described as being about five feet, eight inches, and about twenty years old. (Tony was then twenty-seven, and is over six feet tall.) The two men, the black and the white, then walked away, but Kroll and the sailor apparently followed them and another argument ensued, which ended when the black man produced a sawed-off shotgun from beneath his jacket and shot the Marine in the head, killing him instantly. Then, the two men ran away. The claim was that all this happened because the black man had made an indecent proposal to the sailor.

"Can you see me doing that?" Tony asked. His face was extraordinarily vivid with the scorn he felt for so much of the human race. "Since when have I even *talked*"—his face convulsed as though he were vomiting—"to punks like that?"

And, truly, anyone knowing Tony, and hearing such a description of his conduct, would have been forced to the conclusion that Tony had suddenly gone mad. Tony barely spoke when spoken to by strangers—when we worked together, it was his unending complaint that I was "too nice to these mothers"; he treated nearly everyone not within his immediate entourage with a bored, patient contempt. It was impossible to imagine the arrogant Tony walking through Village streets accosting strangers. As for the indecent proposal, the only way *that* could be explained was for the sailor to have mistaken a curse for an invitation. But it was difficult to imagine Tony speaking to him at all, and also hard to imagine that the sailor would have accosted him. Tony looks dangerous. And Tony could not have engaged in such conduct even if he were drunk, for the very good reason that he could not *get* drunk—long before he got drunk, he got sick. In short, in order to believe any of this, it would be necessary to invent a Tony whom no one knew.

But that, of course, would pose no difficulty for the police or the jury or the judge.

"Before I left New York"—this is another black friend of mine speaking to me, in Paris, many years ago—"well, you know, I was living with this white chick and we went around together, naturally, and we used to have coffee late at night, or early in the morning in this joint on Sheridan Square. And the neighborhood people didn't like it, and the cops didn't like it. And sometimes the cops would come in and give us a very rough time—making wisecracks, asking me for my draft card, and wanting to know where I lived, and all. You see, they didn't really *do* anything. We weren't bothering anybody and we weren't on dope, or anything, and although her family didn't *like* the situation, still, she was white, and the cops didn't know what her family might do if they really got rough with their daughter. Her family was respectable and had some money. But if *they* didn't do anything, you can just imagine the effect they had on the people—they were telling the people that it was all right to go ahead and beat the shit out of us. One of the cops saw me one day when I was alone, and he said, 'I'm going to get you.' Just like that, looking me in the eye. I started dreaming about that cop. He never spoke to me again, just looked at me like that every time we passed each other on the street. I knew he meant it. If I hung around too long, he'd find a way. And so I got some change together, and I hauled ass."

I knew a blond girl in the Village a long time ago, and, eventually, we never walked out of the house together. She was far safer walking the streets alone than when walking with me—a brutal and humiliating fact which thoroughly destroyed whatever relationship this girl and I might have been able to achieve. This happens all the time in America, but Americans have yet to realize what a sinister fact this is, and what it says about them. When we walked out in the evening, then, she would leave ahead of me, alone. I would give her about five minutes, and then I would walk out alone, taking another route, and meet her on the subway platform. We would not acknowledge each other. We would get into the same subway car, sitting at opposite ends of it, and walk, separately, through the streets of the free and the brave, to wherever we were going—a friend's house, or the movies. There was only one restaurant, eventually, in which we ever ate together, and it was run by a black woman. We were fighting for our lives, and we were very young. As for the police, our protectors, we would never have dreamed of calling one. Our connection caused us to be menaced by the police in ways indescribable and nearly inconceivable; and the police egged on the populace, stood laughing and talking while we were spit on, and cursed. When with a girl, I never ran, I couldn't: except once, when a girl I had been sleeping with slapped me in the face in the middle of Washington Square Park. She was pulling rank, she was crying *Rape!*—and then I ran. I still remember the day and the hour, and the sunlight, the faces of the people, and the girl's face—she had short red hair—and I will never forgive that girl. I am astonished until today that I have both my eyes and most of my teeth and functioning kidneys and my sexual equipment: but small black boys have the advantage of being able to curl themselves into knots, and roll with the kicks and the punches. Of course, I was a target for the police. I was black and visible and helpless and the word was out to "get" me, and so, soon, I, too, hauled ass. And the prisons of this country are full of boys like the boy I was.

"All right," cried Tony, with tears in his eyes, "I'm twenty-eight, and I'm a criminal, right? I've got a record—now they can do anything they want!"

Tony had been arrested about four years earlier, as a civil rights demonstrator—that stays on the books; then on a narcotics charge; then charged with stealing an overcoat—"I was running a business—who's going to steal an overcoat out of his own shop!"—and then charged with stealing a car. He was prosecuted only on the car-theft charge, which has since been dropped. Nevertheless, the car-theft charge marked the most important turning point of his life. He was held for something like two months—this was after the murder, and long before he was connected with it—and then released on bail. But a thoroughly shaken Tony, having been assured by the police that they would "get" him, jumped bail and went to Germany. He had been there before and had been happy there. His flight turned out to be his greatest error: but he could not have supposed that he would be arrested in Germany for having been accused of stealing a car—particularly as Tony's brand of arrogance causes him to act as if his private knowledge of his innocence constitutes irrefutable public proof. With his lofty *I would never do a thing like that*, he dismisses the accusation and is affronted—and surprised—when others do not take him at what he supposes to be his sacred word. And, in fact, almost the very first thing he did in Germany was to register his presence with the American Embassy and give them his address—unlikely conduct indeed for anyone supposing himself to be suspected of murder.

The murder occurred in April. The alleged car theft took place before the murder, but Tony was indicted on the car-theft charge well after the murder occurred, sometime in May. He was in jail for about two months and then released on bail. He arrived in Hamburg on October 22. On October 25, a Detective Hanst, in New York, swore out a complaint which declared that "as a result of information received and investigation made," Maynard was guilty of homicide. On October 27, a Judge Weaver, in New York, cabled the Hamburg chief of police demanding Maynard's arrest. It is not until October 31 that the deposition on which the entire case rests makes its appearance. This is signed by a certain Dennis Morris, whose address is in Brooklyn, and he identifies Tony Maynard by means of a passport-size snapshot. His deposition reads: "That on the morning of April 3, 1967 [but the crime is alleged to have taken place on the morning of the fourth] I was on West 4th Street, near Sixth Avenue, in the city, county, and state of New York, and saw a man, now known to me as Wm. A. Maynard, Jr., whose photograph on which I have placed my initials appears below and is part hereof, shoot and kill a man now known to me as Michael E. Kroll. I then saw said Wm. A. Maynard, Jr. run away from the scene of the crime."

This document, to say nothing of the date of its appearance, strikes me as extraordinary. It appears six days after Hanst's warrant and four days after Judge Weaver's cable—to say nothing of the fact that this authoritative identification of the murderer, by means of a photograph, occurs seven months after the event. Dennis Morris has made no appearance until this moment, and no one knows anything about him. The logical eyewitness, Crist, who was locked in an eyeball to eyeball confrontation with the murderer, has entirely disappeared. (He is to reappear during Tony's trial, armed with a most engaging reason for having been away so long.) In any case, Maynard had been under police surveillance for months, during which time the police were presumably investigating the murder, presumably picking up blacks and whites by the scores, and placing them in line-ups, and it seems never to have occurred to them to connect Maynard with the murder. Incidentally, the white assailant disappears completely and forever from this investigation, as though he had never existed.

That, roughly, was the case until that moment, as it could be reconstructed from Germany. Time was to reveal several unnerving details, but this outline never changed. It was to prove important, later, that during this time Tony had been involved with two white women, one of whom, Giselle Nicole, claiming extreme police harassment, disappeared. The other, Mary Quinn, he married. They did not live happily ever after, and Mary Quinn's subsequent conduct was scarcely that of a loving wife.

According to the treaty between Germany and America, two classes of prisoners are not subject to extradition: political prisoners, and those facing the death penalty. Tony wanted to fight the extradition proceedings, for he was certain that he would be murdered on the way back home. This fear may strike the ordinary American as preposterous, in spite of what they themselves know concerning the violence which is the heritage and the scourge of their country. I could not, of course, agree with Tony, but I didn't find his terror, which was exceedingly controlled and therefore very moving, in the least preposterous. But I had no remote notion how to go about fighting his extradition. Ironically, the very greatest obstacle lay in the fact that New York had abolished the death penalty. The plea could be made, then, only on political grounds. I agree with the Black Panther position concerning black prisoners: not one of them has ever had a fair trial, for not one of them has ever been tried by a jury of his peers. White middle-class America is always the jury, and they know absolutely nothing about the lives of the people on whom they sit in judgment: and this fact is not altered, on the contrary it is rendered more implacable by the presence of one or two black faces in the jury box.

But it would be difficult indeed to convey to a German court the political implications of a black man's arrest: difficult if not impossible to convey, especially to a nation "friendly" to the United States, to what extent black Americans are political prisoners. Muhammad Ali, formerly Cassius Clay, is a vivid example of what can happen to a black man who obeys the American injunction, *be true to your faith*, but his press has been so misleading that he is also an unwieldy and intimidating example. Muhammad Ali is one of the best of the "bad niggers" and has been publicly hanged like one, but since I had to avoid the religious issue, which had nothing to do with Tony's case, I could not cite him as an example. Neither was the Maynard case likely to interest civil rights organizations, or the NAACP; it was, in fact, simply another example of a black hustler being thrown into jail. The complex of reasons dictating such a fate could scarcely be articulated in a letter to the German court. There was also the enormous and delicate problem of publicity. Though I had no choice in the matter, for I certainly couldn't abandon him, I was terrified that my presence in the case would work strongly to Tony's disadvantage. I intended to fight the extradition proceedings as hard as I knew how, but I knew how unlikely it was that we would win. In the event that we lost, Tony would be brought to trial and any publicity prior to that trial could certainly be considered prejudicial. On the other hand, both Tony and my German editor felt that an appeal to the press would work strongly in Tony's favor. It is really rather awful to find oneself in a position in which any move one makes may result in irreparable harm to another, and I was torn in two by this question for some time. But the question was brutally taken out of my hands.

One dark, Gothic evening, much delayed by the fact that we had spent hours trying to arrive at a strategy—no easy matter if one's strategy must be dictated by the laws of two different countries, and the psychology of two not so very different peoples—the German lawyer, my German editor, and myself, arrived at the door of the Holstenglacis prison. *We* were rattled because, though we were not exactly late, we knew that we were arriving at just about the time that prisoners were due to be taken upstairs for meals; and, furthermore, again a trick accomplished by my German publishers, by this time Tony and I no longer met in the public waiting room, but in another, smaller and private, where we could smoke, where we could talk. This was an enormous concession, and being late could possibly mean losing it.

Only the lawyer and I had passes to enter. My German editor—Fritz Raddadtz, an anti-Nazi German, who has the scars to prove it—had no right to enter at all. But the guard who opened the door also seemed rattled and, without examining anybody's pass, led us all into the room in which he knew I always awaited Tony.

And there we waited, for quite some time. Another rattled functionary appeared, explaining that Tony was not in his cell and could not be seen that night. My German editor, smelling a rat—I didn't, yet, and the lawyer seemed bewildered—pointed out that Tony, in his cell or not, was, nevertheless, somewhere in the prison, and that we were perfectly prepared to wait in this room until morning, or for weeks, if it came to that: that we would not, in short, leave until we saw Tony. The rattled functionary disappeared again. Then, after quite a long while, they brought in the birthday boy.

Someone had goofed in that prison, very badly; after this visit, heads surely rolled. Tony had been beaten, and beaten very hard; his cheekbones had disappeared and one of his eyes was crooked; he looked swollen above the neck, and he took down his shirt collar, presently, to show us the swelling on his shoulders. And he was weeping, trying not to—I had seen him with tears in his eyes, but I had never seen him weeping.

But when I say that heads surely rolled and that someone had goofed, I do not mean that they goofed because they beat him. They goofed because they let us see him. No one would have taken my word for this beating, or our lawyer's word. But Fritz knows what it means to be beaten in prison. And he, therefore, not only alerted the German press, but armed with the weight of one of the most powerful of German publishing houses, sued the German state. So, there it was, after all, anyway, in the newspapers, and I, too, had to meet the press.

"I've got a religious medallion," Tony said—he has become a kind of Muslim, or, at least, an anti-Christian—"and the guard told me the other day that they were going to let me have it back again. Because they took it, you know. And I wanted it back. It means a lot to me—I'm not about to kill myself with it, I'm not about to kill myself. So, when the guard walked in, I asked him for it because he said he would bring it to me Friday night." (And this was Friday.) "Well, I don't know, he jumped salty and he walked out. And I started beating on the door of my cell, trying to make him come back, to listen to me, at least to explain to me *why* I couldn't have it, after he'd promised. And then the door opened and fifteen men walked in and they beat me up—fifteen men!"

The headline on one of the German newspapers, which, incongruously or cunningly enough also has beneath the headline an old photograph of myself, laughing, is: "Tony Never Lies"! This means at least two things, for it is not humanly possible for it to mean what it says. It means that Tony has never lied to me, though I have frequently watched him attempt to delude me into his delusions: but we human beings do this with each other all the time. Friends and lovers are able, sometimes, not always, to resist and correct the delusions. But it also means something exceedingly difficult to capture, which is that some people are liars, and some people are not. We will return to this speculation later. Somewhere in the Bible there is the chilling observation: *Ye are liars, and the truth's not in you.*

I had been in London when Malcolm was murdered. The sister who worked for me then, Gloria, had the habit, whenever she decided that it was time to get me out of town, of simply arbitrarily picking up an invitation, it scarcely mattered to where, and putting me on a plane; so, for example, we once found ourselves in the midnight sun of Helsinki. This time, we were the guests of my British publishers, in London, and we were staying at the Hilton. On this particular night, we were free and we had decided to treat ourselves to a really fancy, friendly dinner. There we were, at the table, all dressed up, and we'd ordered everything, and we were having a very nice time with each other. The headwaiter came, and said there was a phone call for me, and Gloria rose to take it. She was very strange when she came back—she didn't say anything, and I began to be afraid to ask her anything. Then, nibbling at something she obviously wasn't tasting, she said, "Well, I've got to tell you because the press is on its way over here. They've just killed Malcolm X."

The British press said that I accused innocent people of this murder. What I tried to say then, and will try to repeat now, is that whatever hand pulled the trigger did not buy the bullet. That bullet was forged in the crucible of the West, that death was dictated by the most successful conspiracy in the history of the world, and its name is white supremacy.

Years and years and years ago, a black friend of mine killed himself partly because of what he had been forced to endure at the hands of his countrymen because he was in love with a white girl. I had been away and didn't know that he was dead. I came out of the subway one evening, at West 4th Street, just as the train came in on the other side of the platform. A man I knew came running down the steps to catch this train. He saw me, and he yelled, "Did you hear what happened to Gene?" "No," I cried, "what happened?" "He's dead," shouted the hurrying man, and the subway doors closed and the train pulled out of the station.

When George Bernard Shaw wrote *Saint Joan*, he had the immense advantage of having never known her. He had never seen her walk, never heard her talk, could never have been haunted by any of those infinitesimal, inimitable tones, turns, tics, quirks, which are different in every human being, and which make love and death such inexorably private affairs. He had the advantage of the historical panorama: the forces responsible for Joan's death, as well as the ways in which she herself was responsible, were ranged as clearly as chessmen on a chessboard. The forces responsible for that death, and the forces released by it, had had a long time to make themselves felt, and, while Joan was a riddle for her time, she was not a riddle by the time Shaw got around to her: the riddle could be read in her effect in time. She had been safely burned, and somewhat more thoughtfully canonized and no longer posed any conceivable threat to anyone alive. She was, as Shaw points out, one of the world's first nationalists and terrified, equally, the feudal landlords and the princes of the church by refusing to concede their validity. They had no choice but to burn her, which did not, of course, by the merest iota, alter the exactness of her prophecy or the inevitability of their fate.

But it is a very different matter to attempt to deal with the present, in the present, and with a contemporary, younger than oneself, hideously dead too soon, and one who became, furthermore, long before he died, a much disputed legend. And there is, since his death, a Malcolm, virtually, for every persuasion. People who hated him, people who despised him, people who feared him, and people who, in their various ways and degrees, according to their various lights and darknesses, loved him, all claim him now. It is easy to claim him now, just as it was easy for the church to claim Saint Joan.

But, though this storm of human voices creates a great difficulty, it does not create the greatest one.

The greatest difficulty is to accept the fact that the man is dead. It is one thing to *know* that a friend is dead and another thing to accept, within oneself, that unanswering silence: that not many of us are able to accept the reality of death is both an obvious and a labyrinthine statement. The imagination, then, which has been assigned the job of re-creating and interpreting a life one witnessed and loved simply kicks like a stalled motor, refuses to make contact, and will not get the vehicle to move. One no longer knows if one ever really knew the person, but, what's worse, that no longer makes any difference: one's stuck with whatever it is one thought one knew, with whatever filtered through the complex screen of one's limitations. That's one's legacy, that's all there is: and now only that work which is love and that love which is work will allow one to come anywhere near obeying the dictum laid down by the great Ray Charles, and—tell the truth.

Every new environment, particularly if one knows that one must make the effort to accustom oneself to working in it, risks being more than a little traumatic. One finds oneself nervously examining one's new surroundings, searching for the terms of the adjustment; therefore, in the beginning, I made a somewhat too conscious effort to be pleased by Hollywood. There was the sky, after all, which New Yorkers seldom see, and there was space, which New Yorkers have forgotten, there was the mighty and dramatic Pacific, there were the hills. Some very valuable and attractive people had lived and functioned here for years, I reminded myself, and there was really no reason why I could not—so I insisted to myself. I had a few friends and acquaintances here already, scattered from Watts to Baldwin Hills to Mulholland Drive, and I was sure they'd be happy if I decided to stay. If I were going to be in Hollywood for months, there was no point in raising the odds against me by hating it, or despising it; besides, such an attitude seemed too obvious a defense against my fear of it. As hotels go, the Beverly Hills is more congenial than most, and certainly everyone there was very nice to me. And so I tried—too hard—to look about me with wonder, and be pleased. But I was already in trouble, and the odds against the venture were very long odds indeed.

I was actually in the Beverly Hills until more permanent lodging could be found. This was not easy, since it involved finding someone to take care of me—to keep house, cook, and drive. *I* was no help, since I was still, at the beginning of 1968, committed to various fund-raising functions in the East, and, more particularly, to the question of a lawyer for Tony Maynard, who had been extradited from Germany and placed in the Tombs, in New York. He had been extradited very shortly after I left Hamburg, so speedily indeed that I was unable to fly from the Coast to meet him in New York, as I had promised. I had engaged, at his suggestion, a lawyer named S. J. Siegel, a very sharp, spry old man, who must have been close to eighty, and who was to teach me a great deal about criminal lawyers. Part of the irreducible conflict which was to drive both Columbia and myself up the wall was already implicit during those early days at the Beverly Hills hotel. The conflict was simply between my life as a writer and my life as—not spokesman exactly, but as public witness to the situation of black people. I had to play both roles: there was nothing anyone, including myself, could do about it. This was an unprecedented situation for Columbia, which, after all, had me under exclusive contract and didn't really like my dashing off, making public appearances. It was an unprecedented situation for me, too, since I had never before been under exclusive contract, and had always juggled my conflicting schedules as best I could. I had lived with my two roles for a long time, and had even, insofar as this is ever true, begun to get used to them—I accepted, anyway, that the dichotomy wasn't likely to end soon. But it didn't make the Hollywood scene any easier. It wasn't a matter of wiping the slate clean of existing commitments and then vanishing behind the typewriter, nor was it even a matter of keeping outside commitments to a minimum, though I tried: events were moving much faster than that, creating perpetual crises and making ever new demands. Columbia couldn't but be concerned about the time and energy I expended on matters remote from the scenario. On the other hand, I couldn't really regret it, since it seemed to me that in this perpetual and bitter ferment I was learning something which kept me in touch with reality and would deepen the truth of the scenario.

But I anticipate. People have their environments: the Beverly Hills Hotel was not mine. For no reason that I could easily name, its space, its opulence, its shapelessness, depressed and frightened me. The people in the bar, the lounge, the halls, the walks, the swimming pools, the shops, seemed as rootless as I, seemed unreal. In spite—perhaps because of—all my efforts to feel relaxed and free and at home (for America *is* my home!) I began to feel unreal—almost as though I were playing an unworthy part in a cheap, unworthy drama. I, who have spent half my life in hotels, sometimes woke up in the middle of the night, terrified, wondering where I was. But, though I scarcely realized it, and might even have been ashamed to admit it to myself, I think that this had partly to do with the fact that I was the only black person in the hotel. I must stress that in no way whatever did anyone in the hotel ever make me feel this, nor, indeed, did I ever consciously feel it—it's only now, in looking back, that I suspect it had to be partly that. My presence in the hotel was absolutely unquestioned, even by people who did not know who I was, or who thought I was Sammy Davis. It was simply taken for granted that I would not have been in the hotel if I had not belonged there. This, irrationally enough, got to me—*did* I belong there? In any case, thousands of black people, miles away, did not belong there, though some of them sometimes came to visit me there. (People had to come and get me, or come to visit me, because I do not drive.) The drive from Beverly Hills to Watts and back again is a long and loaded drive—I sometimes felt as though my body were being stretched across those miles. I don't think I felt anything so trivial as guilt, guilt at what appeared to be my comparative good fortune, I knew more about comparative fortunes than that, but I felt a stunning helplessness. These two worlds would never meet, and that fact prefigured disaster for my countrymen, and me. It caused me to look about me with an intensity of wonder which had no pleasure in it. Perhaps even more than the drive from Beverly Hills to Watts, the effect of this ruthless division was summed up for me by a visit I received from a young, very bright black man whom I had met years before, in Boston, after a lecture. Then, he had been very bright indeed, eager, full of ideas for his future, and the future of black people. A few years later, I had run across him, briefly, in Helsinki—he was studying, and seeing the world. Beautiful, I had thought then, make it, baby—it's wonderful to see a black cat at large in the world. Alas, to be at large in the world is also distinctly to risk being lost in it, and now, one afternoon, I received a message from a Prince of Abyssinia and I forget how many other territories, he was downstairs. In spite of the exotic titles, I recognized the domestic name, and I had him sent up. Here he came, then, a piteous, mad, unutterably moving wreck; he could scarcely have passed his thirtieth birthday. He wanted me to deposit ten thousand dollars in one of the many bank accounts he had around the world. He had a map, and a list of the banks, his patrons, and his titles, all impeccably handwritten. When confronting madness, it is usually best to hold one's peace, and so I do not know what I could have said. I did not question his titles, or his fortune, but indicated that I did not have ten thousand dollars. He took this with very good grace, had another drink, and bade me farewell—he had a pressing appointment with a fellow potentate. It was dark when he left, and black people—or white people, for that matter—walking in Beverly Hills do not walk far unnoticed. I almost started to call him a cab, but his regal bearing forbade it, and I then realized that there was nothing I could do.

I, of course, will always believe that this boy would not have been so quickly broken on the wheel of life if he had not been born black, in America. Many of my countrymen will not agree with me and will accuse me of special pleading. Neither they, nor I, can hope to come anywhere near the truth of the matter, so long as a man's color exerts so powerful a force on his fate. In the long meantime, I can only say that the authority of my countrymen in these matters is not equal to my own, since I know what black Americans endure—know it in my own flesh and spirit, know it by the human wreckage through which I have passed.

Therefore, my desire to be seduced, charmed, was a hope poisoned by despair: for better or for worse, it simply was not in me to make a separate peace. It was a symptom of how bitterly weary I was of wandering, how I hoped to find a resting place, reconciliation, in the land where I was born. But everything that might have charmed me merely reminded me of how many were excluded, how many were suffering and groaning and dying, not far from a paradise which was itself but another circle of hell. Everything that charmed me reminded me of someplace else, someplace where I could walk and talk, someplace where I was freer than I was at home, someplace where I could live without the stifling mask—made me homesick for a liberty I had never tasted here, and without which I could never live or work. In America, I was free only in battle, never free to rest—and he who finds no way to rest cannot long survive the battle.

Watts doesn't immediately look like a slum, if you come from New York; but it does if you drive from Beverly Hills. I have said that it is a very long drive, long and increasingly ugly; then one is in the long, flat streets of Watts, low, flat houses on either side. For a New Yorker, where the filth is piled so high that the light can never break through, Watts looks, at first, like a fine place to raise a child. There are little patches of yard, which can be enclosed by a fence, and a tree to which one can attach a swing, and space for a barbecue pit.

But, then, one looks again and sees how spare, shabby, and dark the houses are. One sees that garbage collection is scarcely more efficient here than it is in Harlem. One walks the long street and sees all that one sees in the East: the shabby pool halls, the shabby bars, the boarded-up doors and windows, the plethora of churches and lodges and liquor stores, the shining automobiles, the wine bottles in the gutter, the garbage-strewn alleys, and the young people, boys and girls, in the streets. Over it all hangs a miasma of fury and frustration, a perceptible darkening, as of storm clouds, of rage and despair, and the girls move with a ruthless, defiant dignity, and the boys move against the traffic as though they are moving against the enemy. The enemy is not there, of course, but his soldiers are, in patrol cars, armed.

And yet—I have been to Watts to give high-school lectures, for example, and these despised, maligned, and menaced children have an alertness, an eagerness, and a depth which I certainly did not find in—or failed to elicit from—students at many splendid universities. The future leaders of this country (in principle, anyway) do not impress me as being the intellectual equals of the most despised among us. I am not being vindictive when I say that, nor am I being sentimental or chauvinistic; and indeed the reason that this would be so is a very simple one. It is only very lately that white students, in the main, have had any reason to question the structure into which they were born; it is the very lateness of the hour, and their bewildered resentment—their sense of having been betrayed—which is responsible for their romantic excesses; and a young, white revolutionary remains, in general, far more romantic than a black one. For it is a very different matter, and results in a very different intelligence, to grow up under the necessity of questioning everything—everything, from the question of one's identity to the literal, brutal question of how to save one's life in order to begin to live it. White children, in the main, and whether they are rich or poor, grow up with a grasp of reality so feeble that they can very accurately be described as deluded—about themselves and the world they live in. White people have managed to get through entire lifetimes in this euphoric state, but black people have not been so lucky: a black man who sees the world the way John Wayne, for example, sees it would not be an eccentric patriot, but a raving maniac. The reason for this, at bottom, is that the doctrine of white supremacy, which still controls most white people, is itself a stupendous delusion: but to be born black in America is an immediate, a mortal challenge. People who cling to their delusions find it difficult, if not impossible, to learn anything worth learning: a people under the necessity of creating themselves must examine everything, and soak up learning the way the roots of a tree soak up water. A people still held in bondage must believe that *Ye shall know the truth, and the truth shall make ye free.*

But, of course, what black people are also learning as they learn is the truth about white people: and that's the rub. Actually, black people have known the truth about white people for a long time, but now there is no longer any way for the truth to be hidden. The whole world knows it. The truth which frees black people will also free white people, but this is a truth which white people find very difficult to swallow.

They need desperately to be released, for one thing, from the necessity of lying all the time. I remember visiting a correctional school in Watts where the boys were being taught a "useful" trade. I visited some of the shops—they were being taught to make wooden frames for hassocks—nonsense like that. The boys knew it was a bullshit trip, the teachers knew it, the principal, escorting me through the school, knew it. He looked ashamed of himself, and he should have been ashamed. The truth is that this country does not know what to do with its black population now that the blacks are no longer a source of wealth, are no longer to be bought and sold and bred, like cattle; and they especially do not know what to do with young black men, who pose as devastating a threat to the economy as they do to the morals of young white cheerleaders. It is not at all accidental that the jails and the army and the needle claim so many, but there are still too many prancing about for the public comfort. Americans will, of course, deny, with horror, that they are dreaming of anything like "the final solution"—those Americans, that is, who are likely to be asked: what goes on in the great, vast, private hinterland of the American heart can only be guessed at by observing the way the country goes these days. Some pale, compelling nightmare—an overwhelming collection of private nightmares—is responsible for the irresponsible ferocity of the Omnibus Crime Control and Safe Streets Act. Some vindictive terror on the part of the people made possible the Government's indefensible and obscene performance in Chicago. Something has gone violently wrong in a nation when the government dares attempt to muzzle the press—a press already quite supine enough—and to intimidate reporters by the use of the subpoena. Black men have been burned alive in this country more than once—many men now living have seen it with their own eyes; black men and boys are being murdered here today, in cold blood, and with impunity; and it is a very serious matter when the government which is sworn to protect the interests of all American citizens publicly and unabashedly allies itself with the enemies of black men. Let us tell it like it is: the rhetoric of a Stennis, a Maddox, a Wallace, historically and actually, has brought death to untold numbers of black people and it was meant to bring death to them. This is absolutely true, no matter who denies it—no black man can possibly deny it. Now, in the interest of the public peace, it is the Black Panthers who are being murdered in their beds, by the dutiful and zealous police. But, for a policeman, all black men, especially young black men, are probably Black Panthers and all black women and children are probably allied with them: just as, in a Vietnamese village, the entire population, men, women, children, are considered as probable Vietcong. In the village, as in the ghetto, those who were not dangerous before the search-and-destroy operation assuredly become so afterward, for the inhabitants of the village, like the inhabitants of the ghetto, realize that they are identified, judged, menaced, murdered, solely because of the color of their skin. This is as curious a way of waging a war for a people's freedom as it is of maintaining the domestic public peace.

The ghetto, beleaguered, betrayed by Washington, by the total lack of vision of the men in Washington, determined to outwit, withstand, survive, this present, overwhelming danger, yet lacks a focus, a rallying point, a spokesman. And many of us looked at each other and sighed, saying, *Lord, we really need Malcolm now.*

Hollywood, or a segment of it, at least, was becoming increasingly active on the question of civil rights—now, I thought, sourly, and somewhat unjustly, that the question had been rendered moribund. Just the same, there was a groundswell to replace the toothsome, grimly folksy mayor, Sam Yorty, who had been in office since 1911, with someone who had heard of the twentieth century, in this case, Tom Bradley, a Negro. People like Jack Lemmon, Jean Seberg, Robert Culp, and France Nuyen were actively supporting Martin Luther King, pledging money and getting others to pledge, and some were helping to raise money for a projected Malcolm X Foundation.

Marlon Brando was very much in the forefront of all this. He had a strong interest in the Black Panthers and was acquainted with many of them. On April 6, Eldridge Cleaver was wounded, and Bobby Hutton was killed, in Oakland, in what the police describe as a "shoot-out." Marlon called me to say that he was going up to Oakland. I wanted to go with him, but Martin Luther King had been murdered two days before, and, to tell the truth, I was in a state resembling shock. I can't describe this, or defend it, and I won't dwell on it. Marlon flew up to Oakland to deliver the eulogy for seventeen-year-old Bobby Hutton, shot down, exactly, by the dutiful police, like a mad dog in the streets. The Oakland Police Force was outraged, naturally, and I think they threatened to sue him, probably for defamation of character. The Grand Jury had judged their shooting of an unarmed, black adolescent as "justifiable homicide": the names of these jurors, many of whom can claim as their intimates eminent judges and lawyers, could scarcely have been found on the Master Panel if it were supposed that they were capable of bringing in any other verdict.

(I went to Oakland to visit the house where Hutton was killed, and Cleaver wounded. The house where the Panthers were is wedged between two houses just like it. There are windows on either side of the house, facing the alley; facing the street, there is only an enormous garage door, from which, needless to say, no one could hope to shoot, and live. The house, particularly the basement, where the people were, looks like something from a search-and-destroy operation. The warehouse across the street, where the cops were, doesn't have a scratch on it: so much for the official concept of a shoot-out. When I was there, there were flowers on a rock, marking the spot where Bobby fell: the people of the neighborhood had made of the place a shrine.)

I think it was in March, but it may have been somewhat earlier, that Martin Luther King came to town, to speak in a private dwelling in the Hollywood hills to raise money for the Southern Christian Leadership Conference. I had not seen Martin in quite some time, and I looked forward to seeing him in a setting where we might be able to talk a little bit before he had to dash off and grab some sleep before catching the next plane. For years, most of us had seen each other only at airports, or, wearily, marching, marching.

It always seems—unfairly enough, perhaps, in many cases—incongruous and suspect when relatively wealthy and certainly very worldly people come together for the express purpose of declaring their allegiance to a worthy cause and with the intention of parting with some of their money. I think that someone like myself can scarcely avoid a certain ambivalence before such a spectacle—someone like myself being someone significantly and crucially removed from the world which produced these people. In my own experience, genuine, disinterested compassion or conviction are very rare; yet, it is as well to remember that, rare as these are, they are real, they exist. Giving these people the benefit of the necessary doubt—assuming, that is, for example, that if they were called to serve on a Grand Jury investigating the legal murder of a black, they would have the courage to vote their conscience instead of their class—I would hazard that, in the case of most people in gatherings such as these, their presence is due to a vivid, largely incoherent uneasiness. They are nagged by a sense that something is terribly wrong, and that they must do what they can to put it right: but much of their quality, or lack of it, depends on what they perceive to be wrong. They do not, in any case, know what to do—who does? it may be asked—and so they give their money and their allegiance to whoever appears to be doing what they feel should be done. Their fatal temptation, to which, mostly, they appear to succumb, is to assume that they are, then, off the hook. But, on the other hand, always assuming that they are serious, the crucial lack in their perception is that they do not quite see where, when the chips are down, their allegiance is likely to land them—*à la lanterne!* or to recantation: they do not know how ruthless and powerful is the evil that lives in the world. Years before, for example, I remember having an argument—a most melancholy argument—with a friend of mine concerning our relation to Martin. It was shortly after our celebrated and stormy meeting with Bobby Kennedy, and I was very low. I said that we could petition and petition and march and march and raise money and give money until we wore ourselves out and the stars began to moan: none of this endeavor would or could reach the core of the matter, it would change nobody's fate. The thirty thousand dollars raised tonight would be gone in bail bonds in the morning, and so it would continue until we dropped. Nothing would ever reach the conscience of the people of this nation—it was a dream to suppose that the people of any nation had a conscience. Some individuals within the nation might, and the nation always saw to it that these people came to a bad, if not a bloody end. Nothing we could do would prevent, at last, an open confrontation. And where, then, when the chips were down, would we stand?

We were seated near a fireplace, and my friend's face was very thoughtful. He looked over at me, almost as though he were seeing me for the first time.

"You really believe that, don't you?"

I said, "I wish I didn't. But I'm afraid I do."

"Well," he said, at last, "if you're black, you don't have to worry too much about where you stand. They've got *that* covered, I believe."

Indeed, they do. And, therefore, people like the people in the Hollywood hills can be looked on as the highly problematical leaven in the loaf. Instinctively, when speaking before them, one attempts to fan into a blaze, or at least into positive heat, their somewhat chilled apprehension of life. In attempting to lessen the distance between them and oneself, one is also, unconsciously and inevitably, suggesting that they lessen the distance between themselves and their deepest hopes and fears and desires; even that they dispense with that middleman they call doctor, who is one of their greatest, most infantile self-indulgences. One senses sometimes in their still faces an intense, speculative hesitation. Bobby Seale insists that one of the things that most afflict white people is their disastrous concept of God; they have never accepted the dark gods, and their fear of the dark gods, who live in them at least as surely as the white God does, causes them to distrust life. It causes them, profoundly, to be fascinated by, and more than a little frightened of the lives led by black people: it is this tension which makes them problematical. But, on the other hand, it must be becoming increasingly clear to some, at least, that all of us are standing in the same deep shadow, a shadow which can only be lifted by human courage and honor. Many still hope to keep their honor and their safety, too. No one can blame them for this hope, it is impossible indeed not to share it: but when queried as to the soundness of such a hope, for a people caught in a civilization in crisis, history fails to give any very sanguine answers.

Eventually, Martin arrived, in a light blue suit, accompanied by Andrew Young, and they both looked very tired. We were very glad to see each other. We sat down in a relatively secluded corner and tried to bring each other up to date.

Alas, it would never be possible for us to bring each other up to date. We had first met during the last days of the Montgomery bus boycott—and how long ago was that? It was senseless to say, eight years, ten years ago—it was longer ago than time can reckon. Martin and I had never got to know each other well, circumstances, if not temperament, made that impossible, but

I had much respect and affection for him, and I think Martin liked me, too. I told him what I was doing in Hollywood, and both he and Andrew, looking perhaps a trifle dubious, wished me well. I don't remember whether it was on this evening that we arranged to appear together a few weeks later at Carnegie Hall, or if this had already been arranged. Presently, Marlon, very serious, and even being, as I remember, a little harsh with the assembled company—wanting to make certain that they understood the utter gravity of our situation, and the speed with which the time for peaceful change was running out— took the floor, and introduced Dr. Martin Luther King, Jr.

As our situation had become more complex, Martin's speeches had become simpler and more concrete. As I remember, he spoke very simply that evening on the work of the Southern Christian Leadership Conference, what had been done, what was being done, and the enormity of the tasks that lay ahead. But I remember his tone more than his words. He spoke very humbly, as one of many workers, speaking to his co-workers. I think he made everyone in that room feel that whatever they were doing, whatever they could do, was important, was of the utmost importance. He did not flatter them—very subtly, he challenged them, challenged them to live up to their moral obligations. The room was quite remarkable when he finished—still, thoughtful, grateful: perhaps, in the most serious sense of that weary phrase, profoundly honored.

And yet—how striking to compare his tone that night with what it had been not many years before! Not many years before, we had all marched on Washington. Something like two hundred and fifty thousand people had come to the nation's capital to petition their government for a redress of grievances. They had come from all over the nation, in every condition, in every conceivable attire, and in all kinds of vehicles. Even a skeptic like myself, with every reason to doubt that the petition would, or could, be heard, or acted on, could not fail to respond to the passion of so many people, gathered together, for that purpose, in that place. Their passion made one forget that a terrified Washington had bolted its doors and fled, that many politicians had been present only because they had been afraid not to be, that John Lewis, then of SNCC, had been forced to tone down his speech because of the insuperable arrogance of a Boston archbishop, that the administration had done everything in its power to prevent the March, even to finding out if I, who had nothing whatever to do with the March as organized, would use my influence to try to prevent it. (I said that such influence as I had, which wasn't much, would certainly not be used against the March, and, perhaps to prove this, I led the March on Washington from the American Church, in Paris, to the American Embassy, and brought back from Paris a scroll bearing about a thousand names. I wonder where it is now.)

In spite of all that one knew, and feared, it was a very stirring day, and one very nearly dared, in spite of all that one knew, to hope—to hope that the need and the passion of the people, so nakedly and vividly, and with such dignity revealed, would not be, once again, betrayed. (The People's Republic of China had sent a telegram in our support, which was repudiated by Roy Wilkins, who said, in effect, that we would be glad to accept such a telegram on the day that the Chinese were allowed to petition *their* government for redress of grievances, as we were petitioning ours. I had an uneasy feeling that we might live to hear this boast ring somewhat mockingly in our ears.)

But Martin had been quite moving that day. Marlon (carrying a cattle prod, for the purpose of revealing the depravity of the South) and Sidney Poitier and Harry Belafonte, Charlton Heston, and some others of us had been called away to do a Voice of America show for Ed Murrow, and so we watched and listened to Martin on television. All of us were very silent in that room, listening to Martin, feeling the passion of the people flowing up to him and transforming him, transforming us. Martin finished with one hand raised: "Free at last, free at last, praise God Almighty, I'm free at last!" That day, for a moment, it almost seemed that we stood on a height, and could see our inheritance; perhaps we could make the kingdom real, perhaps the beloved community would not forever remain that dream one dreamed in agony. The people quietly dispersed at nightfall, as had been agreed. Sidney Poitier took us out to dinner that night, in a very, very quiet Washington. The people had come to their capitol, had made themselves known, and were gone: no one could any longer doubt that their suffering was real. Ironically enough, after Washington, I eventually went on the road, on a lecture tour which carried me to Hollywood. So I was in Hollywood when, something like two weeks later, my phone rang, and a nearly hysterical, white, female CORE worker told me that a Sunday school in Birmingham had been bombed, and that four young black girls had been blown into eternity. That was the first answer we received to our petition.

The original plans for the March on Washington had been far from polite: the original plan had been to lie down on airport runways, to block the streets and offices, to immobilize the city completely, and to remain as long as we had to, to force the government to recognize the urgency and the justice of our demands. Malcolm was very caustic about the March on Washington, which he described as a sell-out. I think he was right. Martin, five years later, was five years wearier and five years sadder, and still petitioning. But the impetus was gone, because the people no longer believed in their petitions, no longer believed in their government. The reasoning behind the March on Washington, as it eventually evolved—or as it was, in Malcolm's words, "diluted"—was that peaceful assembly would produce the best results. But, five years later, it was very hard to believe that the frontal assault, as planned, on the capitol, could possibly have produced more bloodshed, or more despair. Five years later, it seemed clear that we had merely postponed, and not at all to our advantage, the hour of dreadful reckoning.

Martin and Andrew and I said good night to each other, and promised to meet in New York.

Siegel, the first lawyer I engaged for Tony, was a refugee from *Bleak House*, and I wish I'd met him in those pages and not in life. Spry, as I have said, white-haired, cunning, with a kind of old-fashioned, phony courtliness, he was eventually to make me think of vultures. He had been a criminal lawyer for a long time, practically since birth, and he had, I was told, a "good" reputation. But I was to discover that to have a "good" reputation as a criminal lawyer does not necessarily reflect any credit on said lawyer's competence or dedication; still less does it indicate that he has any interest in his clients: the term seems to refer almost exclusively to the lawyer's ability to wheel and deal and to his influence with other lawyers and judges, and district attorneys. A criminal lawyer's reputation—except, of course, for the one or two titans in the field—would appear to depend on his standing in this club. The fate of his client depends, to put it brutally, on the client's money: one may say, generally, that, if a poor man in trouble with the law receives justice, one can suppose heavenly intervention.

A poor man is always an isolated man, in the sense that his intimates are as ignorant and as helpless as he. Tony has been in prison since October 27, 1967, and remains in prison still. He had been brought to trial once in all that time; the trial resulted in a hung jury. A citizen more favorably placed than Tony would never have been treated in this way. It would appear, for example, that Tony's constitutional rights were violated at the very moment he was arrested because of the means used to identify him. This question has never been brought up, though Tony has insisted on it time and again. The police are very sensitive about being accused of violating a suspect's constitutional rights—they are, indeed, as sensitive to any and all criticism as aging beauty queens—and would never have arrested Tony in the way that they did if they had not been certain that his accusation could never be heard. Tony had almost nothing going for him, except his devoted sister, Valerie, and me. But neither Valerie nor I are equipped to deal with the world into which we found ourselves so suddenly plunged, and I found myself severely handicapped in this battle by being forced to fight it from three thousand miles away.

This meant that there was a vacuum where Tony's witness should have been. This would not have been so if the system worked differently, or if it were served by different people. But the system works as it works, and it attracts the people it attracts. The poor, the black, and the ignorant become the stepping stones of careers; for the people who make up this remarkable club are judged by their number of arrests and convictions. These matter far more than justice, if justice can be said to matter at all. It is clearly much easier to drag some ignorant wretch to court and burden him with whatever crimes one likes than it is to undergo the inconvenience and possible danger of finding out what actually happened, and who is actually guilty. In my experience, the defenders of the public peace do not care who is guilty. I have been arrested by the New York police, for example, and charged guilty before the judge, and had the charge entered in the record, without anyone asking me how I chose to plead, and without being allowed to speak. (I had the case thrown out of court, and if I'd had any means, I would have sued the city. The judge, when asked to explain his oversight, said that the court was crowded that day, and that the traffic noises, coming in from the streets, distracted him.)

In Tony Maynard's case, the question of justice is simply mocked when one considers that no attempt appears to have been made to discover the white assailant, and also by the fact that Tony has been asked to plead guilty and promised a light sentence if he would so plead. I know this to be a fact because, during Tony's trial, while the jury was out—and the jury was out much longer than anyone expected it to be—Galena, the D.A. who was prosecuting Tony, took me aside, in the presence of Tony's sister, Valerie, and the second lawyer I engaged for Tony, Selig Lenefsky, to ask me to use my influence to persuade Tony to accept the deal. He also told me that they would "get" him, anyway. Lenefsky and Galena are partners now, a perfectly normal development, which enhances the respectful trust and affection with which the poor regard their protectors.

But I anticipate. My absence from New York meant that there was virtually no pressure on Siegel, and Siegel, as far as I could discover, did nothing whatever. Most of his correspondence with me mentions money. I had paid him a retainer, and I wasn't trying to beat him out of his fee; but I was naturally reluctant, especially as time wore on, with no progress being made, to continue throwing good money after bad. This led, really, to a stalemate, and Valerie and I found ourselves thoroughly at a loss. I wanted to fire Siegel, but on what basis would I hire the next lawyer? No one I knew knew anything about criminal lawyers; the lawyers I knew dismissed them as a "scurvy breed." I thought of Melvin Belli, but he operates in California; I thought of Louis Nizer, and, in fact, tried to see him: but I knew I couldn't pay the fee for either of these lawyers. I thought of publicity, but it is not so easy to get publicity for a case which is, alas, so unremarkable. I didn't feel that my unsupported testimony would mean very much, and I couldn't get the groundswell going which might lead to a public hue and cry. I couldn't work at it full time because I was under contract in California and had to get back there. And, furthermore, I now had to finish that screenplay, if only to collect my fee: what price justice indeed!

Val and I would meet in Siegel's office, to learn that the trial had been postponed again, but that this might be all to the good because it meant that Judge So-and-So instead of Judge What-not would be sitting—at least, he would try to make certain that it was Judge What-not instead of Judge So-and-So. He, Siegel, was on friendly terms with Judge What-not, he'd call him later in the evening. And he would smile in a very satisfied way, as though to say, You see how I'm putting myself out for you, how much I take your interests to heart. No, his private investigators had failed to locate Dennis Morris. (Morris is the unknown who identified Tony by means of a photograph.) Morris had disappeared. No one seemed to know where he was. No, there was no word about the whereabouts of Michael Crist, either. All of this took time and money—and he would light a cigar, his bright blue eyes watching me expectantly.

Well, what in the world could we say to this terrifying old man? How could we know whether he had spoken to a single person, or made the remotest phone call on Tony's behalf? We could spend the rest of our lives in this office, while Tony was perishing in jail, and never know. He didn't care about Tony, but we hadn't expected him to—we had supposed that he cared about something else. What? his honor as a criminal lawyer? Probably—which proved what fools we were. His honor as a criminal lawyer was absolutely unassailable, he was a lifetime member of the club. We had no way whatever of lighting a fire under his ass and making him do what we were paying him to do. He didn't need us. There were thousands like us, yes, and black like us, who would keep him in cigars forever, turning over their nickels and dimes to get their loved ones out of trouble. And sometimes he would get them out—he had no objection to getting people out of trouble. But it was a lottery; it depended on whose number came up; and he certainly wasn't bucking the machine. Day after day after day, we would leave him and go to the Tombs, and I would see Tony: who was bearing up fantastically well; I'd not have believed he could be so tough. Seeing him, I felt guilty, frustrated, and helpless, felt time flowing through my hands like water. Val would be waiting for me when I came down, we might walk around a bit, and then I would leave her with the others, who were waiting for the six o'clock visit.

Whoever wishes to know who is in prison in this country has only to go to the prisons and watch who comes to visit. We spent hours and hours, days and days, eternities, down at the Tombs, Val and I, and, later, my brother, David. I suppose there must have been white visitors; it stands, so to speak, to reason, but they were certainly overwhelmed by the dark, dark mass. Black, and Puerto Rican matrons, black, and Puerto Rican girls, black, and Puerto Rican boys, black, and Puerto Rican men: such are the fish trapped in the net called justice. Bewilderment, despair, and poverty roll through the halls like a smell: the visitors have come, looking for a miracle. The miracle will be to find someone who really cares about the people in prison. But no one can afford to care. The prison is overcrowded, the calendars full, the judges busy, the lawyers ambitious, and the cops zealous. What does it matter if someone gets trapped here for a year or two, gets ruined here, goes mad here, commits murder or suicide here? It's too bad, but that's the way the cookie crumbles sometimes.

I do not claim that everyone in prison here is innocent, but I do claim that the law, as it operates, is guilty, and that the prisoners, therefore, are all unjustly imprisoned. Is it conceivable, after all, that any middle-class white boy—or, indeed, almost any white boy—would have been arrested on so grave a charge as murder, with such flimsy substantiation, and forced to spend, as of this writing, three years in prison? What force, precisely, is operating when a prisoner is advised, requested, ordered, intimidated, or forced, to confess to a crime he has not committed, and promised a lighter sentence for so perjuring and debasing himself? Does the law exist for the purpose of furthering the ambitions of those who have sworn to uphold the law, or is it seriously to be considered as a moral, unifying force, the health and strength of a nation? The trouble with these questions, of course, is that they sound rhetorical, and have the effect of irritating the reader, who does not wish to be told that the administration of justice in this country is a wicked farce. Well, if one really wishes to know how justice is administered in a country, one does not question the policemen, the lawyers, the judges, or the protected members of the middle class. One goes to the unprotected—those, precisely, who need the law's protection most!—and listens to their testimony. Ask any Mexican, any Puerto Rican, any black man, any poor person—ask the wretched how they fare in the halls of justice, and then you will know, not whether or not the country is just, but whether or not it has any love for justice, or any concept of it. It is certain, in any case, that ignorance, allied with power, is the most ferocious enemy justice can have.

I saw Martin in New York, and we did our Carnegie Hall gig. Everything I had was dirty, and I had to rush out and buy a dark suit for the occasion. After two or three murderously crowded days, I was on the plane again, flying West. Each time I left New York, I felt that I had heartlessly abandoned Valerie and Tony, and was always tempted to abandon the script instead, and see the battle in New York through. But I knew, of course, that I couldn't do that; in a way they were the same battle: yet, I couldn't help wondering if I were destined to lose them both.

There is a day in Palm Springs that I will remember forever, a bright day. I had moved there from the Beverly Hills Hotel, into a house the producer had found for me. Billy Dee Williams had come to town, and he was staying at the house; and a lot of the day had been spent with a very bright, young, lady reporter, who was interviewing me about the film version of Malcolm. I felt very confident that day—I was never to feel so confident again—and I talked very freely to the reporter. (Too freely, Marvin Worth, the producer, was to tell me later.) I had decided to lay my cards on the table and to state, as clearly as I could, what I felt the movie was about and how I intended to handle it. I thought that this might make things simpler later on, but I was wrong about that. The studio and I were at loggerheads, really, from the moment I stepped off the plane. Anyway, I had opted for candor, or a reasonable facsimile of same, and sounded as though I were in charge of the film, as, indeed, by my lights, for that moment, certainly, I had to be. I was really in a difficult position because, by both temperament and experience, I tend to work alone, and I dread making announcements concerning my work. But I was in a very public position, and I thought that I had better make my own announcements rather than have them made for me. The studio, on the other hand, did not want me making announcements of any kind at all. So there we were, and this particular tension, since it got to the bloody heart of the matter—the question of by whose vision, precisely, this film was to be controlled—was not to be resolved until I finally threw up my hands and walked away.

I very much wanted Billy Dee for Malcolm, and since no one else had any other ideas, I didn't see why this couldn't work out. In brutal Hollywood terms, Poitier is the only really big, black box-office star, and this fact, especially since Marvin had asked me to "keep an eye out" for an actor, gave me, as I considered it, a free hand. To tell the bitter truth, from the very first days we discussed it, I had never had any intention of allowing the Columbia brass to cast this part: I was determined to take my name off the production if I were overruled. Call this bone-headed stupidity, or insufferable arrogance, or what you will—I had made my decision, and once I had made it, nothing could make me waver, and nothing could make me alter it. If there were errors in my concept of the film, and if

I made errors in the execution, well, then, I would have to pay for my errors. But one can learn from one's errors. What one cannot survive is allowing other people to make your errors for you, discarding your own vision, in which, at least, you believe, for someone else's vision, in which you do *not* believe.

Anyway, all that shit had yet to hit the fan. This day, the girl, and Billy, and I had a few drinks by the swimming pool. Walter, my cook-chauffeur, was about to begin preparing supper. The girl got up to leave, and we walked her to her car, and came back to the swimming pool, jubilant.

The phone had been brought out to the pool, and now it rang. Billy was on the other side of the pool, doing what I took to be African improvisations to the sound of Aretha Franklin. And I picked up the phone.

It was David Moses. It took awhile before the sound of his voice—I don't mean the *sound* of his voice, something *in* his voice—got through to me.

He said, "Jimmy—? Martin's just been shot," and I don't think I said anything, or felt anything. I'm not sure I knew who *Martin* was. Yet, though I know—or I think—the record player was still playing, silence fell. David said, "He's not dead yet"—*then* I knew who Martin was—"but it's a head wound—so—"

I don't remember what I said; obviously, I must have said something. Billy and Walter were watching me. I told them what David had said.

I hardly remember the rest of that evening at all, it's retired into some deep cavern in my mind. We must have turned on the television set, if we had one, I don't remember. But we must have had one. I remember weeping, briefly, more in helpless rage than in sorrow, and Billy trying to comfort me. But I really don't remember that evening at all. Later, Walter told me that a car had prowled around the house all night.

The very last time I saw Medgar Evers, he stopped at his house on the way to the airport so I could autograph my books for him and his wife and children. I remember Myrilie Evers standing outside, smiling, and we waved, and Medgar drove to the airport and put me on the plane. He grinned that kind of country boy preacher's grin of his, and we said we'd see each other soon.

Months later, I was in Puerto Rico, working on the last act of my play. My host and hostess, and my friend, Lucien, and I, had spent a day or so wandering around the island, and now we were driving home. It was a wonderful, bright, sunny day, the top to the car was down, we were laughing and talking, and the radio was playing. Then the music stopped, and a voice announced that Medgar Evers had been shot to death in the carport of his home, and his wife and children had seen that big man fall.

No, I can't describe it. I've thought of it often, or been haunted by it often. I said something like, "That's a friend of mine—!" but no one in the car really knew who he was, or what he had meant to me, and to so many people. For some reason, I didn't see him: I saw Myrilie, and the children. They were quite small children. The blue sky seemed to descend like a blanket, and the speed of the car, the wind against my face, seemed stifling, as though the elements were determined to stuff something down my throat, to fill me with something I could never contain. And I couldn't say anything, I couldn't cry; I just remembered his face, a bright, blunt, handsome face, and his weariness, which he wore like his skin, and the way he said *ro-aad* for road, and his telling me how the tatters of clothes from a lynched body hung, flapping, in the tree for days, and how he had to pass that tree every day. Medgar. Gone.

I went to Atlanta alone, I do not remember why. I wore the suit I had bought for my Carnegie Hall appearance with Martin. I seem to have had the foresight to have reserved a hotel room, for I vaguely remember stopping in the hotel and talking to two or three preacher type looking men, and we started off in the direction of the church. We had not got far before it became very clear that we would never get anywhere near it. We went in this direction and then in that direction, but the press of people choked us off. I began to wish that I had not come incognito, and alone, for now that I was in Atlanta, I wanted to get inside the church. I lost my companions and sort of squeezed my way, inch by inch, closer to the church. But, directly between me and the church, there was an impassable wall of people. Squeezing my way up to this point, I had considered myself lucky to be small; but now my size worked against me, for, though there were people on the church steps who knew me, whom I knew, they could not possibly see me, and I could not shout. I squeezed a few more inches and asked a very big man ahead of me please to let me through. He moved, and said, "Yeah, let me see you get through this big Cadillac." It was true—there it was, smack in front of me, big as a house. I saw Jim Brown at a distance, but he didn't see me. I leaned up on the car, making frantic signals, and, finally, someone on the church steps did see me and came to the car and sort of lifted me over. I talked to Jim Brown for a minute, and then somebody led me into the church and I sat down.

The church was packed, of course, incredibly so. Far in the front, I saw Harry Belafonte sitting next to Coretta King. I had interviewed Coretta years ago, when I was doing a profile on her husband. We had got on very well; she had a nice, free laugh. Ralph David Abernathy sat in the pulpit. I remembered him from years ago, sitting in his shirtsleeves in the house in Montgomery, big, black, and cheerful, pouring some cool soft drink, and, later, getting me settled in a nearby hotel. In the pew directly before me sat Marlon Brando, Sammy Davis, Eartha Kitt—covered in black, looking like a lost ten-year-old girl—and Sidney Poitier, in the same pew, or nearby. Marlon saw me and nodded. The atmosphere was black, with a tension indescribable—as though something, perhaps the heavens, perhaps the earth, might crack. Everyone sat very still.

The actual service sort of washed over me, in waves. It wasn't that it seemed unreal; it was the most real church service I've ever sat through in my life, or ever hope to sit through; but I have a childhood hangover thing about not weeping in public, and I was concentrating on holding myself together. I did not want to weep for Martin; tears seemed futile. But I may also have been afraid, and I could not have been the only one, that if I began to weep, I would not be able to stop. There was more than enough to weep for, if one was to weep—so many of us, cut down, so soon. Medgar, Malcolm, Martin: and their widows, and their children. Reverend Ralph David Abernathy asked a certain sister to sing a song which Martin had loved—"once more," said Ralph David, "for Martin and for me," and he sat down.

The long, dark sister, whose name I do not remember, rose, very beautiful in her robes, and in her covered grief, and began to sing. It was a song I knew: "My Heavenly Father Watches Over Me." The song rang out as it might have over dark fields, long ago; she was singing of a covenant a people had made, long ago, with life, and with that larger life which ends in revelation and which moves in love.

> *He guides the eagle through the pathless air.*

She stood there, and she sang it. How she bore it, I do not know; I think I have never seen a face quite like that face that afternoon. She was singing it for Martin, and for us.

> *And surely, He*
> *Remembers me.*
> *My heavenly Father watches over me.*

At last, we were standing, and filing out, to walk behind Martin, home. I found myself between Marlon and Sammy.

I had not been aware of the people when I had been pressing past them to get to the church. But, now, as we came out, and I looked up the road, I saw them. They were all along the road, on either side, they were on all the roofs, on either side. Every inch of ground, as far as the eye could see, was black with black people, and they stood in silence. It was the silence that undid me. I started to cry, and I stumbled, and Sammy grabbed my arm. We started to walk.

A week or so later, Billy and I were having a few drinks in some place like The Factory, I think, and one of the young Hollywood producers came over to the table to insist that the

Martin Luther King story should be done at once, and that I should write it. I said that I couldn't, because I was tied up with Malcolm. (I also thought that it was a terrible idea, but I didn't bother to say so.)

Well, if I couldn't, what black writer could? He asked me to give him some names, and I did. But he shook his head, finally, and said, No, I was the only one who could do it.

I was still not reacting very quickly. But Billy got mad.

"You don't really mean any of that crap," he said, "about Jimmy being the greatest, and all that. That's bullshit. You mean that Jimmy's a commercial name, and if you get that name on a marquee linked with Martin Luther King's name, you'll make yourself some bread. That's what *you* mean."

Billy spoke the truth, but it's hard to shame the devil.

In February, the Panthers in Oakland gave a birthday party for the incarcerated Huey Newton. They asked me to "host" this party, and so I flew to Oakland. The birthday party was, of course, a rally to raise money for Huey's defense, and it was a way of letting the world know that the sorely beleaguered Panthers had no intention of throwing in the towel. It was also a way of letting the world—and Huey—know how much they loved and honored the very young man who, along with Bobby Seale, had organized The Black Panther Party for Self Defense, in the spring of 1966. That was the original name of the Party, and the name states very succinctly the need which brought the Party into existence.

It is a need which no black citizen of the ghetto has to have spelled out. When, as white cops are fond of pointing out to me, ghetto citizens "ask for more cops, not less," what they are asking for is more police protection: for crimes committed by blacks against blacks have never been taken very seriously. Furthermore, the prevention of crimes such as these is not the reason for the policeman's presence. That black people need protection *against* the police is indicated by the black community's reaction to the advent of the Panthers. Without community support, the Panthers would have been merely another insignificant street gang. It was the reaction of the black community which triggered the response of the police: these young men, claiming the right to bear arms, dressed deliberately in guerrilla fashion, standing nearby whenever a black man was accosted by a policeman to inform the black man of his rights and insisting on the right of black people to self defense, were immediately marked as "trouble-makers."

But white people seem affronted by the black distrust of white policemen, and appear to be astonished that a black man, woman, or child can have any reason to fear a white cop. One of the jurors challenged by Charles Garry during the *voir dire* proceedings before Huey's trial had this to say:

"As I said before, that I feel, and it is my opinion that racism, bigotry, and segregation is something that we have to wipe out of our hearts and minds, and not on the street. I have had an opinion that—and been taught never to resist a police officer, that we have courts of law in which to settle—no matter how much I thought I was in the right, the police officer would order me to do something, I would do it expecting if I thought I was right in what I was doing, that I could get justice in the courts"—And, in response to Garry's question, "Assuming the police officer pulled a gun and shot you, what would you do about it?" the prospective juror, at length, replied, "Let me say this. I do not believe a police officer will do that."

This is a fairly vivid and accurate example of the American piety at work. The beginning of the statement is revealing indeed: "—racism, bigotry, and segregation is something that we have to wipe out of our hearts and minds, and not on the street." One can wonder to whom the "we" here refers, but there isn't any question as to the object of the tense, veiled accusation contained in "not on the street." Whoever the "we" is, it is probably not the speaker—to leave it at that: but the anarchy and danger "*on the street*" are the fault of the blacks. Unnecessarily: for the police are honorable, and the courts are just.

It is no accident that Americans cling to this dream. It involves American self-love on some deep, disastrously adolescent level. And Americans are very carefully and deliberately conditioned to believe this fantasy: by their politicians, by the news they get and the way they read it, by the movies, and the television screen, and by every aspect of the popular culture. If I learned nothing else in Hollywood, I learned how abjectly the purveyors of the popular culture are manipulated. The brainwashing is so thorough that blunt, brutal reality stands not a chance against it; the revelation of corruption in high places, as in the recent "scandals" in New Jersey, for example, has no effect whatever on the American complacency; nor have any of our recent assassinations had any more effect than to cause Americans to arm—thus proving their faith in the law!—and double-lock their doors. No doubt, behind these locked doors, with their weapons handy, they switch on the tube and watch *The F.B.I.*, or some similarly reassuring fable. It means nothing, therefore, to say to so thoroughly insulated a people that the forces of crime and the forces of law and order work hand in hand in the ghetto, bleeding it day and night. It means nothing to say that, in the eyes of the black and the poor certainly, the principal distinction between a policeman and a criminal is to be found in their attire. A criminal can break into one's house without warning, at will, and harass or molest everyone in the house, and even commit murder, and so can a cop, and they do; whoever operates whatever hustle in the ghetto without paying off the cops does not stay in business long; and it will be remembered—Malcolm certainly remembered it—that the dope trade flourished in the ghetto for years without ever being seriously molested. Not until white boys and girls began to be hooked—not until the plague in the ghetto spread outward, as plagues do—was there any public uproar. As long as it was only the niggers who were killing themselves and paying white folks handsomely for the privilege, the forces of law and order were silent. The very structure of the ghetto is a nearly irresistible temptation to criminal activity of one kind or another: it is a very rare man who does not victimize the helpless. There is no pressure on the landlord to be responsible for the upkeep of his property: the only pressure on him is to collect his rent; that is, to bleed the ghetto. There is no pressure on the butcher to be honest: if he can sell bad meat at a profit, why should he not do so? buying cheap and selling dear is what made this country great. If the storekeeper can sell, on the installment plan, a worthless "bedroom suite" for six or seven times its value, what is there to prevent him from doing so, and who will ever hear, or credit, his customer's complaint? in the unlikely event that the customer has any notion of where to go to complain. And the ghetto is a goldmine for the insurance companies. A dime a week, for five or ten or twenty years, is a lot of money, but rare indeed is the funeral paid for by the insurance. I myself do not know of any. Some member of my family had been carrying insurance at a dime a week for years and we finally persuaded her to drop it and cash in the policy—which was now worth a little over two hundred dollars. And let me state candidly, and I know, in this instance, that I do not speak only for myself, that every time I hear the black people of this country referred to as "shiftless" and "lazy," every time it is implied that the blacks deserve their condition here (look at the Irish! look at the Poles! Yes. Look at them.) I think of all the pain and sweat with which these greasy dimes were earned, with what trust they were given, in order to make the difficult passage somewhat easier for the living, in order to show honor to the dead, and I then have no compassion whatever for this country, or my countrymen.

Into this maelstrom, this present elaboration of the slave quarters, this rehearsal for a concentration camp, we place, armed, not for the protection of the ghetto but for the protection of American investments there, some blank American boy who is responsible only to some equally blank elder patriot—Andy Hardy and his pious father. Richard Harris, in his New Yorker article, *The Turning Point*, observes that "Back in 1969, a survey of three hundred police departments around the country had revealed that less than one percent required any college training. Three years later, a pilot study ordered by the President showed that most criminals were mentally below average, which suggested that that policemen who failed to stop or find them might not be much above it."

The white cop in the ghetto is as ignorant as he is frightened, and his entire concept of police work is to cow the natives. He is not compelled to answer to these natives for anything he does; whatever he does, he knows that he will be protected by his brothers, who will allow nothing to stain the honor of the force. When his working day is over, he goes home and sleeps soundly in a bed miles away—miles away from the niggers, for that is the way he really thinks of black people. And he is assured of the rightness of his course and the justice of his bigotry every time Nixon, or Agnew, or Mitchell—or the Governor of the State of California—open their mouths.

Watching the Northern reaction to the Black Panthers, observing the abject cowardice with which the Northern populations allow them to be menaced, jailed, and murdered, and all this with but the faintest pretense to legality, can fill one with great contempt for that emancipated North which, but only yesterday, was so full of admiration and sympathy for the heroic blacks in the South. Luckily, many of us were skeptical of the righteous Northern sympathy then, and so we are not overwhelmed or disappointed now. Luckily, many of us have always known, as one of my brothers put it to me something like twenty-four years ago, that "the spirit of the South is the spirit of America." Now, exactly like the Germans at the time of the Third Reich, though innocent men are being harassed, jailed, and murdered, in all the Northern cities, the citizens know nothing, and wish to know nothing, of what is happening around them. Yet the advent of the Panthers was as inevitable as the arrival of that day in Montgomery, Alabama, when Mrs. Rosa Parks refused to stand up on that bus and give her seat to a white man. That day had been coming for a very long time; danger upon danger, and humiliation upon humiliation, had piled intolerably high and gave Mrs. Parks her platform. If Mrs. Parks had merely had a headache that day, and if the community had had no grievances, there would have been no bus boycott and we would never have heard of Martin Luther King.

Just so with the Panthers: it was inevitable that the fury would erupt, that a black man, openly, in the sight of all his fellows, should challenge the policeman's gun, and not only that, but the policeman's right to be in the ghetto at all, and that man happened to be Huey. It is not conceivable that the challenge thus thrown down by this rather stubby, scrubbed-looking, gingerbread-colored youth could have had such repercussions if he had not been articulating the rage and repudiating the humiliation of thousands, more, millions of men.

Huey, on that day, the day which prompted Bobby Seale to describe Huey as "the baddest motherfucker in history," restored to the men and women of the ghetto their honor. And, for this reason, the Panthers, far from being an illegal or a lawless organization, are a great force for peace and stability in the ghetto. But, as this suggests an unprecedented measure of autonomy for the ghetto citizens, no one in authority is prepared to face this overwhelmingly obvious fact. White America remains unable to believe that black America's grievances are real; they are unable to believe this because they cannot face what this fact says about themselves and their country; and the effect of this massive and hostile incomprehension is to increase the danger in which all black people live here, especially the young. No one is more aware of this than the Black Panther leadership. This is why they are so anxious to create work and study programs in the ghetto—everything from hot lunches for school children to academic courses in high schools and colleges to the content, format, and distribution of the Black Panther newspapers. All of these are antidotes to the demoralization which is the scourge of the ghetto, are techniques of self-realization. This is also why they are taught to bear arms—not, like most white Americans, because they fear their neighbors, though indeed they have the most to fear, but in order, this time, to protect *their* lives, *their* women and children, *their* homes, rather than the life and property of an Uncle Sam who has rarely been able to treat his black nephews with more than a vaguely benign contempt. For the necessity, now, which I think nearly all black people see in different ways, is the creation and protection of a nucleus which will bring into existence a new people.

The Black Panthers made themselves visible—made themselves targets, if you like—in order to hip the black community to the presence of a new force in its midst, a force working toward the health and liberation of the community. It was a force which set itself in opposition to that force which uses people as things and which grinds down men and women and children, not only in the ghetto, into an unrecognizable powder. They announced themselves especially as a force for the rehabilitation of the young—the young who were simply perishing, in and out of schools, on the needle, in the Army, or in prison. The black community recognized this energy almost at once and flowed toward it and supported it; a people's most valuable asset is the well-being of their young. Nothing more thoroughly reveals the actual intentions of this country, domestically and globally, than the ferocity of the repression, the storm of fire and blood which the Panthers have been forced to undergo merely for declaring themselves as men—men who want "land, bread, housing, education, clothing, justice, and peace." The Panthers thus became the native Vietcong, the ghetto became the village in which the Vietcong were hidden, and in the ensuing search-and-destroy operations, everyone in the village became suspect.

Under such circumstances, the creation of a new people may seem as unlikely as fashioning the proverbial bricks without straw. On the other hand, though no one appears to learn very much from history, the rulers of empires assuredly learn the least. This unhappy failing will prove to be especially aggravated in the case of the American rulers, who have never heard of history and who have never read it, who do not know what the passion of a people can withstand or what it can accomplish, or how fatal is the moment, for the kingdom, when the passion is driven underground. They do not, for that matter, yet realize that they have already been forced to do two deadly things. They have been forced to reveal their motives, themselves, in all their unattractive nakedness; hence the reaction of the blacks, on every level, to the "Nixon Administration," which is of a stunning, unprecedented unanimity. The administration, increasingly, can rule only by fear: the fears of the people who elected them, and the fear that the administration can inspire. In spite of the tear gas, mace, clubs, helicopters, bugged installations, spies, *provocateurs*, tanks, machine guns, prisons, and detention centers, this is a shaky foundation. And they have helped to create a new pantheon of black heroes. Black babies will be born with new names hereafter and will have a standard to which to aspire new in this country, new in the world. The great question is what this will cost. The great effort is to minimize the damage. While I was on the Coast, Eldridge Cleaver and Bobby Seale and David Hilliard were still free, Fred Hampton and Mark Clark were still alive. Now, every day brings a new setback, frequently a bloody one. The government is absolutely determined to wipe the Black Panthers from the face of the earth: which is but another way of saying that it is absolutely determined to keep the nigger in his place. But this merciless and bloody repression, which is carried out, furthermore, with a remarkable contempt for the sensibilities and intelligence of the black people of this nation—for who can believe the police reports?—causes almost all blacks to realize that neither the government, the police, nor the populace are able to distinguish between a Black Panther, a black school child, or a black lawyer. And this reign of terror is creating a great problem in prisons all over this country. "Now, look," said a harassed prison official to Bobby Seale, "you got a lot of notoriety. We don't want no organizing here, or nothing else. We ain't got no Panthers, we ain't got no Rangers, we ain't got no Muslims. All we got is in-mates." All he's got is trouble. All he's got is black people who know why they're in prison, and not all of them can be kept in solitary. These blacks have unforgiving relatives, to say nothing of unforgiving children, at every level of American life. The government cannot afford to trust a single black man in this country, nor can they penetrate any black's disguise, or apprehend how devious and tenacious black patience can be, and any black man that they appear to trust is useless to them, for he will never be trusted by the blacks. It is true that our weapons do not appear to be very formidable, but, then, they never have. Then, as now, our greatest weapon is silence. As black poet Robert E. Hayden puts it in his poem to Harriet Tubman, "Runagate, Runagate": *Mean mean mean to be free.*

*

I first met Huey in San Francisco, shortly before his fateful encounter with Officers Frey and Heanes. This encounter took place at 5 A.M., in Oakland, on October 28, 1967—on the same day, oddly enough, that Tony Maynard, halfway across the world, was also being arrested for murder.

I had been in San Francisco with my sister, Gloria, I to hide out in a friend's house, working, and she to look after me, and also, poor girl, to rest. It had been a hard, embattled year and we were simply holding our breath, waiting for it to end. We hoped, with that apprehension refugees must feel when they are approaching a border, that the passage would be unnoticeable and that no further disasters would whiten the bleaching year.

A very old friend of mine, a black lady—old in the sense of friendship, indeterminate as to age—made a big West Indian dinner for us in her apartment, and it was also on this evening that I first met Eldridge Cleaver. I'd heard a lot about Cleaver, but all that I knew of Huey Newton was that poster of him in that elaborate chair, as the Black Panthers' Minister of Defense. I talked to him very little that evening. He and Gloria talked, and, as I remember, they scarcely talked to anyone else. I was very impressed by Huey—by his youth, his intelligence, and by a kind of vivid anxiety of hope in him which made his face keep changing as lights failed or flared within. Gloria was impressed by his manners. She had expected, I know, an intolerant, rabble-rousing type who might address her, sneeringly, as "sister," and put her down for not wearing a natural, and give her an interminable, intolerable, and intolerant lecture on the meaning of "black." "I am *tired*," Gloria sometimes said, "of these middle-class, college-educated *darkies* who never saw a rat or a roach in their lives and who never starved or worked a day—who just turned black last *week*—coming and telling *me* what it means to be black." Huey wasn't and isn't like that at all. Huey talks a lot—he has a lot to talk about—but Huey listens.

Anyway, the two of them got on famously. Before we parted, Huey gave me several Black Panther newspapers (the beginning of *my* file on the Panthers, Mr. Mitchell) and he and Eldridge and I promised to keep in touch, and to see each other soon.

I was very much impressed by Eldridge, too—it's impossible

not to be impressed by him—but I felt a certain constraint between us. I felt that he didn't like me—or not exactly that: that he considered me a rather doubtful quantity. I'm used to this, though I can't claim to like it. I knew he'd written about me in *Soul on Ice*, but I hadn't yet read it. Naturally, when I did read it, I didn't like what he had to say about me at all. But, eventually—especially as I admired the book, and felt him to be valuable and rare—I thought I could see why he felt impelled to issue what was, in fact, a warning: he was being a zealous watchman on the city wall, and I do not say that with a sneer. He seemed to feel that I was a dangerously odd, badly twisted, and fragile reed, of too much use to the Establishment to be trusted by blacks. I felt that he used my public reputation against me both naïvely and unjustly, and I also felt that I was confused in his mind with the unutterable debasement of the male—with all those faggots, punks, and sissies, the sight and sound of whom, in prison, must have made him vomit more than once. Well, I certainly hope I know more about myself, and the intention of my work than that, but I *am* an odd quantity. So is Eldridge; so are we all. It is a pity that we won't, probably, ever have the time to attempt to define once more the relationship of the odd and disreputable artist to the odd and disreputable revolutionary; for the revolutionary, however odd, is rarely disreputable in the same way that an artist can be. These two seem doomed to stand forever at an odd and rather uncomfortable angle to each other, and they both stand at a sharp and not always comfortable angle to the people they both, in their different fashions, hope to serve. But I think that it is just as well to remember that the people are one mystery and that the person is another. Though I know what a very bitter and delicate and dangerous conundrum this is, it yet seems to me that a failure to respect the person so dangerously limits one's perception of the people that one risks betraying them and oneself, either by sinking to the apathy of cynical disappointment, or rising to the rage of knowing, better than the people do, what the people want. Ultimately, the artist and the revolutionary function as they function, and pay whatever dues they must pay behind it because they are both possessed by a vision, and they do not so much follow this vision as find themselves driven by it. Otherwise, they could never endure, much less embrace, the lives they are compelled to lead. And I think we need each other, and have much to learn from each other, and, more than ever, now.

Huey and I were supposed to meet again one afternoon, but something happened and Huey couldn't make it. Shortly thereafter Gloria and I returned to New York; eventually we received a phone call from a friend, telling us what had happened to Huey. Gloria's reaction was, first—"That nice boy!" and then a sombre, dry, bitter, "At least he isn't dead."

Many months later, I went to see him, with Charles Garry, his lawyer, and some other journalists, in the Alameda County Courthouse. I remember it as being a hot day; the little room in which we sat was very crowded. Huey looked somewhat thinner and paler than when we had first met, but he was very good-natured and lucid.

Huey is a hard man to describe. People surrounded by legend rarely look the parts they've been assigned, but, in Huey's case, the Great Casting Director decided to blow everybody's mind. Huey looks like the cleanest, most scrubbed, most well-bred of adolescents—everybody's favorite baby-sitter. He is old-fashioned in the most remarkable sense, in that he treats everyone with respect, especially his elders. One can see him—almost—a few years hence working quietly for a law firm, say, able but not distinguished, with a pretty wife and a couple of sturdy children, smoking a pipe, living peacefully in a more or less integrated suburb. I say "almost" because the moment one tries to place him in any ordinary, respectable setting something goes wrong with the picture, leaving a space where one had thought to place Huey. There is in him a dedication as gentle as it is unyielding, absolutely single-minded. I began to realize this when I realized that Huey was always listening and always watching. No doubt he can be fooled, he's human, though he certainly can't be fooled easily; but it would be a very great mistake to try to lie to him. Those eyes take in everything, and behind the juvenile smile, he keeps a complicated scoreboard. It has to be complicated. That day, for example, he was dealing with the press, with photographers, with his lawyer, with me, with prison regulations, with his notoriety in the prison, with the latest pronouncements of Police Chief Gain, with the shape of the terror speedily engulfing his friends and co-workers, and he was also, after all, at that moment, standing in the shadow of the gas chamber.

Anyone, under such circumstances, can be pardoned for being rattled or even rude, but Huey was beautiful, and spoke with perfect candor of what was on his mind. Huey believes, and I do, too, in the necessity of establishing a form of socialism in this country—what Bobby Seale would probably call a "Yankee-Doodle type" socialism. This means an indigenous socialism, formed by, and responding to, the real needs of the American people. This is not a doctrinaire position, no matter how the Panthers may seem to glorify Mao or Che or Fanon. (It may perhaps be noted that these men have something to say to the century, after all, and may be read with profit, and are not, as public opinion would seem to have it, merely more subtle, or more dangerous, heroin peddlers.) The necessity for a form of socialism is based on the observation that the world's present economic arrangements doom most of the world to misery; that the way of life dictated by these arrangements is both sterile and immoral; and, finally, that there is no hope for peace in the world so long as these arrangements obtain.

But not only does the world make its arrangements slowly, and submit to any change only with the greatest reluctance; the idea of a genuine socialism in America, of all places, is an utterly intolerable idea, and those in power, as well as the bulk of the people, will resist so tremendous a heresy with all the force at their command; for which reason, precisely, Huey sits in prison and the blacks of the nation walk in danger. Watching Huey, I wondered what force sustained him, and lent him his bright dignity—then I suddenly did not wonder. The very fact that the odds are so great, and the journey, barely begun, so dangerous means that there is no time to waste, and it invests every action with an impersonal urgency. It may, for example, seem nothing to feed hot lunches to children at school, but it must be done, for the sake of the health and morale of the child, for the sake of the health and morale of his elders. It may seem nothing to establish a Liberation school, or to insist that all adult Panther members take Political Education classes, but that school, and those classes, can be very potent antidotes to the tranquilizers this country hands out as morality, truth, and history. A needle, or a piece of bread are nothing, but it is very important that all Panther members are forbidden to steal or take even that much from the people: and it changes a person when he conceives of himself, in Huey's words, as "an ox to be ridden by the people." To study the economic structure of this country, to know which hands control the wealth, and to which end, seems an academic exercise—and yet it is necessary, all of it is necessary, for discipline, for knowledge, and for power. Since the blacks are so seriously outnumbered, it is possible to dismiss these passionate exercises as mere acts of faith, preposterous to everyone but the believer: but no one in power appears to find the Panthers even remotely preposterous. On the contrary, they have poured out on these black, defenseless, outnumbered heads a storm of retribution so unspeakably vindictive as to have attracted the wondering and skeptical notice of the world—which does not accept the American version of reality as gospel; and they apparently consider the Panthers so dangerous that nations—or, rather, governments—friendly to the United States have refused to allow individual Panthers to land on their shores, much to the displeasure of their already restive and distinctly crucial student populations. This is to sum up the effect of the Panthers negatively, but this effect reveals volumes about America, and our role in the world. Those who rule in this country now—as distinguished, it must be said, from governing it—are determined to smash the Panthers in order to hide the truth of the American black situation. They want to hide this truth from black people—by making it impossible for them to respond to it—and they would like to hide it from the world; and not, alas, because they are ashamed of it but because they have no intention of changing it. They cannot afford to change it. They would not know how to go about changing it, even if their imaginations were capable of encompassing the concept of black freedom.

But this concept lives in their imaginations, and in the popular imagination, only as a nightmare. Blacks have never been free in this country, never was it intended that they should be free, and the spectre of so dreadful a freedom—the idea of a license so bloody and abandoned—conjures up another, unimaginable country, a country in which no decent, God-fearing white man or woman can live. A civilized country is, by definition, a country dominated by whites, in which the blacks clearly know their place. This is really the way the generality of white Americans feel, and they consider—quite rightly, as far as any concern for their interest goes—that it is they who, now, at long last, are being represented in Washington. And, of course, any real commitment to black freedom in this country would have the effect of reordering all our priorities, and altering all our commitments, so that, for horrendous example, we would be supporting black freedom fighters in South Africa and Angola, and would not be allied with Portugal, would be closer to Cuba than we are to Spain, would be supporting the Arab nations instead of Israel, and would never have felt compelled to follow the French into Southeast Asia. But such a course would forever wipe the smile from the face of that friend we all rejoice to have at Chase Manhattan. The course we *are* following is bound to have the same effect, and with dreadful repercussions, but to hint such things now is very close to treason. In spite of our grim situation, and even facing the possibility that the Panthers may be smashed and driven underground, they—that is, the black people here—yet have more going for them than did those outnumbered Christians, running through the catacombs: and digging the grave, as Malcolm put it, of the mighty Roman empire.

In this place, and more particularly, in this time, generations appear to flower, flourish, and wither with the speed of light. I don't think that this is merely the inevitable reflection of middle age: I suspect that there really has been some radical alteration in the structure, the nature, of time. One may say that there are no clear images; everything seems superimposed on, and at war with something else. There are no clear vistas: the road that seems to pull one forward into the future is also pulling one backward into the past. I felt, anyway, kaleidoscopic, fragmented, walking through the streets of San Francisco, trying to decipher whatever it was that my own consciousness made of all the elements in which I was entangled, and which were all tangled up in me. In spite of the fact that my reasons for being in San Francisco were rather chilling, there were compensations. Looking into Huey's face, even though he was in jail, had been a kind of compensation—at least I knew that he was holding on. Talking to Charles Garry, because he is intelligent, honest, and vivid, and devoted to Huey, had been a compensation, and meeting Huey's brother, Melvin, and simply walking through the streets of San Francisco, by far my favorite town—my favorite American town.

I had first been in San Francisco at the height of the civil rights movement, first on an *Esquire* junket, then on a lecture tour. There had been no flower children here then, only earnest, eager students anxious to know what they could "do." Would black people take it amiss if the white kids came into the neighborhood, and—fraternized is probably the only word—with the kids in the pool halls, the bars, the soda fountains? Would black people take it amiss if some of them were to visit a black church? Could they invite members of the black congregation to their white churches, or would the black people feel uncomfortable? Wouldn't it be a good idea if the black and white basketball teams played each other? And there wouldn't be any trouble about the dance afterward, because all the fellows would invite their own dates. Did I think they should go south to work on voting registration this summer, or should they stay home and work in their own communities? Some of them wanted to get a discussion started on open housing—on Proposition Fourteen—and would I come and speak and answer questions? What do you do about older people who are *very nice, really*, but who just—well, who just don't seem to understand the issues—what do you say to them, what do you do? And the black kids: It's another way of life—you have to understand that. *Yeah*, a whole lot of black people are going to put you down, you have to understand *that*. Man, I know my mother don't really want to come to your church. We got more life in *our* church. Mr. B., Brother Malcolm says that no people in history have ever been respected who did not own their own land. What do you say about that, and how are we going to *get* the land? My parents think I shouldn't be sitting in and demonstrating and all that, that I should be getting an education first. What do you think about that? Mr. B., what do you say to an older black man who just feels discouraged about everything? Mr. B., what are we going to do about the dope traffic in the ghetto? Mr. B., do you think black people should join the Army? Mr. B., do you think the Muslims are right and we should be a separate state? Mr. B., have you ever been to Africa? Mr. B., don't you think the first thing our people need is unity? How can we trust those white people in Washington? they don't really care about black people. Mr. B., what do you think of integration? Don't you think it might just be a trap, to brainwash black people? I come to the conclusion that the man just ain't never going to do right. He a devil, just like Malcolm says he is. I told my teacher I wasn't going to salute the flag no more—don't you think I was right? You mean, if we have a dance after the basketball game, all the brothers is going to have to dance with the *same girl* all night? What about the white guys? Oh, they can dance with *your* girl. Laughter, embarrassment, bewildered ill-feeling. Mr. B., What do *you* think of intermarriage?

Real questions can be absurdly phrased, and probably can be answered only by the questioner, and, at that, only in time. But real questions, especially from the young, are very moving and I will always remember the faces of some of those children. Though the questions facing them were difficult, they appeared, for the most part, to like the challenge. It is true that the white students seemed to look on the black students with some apprehension and some bewilderment, and they also revealed how deeply corrupted they were by the doctrine of white supremacy in many unconscious ways. But the black students, though they were capable of an elaborate, deliberate, and overpowering condescension, seemed, for the most part, to have their tongue in their cheek and exhibited very little malice or venom—toward the students: they felt toward their white elders a passionate contempt.

What seemed most to distress the white students—distress may be too strong a word; what rendered them thoughtful and uneasy—was the unpromising nature of their options. It was not that they had compared their options with those of the black student and been upset by the obvious, worldly injustice. On the contrary, they seemed to feel, some dimly and some desperately, that the roles which they, as whites, were expected to play were not very meaningful, and perhaps—therefore—not very honorable. I remember one boy who was already set to become an executive at one of the major airlines—for him, he joked, bleakly, the sky would be the limit. But he wondered if he could "hold on" to himself, if he could retain the respect of some of the people who respected him now. What he meant was that he hoped not to be programmed out of all meaningful human existence, and, clearly, he feared the worst. He, like many students, was being forced to choose between treason and irrelevance. Their moral obligations to the darker brother, if they were real, and if they were really to be acted on, placed them in conflict with all that they had loved and all that had given them an identity, rendered their present uncertain and their future still more so, and even jeopardized their means of staying alive. They were far from judging or repudiating the American state as oppressive or immoral—they were merely profoundly uneasy. They were aware that the blacks looked on the white commitment very skeptically indeed, and they made it clear that they did not depend on the whites. They could not depend on the whites until the whites had a clearer sense of what they had let themselves in for. And what the white students had not expected to let themselves in for, when boarding the Freedom Train, was the realization that the black situation in America was but one aspect of the fraudulent nature of American life. They had not expected to be forced to judge their parents, their elders, and their antecedents, so harshly, and they had not realized how cheaply, after all, the rulers of the republic held their white lives to be. Coming to the defense of the rejected and destitute, they were confronted with the extent of their own alienation, and the unimaginable dimensions of their own poverty. They were privileged and secure only so long as they did, in effect, what they were told: but they had been raised to believe that they were free.

I next came to San Francisco at the time of the flower children, when everyone, young and not so young, was freaking out on whatever came to hand. The flower children were all up and down the Haight-Ashbury section of San Francisco—and they might have been everywhere else, too, but for the vigilance of the cops—with their long hair, their beads, their robes, their fancied resistance, and, in spite of a shrewd, hard skepticism as unnerving as it was unanswerable, really tormented by the hope of love. The fact that their uniforms and their jargon precisely represented the distances they had yet to cover before arriving at that maturity which makes love possible—or no longer possible—could not be considered their fault. They had been born into a society in which nothing was harder to achieve, in which perhaps nothing was more scorned and feared than the idea of the soul's maturity. Their flowers had the validity, at least, of existing in direct challenge to the romance of the gun; their gentleness, however specious, was nevertheless a direct repudiation of the American adoration of violence. Yet they looked—alas—doomed. They seemed to sense their doom. They really were flower children, having opted out on the promises and possibilities offered them by the shining and now visibly perishing republic. I could not help feeling, watching them, knowing them to be idealistic, fragmented, and impotent, that, exactly as the Third Reich had had first to conquer the German opposition before getting around to the Jews, and then the rest of Europe, my republic, which, unhappily, I was beginning to think of as the Fourth Reich, would be forced to plow under the flower children—in all their variations—before getting around to the blacks and then the rest of the world.

The blacks, for the most part, were not to be found with the flower children. In the eerie American way, they walked the same streets, were to be found in the same neighborhoods, were the targets of the very same forces, seemed to bear each other no ill will—on the contrary indeed, especially from the point of view of the forces watching them—and yet they seemed to have no effect on each other, and they certainly were not together. The blacks were not putting their trust in flowers. They were putting their trust in guns.

An historical wheel had come full circle. The descendants of the cowboys, who had slaughtered the Indians, the issue of those adventurers who had enslaved the blacks, wished to lay down their swords and shields. But these could be laid down only at Sambo's feet, and this was why they could not be together: I felt like a lip-reader watching the communication of despair.

It was appalling, anyway, with or without flowers, to find so many children in the streets. In benighted, incompetent Africa, I had never encountered an orphan: the American streets resembled nothing so much as one vast, howling, unprecedented orphanage. It has been vivid to me for many years that what we call a race problem here is not a race problem at all: to keep calling it that is a way of avoiding the problem. The problem is rooted in the question of how one treats one's flesh and blood, especially one's children. The blacks are the despised and slaughtered children of the great Western house—nameless and unnameable bastards. This is a fact so obvious, so speedily verifiable, that it would seem pure insanity to deny it, and yet the life of the entire country is predicated on this denial, this monstrous and pathetic lie. For many generations, many a white American has gone—sometimes shrieking—to his grave, knowing that his own son, the issue of his loins, was denied, and sometimes murdered by him. Many a white American woman has gone through life carrying the knowledge that she is responsible for the slaughter of her lover, and also for the destruction of that love's issue. *Ye are liars and the truth's not in you:* it cannot be pretty to be forced, with every day the good Lord sends, to tell so many lies about everything. It demands a tremendous effort of the will and an absolute surrender of the personality to act on the lies one tells oneself. It is not true that people become liars without knowing it. A liar always knows he is lying, and that is why liars travel in packs: in order to be reassured that the judgment day will never come for them. They need each other for the well-being, the health, the perpetuation of their lie. They have a tacit agreement to guard each other's secrets, for they have the same secret. That is why all liars are cruel and filthy minded—one's merely got to listen to their dirty jokes, to what they think is funny, which is also what they think is real.

The flower children seemed completely aware that the blacks were their denied brothers, seemed even to be patiently waiting for the blacks to recognize that they had repudiated the house. For it seemed to have struck the flower children—I judged this from their conduct, from what seemed to be their blind and moving need to become organic, autonomous, loving and joyful creatures; their desire to connect love, joy, and eroticism, so that all flowed together as one—that they were themselves the issue of a dirty joke, the dirty joke which has always been hidden at the heart of the legend of the Virgin birth. They were in the streets in the hope of becoming whole. They had taken the first step—they had said, No. Whether or not they would be able to take the second step, the harder step—of saying, Yes, and then going for their own most private broke—was a question which much exercised my mind, as indeed it seemed to exercise the minds, very loosely speaking, of all the tourists and policemen in the area. When the heir of a great house repudiates the house, the house cannot continue, unless it looks to alien blood to save it; and here were the heirs and heiresses of all the ages, in the streets, along with that blood always considered to be most alien, never lawfully to be mixed with that of the sons and daughters of the great house.

I seemed to observe in some of the eyes that watched them that same bright, paranoid, flinching bewilderment I have seen in the eyes of some white Americans when they encounter a black man abroad. In the latter case, one sometimes had the feeling that they were ducking a blow—that they had encountered their deadliest enemy on a lonely mountain road. The eyes seemed to say, *I didn't do it! Let me pass!* and in such a moment one recognized the fraudulent and expedient nature of the American innocence which has always been able to persuade itself that it does not know what it knows too well. Or, it was exactly like watching someone who finds himself caught in a lie: for a black man abroad is no longer one of "our" niggers, is a stranger, not to be controlled by anything his countrymen think or say or do. In a word, he is free and thus discovers how little equipped his countrymen are to behold him in that state. In San Francisco, the eyes that watched seemed to feel that the children were deliberately giving away family secrets in the hope of egging on the blacks to destroy the family. And that is precisely what they *were* doing—helplessly, unconsciously, out of a profound desire to be saved, to live. But the blacks already knew the family secrets and had no interest in them. Nor did they have much confidence in these troubled white boys and girls. The black trouble was of a different order, and blacks had to be concerned with much more than their own private happiness or unhappiness. They had to be aware that this troubled white person might suddenly decide not to be in trouble and go home—and when he went home, he would be the enemy. Therefore, it was best not to speak too freely to anyone who spoke too freely to you, especially not on the streets of a nation which probably has more hired informers working for it, here and all over the world, than any nation in history. True rebels, after all, are as rare as true lovers, and, in both cases, to mistake a fever for a passion can destroy one's life.

The black and white confrontation, whether it be hostile, as in the cities and the labor unions, or with the intention of forming a common front and creating the foundations of a new society, as with the students and the radicals, is obviously crucial, containing the shape of the American future and the only potential of a truly valid American identity. No one knows precisely how identities are forged, but it is safe to say that identities are not invented: an identity would seem to be arrived at by the way in which the person faces and uses his experience. It is a long drawn-out and somewhat bewildering and awkward process. When I was young, for example, it was an insult to be called black. The blacks have now taken over this once pejorative term and made of it a rallying cry and a badge of honor and are teaching their children to be proud that they are black.

It is true that the children are as vari-colored—tea, coffee, chocolate, mocha, honey, eggplant coated with red pepper, red pepper dipped in eggplant—as it is possible for a people to be; black people, here, are no more uniformly black than white people are physically white; but the shades of color, which have been used for so long to distress and corrupt our minds and set us against each other, now count, at least in principle, for nothing. Black is a tremendous spiritual condition, one of the greatest challenges anyone alive can face—this is what the blacks are saying. Nothing is easier, nor, for the guilt-ridden American, more inevitable, than to dismiss this as chauvinism in reverse. But, in this, white Americans are being—it is a part of their fate—inaccurate. To be liberated from the stigma of blackness by embracing it is to cease, forever, one's interior agreement and collaboration with the authors of one's degradation. It abruptly reduces the white enemy to a contest merely physical, which he can win only physically. White men have killed black men for refusing to say, "Sir": but it was the corroboration of their worth and their power that they wanted, and not the corpse, still less the staining blood. When the black man's mind is no longer controlled by the white man's fantasies, a new balance or what may be described as an unprecedented inequality begins to make itself felt: for the white man no longer knows who he is, whereas the black man knows them both. For if it is difficult to be released from the stigma of blackness, it is clearly at least equally difficult to surmount the delusion of whiteness. And as the black glories in his newfound color, which is *his* at last, and asserts, not always with the very greatest politeness, the unanswerable validity and power of his being—even in the shadow of death—the white is very often affronted and very often made afraid. He has his reasons, after all, not only for being weary of the entire concept of color, but fearful as to what may be made of this concept once it has fallen, as it were, into the wrong hands. And one may indeed be wary, but the point is that it was inevitable that black and white should arrive at this dizzying height of tension. Only when we have passed this moment will we know what our history has made of us.

Many white people appear to live in a state of carefully

repressed terror in relation to blacks. There is something curious and paradoxical about this terror, which is involved not only with the common fear of death, but with a sense of its being considered utterly irrelevant whether one is breathing or not. I think that this has something to do with the fact that, whereas white men have killed black men for sport, or out of terror or out of the intolerable excess of terror called hatred, or out of the necessity of affirming their identity as white men, none of these motives appear necessarily to obtain for black men: it is not necessary for a black man to hate a white man, or to have any particular feelings about him at all, in order to realize that he must kill him. Yes, we have come, or are coming to this, and there is no point in flinching before the prospect of this exceedingly cool species of fratricide—which prospect white people, after all, have brought on themselves. Of course, whenever a black man discusses violence he is said to be "advocating" it. This is very far indeed from my intention, if only because I have no desire whatever to see a generation perish in the streets. But the shape and extent of whatever violence may come is not in the hands of people like myself, but in the hands of the American people, who are at present among the most dishonorable and violent people in the world. I am merely trying to face certain blunt, human facts. I do not carry a gun and do not consider myself to be a violent man: but my life has more than once depended on the gun in a brother's holster. I know that when certain powerful and blatant enemies of black people are shoveled, at last, into the ground I may feel a certain pity that they spent their lives so badly, but I certainly do not mourn their passing, nor, when I hear that they are ailing, do I pray for their recovery. I know what I would do if I had a gun and someone had a gun pointed at my brother, and I would not count ten to do it and there would be no hatred in it, nor any remorse. People who treat other people as less than human must not be surprised when the bread they have cast on the waters comes floating back to them, poisoned.

I'm black and I'm proud: yet, I suppose that the most accurate term, now, for this history, this particular and peculiar danger, as well as for all persons produced out of it and struggling in it, is: Afro-American. Which is but a wedding, however, of two confusions, an arbitrary linking of two undefined and currently undefineable proper nouns. I mean that, in the case of Africa, Africa is still chained to Europe, and exploited by Europe, and Europe and America are chained together; and as long as this is so, it is hard to speak of Africa except as a cradle and a potential. Not until the many millions of people on the continent of Africa control their land and their resources will the African personality flower or genuinely African institutions flourish and reveal Africa as she is. But it is striking that that part of the North American continent which calls itself, arrogantly enough, *America* poses as profound and dangerous a mystery for human understanding as does the fabled dark continent of Africa. The terms in which the mystery is posed, as well as the mysteries themselves, are very different. Yet, when one places the mysteries side by side—ponders the history and possible future of Africa, and the history and possible future of America—something is illuminated of the nature, the depth and the tenacity of the great war between black and white life styles here. Something is suggested of the nature of fecundity, the nature of sterility, and one realizes that it is by no means a simple matter to know which is which: the one can very easily resemble the other. Questions louder than drums begin beating in the mind, and one realizes that what is called civilization lives first of all in the mind, has the mind above all as its province, and that the civilization, or its rudiments, can continue to live long after its externals have vanished—they can never entirely vanish from the mind. These questions—they are too vague for questions, this excitement, this discomfort—concern the true nature of any inheritance and the means by which that inheritance is handed down. There is a reason, after all, that some people wish to colonize the moon, and others dance before it as before an ancient friend. And the extent to which these apprehensions, instincts, relations, are modified by the passage of time, or the accumulation of inventions, is a question that no one seems able to answer. All men, clearly, are primitive, but it can be doubted that all men are primitive in the same way; and if they are not, it can only be because, in that absolutely unassailable privacy of the soul, they do not worship the same gods. Both continents, Africa and America, be it remembered, were "discovered"—what a wealth of arrogance that little word contains!—with devastating results for the indigenous populations, whose only human use thereafter was as the source of capital for white people. On both continents the white and the dark gods met in combat, and it is on the outcome of this combat that the future of both continents depends.

To be an Afro-American, or an American black, is to be in the situation, intolerably exaggerated, of all those who have ever found themselves part of a civilization which they could in no wise honorably defend—which they were compelled, indeed, endlessly to attack and condemn—and who yet spoke out of the most passionate love, hoping to make the kingdom new, to make it honorable and worthy of life. Whoever is part of whatever civilization helplessly loves some aspects of it, and some of the people in it. A person does not lightly elect to oppose his society. One would much rather be at home among one's compatriots than be mocked and detested by them. And there is a level on which the mockery of the people, even their hatred, is moving because it is so blind: it is terrible to watch people cling to their captivity and insist on their own destruction. I think black people have always felt this about America, and Americans, and have always seen, spinning above the thoughtless American head, the shape of the wrath to come.

EPILOGUE
WHO HAS BELIEVED OUR REPORT?

THIS BOOK HAS been much delayed by trials, assassinations, funerals, and despair. Nor is the American crisis, which is part of a global, historical crisis, likely to resolve itself soon. An old world is dying, and a new one, kicking in the belly of its mother, time, announces that it is ready to be born. This birth will not be easy, and many of us are doomed to discover that we are exceedingly clumsy midwives. No matter, so long as we accept that our responsibility is to the newborn: the acceptance of responsibility contains the key to the necessarily evolving skill.

This book is not finished—can never be finished, by me. As of this writing, I am waiting to hear the fate of Tony Maynard, whose last address was Attica. Though the cops have been buried, with much patriotic grief, the blacks are still waiting to hear who is alive or dead. Mr. Nixon has congratulated Mr. Rockefeller, who has congratulated the police: so much for that. As to the effect of all this—and so much more!—on the Black Panther leadership and on black or non-white people, in this country, and all over the world, time will give a sufficiently authoritative answer. People, even if they are so thoughtless as to be born black, do not come into this world merely to provide mink coats and diamonds for chattering, trivial, pale matrons, or genocidal opportunities for their unsexed, unloved, and, finally, despicable men—oh, pioneers!

There will be bloody holding actions all over the world, for years to come: but the Western party is over, and the white man's sun has set. Period.

Angela Davis is still in danger. George Jackson has joined his beloved baby brother, Jon, in the royal fellowship of death. And one may say that Mrs. Georgia Jackson and the alleged mother of God have, at last, found something in common.

Now, it is the Virgin, the alabaster Mary, who must embrace the despised black mother whose children are also the issue of the Holy Ghost.

*New York, San Francisco, Hollywood, London, Istanbul,
St. Paul de Vence,
1967–1971.*

THE DEVIL
FINDS WORK

AN ESSAY

for Paula-Maria, on her birthday,
and John Latham
and brother, David Moses

For our God is a consuming fire.

HEBREWS 12:29

ONE
CONGO SQUARE

JOAN CRAWFORD'S STRAIGHT, narrow, and lonely back. We are following her through the corridors of a moving train. She is looking for someone, or she is trying to escape from someone. She is eventually intercepted by, I think, Clark Gable.

I am fascinated by the movement on, and of, the screen, that movement which is something like the heaving and swelling of the sea (though I have not yet been to the sea): and which is also something like the light which moves on, and especially beneath, the water.

I am about seven. I am with my mother, or my aunt. The movie is *Dance, Fools, Dance*.

I don't remember the film. A child is far too self-centered to relate to any dilemma which does not, somehow, relate to him—to his own evolving dilemma. The child escapes into what he would like his situation to be, and I certainly did not wish to be a fleeing fugitive on a moving train; and, also, with quite another part of my mind, I was aware that Joan Crawford was a white lady. Yet, I remember being sent to the store sometime later, and a colored woman, who, to me, looked exactly like Joan Crawford, was buying something. She was so incredibly beautiful—she seemed to be wearing the sunlight, rearranging it around her from time to time, with a movement of one hand, with a movement of her head, and with her smile—that, when she paid the man and started out of the store, I started out behind her. The storekeeper, who knew me, and others in the store who knew my mother's little boy (and who also knew my Miss Crawford!) laughed and called me back. Miss Crawford also laughed and looked down at me with so beautiful a smile that I was not even embarrassed. Which was rare for me.

Tom Mix, on his white horse. Actually, it was Tom Mix's hat, a shadow in the shadow of the hat, a kind of rocky background (which, again, was always moving) and the white horse. Tom Mix was a serial. Every Saturday, then, if memory serves, we left Tom Mix and some bleakly interchangeable girl in the most dreadful danger—or, rather, we left the hat and the shadow of the hat and the white horse: for the horse was not interchangeable and the serial could not have existed without it.

The Last of the Mohicans: Randolph Scott (a kind of fifteenth-rate Gary Cooper) and Binnie Barnes (a kind of funky Geraldine Fitzgerald), Heather Angel (a somewhat more bewildered Olivia de Havilland) and Philip Reed (a precursor of Anthony Quinn). Philip Reed was the Indian, Uncas, whose savage, not to say slavish adoration of Miss Angel's fine blonde frame drives her over a cliff, headlong, to her death. She has chosen death before dishonor, which made perfect sense. The erring Uncas eventually pays for his misguided lust with his life, and a tremulous, wet-eyed, brave couple, Randolph Scott and Binnie Barnes, eventually, hand in hand, manage to make it out of the wilderness. Into America, or back to England, I really do not remember, and I don't suppose that it matters.*

20,000 Years in Sing Sing: Spencer Tracy and Bette Davis. By this time, I had been taken in hand by a young white schoolteacher, a beautiful woman, very important to me. I was between ten and eleven. She had directed my first play and endured my first theatrical tantrums and had then decided to escort me into the world. She gave me books to read and talked to me about the books, and about the world: about Spain, for example, and Ethiopia, and Italy, and the German Third Reich; and took me to see plays and films, plays and films to which no one else would have dreamed of taking a ten-year-old boy. I loved her, of course, and absolutely, with a child's love; didn't understand half of what she said, but remembered it; and it stood me in good stead later. It is certainly partly because of her, who arrived in my terrifying life so soon, that I never really managed to hate white people—though, God knows, I have often

---

* The novel, which I read much later, is not my favorite novel, and, on some other day, I may detail my quarrel with it; but it is far more honest and courageous than the film.

wished to murder more than one or two. But Bill Miller—her name was Orilla, we called her Bill—was not white for me in the way, for example, that Joan Crawford was white, in the way that the landlords and the storekeepers and the cops and most of my teachers were white. She didn't baffle me that way and she never frightened me and she never lied to me. I never felt her pity, either, in spite of the fact that she sometimes brought us old clothes (because she worried about our winters) and cod-liver oil, especially for me, because I seemed destined, then, to be carried away by whooping cough.

I was a child, of course, and, therefore, unsophisticated. I don't seem ever to have had any innate need (or, indeed, any innate ability) to distrust people: and so I took Bill Miller as she was, or as she appeared to be to me. Yet, the difference between Miss Miller and other white people, white people as they lived in my imagination, and also as they were in life, had to have had a profound and bewildering effect on my mind. Bill Miller was not at all like the cops who had already beaten me up, she was not like the landlords who called me nigger, she was not like the storekeepers who laughed at me. I had found white people to be unutterably menacing, terrifying, mysterious—wicked: and they were mysterious, in fact, to the extent that they were wicked: the unfathomable question being, precisely, this one: what, under heaven, or beneath the sea, or in the catacombs of hell, could cause any people to act as white people acted? From Miss Miller, therefore, I began to suspect that white people did not act as they did because they were white, but for some other reason, and I began to try to locate and understand the reason. She, too, anyway, was treated like a nigger, especially by the cops, and she had no love for landlords.

My father said, during all the years I lived with him, that I was the ugliest boy he had ever seen, and I had absolutely no reason to doubt him. But it was not my father's hatred of *my* frog-eyes which hurt me, this hatred proving, in time, to be rather more resounding than real: I have my mother's eyes. When my father called me ugly, he was not attacking me so much as he was attacking my mother. (No doubt, he was also attacking my real, and unknown, father.) And I loved my mother. I knew that she loved me, and I sensed that she was paying an enormous price for me. I was a boy, and so I didn't really too much care that my father thought me hideous. (So I said to myself—this judgment, nevertheless, was to have a decidedly terrifying effect on my life.) But I thought that he must have been stricken blind (or was as mysteriously wicked as white people, a paralyzing thought) if he was unable to see that my mother was absolutely beyond any question the most beautiful woman in the world.

So, here, now, was Bette Davis, on that Saturday afternoon, in close-up, over a champagne glass, pop-eyes popping. I was astounded. I had caught my father, not in a lie, but in an infirmity. For, here, before me, after all, was a *movie star: white:* and if she was white and a movie star, she was *rich:* and she was *ugly.* I felt exactly the same way I felt, just before this moment, or just after, when I was in the street, playing, and I saw an old, very black, and very drunk woman stumbling up the sidewalk, and I ran upstairs to make my mother come to the window and see what I had found: *You see? You see? She's uglier than you, Mama! She's uglier than me!* Out of bewilderment, out of loyalty to my mother, probably, and also because I sensed something menacing and unhealthy (for me, certainly) in the face on the screen, I gave Davis's skin the dead-white greenish cast of something crawling from under a rock, but I was held, just the same, by the tense intelligence of the forehead, the disaster of the lips: and when she moved, she moved just like a nigger. Eventually, from a hospital bed, she murders someone, and Tracy takes the weight, to Sing Sing. In his arms, Davis cries and cries, and the movie ends. "What's going to happen to her now?" I asked Bill Miller. "We don't know," said Bill, conveying to me, nevertheless, that she would probably never get over it, that people pay for what they do.

I had not yet heard Bessie Smith's *"why they call this place the Sing Sing?!Come stand here by this rock pile, and listen to these hammers ring,"* and it would be seven years before I would begin working on the railroad. It was to take a longer time than that before I would cry; a longer time than that before I would cry in anyone's arms; and a long long long long time before I would begin to realize what I myself was doing with my enormous eyes—or vice versa. This had nothing to do with Davis, the actress, or with all those hang-ups I didn't yet know I had: I had discovered that my infirmity might not be my doom; my infirmity, or infirmities, might be forged into weapons.

For, I was not only considered by my father to be ugly. I was considered by everyone to be "strange," including my poor mother, who didn't, however, beat me for it. Well, if I was "strange"—and I knew that I must be, otherwise people would not have treated me so strangely, and I would not have been so miserable—perhaps I could find a way to use my strangeness. A "strange" child, anyway, dimly and fearfully apprehends that the years are not likely to make him less strange. Therefore, if he wishes to live, he must calculate, and I knew that I had to live. I very much wanted my mother to be happy and to be proud of me, and I very much loved my brothers and my sisters, who, in a sense, were all I had. My father showed no favoritism, he did not beat me worse than the others because I was not his son. (I didn't know this then, anyway, none of the children did, and by the time we all found out, it became just one more detail of the peculiar journey we had made in company with each other.) I knew, too, that my mother depended on me. I was not always dependable, for no child can be, but I tried: and I knew that I might have to prepare myself to be, one day, the actual head of my family. I did not actually do this, either, for we were all forced to take on our responsibilities each for the other, and to discharge them in our different ways. The eldest can be, God knows, as much a burden as a help, and is doomed to be something of a mystery for those growing up behind him—a mystery when not, indeed, an intolerable exasperation. *I*, nevertheless, was the eldest, a responsibility I did not intend to fail, and my first conscious calculation as to how to go about defeating the world's intentions for me and mine began on that Saturday afternoon in what we called *the movies*, but which was actually my first entrance into the cinema of my mind.

I read *Uncle Tom's Cabin* over and over and over again—this is the first book I can remember having read—and then I read *A Tale of Two Cities*—over and over and over again. Bill Miller takes me to see *A Tale of Two Cities*, at the Lincoln, on 135th Street. I am twelve.

I did not yet know that virtually every black community in America contains a movie house, or, sometimes, in those days, an actual theater, called the Lincoln, or the Booker T. Washington, nor did I know why; any more than I knew why The Cotton Club was called The Cotton Club. I knew about Lincoln only that he had freed the slaves (in the South, which made the venture remote from me) and then had been shot, dead, in a theater, by an actor; and a movie I was never to see, called *The Prisoner of Shark Island*, had something to do with the murder of Lincoln. How I knew this, I do not remember precisely. But I know that I read everything I could get my hands on, including movie advertisements, and *Uncle Tom's Cabin* had had a tremendous impact on me, and I certainly reacted to the brutal conjunction of the words, *prisoner*, and *shark*, and *island*. I may have feared becoming a prisoner, or feared that I was one already; had never seen a shark—I hoped: but I was certainly trapped on an island. And, in any case, the star of this film, Warner Baxter, later, but during the same era, made a film with the female star of *A Tale of Two Cities*, called *Slave Ship:* which I did not see, either.

I knew about Booker T. Washington less than I knew about my father's mother, who had been born a slave, and who died in our house when I was little: a child cannot make the connection between *slave* and *grandmother*, and it was to take me a while (mainly because I had discovered the Schomburg collection at the 135th Street Library) to read *Up From Slavery:* but, when I read it, I no longer knew which way was up. As for The Cotton Club, I knew only that it was a dance hall which gave out free Thanksgiving dinners every Thanksgiving (!) for which my brother, George, and I, stood in line. Which means that I knew that I was poor, and knew that I was black, but did not yet know what being black really meant, what it meant, that is, in the history of my country, and in my own history. Bill could instruct me as to how poverty came about and what it meant and what it did, and, also, what it was meant to do: but she could not instruct me as to blackness, except obliquely, feeling that she had neither the right nor the authority, and also knowing that I was certain to find out. Thus, she tried to suggest to me the extent to which the world's social and economic arrangements are responsible for (and to) the world's victims. But a victim may or may not have a color, just as he may or may not have virtue: a difficult, not to say unpopular notion, for nearly everyone prefers to be defined by his status, which, unlike his virtue, is ready to wear.

The 1936 Metro-Goldwyn-Mayer production of *A Tale of Two Cities* ends with this enormity sprawled across the screen:

> *I am the resurrection and the life, saith the Lord: he that believeth in me, though he were dead, yet shall he live; and he that believeth in me shall never die.*

I had lived with this text all my life, which made encountering it on the screen of the Lincoln Theater absolutely astounding: and I had lived with the people of *A Tale of Two Cities* for very nearly as long. I had no idea what *Two Cities* was really about, any more than I knew what *Uncle Tom's Cabin* was really about, which was why I had read them both so obsessively: they had something to tell me. It was this particular child's way of circling around the question of what it meant to be a nigger. It was the reason that I was reading Dostoevski, a writer—or, rather, for me, a messenger—whom I would have had to understand, obviously, even less: my relentless pursuit of *Crime and Punishment* made my father (vocally) and my mother (silently) consider the possibility of brain fever. I was intrigued, but not misled, by the surface of these novels—Sydney Carton's noble renunciation of his life on the spectacular guillotine, Tom's forbearance before Simon Legree, the tracking down of Raskolnikov: the time of my time was to reduce all these images to the angel dancing on the edge of the junkie's needle: I did not believe in any of these people so much as I believed in their situation, which I suspected, dreadfully, to have something to do with my own.

And it had clearly escaped everyone's notice that I had already been bull-whipped through the Psalms of David and The Book of Job, to say nothing of the arrogant and loving Isaiah, the doomed Ezekiel, and the helplessly paranoiac Saint Paul: such a forced march, designed to prepare the mind for conciliation and safety, can also prepare it for subversion and danger. For, I was on Job's side, for example, *though He slay me, yet will I trust Him, and I will maintain mine own ways before Him*—You will not talk to *me* from the safety of your whirlwind, never—and, yet, something in me, out of the unbelievable pride and sorrow and beauty of my father's face, caused me to understand—I did not understand, perhaps I still do not understand, and never will, caused me to begin to accept the fatality and the inexorability of that voice out of the whirlwind, for if one is not able to live with so crushing and continuing a mystery, one is not able to live.

The pride and sorrow and beauty of my father's face: for that man I called my father really *was* my father in every sense except the biological, or literal one. He formed me, and he raised me, and he did not let me starve: and he gave me something, however harshly, and however little I wanted it, which prepared me for an impending horror which he could not prevent. This is not a Western idea, but fathers and sons arrive at that relationship only by claiming that relationship: that is, by paying for it. If the relationship of father to son could really be reduced to biology, the whole earth would blaze with the glory of fathers and sons. (But to pursue this further carries us far beyond the confines of the present discussion.)

In the novel, *A Tale of Two Cities*, it had been Madame Defarge who most struck me. I recognized that unrelenting hatred, for it was all up and down my streets, and in my father's face and voice. The wine cask, *shattered like a walnut shell*, shattered every Saturday night on the corner of our street, and, yes, Dickens was right, the gutters turned a bright and then a rusty red. I understood the knitted registers as hope and fate, for I knew that everything (including my own name) had long been written in The Book: *you may run on a great long time but great God Almighty's going to cut you down!* I understood the meaning of the rose in the turban of Madame Defarge as she sits knitting in the wine shop, the flower in the headdress meant to alert the neighborhood to the presence of a spy. We lived by such signals, and long before it was safe to say *there is a rose in Spanish Harlem!*

When, at last, in the film, the people rise and fill the streets and alleys and hurl themselves onto the drawbridge of the Bastille, I was tremendously stirred and frightened. I did not really know who these people were, or why they were in the streets— they were white: and a white mob can be in no way reassuring to a black boy (even though, or if, he cannot say why). If, in the novel, it was Madame Defarge who most held me, in the film two images and one moment stand out, even from this distance. The first is a long climb up an outside staircase, in Paris, when Lucie Manette and Dr. Lorry and Ernest Defarge go to retrieve Lucie's father, Dr. Manette: for I knew about staircases. The second is when the carriage of the Marquis races headlong through a provincial village. We are confronted with the speeding wheels of the carriage, the relentless hooves of the horses, and a small, running, ragged boy, trying to get out of the way. He is knocked down, he is run over, he is killed; and I knew something about that. The moment that most stands out, for me, is that moment in the tumbril, near the end of the film, when the seamstress (Isabel Jewell) recognizes that Sydney Carton (Ronald Colman) is dying in his friend's stead. I knew nothing about *that*, but I had been taught *greater love hath no man than this*, and something in me believed it. Yet, when Bill whispered to me, during the scene of the storming of the Bastille, "Every time somebody drops from the drawbridge, they die," though I watched the people dropping off the drawbridge like so many dead cockroaches being swept into the dust pan, I was also aware that Bill was not telling me that Metro-Goldwyn-Mayer was murdering all these people, any more than that that guillotine was really going to chop off Ronald Colman's head. The guillotine was going to chop off *Sydney Carton's* head: my first director was instructing me in the discipline and power of make-believe.

For, while believing it all, and *really* believing it, I still knew that Madame Defarge was really an actress named Blanche Yurka, and that Lucie Manette was really an English girl, named Elizabeth Allan. Something implacable in the set of Yurka's mouth probably reminded me of my grandmother, and I knew that Elizabeth Allan-Lucie Manette reminded me of my music teacher, a Miss Taub, with whom I was desperately in love. When Lucie Manette and Charles Darnay are torn from each other's arms in the courtroom, tears rose to my eyes, for I knew something about *that:* yet, at the very same time, I also knew that Charles Darnay was really an actor, named Donald Woods. This was the first time in my life, after all, that I had seen a *screen rendition* (so the ads and the press put it) of a novel, which, considering my age, I could claim to know. And I felt very close to the actors, who had not betrayed the friends I had lived with for nearly as long as I had lived with the people of *Uncle Tom's Cabin.*

I had read *Uncle Tom's Cabin* compulsively, the book in one hand, the newest baby on my hipbone. I was trying to find out something, sensing something in the book of some immense import for me: which, however, I knew I did not really understand.

My mother got scared. She hid the book. The last time she hid it, she hid it on the highest shelf above the bathtub. I was somewhere around seven or eight. God knows how I did it, but I somehow climbed up and dragged the book down. Then, my mother, as she herself puts it, "didn't hide it anymore," and, indeed, from that moment, though in fear and trembling, began to let me go.

I understood, as Bill had intended me to, something of revolution—understood, that is, something of the universal and inevitable human ferment which explodes into what is called a revolution. *Revolution:* the word had a solemn, dreadful ring: what was going on in Spain was a *revolution.* Revolution was the only hope of the American working class—the *proletariat:* and world-wide revolution was the only hope of the world. I could understand (or, rather, accept) all this, as it were, negatively. I could not see where I fit in this formulation, and I did not see where blacks fit. I don't think that I ever dared pose this question to Bill, partly because I hadn't yet really accepted, or understood, that *I* was black and also because I knew (and didn't want her to know, although, of course, she did) how much my father distrusted and disliked her. My father was certainly a proletarian, but I had been sent downtown often to pay his union dues, and I knew how much he hated these greasy, slimy men—also proletarians—whom he called, quite rightly, robbers.

In the film, I was not overwhelmed by the guillotine. The guillotine had been very present for me in the novel because I already wanted, and for very good reasons, to lop off heads. But: once begun, how to distinguish one head from another, and how, where, and for what reason, would the process stop? Beneath the resonance of the word, *revolution*, thundered the word, *revenge*. But: *vengeance is mine, saith the Lord:* a hard saying, the identity of *the Lord* becoming, with the passage of time, either a private agony or an abstract question. And, to put it as simply as it can be put, unless one can conceive of (and endure) an abstract life, there can be no abstract questions. A question is a threat, the door which slams shut, or swings open: on another threat.

I was haunted, for example, by Alexandre Manette's document, in *A Tale of Two Cities*, describing the murder of a peasant boy—who, dying, speaks: *I say, we were so robbed, and hunted, and were made so poor, that our father told us it was a dreadful thing to bring a child into this world, and that what we should most pray for was that our women might be barren and our miserable race die out!* (*I had never before*, observes Dr. Manette, *seen the sense of being oppressed, bursting forth like a fire.*)

Dickens has not seen it at all. The wretched of the earth do not decide to become extinct, they resolve, on the contrary, to multiply: life is their only weapon against life, life is all that they have. This is why the dispossessed and starving will never be convinced (though some may be coerced) by the population-control programs of the civilized. I have watched the dispossessed and starving laboring in the fields which others own, with their transistor radios at their ear, all day long: so they learn, for example, along with equally weighty matters, that the Pope, one of the heads of the civilized world, forbids to the civilized that abortion which is being, literally, forced on them, the wretched. The civilized have created the wretched, quite coldly and deliberately, and do not intend to change the *status quo;* are responsible for their slaughter and enslavement; rain down bombs on defenseless children whenever and wherever they decide that their "vital interests" are menaced, and think nothing of torturing a man to death: these people are not to be taken seriously when they speak of the "sanctity" of human life, or the "conscience" of the civilized world. There is a "sanctity" involved with bringing a child into this world: it is better than bombing one out of it. Dreadful indeed it is to see a starving child, but the answer to that is not to prevent the child's arrival but to restructure the world so that the child can live in it: so that the "vital interest" of the world becomes nothing less than the life of the child. However—I would not have said any of this then, nor is so absurd a notion about to engulf the world now. But we were all starving children, after all, and none of our fathers, even at their most embittered and enraged, had ever suggested that we "die out." It was not *we* who were supposed to *die out:* this was, of all notions, the most forbidden, and we learned this from the cradle. Every trial, every beating, every drop of blood, every tear, were meant to be used by us for a day that was coming—for a day that was certainly coming, absolutely certainly, certainly coming: not for us, perhaps, but for our children. The children of the despised and rejected are menaced from the moment they stir in the womb, and are therefore sacred in a way that the children of the saved are not. And the children know it, which is how they manage to raise their children, and why they will not be persuaded—by their children's murderers, after all—to cease having children.

But I was haunted, too, by the fact that it is Dr. Manette's testimony, written in prison, and recuperated by Ernest Defarge upon the storming of the Bastille, which dooms his son-in-law to death. The Defarges seize and hide this document in order to use it against the son-in-law at the latter's trial: at which trial, Dr. Manette is chief witness for the defense—or, in other words, in fact, his son-in-law's only hope.

Manette wrote his testimony in agony and silence, never expecting to see his daughter again, and unable, of course, to imagine that his daughter would marry one of the descendants of the house which had condemned him to a living death. His testimony ends: *them and their descendants, to the last of their race, I . . . denounce them to Heaven and to earth.* His son-in-law is the descendant of the "race" which had imprisoned him, and the "last" of that race, denounced by him, is flesh of his flesh, his granddaughter. Which connected for me, horribly, with the testimony of Madame Defarge, sister of the murdered boy: *that brother was my brother, that father was my father, those dead are my dead and that summons to answer for all those things descends to me!* Her husband reluctantly agrees that this is so, whereupon Madame Defarge says, *Then tell wind and fire where to stop, but don't tell me!*

I understood *that:* I had seen it in the face, heard it in the voice of many a black man or woman, sweeping the pavement, wrestling with the garbage cans, men and women whose children were dying faster than those MGM extras dropping from the drawbridge. *If I love you, I love you, and I don't give a damn. You my nigger, nigger, if you don't get no bigger. I will cut your dick off, I will cut your balls out. I ain't got to do nothing but stay black and die and I'm black already! Honey. Don't be like that. Honey. Don't do me like that. We in this shit together, and you need me and I need you, now ain't that so?* Who *going to take care of us if we don't take care of each other?*

I feared, feared—like a thief in the night, as one of my brothers would put it—to connect all this with my father and mother and everyone I knew, and with myself, and to connect all this with black Uncle Tom: no more than I had wished to be that fleeing fugitive on that moving train did I desire to endure his destiny or meet his end. Uncle Tom really believed *vengeance is mine, saith the Lord,* for he believed in the Lord, as I flattered myself I did not: this inconvenient faith (described, furthermore, by a white woman) obscured the fact that Tom allowed himself to be murdered for refusing to disclose the road taken by the runaway slave. Because Uncle Tom would not take vengeance into his own hands, he was not a hero for me. Heroes, as far as I could then see, were white, and not merely because of the movies but because of the land in which I lived, of which movies were simply a reflection: I despised and feared those heroes because they *did* take vengeance into their own hands. They thought that vengeance was theirs to take. This difficult coin did not cease to spin, it had neither heads nor tails: for what white people took into their hands could scarcely even be called vengeance, it was something less and something more. The Scottsboro boys, for example—for the Scottsboro Case has begun—were certainly innocent of anything requiring vengeance. My father's youngest son by his first marriage, nine years older than I, who had vanished from our lives, might have been one of those boys, now being murdered by my fellow Americans on the basis of the rape charge delivered by two white whores: and I was reading Angelo Herndon's *Let Me Live*. Yes. I understood *that:* my countrymen were my enemy, and I had already begun to hate them from the bottom of my heart.

Angelo Herndon was a young, black labor organizer in the Deep South, railroaded to prison, who lived long enough, at least, to write a book about it—the George Jackson of the era. No one resembling him, or anyone resembling any of the Scottsboro Boys, nor anyone resembling my father, has yet made an appearance on the American cinema scene. Perhaps to compensate for this, Bill now takes me to see Sylvia Sidney and Henry Fonda in the Walter Wanger production of Fritz Lang's *You Only Live Once*. I, also, either with her or without her, I don't remember, see the Warner Brothers production (or *screen rendition*, which pompous formulation I adored) of a novel I had read, Ward Greene's *Death in the Deep South*, brought to the screen by (I think) Mervyn LeRoy, as *They Won't Forget*, starring Claude Rains; and Samuel Goldwyn's production of William Wyler's *Dead End*, again starring Sylvia Sidney. Who also starred in the film version of a play Bill took me to see, the WPA Living Newspaper production,—*one third of a nation*—.

It is not entirely true that no one from the world I knew had yet made an appearance on the American screen: there were, for example, Stepin Fetchit and Willie Best and Manton Moreland, all of whom, rightly or wrongly, I loathed. It seemed to me that they lied about the world I knew, and debased it, and certainly I did not know anybody like them—as far as I could tell; for it is also possible that their comic, bug-eyed terror contained the truth concerning a terror by which I hoped never to be engulfed.

Yet, I had no reservations at all concerning the terror of the black janitor in *They Won't Forget*. I think that it was a black actor named Clinton Rosewood who played this part, and he looked a little like my father. He is terrified because a young white girl, in this small Southern town, has been raped and murdered, and her body has been found on the premises of which he is the janitor. (Lana Turner, in her first movie, is the raped and murdered girl, which is, perhaps, a somewhat curious beginning for so gold-plated a career.) The role of the janitor is small, yet the man's face hangs in my memory until today: and the film's icy brutality both scared me and strengthened me. The Southern politician (Rains) needs an issue on which to be re-elected. He decides, therefore, that to pin the rape and murder of the white girl on a black man is insufficiently sensational. He very coldly frames a white Northern schoolteacher for this crime, and brings about his death at the hands of a lynch mob. (And I knew that this was exactly what would have happened to Bill, if such a mob had ever got its hands on her.) Unlike the later *Ox-Bow Incident*, in which a similar lynching is partially redeemed by the reading of a letter, which, presumably, will cause the members of the mob to repent the horror of what they have done and resolve to become better men and women, and also unlike the later *Intruder in the Dust*, which suggests the same hopeful improbability, *They Won't Forget* ends with the teacher dead and the politician triumphantly re-elected. As he watches the widow walk down the courthouse steps, he mutters, seeming, almost, to stifle a yawn, *I wonder if he really did it, after all*.

And, yes: I was beginning to understand *that*.

*

Sylvia Sidney was the only American film actress who reminded me of a colored girl, or woman—which is to say that she was the only American film actress who reminded me of reality. All of the others, without exception, were white, and, even when they moved me (like Margaret Sullavan or Bette Davis or Carole Lombard) they moved me from that distance. Some instinct caused me profoundly to distrust the sense of life they projected: this sense of life could certainly never, in any case, be used by me, and, while *His* eye might be on the sparrow, mine had to be on the hawk. And, similarly, while I admired Edward G. Robinson and James Cagney (and, on a more demanding level, Fredric March), the only actor of the era with whom I identified was Henry Fonda. I was not alone. A black friend of mine, after seeing Henry Fonda in *The Grapes of Wrath*, swore that Fonda had colored blood. You could tell, he said, by the way Fonda walked down the road at the end of the film: *white men don't walk like that!* and he imitated Fonda's stubborn, patient, wide-legged hike away from the camera. My reaction to Sylvia Sidney was certainly due, in part, to the kind of film she appeared in during that era—*Fury*; *Mary Burns, Fugitive*; *You and Me*; *Street Scene* (I was certain, even, that I knew the meaning of the title of a film she made with Gene Raymond, which I never saw, *Behold My Wife*). It was almost as though she and I had a secret: she seemed to know something I knew. *Every street in New York ends in a river:* this is the legend which begins the film, *Dead End*, and I was enormously grateful for it. I had never thought of that before. Sylvia Sidney, facing a cop in this film, pulling her black hat back from her forehead: *One of you lousy cops gave me that*. She was always being beaten up, victimized, weeping, and she should have been drearier than Tom Mix's girl friends. But I always believed her—in a way, she reminded me of Bill, for I had seen Bill facing hostile cops. Bill took us on a picnic downtown once, and there was supposed to be ice cream waiting for us at a police station. The cops didn't like Bill, didn't like the fact that we were colored kids, and didn't want to give up the ice cream. I don't remember anything Bill said. I just remember her face as she stared at the cop, clearly intending to stand there until the ice cream all over the world melted or until the earth's surface froze, and she got us our ice cream, saying *Thank you*, I remember, as we left. *You Only Live Once* was the most powerful movie I had seen until that moment. The only other film to hit me as hard, at that time of my life, was *The Childhood of Maxim Gorky*, which, for me, had not been about white people. Similarly, while *20,000 Years in Sing Sing* had concerned the trials of a finally somewhat improbable white couple, *You Only Live Once* came much much closer to home.

It is the top of 1937. I am not yet thirteen.

Fury, MGM, 1936, is, I believe, Lang's first American film. It is meant to be a study of mob violence, on which level it is indignant, sincere, and inept. Since the mob separates the lovers almost at the beginning of the film, the film works as a love story only intermittently, and to the extent that one responds to the lovers (Sylvia Sidney and Spencer Tracy). It is an exceedingly uneasy and uneven film, with both the lovers and the mob placed, really, in the German Third Reich, which Lang has not so much fled as furiously repudiated, and to which he is still reacting. (The railroad station at which the lovers separate is heavy with menace, and the train which carries Sidney away to go to work in another town is rather like the train to a bloody destination unknown.) Lang's is the *fury* of the film: but his grasp of the texture of American life is still extremely weak: he has not yet really left Germany. His fury, nevertheless, manages to convey something of the idle, aimless, compulsive wickedness of idle, terrified, aimless people, who can come together only as a mob: but his hatred of these people also makes them, at least, unreal. God knows what Lang had already seen, in Germany.

By the time of *You Only Live Once*, Lang had found his American feet. He never succeeded quite so brilliantly again. Considering the speed with which we moved from the New Deal to World War II, to Yalta, to the Marshall Plan, the Truman Doctrine, to Korea, and the House Un-American Activities Committee, this may not be his fault.

(One of the last of his films, entitled *Beyond a Reasonable Doubt*, starring Joan Fontaine, Dana Andrews, and Sydney Blackmer, is an utterly shameless apology for American justice, the work of a defeated man. But, children, yes, it be's that way sometimes.)

Lang's concern, or obsession, was with the fact and the effect of human loneliness, and the ways in which we are all responsible for the creation, and the fate, of the isolated monster: whom we isolate because we recognize him as living within us. This is what his great German film, *M*, which launched Peter Lorre, is all about. In the American context, there being no way for him to get to the *nigger*, he could use only that other American prototype, the criminal, *le gangster*. The premise of *You Only Live Once* is that Eddie Taylor (Henry Fonda) is an ex-convict who wants to go "straight": but the society will not allow him to live down, or redeem, his criminal past. This apparently banal situation is thrust upon us with so heavy a hand that one is forced—as I was, even so long ago—to wonder if one is resisting the film or resisting the truth. But, however one may wish to defend oneself against Lang's indictment of the small, faceless people, always available for any public ceremony and absent forever from any private one, who *are* society, one is left defenseless before his study of the result, which is the isolation and the doom of the lovers.

Very early in the film we meet the earnest and popular prison chaplain—a priest: we meet him as he pitches the ball to the men who are playing baseball in the prison courtyard. It is a curiously loaded moment, a disturbing image: perhaps only an exiled German, at that period of our history, would have dreamed of so connecting games and slaughter, thus foreshadowing the fate of the accomplice, who is, in this case, the priest. The film does not suggest that the priest's popularity has anything to do with the religious instruction he, presumably, brings to the men—his popularity is due to his personal qualities, which include a somewhat overworked cheerfulness: and his function, at bottom, is to prepare the men for death. His role, also, is to make the prison more bearable, both for the men in the courtyard and the guard behind the machine gun in the tower. And he is, also, of course, to prepare these men for their eventual freedom beyond these walls—which freedom, according to Lang's savage and elaborately articulated vision, does not and probably cannot exist.

The film has a kind of claustrophobic physicality—Sidney is first seen, for example, behind a desk, trapped, and Lang forces us to concentrate on her maneuvers to free herself, smiling all the way. (She's trapped behind her desk by a telephone and an apple vendor who has come to City Hall, where Sidney works, to complain that policemen eat his apples for free.) The first reunion of the lovers takes place with bars between them: it takes a moment before they realize that the gate is open, the man is being set free. There is a marvelous small moment in the flop house, with Fonda pacing the room the way he paced the cell, and pausing at the window to listen to the Salvation Army Band outside, singing, *if you love your mother, meet her in the skies*. I cannot imagine any native-born white American daring to use, so laconically, a banality so nearly comic in order to capture so deep a distress.

The genuine indignation which informs this film is a quality which was very shortly to disappear out of the American cinema, and severely to be menaced in American life. In a way, we were all niggers in the thirties. I do not know if that really made us more friendly with each other—at bottom, I doubt that, for more would remain of that friendliness today—but it was harder then, and riskier, to attempt a separate peace, and benign neglect was not among our possibilities. The Okies, of *The Grapes of Wrath*, were still crossing the plains in their jalopy and had not yet arrived in California, there, every single one of them, to encounter running water, and to become cops. Neither Steinbeck nor Dos Passos had yet said, *my country, right or wrong*, nor did anyone suppose that they ever could—but they did; and Hemingway was as vocal concerning the Spanish revolution as he was to be silent concerning the Cuban one.

There is that moment in the film, in prison, when Fonda whispers to Sidney, through jailhouse glass, *Get me a gun*.

Sidney said, *I can't get you a gun. You'll kill somebody!* and Fonda says, *What do you think they're going to do to me?*

I understood *that:* it was a real question. I was living with that question.

It is the priest who covers for the trapped and weary girl when she attempts to smuggle a gun into the prison, and it is the priest whom Fonda murders, with a gun. And I wondered about that, the well-meaning accomplice and his fate: he is murdered because Fonda does not believe him, even though he is, in fact, speaking the truth. But the prisoner has no way of knowing with whom the priest is playing ball at the moment and so dares not risk believing him. This dread is underscored by the film's last line, delivered (in the dying prisoner's memory) by the priest: *the gates are open.* I knew damn well that the gates were *not* open, and, by this time, in any case, the lovers were dead.

Dead End, on the other hand, left me cold, and so did *Street Scene*, for the same reason: my streets were funkier and more dangerous than that. I had seen the gangster, Baby-Face Martin (Humphrey Bogart), in *my* streets, with his one-hundred-dollar suits, and his silk shirts, and his hat: sometimes he was a pimp and sometimes he was a preacher and often he was both: but Baby-Face always had the same taste in women, boys, and cars. I knew no one like the heroine, Drina (Sylvia Sidney), except certain high-yellow bitches, whose concern for their younger brother, if they had any concern, would long before have forced them to hit the block, hit the road, or hit a clean old banker, and steal the keys to the long old highway; or, in other words, the severity of the social situation which *Dead End* so romanticizes (somewhat like its direct descendant, *West Side Story*) utterly precludes the innocence of its heroine. Much closer to the truth are the gangster, his broken mother, and his broken girl—yes: I had seen *that.* The script is unable to face the fact that it is merely another version of that brutal fantasy known as the American success story: this helpless dishonesty is revealed by the script's resolution. I was by no means certain that I approved of the hero's decision to inform on Baby-Face, to turn him over to the police, and bring about his death. In my streets, we never called the cops, and whoever turned anyone in to the cops was a pariah. I did not believe, though the film insists on it, that the hero (Joel McCrea) turned in the gangster in order to save the children. I had never seen any children saved that way. In my own experience, on the contrary, and not only because I was watching Bill, I had observed that those who really wished to save the children became themselves, immediately, the target of the police. I could believe—though the film pretends that this consideration never entered the hero's mind—that the hero turned in the gangster in order to collect the reward money: that reward money which will allow the hero and heroine to escape from the stink of the children: for I had certainly seen attempts at *that*. Should the hero and heroine take the younger brother with them into that so celebrated American mainstream, the boy, having no friends, and finding, therefore, no resonance, no corroboration of himself anywhere, will become either a derelict, or the most monstrous of patriots. Or, perhaps (trying to escape and atone, or, perhaps, simply trying to live) the boy will become a kind of revolutionary, a superior and dedicated gangster: for there is a reason that the heroes of the poor resemble so little (and yet so closely resemble!) the heroes of the rich. I do not wish to be misunderstood as suggesting, for example, that the late Adam Clayton Powell was in any way whatever a bandit, but that is what the white world called him. Harlem's position, therefore, as concerned Adam, was that Adam might have his faults, but that he was certainly a better man than any of his accusers, his accusers being on our backs: and that is why Harlem never abandoned him. Of course, I could not have said any of that then, either. I knew about Adam only that he was the son of "old" Adam, the pastor of Abyssinian Baptist Church, of which church we had been members when I was little; and that he had been instrumental, in the wake of the 1935 Harlem riot, in getting black people hired—for the first time—in the stores on 125th Street where we spent so much of our money—the word, "money," here being meant to convey the image of black fistfuls of nickels and dimes.

In any case, the happy resolution of *Dead End* could mean nothing to me, since, even with some money, black people could move only into black neighborhoods: which is not to be interpreted as meaning that we wished to move into white neighborhoods. We wished, merely, to be free to move. At the time that I am speaking of we had not yet even begun to move across the river, into the Bronx.

Bill takes me to see my first play, the Orson Welles production of *Macbeth*, with an all-black cast, at the Lafayette Theater, on 132nd Street and Seventh Avenue, in Harlem.

I do not remember if I had already read *Macbeth*. My impression is that I read the play when Bill told me she was taking me to see it. In any case, before the curtain rose, I knew the play by heart.

I don't think that the name, *Shakespeare*, meant very much to me in those years. I was not yet intimidated by the name—that was to come later. I had read a play which took place in Scotland. Bill had not warned me—she may not have known—that Welles had transposed the play to Haiti.

I am still about twelve or thirteen. I can be fairly certain about all this, because my life changed so violently when I entered the church, and I entered the church around the time of fourteen. When I entered the church, I ceased going to the theater. It took me awhile to realize that I was working in one.

There is an enormous difference because the first time I ever really saw black actors at work was on the stage: and it is important to emphasize that the people I was watching were black, like me. Nothing that I had seen before had prepared me for this—which is a melancholy comment indeed, but I cannot be blamed for an ignorance which an entire republic had deliberately inculcated.

The distance between oneself—the audience—and a screen performer is an absolute: a paradoxical absolute, masquerading as intimacy. No one, for example, will ever really know whether Katharine Hepburn or Bette Davis or Humphrey Bogart or

Spencer Tracy or Clark Gable—or John Wayne—can, or could, really act, or not, nor does anyone care: acting is not what they are required to do. Their acting ability, so far from being what attracts their audience, can often be what drives their audience away. One does not go to see them act: one goes to watch them *be*. One does not go to see Humphrey Bogart, *as Sam Spade:* one goes to see Sam Spade, *as Humphrey Bogart*. I don't wish, here, to belabor a point to which we shall, presently, and somewhat elaborately, be compelled to return: but, *no one*, I read somewhere, a long time ago, *makes his escape personality black*. That the movie star is an "escape" personality indicates one of the irreducible dangers to which the moviegoer is exposed: the danger of surrendering to the corroboration of one's fantasies as they are thrown back from the screen. The danger is as great for the performer: Bette Davis may have longed, all these years, to play Mrs. Alving, in *Ghosts*, and Spencer Tracy may have carried with him to the grave an unfulfilled *King Lear*—nobody was about to let them try it, for fear that their public would feel themselves betrayed. This is one of the reasons that Joan Crawford, for example, doesn't like the film *Rain*, in which she starred. God knows that it's not a very good picture, but Crawford didn't write the abysmal script. She made the mistake, and very honorably, after all, of trying to be Miss Sadie Thompson instead of Miss Joan Crawford, and the kids didn't like that at all.

For the tension in the theater is a very different, and very particular tension: this tension between the real and the imagined *is* the theater, and this is why the theater will always remain a necessity. One is not in the presence of shadows, but responding to one's flesh and blood: in the theater, we are re-creating each other. Clearly, now, when speaking of the theater, I am not referring to those desperate and debilitating commercial ventures on which Broadway embarks each season, or those grim "revivals" of stillborn plays of which London is so fond, or those "adaptations" of American monstrosities which have been the rage of Paris for so long. Nor, in the present instance, is the term, "one's flesh and blood" meant to refer, merely, to the spectacle of a black boy seeing, for the first time in his life, living black actors on a living stage: we are *all* each other's flesh and blood.

This is the truth which it is very difficult for the theater to deny, and when it attempts to do so the same thing happens to the theater as happens to the church: it becomes sterile and irrelevant, a blasphemy, and the true believer goes elsewhere—carrying, as it happens, the church and the theater with him, and leaving the form behind. For, the church and the theater are carried within us and it is we who create them, out of our need and out of an impulse more mysterious than our desire. If this seems to be saying that the life of the theater and the life of the church are dependent on maverick freak poets and visionaries, I can only point out that these difficult creatures are *also* our flesh and blood, and are also created by our need and out of an impulse more mysterious than our desire.

In the darkened Lafayette Theater—that moment when the house lights dim in the theater is not at all like the dimming of the house lights in the movies—I watched the narrow, horizontal ribbon of light which connects the stage curtain to the floor of the stage, and which also separates them. That narrow ribbon of light then contains a mystery. That mystery may contain the future—you are, yourself, suspended as mortal as that ribbon. No one can possibly know what is about to happen: it is happening, each time, for the first time, for the only time. For this reason, although I did not know this, I had never before, in the movies, been aware of the audience: in the movies, we knew what was going to happen, and, if we wanted to, we could stay there all afternoon, seeing it happen over and over again.

But I was aware of the audience now. Everyone seemed to be waiting, as I was waiting. The curtain rose.

Between three and four years later, that is, around the time that I was seventeen, my best friend, Emile, took me to a movie at the Irving Place Theater, a Russian movie, since America and Russia were allies then. My friend is a Jew—an American Jew, of Spanish descent: he was then, and is today, one of the most honest and honorable people I have ever known. He took me to the movie because he was trying to help me leave the church. I had not been to a film, or a theater from the time of my conversion, which came hard upon the heels of *Macbeth*.

At this time of my life, Emile was the only friend I had who knew to what extent my ministry tormented me. I knew that I could not stay in the pulpit. I could not make my peace with that particular lie—a lie, in any case, for me. I did not want to become Baby-Face Martin—I could see that coming, and, indeed, it demanded no spectacular perception, since I found myself surrounded by what I was certain to become. But neither did I know how to leave—to jump: it could not be explained to my brothers and sisters, or my mother, and my father had begun his descent into the valley. Emile took me to this film, of which I remember only a close-up of a tambourine. I played the tambourine, in church: the tambourine on the screen might as well have been Gabriel's trumpet. I collapsed, weeping, terrified, and Emile led me out. He walked me up to Herald Square. It was night. He talked to me; he tried to make me see something—tried to do something only a friend can do: and challenged me, thus:

Even if what I was preaching was gospel, I had no right to preach it if I no longer believed it. To stay in the church merely because I was afraid of leaving it was unutterably far beneath me, and too despicable a cowardice for him to support in any friend of his. Therefore, on the coming Sunday, he would buy two tickets to a Broadway matinee and meet me on the steps of the 42nd Street Library, at two o'clock in the afternoon. He knew that I spent all day Sunday in church—the point, precisely, of the challenge. If I were not on the steps of the library (in the bookshelves of which so much of my trouble had begun!) then he would be ashamed of me and never speak to me again, and I would be ashamed of myself.

(I cannot resist observing that this still seems to me a quite extraordinary confrontation between two adolescents, one white and one black: but, then, I had never forgotten Bill's quiet statement, when I went down to her house on 12th Street to tell her that I had been "saved" and would not be going to the movies, or the theater anymore—which meant that I would not be seeing her anymore: *I've lost a lot of respect for you.* Perhaps, in the intervening time, I had lost a lot of respect for myself.)

But beneath all this, as under a graveyard pallor, or the noonday sun, lay the fact that the leap demanded that I commit myself to the clear impossibility of becoming a writer, and attempting to save my family that way. I do not think I said this. I think Emile knew it.

I had hoped for a reprieve, hoped, on the marked Sunday, to get away, unnoticed: but I was the "young" Brother Baldwin, and I sat in the front row, and the pastor did not begin his sermon until about a quarter past one. Well. At one thirty, I—*tiptoed*—out. The further details of my departure do not concern us here: that was how I left the church.

I am fairly certain that the matinee, that Sunday, was *Native Son* (also directed by Orson Welles) at the St. James Theatre. We were in the balcony, and I remember standing up, abruptly and unwisely, when the play ended, and nearly falling headlong from the balcony to the pit. I did not know that I had been hit so hard: I will not forget Canada Lee's performance as long as I live.

Canada Lee was Bigger Thomas, but he was also Canada Lee: his physical presence, like the physical presence of Paul Robeson, gave me the right to live. He was not at the mercy of my imagination, as he would have been, on the screen: he was on the stage, in flesh and blood, and I was, therefore, at the mercy of *his* imagination.

For that long-ago *Macbeth* had both terrified and exhilarated me. I knew enough to know that the actress (the colored lady!) who played Lady Macbeth might very well be a janitor, or a janitor's wife, when the play closed, or when the curtain came down. Macbeth was a nigger, just like me, and I saw the witches in church, every Sunday, and all up and down the block, all week long, and Banquo's face was a familiar face. At the same time, the majesty and torment on that stage were real: indeed they revealed the play, *Macbeth*. They *were* those people and that torment was a torment I recognized, those were real daggers, it was real blood, and those crimes resounded and compounded, as real crimes do: I did not have to ask, *what happens to them now?* And, if niggers have rhythm, these niggers had the beat—*tomorrow and tomorrow and tomorrow*, and—*thou shalt be King hereafter!* It is not accidental that I was carrying around the plot of a play in my head, and looking, with a new wonder (and a new terror) at everyone around me, when I suddenly found myself on the floor of the church, one Sunday, crying holy unto the Lord. Flesh and blood had proved to be too much for flesh and blood.

For, they were themselves, these actors—these people were themselves. They could *be* Macbeth only because they were themselves: my first real apprehension of the mortal challenge. Here, nothing corroborated any of my fantasies: flesh and blood was being challenged by flesh and blood. It is said that the camera cannot lie, but rarely do we allow it to do anything else, since the camera sees what you point it at: the camera sees what you want it to see. The language of the camera is the language of our dreams.

TWO
WHO SAW HIM DIE? I, SAID THE FLY

> If religion was a thing
> money could buy,
> The rich would live,
> and the poor would die.
>
> **TRADITIONAL**

I SHALL SPIT on Your Graves is a French look at the black American problem. It is, also, an utterly cynical use of the name of Boris Vian, the young Frenchman who wrote the novel on which the film is emphatically *not* based. (I am told that Vian never saw the completed film. During the first screening of the film, he had a heart attack and died. The story may be apocryphal, but I can well believe it.)

Vian himself points out, somewhat savagely, that *I Shall Spit on Your Graves* is not a very good novel: he was enraged (and enlightened) by the vogue it had in France. This vogue was due partly to the fact that it was presented as Vian's translation of an American novel. But this vogue was due also to Vian himself, who was one of the most striking figures of a long-ago Saint-Germain des Prés. I am speaking of the immediate postwar years. Paris was then on bicycles: there were few cars, and gas (along with milk, cheese, and butter) was rationed. Juliette Greco was in the process of becoming famous in *Le Tabou*, and was often to be seen driving an ancient automobile: she was the envy of the neighborhood. Sidney Bechet and Claude Luter were playing together at *Le Vieux Colombier;* Kenny Clarke was soon to arrive. There were jam sessions over a theater in rue Fontaine which lasted until dawn, and sometimes until noon, at one of which jam sessions I first heard Annie Ross.

I was sitting at the Café Flore one afternoon when an enormous car, with baggage piled on the roof, stopped before the café. A large woman opened the car door, leaned out, and yelled, "Is Jean-Paul Sartre here today?" The waiter said, "No, madame," whereupon the car door slammed, and the car drove off. Camus' hour had yet so savagely to strike: and both men eventually disappeared from the Flore. The curious, and, on the whole, rather obvious doctrine of *l'existentialisme* flourished, and the word *négritude*, though it was beginning to be muttered, had yet to be heard. *I Shall Spit on Your Graves,* and Vian himself, and a tense, even rather terrified wonder about Americans, were part of this ferment: and, further, the strait-laced French (who had not yet heard of Jean Genet, and who remain absolutely impervious to Rimbaud and Baudelaire) considered the novel pornographic.

One of the reasons—perhaps *the* reason—that the novel was considered pornographic is that it is concerned with the vindictive sexual aggression of one black man against many women. (At that moment in time, the black G.I. in Europe was a genuinely disturbing conundrum.) The novel takes place in America, and the black man looks like a white man—this double remove liberating both fantasy and hope, which is, perhaps, at bottom, what pornography is all about. This is certainly what that legend created by Rudolph Valentino, in *The Sheik,* is all about, as is made clear by his fan mail—poor boy!—and this fantasy and hope contain the root appeal of *Tarzan* (*King of the Apes!*). Both the Sheik and Tarzan are white men who look and act like black men—act like black men, that is, according to the white imagination which has created them: one can eat one's cake without having it, or one can have one's cake without eating it.

What informs Vian's book, however, is not sexual fantasy, but rage and pain: that rage and pain which Vian (almost alone) was able to hear in the black American musicians, in the bars, dives, and cellars, of the Paris of those years. In his book, a black man who can "cross the line" sets out to avenge the murder of his younger, darker brother; and the primary tool of this vengeance is—his tool. Vian would have known something of this from Faulkner, and from Richard Wright, and from Chester Himes, but he *heard* it in the music, and, indeed, he saw it in the streets. Vian's character is eventually uncovered, but not before he has seduced and murdered two of the richest and most attractive white women he can find. He is caught, and hanged—hung, like a horse, his sex, according to Vian, mocking his murders to the last. Vian did not know that this particular nigger would almost certainly have been castrated: which is but another and deadlier way for white men to be mocked by the terror and the fury by which they are engulfed upon the discovery that the black man is a man: "it hurt," says T. E. Lawrence, in *Seven Pillars of Wisdom*, "that they [the negroes] should possess exact counter-parts of all our bodies."

Vian's social details, as concerns American life, are all askew, but he had the sense to frame his story in such a way as to prevent these details from intruding. And he gets some things right, for example, the idle, self-centered, spoiled, erotic dreaming of a certain category of American youth: there are moments which bring to mind *Rebel Without a Cause*. For these children, the passage of time can mean only the acceleration of hostility and despair. In spite of the book's naïveté, Vian cared enough about his subject to force one into a confrontation with a certain kind of anguish. The book's power comes from the fact that he forces you to see this anguish from the undisguised viewpoint of his foreign, alienated own.

The film is quite another matter, having, for one thing, no viewpoint whatever except that from the window of the Stock Exchange. The film takes place, so we are endlessly informed, in Trenton: which is, in the film, a small, unbelievably unattractive town, just outside of Paris, on the road to New Orleans. In fact, it begins in (I guess) New Orleans, with a black boy, playing a harmonica, sitting on an immense bale of cotton which is being hoisted to the dock. The boy jumps off the bale of cotton, still playing his harmonica, starts walking; is grabbed around the neck by his affectionate, older, light white brother; and, alas, the film begins. The young black boy, who would appear to be about thirteen, seems to have been playing around with a white girl. (We do not, thank heaven, meet her.) His older brother warns him to be careful. Harmonica says that he will be. The brothers separate, and we next see and hear Harmonica in the cool of the evening (not yet in the heat of the night) unconcernedly walking along a deserted country road. Headlights flash behind him; white men leap out of their cars, the boy turns to face them; and the next time we see him, he is hanging from a tree.

His older light white brother cuts him down and carries him

to where the darkies are assembled, beginning to moan—the darkies, that is. The older light white brother vows vengeance, over the Christian plea for forgiveness of the old black preacher, to whom he appears—though certainly not physically—to be related. He puts his brother's body on a table in the cabin, while the darkies watch; douses it with kerosene, while the darkies watch, and moan; lights a match, setting his brother, the cabin, and, presumably, the entire neighborhood aflame, while the darkies keep moaning; and, sensibly enough, leaves.

There follows a somewhat opaque episode, involving the French idea of a drunken, cowardly Southerner—an idea which is not absolutely inaccurate, bearing in mind that *New* Orleans is found in the state of *Louisiana*, for very precise reasons, and leaving aside the Haitian adventure, and to go, for the moment, no further than that—from whom our hero, indisputably *évolué*, needs credentials for Trenton: a city to be found, he has been told, in the North. For he is going North, he is going to "cross the line," and he is, in effect, black-mailing the Southern drunkard into being his accomplice. There is a great deal of unsuspenseful business with a loaded shotgun, but our hero gets the letter, throws the loaded shotgun toward the arms of his drunken friend, gets into his car, and drives off. (None of this paranoia is in Vian's book.) Our hero takes what is, in effect, his letter of racial credit to an aging bookstore owner in Trenton, and so we meet the far from merry maidens of our hero's grim desire.

Vian's book has a certain weary, misogynistic humor—the chicks fuck like rabbits, or minks, and our hero gets a certain charge, or arrives at the mercy of a nearly unbearable ecstasy, out of his private knowledge that they are being fucked by a nigger: he is committing the crime for which his brother was murdered, he is fucking these cunts with his brother's prick. And he comes three times, so to speak, each time he comes, once for his brother, and once for the "little death" of the orgasms to which he always brings the ladies, and, uncontrollably, for the real death to which he is determined to bring them. This intersection, where life disputes with death, is very vivid in the book: and it does not, of course, exist in the film.

In the book, one believes that the hero loved his brother, and to such a depth indeed that he is deliberately destroying his own sexuality—his hope of love—in order to keep faith with his destroyed brother: *the mortification of the flesh*. One may object that this is not exactly what Paul or Peter or The Bank of the Holy Ghost meant to say, but, incontestably, this is what has been accomplished: that the use of one's own body in the act of love is considered a crime against the Holy Ghost. No greater blasphemy against the human being can be imagined. One may remark that the hero's vengeance is not at all what the brother would have wanted, for his brother, but the younger brother is not there to speak for himself. The younger brother lives only in the memory of his older brother, and in the unanswerable light of an unforgivable crime.

This relentless need for something much deeper than revenge comes close to the truth of many lives, black and white: but revenge is not among the human possibilities. Revenge is a human dream. There is no way of conveying to the corpse the reasons you have made him one—you have the corpse, and you are, thereafter, at the mercy of a fact which missed the truth, which means that the corpse has you. On the other hand, the corpse doesn't want his murderer, either, and one is under the iron obligation not to allow oneself to be turned into one. The key is contained in the question of where the power lies—power, literally, and power on a more dreadful level—and Vian's anecdote pivots on the geometry of destruction and self-destruction. This is a delicate tightrope stretched taut and high, above unimaginable chasms, coming close to the truth of many black lives: many have fallen, but many have not. There is, indeed, far beyond and beneath the truth of Vian's anecdote, another truth, a truth which drags us into the icy and fiery center of a mystery: how have we endured? But the key word, there, is *we*.

In the film there is no brother, there are no brothers, there are no women, no passion, and no pain: there is the guilty, furtive, European notion of sex, a notion which obliterates any possibility of communion, or any hope of love. There is also the European dream of America—which, after all, is how we *got* America: a dream full of envy, guilt, condescension, and terror, a dream which began as an adventure in real estate. That song which Europe let out of its heart so long ago, to be sung on ships, and to cross all that water, is now coming back to Europe, perhaps to drive Europe mad: the return of the song will certainly render Europe obsolete, and return the North American wilderness—yet to be conquered!—to a truth which has nothing to do with Europe.

The Birth of a Nation is based on a novel I will almost certainly never read, *The Clansman,* by a certain Thomas Dixon, who achieved it sometime after the Civil War. He did not, oddly enough, write the 1952 film, *Storm Warning,* also about the Klan, starring Ginger Rogers, Steve Cochran, Ronald Reagan, and Doris Day. Unlike, and quite unjustly, *Storm Warning* (possibly because the Ginger Rogers film speaks courageously for the Union, and against the Confederacy), *The Birth of a Nation* is known as one of the great classics of the American cinema: and indeed it is.

It is impossible to do justice to the story, such story as attempts to make an appearance being immediately submerged by the tidal wave of the plot; and, in Griffith's handling of this fable, anyway, the key is to be found in the images. The film cannot be called dishonest: it has the Niagara force of an obsession.

A story is impelled by the necessity to reveal: the aim of the story is revelation, which means that a story can have nothing—at least not deliberately—to hide. This also means that a story resolves nothing. The resolution of a story must occur in us, with what we make of the questions with which the story leaves us. A plot, on the other hand, must come to a resolution, prove a point: a plot must answer all the questions which it pretends to pose. *In the Heat of the Night,* for example, turns on a plot, a plot designed to camouflage exceedingly bitter questions; it can be said, for *The Defiant Ones,* that it attempts to tell a story. The Book of Job is a story, the proof being that the details of Job's affliction never, for an instant, obscure Job from our view. This story has no resolution. We end where we began: everything Job has lost has been returned to him. And, yet, we are not quite where we began. We do not know what that voice out of the whirlwind will thunder next time—and we know that there will certainly be a next time. Job is not the same, nor are we: Job's story has changed Job forever, and illuminated us. By contrast, the elaborate anecdote of Joseph and his brothers turns on a plot, the key to which is that coat of many colors. That coat is meant to blind us to the fact that the anecdote of Joseph and his brothers, so far from being a record of brotherly love and forgiveness, is an absolutely deadly study of frustrated fratricide and frustrated (although elaborately disguised) revenge. When Joseph feeds his brothers, it is not an act of love: he could just as easily have let them starve, which they, very logically, expected him to do. They, just as logically, expected him to die when they threw him into the pit. Having done the unexpected once, Joseph can do it twice: *here is the brother who was thrown into a pit by you, my brothers, and left alone there to die!—help yourself, there's plenty*. Neither Joseph, nor, more importantly, perhaps, his brothers, have got past that day. It is an act which cannot be forgotten, any more than the branding iron on the skin can be forgotten. And, if it cannot be forgotten, which is to say undone, then it will certainly, in one way or another, be repeated: therefore, it cannot be forgiven: a grave matter, if one accepts my central premise, which is that all men are brothers.

Similarly, *The Birth of a Nation* is really an elaborate justification of mass murder. The film cannot possibly admit this, which is why we are immediately placed at the mercy of a plot labyrinthine and preposterous—as follows:

The gallant South, on the edge of the great betrayal by the Northern brethren: this is the pastoral and yet doom-laden weight of the early images. Two brothers, robust, two sisters, fair, a handsome house, a loving and united family, and happy, loyal slaves.

Unhappily, however, for the South, and for us all, a certain eminent Southern politician has a mulatto slave mistress—a house nigger, whose cot he shares when the sun goes down: she does not share his bed, to which he returns shortly before the sun comes up: and the baleful effect of this carnal creature on the eminent Southern politician helps bring about the ruin of the South. I cannot tell you exactly *how* she brings about so devastating a fate, and I defy anyone to tell *me:* but she does. Without attempting to track my way through any more of what we will call the pre-plot: the War comes. The South is shamefully defeated—or, not so much defeated, it would appear, as betrayed: by the influence of the mulattoes. For the previously noted eminent and now renegade Southern politician has also, as it turns out, a mulatto protégé (we do not know how this happened, but we are allowed to suspect the worst) and this mulatto protégé is maneuvered into the previously all-white Congress of the United States. At which point the Carpetbaggers arrive, and the movie begins. For the film is concerned with the Reconstruction, and how the birth of the Ku Klux Klan overcame that dismal and mistaken chapter in our—American—history.

The first image of the film is of the African slave's arrival. The image and the title both convey the European terror before the idea of the black and white, red and white, saved and pagan, confrontation. I think that it was Freud who suggested that the presence of the black man in America foreshadowed America's doom—which America, if it could not civilize these savages, would deserve: it is certainly the testimony of such disparate witnesses as William Faulkner and Isadora Duncan. For Marx and Engels, the presence of the black man in America was simply a useful crowbar for the liberation of whites: an idea which has had its issue in the history of American labor unions. The Founding Fathers shared this view, eminently, Thomas Jefferson, and The Great Emancipator freed those slaves he could not reach, in order to create, hopefully, a fifth column behind the Confederate lines. This ambivalence contains the key to American literature—all the way from *The Scarlet Letter* to *The Big Sleep*. In any case, what Europe really felt about the black presence in America is revealed by the stratagems the European-Americans have used, and use, to avoid it: that is, by American history, or the actual, present condition of any American city.

The first image, then, of *The Birth of a Nation* is immensely and unconsciously revealing. Were it not for their swarthy color—or not even that, so many immigrants having been transformed into white men only upon arrival, and, as it were, by decree—were it not for the title preceding the image: they would look exactly like European passengers, huddled, silent, patient, and hopeful, in the shadow of the Statue of Liberty. (*Give us your poor!* Many of the poor, not only in America, but all over the world, are beginning to find that these famous lines have a somewhat sinister ring.) These slaves look as though they *want* to enter the Promised Land, and are regarding their imminent masters in the hope of being bought.

This is not exactly the way blacks looked, of course, as they entered America, nor were they yet covered by European clothes. Blacks got here nearly as naked as the day they were born, and were sold that way, every inch of their anatomy exposed and examined, teeth to testicles, breast to bottom. That's how darkies were born: more to the point, here, it is certainly how mulattoes were born.

For, the most striking thing about the merciless plot on which *The Birth of a Nation* depends is that, although the legend of the nigger controls it the way the day may be controlled by threat of rain, there are really no niggers in it. The plot is entirely controlled by the image of the mulatto, and there are two of them, one male and one female. All of the energy of the film is siphoned off into these two dreadful and improbable creatures. It might have made sense—that is, might have made a story—if these two mulattoes had been related to each other, or to the renegade politician, whose wards they are: but, no, he seems to have dreamed them up (they *are* like creatures in a nightmare *someone* is having) and they are related to each other only by their envy of white people. The renegade politician, I should already have told you—but this is one of the difficulties of trying to follow a plot—is also the heroine's father. This fact brings about his belated enlightenment, the final victory of the Klan, the film's denouement, and a double wedding.

I am leaving a great deal out, but, in any case, the renegade politician is brought brutally to his senses when his mulatto ward, now a rising congressman, so far forgets himself as to offer himself in marriage to the renegade politician's beautiful daughter, Miss Lillian Gish. The Klan rides out in fury, making short work of the ruffian, and others like him. The niggers are last seen, heads averted and eyes down, returning to their cabins—none of which have been burned, apparently, there being no point in burning empty cabins—and the South rises triumphantly to its feet.

It is not clear what happens to the one presumably remaining mulatto, the female. Neither of the two mulattoes had any sexual interest in the other; given what we see of their charms, this is quite understandable. Both are driven by a hideous lust for whites, she for the master, he for the maid: they are, at least, thank heaven, heterosexual, due, probably, to their lack of imagination.

Their lust for the whites, however, is of such a nature that it suffers from all the manifestations of hysterical hatred. And this is not quite so understandable, except in the gaudy light of the film's intention. The film presents us, after all, with the spectacle of a noble planet, brought to such a pass that even their loyal slaves are subverted. For the sake of the dignity of this temporarily defeated people, and out of a vivid and loving concern for their betrayed and endangered slaves, the violated social order must, at all costs, be re-established. And it *is* re-established by the vision and heroism of the noblest (and, in future, overt), has been brought about, not through any fault of their own, and not because of any defection among their slaves, but by the weak and misguided among them who have given the mulattoes ideas above their station.

But how did so ungodly a creature as the mulatto enter this Eden, and where did he come from?

The film cannot concern itself with this inconvenient and impertinent question, any more than can Governor Wallace, or the bulk of his confreres, North or South. We need not pursue it, except to observe that almost all mulattoes, and especially at that time, were produced by white men, and rarely indeed by an act of love. The mildest possible word is coercion: which is why white men invented the crime of rape, with the specific intention (and effect) of castrating and hanging the nigger. Neither did black men fasten on the word, *mulatto*, to describe the issue of their loins. But white men did—as follows:

The root of the word, *mulatto*, is Spanish, according to Webster, from *mulo*, a mule. The word refers to: (1) a person, one of whose parents is Negro and the other Caucasian, or white; and (2) popularly, any person with mixed Negro and Caucasian ancestry.

A mule is defined as (1) the offspring of a donkey and a horse, especially the offspring of a jackass and a mare—*mules are usually sterile*. And, a further definition: in biology, a hybrid, *especially a sterile hybrid*. (Italics mine.)

The idea of producing a child, on condition, and under the guarantee, that the child cannot reproduce must, after all, be relatively rare: no matter how dim a view one may take of the human race. It argues an extraordinary spiritual condition, or an unspeakable spiritual poverty: to produce a child with the intention of using it to gain a lease on limbo, or, failing that, on purgatory: to produce a child with the extinction of the child as one's hope of heaven. *Mulatto*: for that outpost of Christianity, that segment of the race which called itself white, which found itself stranded among the heathen on the North American continent, under the necessity of destroying all evidence of sin, including, if need be, those children who were proof of abandonment to savage, heathen passion, and under the absolute necessity of preserving its idea of itself by any means necessary, the use of the word, *mulatto*, was by no means inadvertent. It was one of the keys to American history, present, and past. Americans are still destroying their own children: and, infanticide being but a step away from genocide, not only theirs. If we do not know where the mulatto came from, we certainly know where a multitude went, dispatched by their own fathers, and we know where multitudes are, until today, plotting death, plotting life, groaning in the chains in which their fathers have bound them.

Our fathers, indeed, for here we all are: and we encounter an invitation to discover the essential decency of this history (this is known as progress) in the person of the Sheriff in a film made some fifty-odd years later, *In the Heat of the Night*.

This film has no mulattoes: unless one wishes to examine, with a certain rigor, the roles played by some of the townspeople: we will return to this speculation: and, apart from the brief cotton-picking sequence, seen from the window of the Sheriff's moving car, it is hard to locate the niggers. (This, also, is progress.) The man who lodges the black detective comes close to being a nigger. The lady who arranges abortions is dark indeed, but is clearly passing—through; and Mr. Virgil Tibbs comes from freedom-loving Philadelphia, the city of brotherly love. To this haven, he will return, if he lives. But we know that he *will* live. The star of a film is rarely put to death, and certainly not *this* star, and certainly not in this film.

The entire burden, therefore, of such suspense as the film may claim to have falls squarely on the shoulders of the Sheriff (Rod Steiger). The life of Virgil Tibbs (Sidney Poitier) is endangered precisely to the extent that we are concerned about the salvation of the Sheriff's soul. One ought, indeed, I suppose, to be concerned about the soul of any descendant of *The Birth of a Nation,* and the Sheriff is certainly such a descendant, as is the film itself. On the other hand, it is difficult to sustain such a concern when the concern is not reciprocal, and if this concern demands one's complicity in a lie: which state of affairs, having gone beyond progress, is sometimes called brotherhood, the achievement of which state of grace is exactly what *In the Heat of the Night* imagines itself to be about.

The film is breathtaking, not to say vertiginous, in the speed with which it moves from one preposterous proposition to another. We are asked to believe that a grown black man, who knows the South, and who, being a policeman, must know something about his colleagues, both South and North, would elect to change trains in a Southern backwater at that hour of the early morning and sit alone in the waiting room; that the Sheriff imagines that he needs a confession from this black Northern vagrant, and so elects to converse with him before locking him up, turning him over to his deputies, and closing the case. (Of course, it is suggested, at that moment—and quite helplessly, the truth of the white and black male meeting living far beneath the moment of this manipulated scene—that the Sheriff is being something of a sadist, and is playing cat and mouse.) And the film betrays itself, in the early sequences, in quite a curious way. One might suppose, after all, since the film was made *after* the 1964 Civil Rights Act, that the Sheriff might be concerned about the pressure which might be brought to bear by the Federal Government: but this possibility, astoundingly enough, does not appear to enter his mind. He reacts to the fact that the black man makes more money than he does which has the effect of eliciting our sympathy for this doubly poor white man. Virgil's continued presence on the case is due entirely to the reaction of the widow of the murdered man; this man, conveniently enough (as concerns the necessities of the plot) was in the process of bringing new industry to the town when he was murdered. As the man's widow, she now has the power to transfer this potential wealth to another town, which she will do if Virgil is not allowed to continue his investigation of her husband's murder. This convolution of the plot really demands a separate essay: it contains so many oblique and unconscious confessions concerning the roles of money, sex, marriage, greed, and guilt and power. In any case, the widow, having done her bit, disappears, and the town is stuck with Virgil. So is the Sheriff: and the Sheriff just don't know, now, if he glad or if he bad: but he got to do his best to look bad.

What kind of people are you? the widow cries out at one point in the film: as well she might. There is something really stunning—cunning is too loaded a word—in the casting of this film. Poitier's presence gives the film its only real virility, and so emphatically indeed that the emotional climate of the film is that of a mysteriously choked and baffled—and yet compulsive—act of contrition. This virility is not in the least compromised by the fact that he has no woman, visibly: on the contrary, it is thus reinforced, since we know that he is saving himself for Philadelphia, where *"they call me Mr. Tibbs!"* The wealth of his health is presented in very powerful contrast to the poverty and infirmity of the white men by whom he is surrounded, and is the only genuinely positive element the film contains. It coats the film lightly, so to speak, with a kind of desperately boyish, unadmitted anguish. But that the film cannot or dare not pursue the implications of this sorrow is made very clear in that choked and opaque scene between the black detective and the Sheriff, in the latter's living room, over bourbon. The chief deputy, Sam (Warren Oates), in terms of the weights and balances of the film has the best assignment, his role allowing him to be absolutely truthful, though never deep. Sam drives his patrol car, each night, off his route to watch a naked girl through the windows of her house. She is to be found thus, apparently, every night, at the hour that Sam drives by: and, so far as the film informs us, this is their only connection—a rather horrifying thought, when one considers how much of the truth it contains, for lives like that, and in such a town.

The girl is a poor white, and is as marked by this misfortune as are the mulattoes of *The Birth of a Nation,* and she has a poor white brother, who appears to know nothing at all about his sister. There is the white boy, picked up for the murder after Virgil Tibbs's credentials have been established, and Virgil has agreed to remain on the case, or been coerced into doing so: this boy first hates, then learns to love the black cop who clears him, and saves his life. And there is the waiter in the diner, who refuses to serve Virgil Tibbs. This is an utterly grotesque creature, as hysterical as *Nation*'s mulatto maid, presented as being virtually biologically inferior to everyone else. He, it turns out, is the lover of the exhibitionistic girl—a circumstance which one does not believe for a moment, not even in that sleepy little town—and he is the father of the child she is expecting. He is, also, the murderer. He committed the murder because (I think) he needed money for an abortion. The climactic scene, anyway, takes place outside the establishment of the lady who deals in abortions. This is an exciting scene indeed, but before I try to deal with this excitement, there are a couple of other scenes we should consider.

One is the scene in the hothouse of the wealthy horticulturist, who is presented as being one of the most powerful men of the region. In this scene, Tibbs exhibits a somewhat unexpected knowledge of varieties of plant life. This allows his host to make clear his racial bias. ("These plants are delicate. They like the nigras. They need care.") One thing leads to another, so to speak, and, eventually, the wealthy horticulturist slaps Tibbs in the face. Under the eyes of the Sheriff, Tibbs slaps him back. The wealthy host is astonished that the Sheriff does not shoot Tibbs on the spot: the Sheriff, furious that anyone should suppose him capable of so base an action, throws his chewing gum on the ground (of the powerful host) and stalks out, after Virgil. The wealthy landowner ("There was a day when I could have had you shot!") looks on in disbelief, and we leave him weeping, possibly because his day has passed. End of joke.

Then, there is the scene with the lady who deals in abortions. I have described this lady somewhat rudely; she may have passed through the West Indies, or Africa, and, at that, speedily; but she surely do not come from around here. She appears to be looking for a home, and, from the way Virgil Tibbs treats her, no wonder—I would, too. Demanding to know who, in the town, is paying for an abortion, he informs her (speaking of the prison sentence with which he is threatening her) that "there's white time and black time—and ain't nothing worse than black time!" The lady who deals in abortions appears to be utterly astounded and downcast by this news and rolls her eyes toward (I suppose) her suitcase. But she is saved by the arrival of the exhibitionistic girl: who, seeing Virgil Tibbs (they have met before), runs out into the night.

Virgil runs after her (while the lady who deals in abortions flees into the back room, to pack, and book passage to Canada, or Algeria) and picks up the fleeing poor white chick in his arms. In this unlucky posture he is found as headlights flash, before, and behind, and all around him, and white men leap out of their cars: into the heat of the night.

This is the penultimate, exciting scene. One of the white men is the poor white brother of the poor white girl, and, naturally, he intends to lynch the nigger, whose black hands are still on the body of his white sister. With great presence of mind, Mr. Tibbs drops the sister and points to the real killer, who has the money for the abortion in his pocket. The attention of the murderous mob is thus distracted, naturally, from the nigger and the white chick to this creep, who promptly shoots the brother, dead: end of exciting scene.

There remains the obligatory, fade-out kiss. I am aware that men do not kiss each other in American films, nor, for the most part, in America, nor do the black detective and the white Sheriff kiss here. But the obligatory, fade-out kiss, in the classic American film, did not really speak of love, and, still less, of sex: it spoke of reconciliation, of all things now becoming possible. It was a device desperately needed among a people for whom so much had to be made possible. And, no matter how inept one must judge this film to be, in spite of its absolutely appalling distance from reality, in spite of my own helplessly sardonic tone when discussing it, and even in spite of the fact that the effect of such a film is to increase and not lessen white confusion and complacency, and black rage and despair, I still do not wish to be guilty of the gratuitous injustice of seeming to impute base motives to the people responsible for its existence. Our situation would be far more coherent if it were possible to categorize, or dismiss, *In the Heat of the Night* so painlessly. No: the film helplessly conveys—without confronting—the anguish of people trapped in a legend. They cannot live within this legend; neither can they step out of it. The film gave me the impression, according to my notes the day I saw it, of "something strangling, alive, struggling to get out." And I certainly felt this during the final scene, when the white Sheriff takes the black detective's bag as they walk to the train. It is not that the creators of the film were inspired by base motives, but that they could not understand their motives, nor be responsible for the effect of their exceedingly complex motives, in action. (All motives are complex, and it is just as well to remember this: including, or perhaps especially, one's own.) The history which produces such a film cannot, after all, be swiftly understood, nor can the effects of this history be easily resolved. Nor can this history be blamed on any single individual; but, at the same time, no one can be let off the hook. It is a terrible thing, simply, to be trapped in one's history, and attempt, in the same motion (and in this, our life!) to accept, deny, reject, and redeem it—and, also, on whatever level, to profit from it. And: with one's head in the fetid jaws of this lion's mouth, attempt to love and be loved, and raise one's children, and pay the rent, and wrestle with one's mortality. In the final scene at the station, there is something choked and moving, something sensed through a thick glass, dimly, in the Sheriff's sweet, boyish, Southern injunction, to Virgil, "take care, you hear?" and something equally choked and rigid in the black detective's reaction. It reminded me of nothing so much as William Blake's *Little Black Boy*—that remote, that romantic, and that hopeless. Virgil Tibbs goes to where they call him *Mister*, far away, presumably, from South Street, and the Sheriff has gone back to the niggers, who are really his only assignment. And nothing, alas, has been made possible by this obligatory, fade-out kiss, this preposterous adventure: except that white Americans have been encouraged to continue dreaming, and black Americans have been alerted to the necessity of waking up. People who cannot escape thinking of themselves as white are poorly equipped, if equipped at all, to consider the meaning of black: people who know so little about themselves can face very little in another: and one dare hope for nothing from friends like these. This cruel observation is implicit in the script: for what would have happened to our Mr. Tibbs, or, indeed, to our Sheriff, had the widow demanded the black man's blood as the price for the wealth she was bringing into the town? Who, among that manly crew, would have resisted the widow's might? The people of *In the Heat of the Night* can be considered moving and pathetic only if one has the luxury of the assurance that one will never be at their mercy. And that no one in the world has the luxury of this assurance is beginning to be clear: all over the world.

In *The Birth of a Nation,* the Sheriff would have been an officer of the Klan. The widow would, secretly, have been sewing Klan insignia. The murdered man (whether or not he was her husband) would have been a carpetbagger. Sam would have been a Klan deputy. The troublesome poor whites would have been mulattoes. And Virgil Tibbs would have been the hunted, not the hunter. It is impossible to pretend that this state of affairs has really altered: a black man, in any case, had certainly best not believe everything he sees in the movies.

In 1942, Bette Davis, under the direction of John Huston, delivered a ruthlessly accurate (and much underrated) portrait of a Southern girl, in the Warner Brothers production of Ellen Glasgow's novel, *In This, Our Life*. She thus became, and, indeed, remained, the toast of Harlem because her prison scene with the black chauffeur was cut when the movie came uptown. The uproar in Harlem was impressive, and I think that the scene was reinserted; in any case, either uptown or downtown, I saw it. Davis appeared to have read, and grasped, the script—which must have made her rather lonely—and she certainly understood the role. Her performance had the effect, rather, of exposing and shattering the film, so that she played in a kind of vacuum: much the same thing was to happen, later, to Sidney Poitier, with his creation of Noah Cullen, in *The Defiant Ones*.

In *In This, Our Life,* Davis is a spoiled Southern girl, guilty of murder in a hit-and-run automobile accident, and she has blamed this crime on her black chauffeur. (An actor named Ernest Anderson: Hattie McDaniel played his mother.) But he has steadfastly denied having had the car that night. She, armed with her wealth, her color, and her sex, goes to the prison to persuade him to corroborate her story: and what she uses, through jailhouse bars, is her sex. She will pay, for the chauffeur's silence, any price he demands. Indeed, the price is implicit in the fact that she knows he knows that she is guilty: she can have no secrets from him now.

Blacks are often confronted, in American life, with such devastating examples of the white descent from dignity; devastating not only because of the enormity of the white pretensions, but because this swift and graceless descent would seem to indicate that white people have no principles whatever. At the beginning of the Attica uprising, for example, a white guard was heard pleading with a black prisoner: "You can have anything you want," the guard is reported to have said. "You can have *me*. Just don't send me out there."

In the film, the black chauffeur simply does not trust the white girl to keep her end of the bargain—which would involve using her power to save his life—and is far too proud, anyway, to strike such a bargain. But the offer has been made, and the truth about the woman revealed.

The blacks have a song which says, *I can't believe what you say, because I see what you do.* No American film, relating to blacks, can possibly incorporate this observation. This observation—set to music, as are so many black observations—denies, simply, the validity of the legend which is responsible for these films; films which exist for the sole purpose of perpetuating the legend.

Black men, after all, have been the lovers, and victims, of women like the woman in *In This, Our Life:* and these women have also been the victims of black men: and sometimes they have loved each other; and sometimes had to live in hell to pay for it. Even the most thoughtless, even the most deluded black person knows more about his life than the image he is offered as the justification of it. Black men know something about white sheriffs. They know, for one thing, that the sheriff is no freer to become friends with them than they are to become friends with the sheriff: For example:

A white taxi driver once drove me from the airport in Birmingham, Alabama, to the Gaston Motel. This is a long, dark, tree-lined drive, and the taxi driver was breaking the law: for a white taxi driver is not—or was not, it is hard to be accurate concerning the pace of my country's progress—allowed to pick up a black fare. That this was not a wicked man is proven, perhaps, by the fact that I am still here. But I was in his cab only because the idea of waiting another hour at the airport (sitting on my typewriter, which I never carried South again) was too frightening. I had had no choice but to gamble on him. Yet, I could not be at ease about his motives in breaking the law for a black, Northern journalist. It was perfectly possible, after all, that he had no intention of driving me to the Gaston Motel (which had already been bombed three times) but to my death. And there was no way for this thought not to have entered my mind: I would have had to be mindless not to have thought it. And what was he thinking? For, I felt that he wanted to talk to me, and I certainly wanted to talk to him. But neither of us could manage it. It was not his fault, and it was not my fault. We could find no way out of our common trouble, for we had been forbidden—and on pain of death—to trust, or to use, our common humanity, that confrontation and acceptance which is all that can save another human being.

Blacks know something about black cops, too, even those called Mister, in Philadelphia. They know that their presence on the force doesn't change the force or the judges or the lawyers or the bondsmen or the jails. They know the black cop's mother and his father, they may have met the sister, and they know the younger, or the older brother, who may be a bondsman, or a junkie, or a student, in limbo, at Yale. They know how much the black cop has to prove, and how limited are his means of proving it: where I grew up, black cops were yet more terrifying than white ones.

I think that it was T. S. Eliot who observed that the people cannot bear very much reality. This may be true enough, as far as it goes, so much depending on what the word "people" brings to mind: I think that we bear a little more reality than we might wish. In any case, in order for a person to bear his life, he needs a valid re-creation of that life, which is why, as Ray Charles might put it, blacks chose to sing the blues. This is why *Raisin in the Sun* meant so much to black people—on the stage: the film is another matter. In the theater, a current flowed back and forth between the audience and the actors: flesh and blood corroborating flesh and blood—as we say, testifying. The filmed play, which is all, alas, that *Raisin* is on film, simply stayed up there, on that screen. The unimaginative rigidity of the film locked the audience out of it. Furthermore, the people in *Raisin* are not the people one goes to the movies to see. The root argument of the play is really far more subtle than either its detractors or the bulk of its admirers were able to see.

The Defiant Ones, on the other hand, is a film, with people we are accustomed to seeing in the movies. Well: all except one. The irreducible difficulty of this genuinely well-meaning film is that no one, clearly, was able to foresee what Poitier would do with his role—nor was anyone, thereafter, able to undo it—and his performance, which lends the film its only real distinction, also, paradoxically, smashes it to pieces. There is no way to believe both Noah Cullen *and* the story. With the best will in the world, it is virtually impossible to watch Tony Curtis while Sidney is on the screen, or, with the possible exception of Lon Chaney, Jr., anyone else. It is impossible to accept the premise of the story, a premise based on the profound American misunderstanding of the nature of the hatred between black and white. There is a hatred—certainly: though I am now using this word with great caution, and only in the light of the effects, or the results, of hatred. But the hatred is not equal on both sides, for it does not have the same roots. This is, perhaps, a very subtle argument, but black men do not have the same reason to hate white men as white men have to hate blacks. The root of the white man's hatred is terror, a bottomless and nameless terror, which focuses on the black, surfacing, and concentrating on this dread figure, an entity which lives only in his mind. But the root of the black man's hatred is rage, and he does not so much hate white men as simply want them out of his way, and, more than that, out of his children's way. When the white man begins to have in the black man's mind the weight that the black man has in the white man's mind, that black man is going mad. And when he goes under, he does not go under screaming in terror: he goes under howling with rage. A black man knows that two men chained together have to learn to forage, eat, fart, shit, piss, and tremble, and sleep together: they are indispensable to each other, and anything can happen between them, and anyone who has been there knows this. No black man, in such a situation, and especially knowing what Poitier conveys so vividly Noah Cullen knows, would rise to the bait proffered by this dimwitted poor white child, whose only real complaint is that he is a bona-fide mediocrity who failed to make it in the American rat-race. But many, no better than he, and many much worse, make it every day, all the way to Washington: sometimes, indeed, via Hollywood. It is a species of cowardice, grave indeed, to pretend that black men do not know this. And it is a matter of the most disastrous sentimentality to attempt to bring black men into the white American nightmare, and on the same terms, moreover, which make life for white men all but intolerable.

It is this which black audiences resented about *The Defiant Ones:* that Sidney was in company far beneath him, and that the unmistakable truth of his performance was being placed at the mercy of a lie. Liberal white audiences applauded when Sidney, at the end of the film, jumped off the train in order not to abandon his white buddy. The Harlem audience was outraged, and yelled, *Get back on the train, you fool!* And yet, even at that, recognized, in Sidney's face, at the very end, as he sings "Sewing Machine," something noble, true, and terrible, something out of which we come: I have heard exasperated black voices mutter, more than once, *Lord, have mercy on these children, have* mercy—! *they just don't* know.

There is an image in *The Defiant Ones* which suggests the truth it can neither face nor articulate; and there is a sequence which gives the film completely away. The image occurs when the little boy has been disarmed, and, accidentally, knocked unconscious. The two fugitives are anxiously trying to revive him.

When the boy comes to, he looks up and sees Sidney's black face over him: and we see this face from the boy's point of view, and as the boy sees it: black, unreadable, not quite in focus—and, with a moving, and, as I take it, deliberate irony, this image is the single most beautiful image in the film. The boy screams in terror, and turns to the white man for protection; and the white man assures him that he needs no protection from the black man he was cursing when the boy came along.

We are trembling on the edge of confession here, for, of course, the way the little boy sees the black face is exactly the way the man sees it. It is a presence vaguely, but mightily threatening, partly because of its strangeness and privacy, but also because of its beauty: that beauty which lives so tormentedly in the eye of the white beholder. The film cannot pursue this perception, or suspicion, without bringing into focus the question of white maturity, or white masculinity. This is not the ostensible subject of *The Defiant Ones*. Yet, the dilemma with which we are confronted in the film can only begin to be unlocked on that level, precisely, which the film is compelled to avoid.

In the next sequence, they go along to the home of the boy's mother, who lives alone with her child. The husband, or the father, has been long gone. This sequence is crucial, containing the only justification for the ending of the film, and it deserves a little scrutiny.

The woman who now enters the picture has already been abandoned; and, in quite another sense, once she sees the white boy, is anxious to *be* abandoned. She has the tools which allow the two men to destroy the manacles and break the chain which has bound them together for so long.

The logic of actuality would now strongly indicate, given their situation, and what we have seen of their relationship, that they separate. For one thing, each fugitive is safer without the other, and, for another, the woman clearly wishes to be alone with the white boy. She feeds them both, first asking the white boy if he wants her to feed the black one. He says that he does, and they eat. It is unlikely that Noah Cullen would have sat still for this scene, and even more unlikely that he would obligingly fall asleep at the table while the white boy and the woman make love.

Of course, what the film is now attempting to say—consciously—is that the ordeal of the black man and the white man has brought them closer together than they ever imagined they could be. The fact, and the effect, of this particular ordeal is being offered as a metaphor for the ordeal of black-white relations in America, an ordeal, the film is saying, which has brought us closer together than we know. But the only level on which this can be said to be true is that level of human experience—that depth—of which Americans are most terrified. The complex of conflicting terrors which the black-white connection engenders is suggested by the turgidity of the action which ends this film.

For, when the morning comes, the white boy has elected to throw in his lot with the woman, which means that Noah, after all, is to brave the swamps, and ride the rails, alone.

Noah accepts this, with a briefly mocking bitterness, and he goes. The white boy and the woman begin preparing for their journey. The white boy is worried about his black buddy; though it is difficult to guess at what point, precisely, he begins to think of Noah as his buddy; and wonders, aloud, if he'll be all right. Whereupon, the woman tells him that she has deliberately given Noah instructions which will lead him to his death: that he will never get out of the swamps alive.

It is absolutely impossible to locate the woman's motive for conveying this information. Once Noah has walked out of her door, he is long gone, simply, and can pose no threat. It cannot conceivably matter to her whether he lives, or dies: he has left their lives, in any case, never to return. If she, for whatever reason, has found a means to make certain that he dies, it is impossible to believe that she would risk telling her newfound lover this. She does not know enough about him. The woman is presented as a kind of pathetic, unthinking racist. But she cannot be so unthinking (no woman is) as to take for granted that the man she met last night will approve of being made, in fact, her accomplice in murder. After all, she knows only that the man she met last night ordered her to feed the black boy: and the white boy who orders you to feed his black boy may not be willing to authorize you to kill him. This is not only *what every woman knows*, it is, more crucially, what every white Southern woman knows.

It would appear, however, that this revelation on the part of the woman has the effect of opening our white hero's eyes to the bottomless evil of racial hatred, and, after a stormy scene—a scene quite remarkably unconvincing—and, after the little boy has shot him in the shoulder, our hero lights out for the swamps, and Noah. He finds Noah, and they head for the train—Lord, that Hollywood train, forever coming round the bend!—but the gunshot wound slows the white boy up. Noah refuses to leave him—*you're dragging on the chain!* he cries, stretching out his arm. They get to the train, the black man jumps on, but the white boy can't make it, and the black man jumps off the train, it is hard, indeed, to say why.

Well. He jumps off the train in order to reassure white people, to make them know that they are not hated; that, though they have made human errors, they have done nothing for which to be hated. Well, blacks may or may not hate whites, and when they do, as I have tried to indicate, it's in their fashion. Whites may or may not deserve to be hated, depending on how one manipulates one's reserves of energy, and what one makes of history: in any case, the reassurance is false, the need ignoble, and the question, in this context, absolutely irrelevant. The question operates to hide the question: for what has actually happened, at the end of *The Defiant Ones,* is that a white male and a white female have come together, but are menaced by the presence of the black man. The white woman, therefore, eliminates the black man, so that she and the white man can be alone together. But the white man cannot endure this rupture—from what one must, here, perhaps, call his other, better, worse, or deeper self—and so rejects the white woman, crashing through the swamps, and braving death, in order to regain his black buddy. And his black buddy is waiting for him, and, eventually, takes him in his arms. The white boy has given up his woman. The black man has given up his hope of freedom: and what are we to make of such rigorous choices, so rigorously arrived at?

The choices do not involve, for example, that seismographic shudder which the word, *homosexual,* until today, produces in the American mind, or soul: I doubt that Americans will ever be able to face the fact that the word, homosexual, is not a noun. The root of this word, as Americans use it—or, as this word uses Americans—simply involves a terror of any human touch, since any human touch can change you. A black man and a white man can come together only in the absence of women: which is, simply, the American legend of masculinity brought to its highest pressure, and revealed, as it were, in black and white.

*

In black and white: the late James Edwards, and Lloyd Bridges, in the long-ago *Home of the Brave,* love each other, as friends must, and as men do. But the fact that one is black and one is white eliminates the possibility of the female presence, according, that is, to the American theology: *may the best man win!* In the black-white context, this elicits, simply, white paranoia: it is hard to imagine anything more abjectly infantile, or anything more tragic.

The film takes place in the heat of the jungles of the Second World War. The white boy loses his life immediately after a quarrel with the black boy. The quarrel is intense. The black boy imagines—hears, though the word is not spoken—that the white boy, his buddy, is about to call him nigger, or an approximation thereof. The nature of the military crisis forces them, at that precise moment, to separate: the white boy does not join them on the beach, where the boats are waiting to rescue our people from the Japanese. The black boy crawls back through the jungle, to find his dying friend, who dies in his arms. Then, guilt paralyzes him, physically, and he undergoes psychotherapy (the central action of the film) and, cured, able to walk, walks into the sunset with another victim, a white, one-armed veteran, to start a business—one dare not say a life—together. The doomed connect, again without women: *Coward*, says the one-armed white victim to that definitive victim, the black, *take my coward's hand.*

Okay. But why is the price of what should, after all, be a simple human connection so high? Is it really necessary to lose a woman, an arm, or one's mind, in order to say hello? And, let's face it, kids, men suffer from penis envy on quite another level than women do, a crucial matter if yours is black and mine is white: furthermore, no matter what Saint Paul may thunder, love is where you find it. A man can fall in love with a man: incarceration, torture, fire, and death, and, still more, the threat of these, have not been able to prevent it, and never will. It became a grave, a tragic matter, on the North American continent, where white power became indistinguishable from the question of sexual dominance. But the question of sexual dominance can exist only in the nightmare of that soul which has armed itself, totally, against the possibility of the changing motion of conquest and surrender, which is love.

The immense quantity of polish expended on *Guess Who's Coming to Dinner* is meant to blind one to its essential inertia and despair. A black person can make nothing of this film—except, perhaps, *Superfly*—and, when one tries to guess what white people make of it, a certain chill goes down the spine. A thirty-seven-year-old black doctor, for whom the word "prodigy" is simply ridiculously inadequate, has met a white girl somewhere in his travels, and they have come, together, to the home of the girl's parents, in San Francisco, to announce their intention to marry each other. Since the girl does not doubt, and has no reason to doubt, her parents' approval, this trip would not seem to be necessary. However, she may wish, merely, to exhibit her remarkable catch to San Francisco: or, to put it in less speculative terms, we are, again, at the mercy of a plot. The wonder doctor is Sidney Poitier, and the girl's parents are Spencer Tracy and Katharine Hepburn: which means that the question of parental blessing is immediately robbed of the remotest suspense: these winning, intelligent, and forward-looking people can certainly not object. The girl's mother, after an initial shock, is won over, almost at once. The father is dubious, cranky, and crotchety, but we know that his heart is in the right place—otherwise, Spencer Tracy would never have been cast in the part. The wonder doctor's parents (significantly) do not really pose a problem, and they enter the picture late—we will speak of them later.

The suspense, then, concerning this interracial marriage, can be created only by the black doctor. We gather that he has been married before, to a black woman, who died. This informs us that, in spite of his brilliance, he is not presumptuous, and he is not an upstart, unstable adventurer: nothing less than real love would have driven him so far beyond the boundaries of caste. This love is, also, quite remarkably self-effacing. He informs the girl's parents that, even though their daughter may be prepared to marry *him* without their consent, *he* will not marry *her* without it. The girl loves her parents too much, he explains, to be able to endure such a rupture; nor can he himself, for reasons of his own, bear to be the author of such pain.

Since history affords so few examples of this species of restraint on the part of the prospective bridegroom, perhaps we should take a closer look at him: and try to find out what he is actually saying. I scarcely have the heart to indicate the echoes to be found, here, of *In Abraham's Bosom* (yes: the supplicant of Paul Green's *In Abraham's Bosom*) nor do more than indicate the existence of Eugene O'Neill's *All God's Chillun Got Wings,* or the terror underlying *The Hairy Ape:* not now can I tell you: the road was rocky. The setting of *Guess Who's Coming to Dinner* is the key. We are on the heights of San Francisco—at a time not too far removed from the moment when the city of San Francisco reclaimed the land at Hunter's Point and urban-renewalized the niggers out of it. The difficult and terrified city, where the niggers are, lives far beneath these heights. The father is in a perfectly respectable, perhaps even admirable profession, and the mother runs an art gallery. The setting is a brilliant re-creation of a certain—and far from unattractive—level of American life. And the black doctor is saying, among other things, that his presence in this landscape (this hard-won Eden) will do nothing to threaten, or defile it—indeed, since in the event that he marries the girl, they are immediately going to the Far East, or some such place, he will not even be present. One can scarcely imagine striking a bargain more painless; and without even losing a daughter, who will, merely, in effect, be traveling, and broadening her education; keeping in touch via trans-Pacific telephone, and coming home to San Francisco from time to time, with her yet more various, toddling, and exotic acquisitions.

This moment in the film is handled with such skill that one would certainly prefer to believe it, if one could. Only the fact that one does not believe it prevents one from resenting it. No man in love is so easily prepared to surrender his beloved, or travel so many thousands of miles to do so: no one expects such behavior from Steve McQueen. Without belaboring this sufficiently glaring point, the basis for such suspense as the film may hope to claim having now been established, we are confronted with a series of classical tableaux:

We have already met the white, backward, uneducated taxi driver, mightily displeased by the glimpse he catches, in his rearview mirror, of our lovers, kissing. He conveys his displeasure, failing to shake the doctor's cool: indeed, the doctor tips him.

We have already met the mother's assistant at the art gallery, a white woman, along with a particularly gruesome (and very cunningly used) example of modern art. The doctor toys with this dreadful object, as he toys with the woman's avid curiosity, and our lovers leave.

We meet the mother and the father, distressed domestic tête-à-tête, etc.—at which point we are informed of the doctor's staggering achievements—and now we meet the loyal nigger maid.

It so happened that I saw *The Birth of a Nation* and *Guess Who's Coming to Dinner* on the same day—the first in the morning, the second in the afternoon. It happened, also, that I saw both films in the company of a young African girl, a Cameroons journalist. This girl has never seen America, and, understandably, took my testimony concerning my country with enormous grains of salt.

Yet, it was not my testimony which presented us, on the same day, in two films divided from each other by something like half a century, with the same loyal nigger maid, playing the same role, and speaking the same lines. In *The Birth of a Nation,* the loyal nigger maid informs the nigger congressman that she don't like niggers who set themselves up above their station. When our black wonder doctor hits San Francisco, some fifty-odd years later, he encounters exactly the same maid, who tells him exactly the same thing, for the same reason, and in the same words, adding, merely, as a concession, no doubt, to modern times—she has come across our black hero, having entered his room without knocking, holding only a towel between his nakedness and her indignation—"and furthermore to that, you ain't even that handsome!" For she is a part of the family: she would appear to have no family of her own: and is clearly prepared to protect her golden-haired mistress from the clutches of this black ape by any means necessary.

The inclusion of this figure is absolutely obligatory—compulsive—no matter what the film imagines itself to be saying by means of this inclusion. How many times have we seen her! She is Dilsey, she is Mammy, in *Gone with the Wind,* and in *Imitation of Life,* and *The Member of the Wedding*—mother of sorrows, whore and saint, reaching a kind of apotheosis in *Requiem for a Nun.* (And yet, black men have mothers and sisters and daughters who are not like that at all!) In *Guess Who,* her presence is meant to be taken as comic, and the film seems to be using her to suggest that backward people can be found on both sides of the racial fence—a point which can scarcely be made so long as one is sitting on it. In any case, in life, she has a family, she may even have a doctor for a son, and she assuredly does not love the white family so deeply as they are compelled to suppose: she cannot, since she knows how bitterly her black family is endangered by her white one.

Then, there is the scene with the mother and the lady assistant at the art gallery, a scene which Miss Hepburn obviously relishes, and which she plays with a marvelously vindictive skill. The lady assistant is horrified at the news of this impending disastrous marriage, and is full of sympathy for the mother: who reacts with a cold, proud, and even rather terrified contempt. (This is probably the best scene in the film, and it juts out from it because of Hepburn's genuine indignation.) She walks the lady to her car, makes her get into the car, instructs her to pay herself her wages, and a bonus, to start her car motor, to get rid of the artistic monstrosity with which we have seen the doctor amusing himself earlier, and get permanently lost. One down, then, but several more to go, for, now, here come the doctor's father and mother.

The film's high polish does not entirely succeed in blinding us to a kind of incipient reality suggested by these two. Though they come, principally, out of a Hollywood scriptwriter's imagination, they unexpectedly resist being manipulated into total irrelevance—or, in other words, it proved somewhat difficult to find a place for them in this so briefly troubled Eden.

The black mother and the white mother become allies at once, firmly opting for the happiness of their children. The black father and the white father, without becoming allies, nevertheless agree that their children should not marry. I forgot to mention the priest, who is, perhaps, the master stroke of the film. Though, as the film carefully informs us, the Tracy-Hepburn couple are not Catholic, this priest is their best friend, and he is, unequivocally, on the side of the young couple. The two crass, practical fathers find, therefore, that they have taken on those two formidable adversaries, the Church, and mother love—the last being also related to women's intuition. The Church, here, is truculent (rather than militant) and mocks the fears of the white father: and mother love, as projected by Bea Richards in her brief scene with Spencer Tracy, moderately poignant and perceptive. The outcome cannot really very much longer be left in doubt (the film has got to end) but before we can arrive at the film's resolution, there is another matter to be dealt with, and that involves the relationship of the black father to the black son.

It is here that the film's polish cracks—becomes, as it were, unglued. There is no way, simply, for so light and self-serving a fable to deal with a matter so weighty—and so painful. It is not enough for the father to feel that his son has gone mad, and is throwing away his life, or his future, because of a doomed infatuation. The crucial element in such a confrontation is the question—vivid, though nearly unspoken—between the father and the son: what did the father raise the son to respect? For the son can make his lonely decision now only by confronting the nature and the value of that gift. A black man who has raised a son who has achieved his own life, and a son who has also achieved worldly eminence, has great respect for that son. He will offer his judgment, but he will not attempt to impose his will. As for being frightened for that son, the father has been frightened so long that this fear has become no more remarkable to him than the fact that he has to shave; moreover, hiding his fear from his son has been one of the principal conditions of his life, as a father, and a man. And rarely does the father complain about the sacrifices he has made: the subject arrives during adolescence, when the father is attempting to prepare the son for the price *he* will have to pay for his life. All this takes place, anyway, in a kind of short-hand virtually impossible to translate for the bulk of white Americans. But, leaving all that aside, the father has absolutely no motive for this scene. The son is a world-famous doctor, thirty-seven years old, who has already been married, and who has lived all over the world; and who, if he marries the girl, is immediately taking her away with him, out of the United States. The father knows perfectly well that America is not the world: indeed, it would have to be a part of his pride that his effort has helped to release his son from the obscenely crippling pressures of his homeland. It can make absolutely no difference to him who his son marries: if the son is free and happy, the father is, too. And it is worth noting, perhaps, that the film appears completely to forget the wonder doctor's eminence, and the effect that this would have on his parents. As the parents of a world-famous man, they, indisputably, out-rank their hosts, and might very well feel that the far from galvanizing fiancée is not worthy of their son: it is not the black parents who would be ill at ease.

But the American self-evasion, which is all that this country has as history, has created the myth on which this film is based, and this myth cannot endure so treacherous a perception; treacherous to the American self-image, and to what passes, in America, for self-esteem. Only yesterday, if, indeed, it was yesterday, the hotly contested white fiancée cried *death before dishonor!* (or *you yellow dogs!*) and ran out of this life, into the arms of Jesus, in order not to be defiled by the nigger's touch. Today—if it *is* today—she tells her mother, in a scene manipulated with such cool efficiency that it almost seems to be true, that, although she certainly wanted to sleep with her black fiancé, *he* was too honorable to touch *her*: in this day of so many liberations, make of this collision of inadmissible fantasies whatever you will. In any case, it is out of all this that the black son must say, finally, to his black father, and ignobly enough, "You're a colored man. I just want to be a man." Which means that a man exists only in the brutally limited lexicon of those who think of themselves as white, and imagine, therefore, that they control reality and rule the world. And the black son says this to his black father in spite of the fact that he, the wonder doctor, has had to become a living freak, a walking encyclopedia of rare medical knowledge, in order to have the question of his marriage to a white girl *discussed*. The assumptions of *The Last of the Mohicans* and *The Birth of a Nation* are very present here, and, if even the wonder doctor must undergo such trials in order to be able to touch his lady love, heaven help the high-school dropouts: so many of whom found themselves in Attica, for example, not impossibly for trying to be men. Heaven did not help those among the blacks who failed to master their pre-med courses on the day that the Republic, responsive to the will of heaven, decided to uphold what Rockefeller, in one of his nobler statements, described as "the impartial application of the law": he, too, clearly, is a movie fan.

The film does make one despairing attempt to suggest, after Galileo, that the earth may be turning; in that lamentable scene in the city when Tracy tastes a new flavor of ice cream and discovers that he likes it. This scene occurs in a drive-in, and is punctuated by Tracy's backing his car into the car of a young black boy. The black boy's resulting tantrum is impressive—and also entirely false, due to no fault of the actor (D'Urville Martin). The moral of the scene is *They're here now, and we have to deal with them*: or, *The natives are restless. What shall we do?*

Ah. What indeed—short, that is, of bombing them back into the stone age. As concerns *Guess Who's Coming to Dinner,* we can conclude that people have the right to marry whom they choose, especially if we know that they are leaving town as soon as dinner is over.

In Sol Stein's *The Childkeeper,* a short and remarkable novel, a forty-eight-year-old bank vice-president, and his wife, and three of their four children, spend a long weekend together in their country house. The children, who are adolescents, invite some of their adolescent friends, and, among these, is a black boy of nineteen, named Greco. The father finds himself paralyzed by his liberal, or, more accurately, humanitarian presumptions

(presumptions by which he does not live) and by his apprehension that he really knows nothing about his children, nor (he both hopes and fears) they about him. The presence of the black boy, an exceedingly rude and dangerous visitor, drags to the surface the buried terrors of his life, and, helplessly, he kills the boy. He does not mean to kill him, but Eden has a price: and the death of the black boy brings about his own.

The question of identity is a question involving the most profound panic—a terror as primary as the nightmare of the mortal fall. This question can scarcely be said to exist among the wretched, who know, merely, that they are wretched and who bear it day by day—it is a mistake to suppose that the wretched do not know that they are wretched; nor does this question exist among the splendid, who know, merely, that they are splendid, and who flaunt it, day by day: it is a mistake to suppose that the splendid have any intention of surrendering their splendor. An identity is questioned only when it is menaced, as when the mighty begin to fall, or when the wretched begin to rise, or when the stranger enters the gates, never, thereafter, to be a stranger: the stranger's presence making *you* the stranger, less to the stranger than to yourself. Identity would seem to be the garment with which one covers the nakedness of the self; in which case, it is best that the garment be loose, a little like the robes of the desert, through which robes one's nakedness can always be felt, and, sometimes, discerned. This trust in one's nakedness is all that gives one the power to change one's robes.

Lawrence of Arabia, stemming, both dimly and helplessly, from T. E. Lawrence's *Seven Pillars of Wisdom,* is a kind of muted and updated, excruciatingly astute version of Rudyard Kipling's *Gunga Din.* The word "muted" does not refer to the musical score, which must be the loudest in the history of the cinema, and which is absolutely indispensable to the intention of the film.

The song says *There is trouble all over this world*: and our ancestors, the English, made careful note of this, and proceeded to base their imperial policy on this relentless and utilitarian truth. Living on an island, they built boats, and where trouble was, they sailed them; sometimes, they very carefully brought the needed trouble with them, and very often, simply, their presence was trouble enough. The English learned how to use, and foment, trouble to their purposes, and this policy was known as Divide and Rule. Alongside this, and justifying it, was the concept and necessity of Civilization. I point this out, calmly enough, because nothing in *Lawrence of Arabia* really conveys the fact that the British were deliberately using, and backing, an Arab rebellion in order to complete the dismemberment of the Ottoman Empire. This they managed to do, without keeping any of their promises to the Arabs, to the great sorrow and bewilderment of young Lawrence, who does not understand, until Damascus, to what pragmatic ends his idealism has been put. (The Sykes-Picot Treaty contained a secret clause which divided the conquered territory between England, France, and Russia. Lawrence, in his book, is aware of this. But, "In revenge I vowed to make the Arab revolt the engine of its own success, as well as hand-maid to our Egyptian campaign: and vowed to lead it so madly in the final victory that expediency should counsel to the Powers a fair settlement of the Arabs' moral claims.")

The film begins with a long, overhead shot of a motorcycle in a sunlit square. A khaki-clad man appears and begins fooling around with the motorcycle: walks off, comes back. A closer shot reveals that he is trying to get the motorcycle started. He starts it, gets on it, and we ride with him through the English countryside, on a sunny day. For those who know that Lawrence died in a motorcycle accident, the film is beginning at the end of Lawrence's life: later on, we may ask ourselves why.

The motorcycle goes off the road, crashes. We are then present at Lawrence's funeral, a very impressive one, treated to vehemently conflicting views of him—emanating from the military—and the film begins.

Since the Empire must be kept in the background—and yet, always be present, hence the overwhelming music—the great burden of this film is on the shoulders of Lawrence, played by Peter O'Toole. But the star of the film is the desert: the vast, technicolored backdrop of the desert meant to invest with splendor a stammering tale.

For, this overwhelming desert, though it exists geographically, and was actually filmed by an actual camera crew, sent there for that purpose, is put to a use which is as far from reality as are most of the people we encounter in it. The least real of these people is Lawrence himself. This is not O'Toole's fault: but so grave an adventure can scarcely be ascribed to the vagaries and idealism of a single man. Lawrence's courage and steadfastness are given as admirable, because hard-won—here, the film, unconsciously, rather patronizes Lawrence; his complexities are barely—or, rather, perhaps, endlessly—hinted at, that is to say never illuminated. His rapport with the Arabs is of great use to the British, whose attitude toward him, otherwise, is, at best, ambivalent. The film takes the view that he was a valiant maverick, naïve and headstrong, brutally broken in battle, and betrayed, less by his country than by his inability to confront—as do his superiors—the hard facts of life: the hard facts of life, in this case, referring, principally, to the limits and exigencies of power. And it would appear to be true that Lawrence's concept of power existed almost entirely on the messianic level—indeed, on a level far more complex and painful than that—but it is almost impossible to pursue this speculation within the confines described by the film.

The film presents us with an inadvertent martyr to the cause of spreading civilization: the speeding of the light to those in darkness. One of the hazards of this endeavor is that of finding oneself in the hands of the infidels. This is what happens to Lawrence in the film (and in a far more fascinating and terrible way in his book). In the film, he is captured by the Turks, refuses the lustful attentions of a Turkish Bey, and is raped by the soldiers. This precipitates his subsequent slaughter of the fleeing Turkish Army. This slaughter destroys his soul, and, though the desert has now claimed him forever, he no longer has any role in the desert, and so must go home to England, dead, to die.

The film begins with the death of Lawrence in order to

avoid, whether consciously or not, the deepest and most dangerous implications of this story. We are confronted with a fallen hero, and we trace the steps which lead him to his end. But the zeal which drove Lawrence into the desert does not begin at the point at which we meet him in the film, but farther back than that, in that complex of stratifications called England. Of this, Lawrence himself was most tormentedly aware.

The English can be said to exemplify the power of nostalgia to an uncanny degree. Nothing the world holds, from Australia to Africa, to America, India, to China, to Egypt, appears to have made the faintest imprint on the English soul: wherever the English are is—or will resist, out of perversity, or at its peril, becoming—England. (Not, on the other hand, of course, that it can ever truly *be* England: but it can try.) This is a powerful presumption, but why, then, the ruder recipient cannot but demand, do not the English stay in England? It would appear that this island people need endless corroboration of their worth: and the tragedy of their history has been their compulsion to make the world their mirror, and this to a degree not to be equalled in the history of any other people—and with a success, if that is the word, not to be equalled in the history of any other people. *I liked the things beneath me*—Lawrence, from *Seven Pillars of Wisdom,* is speaking—*and took my pleasures and adventures downward. There seemed a certainty in degradation, a final safety. Man could rise to any height, but there was an animal level beneath which he could not fall. It was a satisfaction on which to rest.*

The necessity, then, of those "lesser breeds without the law"—those wogs, barbarians, niggers—is this: one must not become more free, not become more base than they: must not be used as they are used, nor yet use them as their abandonment allows one to use them: therefore, they must be civilized. But, when they *are* civilized, they may simply "spuriously imitate [the civilizer] back again," leaving the civilizer with "no satisfaction on which to rest."

Thus, it may be said that the weary melancholy underlying *Lawrence of Arabia* stems from the stupefying apprehension that, whereas England may have been doomed to civilize the world, no power under heaven can civilize England. I am using England, at the moment, arbitrarily, simply because England is responsible for Lawrence: but the principle illustrates the dilemma of all the civilizing, or colonizing powers, particularly now, as their power begins to be, at once, more tenuous and more brutal, and their vaunted identities revealed as being dubious indeed. The greater the public power, the greater the private, inadmissible despair; the greater this despair, the greater the danger to all human life. The camera remains on Lawrence's face a long time before he finally cries, *No prisoners!* and leads his men to massacre the Turks. This pause is meant to recall to us the intolerable mortification he has endured, and to make comprehensible the savagery of this English schoolboy.

But the mortification of an English schoolboy, in the desert, at the hands of infidels who refuse to be civilized, cannot be used to justify the bloody course of Empire, or the ruthless stratagems of power: this schoolboy is armed with the weight of a nation, and his mortification is, or should be, nothing to the point. If we grant that the Turks are, also, notoriously bloodthirsty, then we must equally grant that rape is not unknown in English public schools: there *is* no "animal level" beneath which "we" cannot fall. The truth is that Lawrence was deliberately formed and deliberately used, and, at that moment, superbly executed the real intentions of the state which had formed him. So, after all, do most of us, without even knowing it: sometimes, the unexpected results—given the short-sightedness of states, and statesmen—are immediate, immense, and retaliatory. For example, there may, one day, be a film, called *Chamberlain, at Munich,* in which we will learn, for the first time, of the mortifications Chamberlain endured and which compelled him, as Prime Minister of England, to sell, as it turned out, all of Europe to the then German Chancellor, in order to protect his island. Looking for all the world like the schoolboy he never ceased to be, he proclaimed to cheering crowds, upon his return from Munich, "*If at first you don't succeed, try, try again!*"

The crowds were cheering their own impending ordeal: one wonders how many of them survived the rage which their loyal schoolboy, superb epitome of themselves, had just unleashed against them.

In 1952, I was in America, just in time for the McCarthy era. I had never seen anything like it.

If I had ever really been able to hate white people, the era of that dimwitted, good-natured, flamboyant representative of the American people would have been pure heaven: for, not even the most vindictive hatred could have imagined the slimy depths to which the bulk of white Americans allowed themselves to sink: noisily, gracelessly, flatulent and foul with patriotism. Though cowardice was certainly the most vividly recognizable color in the tapestry, it was not mere cowardice one was watching, but something much worse, an absolute panic, absolutely infantile. Truman, the honest haberdasher and machine-made politician, in whose wisdom we had dropped the atomic bomb on Japan, had been elected President the year (1948) that I left America. Subsequently, my countrymen (who were still arguing among themselves as to this relationship—their relationship, that is, to blacks) decided to entrust their lives, their fortunes, and their sacred honor, not once, but twice, to Daddy Warbucks Eisenhower, who had nothing against McCarthy, and who was Papa to Richard Nixon. I began to feel a terrified pity for the white children of these white people: who had been sent, by their parents, to Korea, though their parents did not know why. Neither did their parents know why these miserable, incontestably inferior, rice-eating gooks refused to come to heel, and would not be saved. But *I* knew why. I came from a long line of miserable, incontestably inferior, rice-eating, chicken-stealing, hog-swilling niggers—who had acquired these skills in their flight from bondage—who still refused to come to heel, and who would not be saved. If two and two make four, then it is a very simple matter to recognize that people unable to be responsible for their own children, and who care so little about each other, are unlikely instruments for the salvation of the people whom they permit themselves the luxury of despising as inferior to themselves. Even in the case of Korea, we, the blacks at least, knew why our children were there: they had been sent there to be used, in exactly the same way, and for the same reasons, as the blacks had been so widely dispersed out of Africa—an incalculable investment of raw material in what was not yet known as the common market.

Each time the black discontent erupts within the continental limits of the United States—erupts, that is, to the extent of demanding a "police action"—the Republic claims "outside" interference. It is simply not conceivable that American blacks can be so unhappy (or so bright, or so brave) as seriously to menace the only social order that they know; a social order, moreover, in which they have achieved, or have been given— let's hear both points of view, please!—the highest standard of living of any black people in the world. Apart from pointing out that the black suicide rate began to rise impressively about a quarter of a century ago, we will not otherwise challenge this moving article of faith. Unluckily, Americans remain at the mercy of this misapprehension when attempting to deal with the world. They do not know how their slaves endured, nor how they endure, nor do they know what their slaves know about them—they do not dare to know it: and what they dare not know about Little Black Sambo is precisely what they do not dare to know about the world by which they are surrounded. Thus, the disaster in Korea had to be explained away. American error being unthinkable, and American might not to be questioned, the disaster could be explained away only by a species of *inside* interference: America was not being defeated, it was being betrayed, by disloyal Americans.

A disloyal American was any American who disapproved of the course his government was taking: though it is very important to stress that Charles Lindbergh, for example, who disapproved of the course his government was taking, and who addressed an America First Committee Rally in Madison Square Garden to prove it, was never considered anything less than a superb and loyal patriot: as is, today, Governor George Wallace, of Alabama, who would have agreed with Colonel Lindbergh that we were fighting on the wrong side. (Lindbergh's wife, the poetess, Anne Morrow Lindbergh, assured us that the inconveniences of the Third Reich—the foul-smelling camps, the ovens, the gas chambers, the slaughter of, among other human beings, the Jews—were "not in themselves the future," merely "scum on the wave of the future.") The American marked as disloyal was always someone whose disagreement with his government might have begun with his apprehension of the role of Franco's Spain, and Mussolini's Italy, and the Italian adventure in Ethiopia: someone who could see what these piratical rehearsals, carried out with the consent, and the power, of the Western world, meant for the future of the world. It was also someone who could see that it had not been Roosevelt, but a global war, necessitating a war economy, which ended the American, and, subsequently, the Western Depression. A disloyal American was anyone who really believed in equal justice under the law, and his testimony may have begun with the Scottsboro Case, or with the Peekskill riot. A disloyal American was anyone who believed it his right, and his duty, to attempt to feed the hungry, and clothe the naked, and visit those in prison, and he may have been fingered, so to speak, by any Southern senator: he was certainly being scrutinized by the late, and much lamented, J. Edgar Hoover, history's most highly paid (and most utterly useless) *voyeur*.

Americans, then, in order to prove their devotion to American ideals, began informing on each other. I had been living in Europe for nearly four years, and knew refugees from precisely this species of moral and actual nightmare, from Germany, Italy, Spain, and Russia, and Ethiopia: *Give us your poor!* But this species of refugee was not what the hymn of the Statue of Liberty had in mind.

Lives, careers, and loves were smashed on the rock of this cowardice. I was much younger then: the best I can say is that I was appalled, but not—alas—surprised. Still, it was horrible to be confirmed: out of this obscenely fomented hysteria, we are confronted with the nonsense of the pumpkin papers, the self-important paranoia of Whittaker Chambers, such nightshade creatures as Harvey Matusow, Elizabeth Bentley, and Harry Gold, and the breathtaking careers of those remarkable spies, Julius and Ethel Rosenberg: who are about to lose their lives, just the same, in order to astonish, halt, and purify, an erring nation. Yes: and there were others. Some knew it, and some didn't.

I wandered, then, in my confusion and isolation—for almost all the friends I had had were in trouble, and, therefore, in one way or another, *incommunicado*—into a movie, called *My Son, John*. And I will never forget it.

This movie stars Miss Helen Hayes, the late Van Heflin, and the late Robert Walker. Dean Jagger plays the American Legion husband. (Years and years ago, Dean Jagger had appeared in John Wexley's play about the Scottsboro Case, *They Shall Not Die!:* he played the young reporter whose love forces one of the poor white girls to retract her testimony that the black boys had raped her.)

The family is the American family one has seen and seen and seen again on the American screen: the somewhat stolid, but, at bottom, strong, decent, and loving head of the family; the somewhat scatterbrained, but, at bottom, shrewd, loving, and tough wife and mother; and the children of this remarkable unremarkable couple. In *My Son, John,* there are two sons. One of them plays football, which is, literally, all that we ever learn about him. The other son, John, who does not, apparently, play football, has flown the family coop, and has a job in Washington, where he appears to be doing very well. But they don't see very much of him anymore, which causes the mother some distress: she misses her son, John, and this to a somewhat disquieting extent—the movie seems to feel, however, that this morbid worry about the life of her grown son is the normal reaction of any normal American mother.

The mother's distress is considerably augmented by the arrival of the FBI, in the personable person of Van Heflin, who arrives to ask the family discreet questions concerning their maverick relative. Though this FBI agent is the soul of tact and understanding, the mother eventually perceives the gravity of the situation, and agrees to attempt to save her son. The salvation of her son depends on confession, for he is, indeed, a

Communist agent: for the sake of her son's salvation, she must, therefore, cooperate with the FBI. For, if her son does not confess, he is lost: he is anathema. The film concentrates on the struggle in the soul of the mother between mother love and her larger duty. At one point in the film, she cheers him on, exactly as though he were in the football field, urging him to make the touchdown and save the team.

Nothing can possibly redeem so grisly a species of sentimental dishonesty, but Robert Walker's gleefully vicious parody of the wayward American son does a great deal to demystify it. The moment he enters the family house, he makes the reasons for his leaving it very clear: his American Legion father, his adoring mother, his football-playing brother, bore him shitless, and he simply does not want to be like them. This is heresy, of course, and Walker plays it for all it is worth, absolutely heartless and hilarious, acting out all of his mother's terrors, including, and especially, the role of flaming faggot, which is his father's terror, too. It is astonishing that he was allowed to get away with so broad and hostile a put-down— one very nearly expects him to turn up, in black-face, singing "Mammy"—but, on the other hand, this is probably exactly the way the film sees wayward sons. Once they have renounced the American virtues, they are, because of this renunciation, practically Communists already and able to incarnate everything we fear.

Virtue triumphs, at last, of course, but not before the erring son has come to a bloody end. He has been sacrificed to life's larger aims, that is, to the American way of life. The mother says to the father, at the close of the film—the father having more swiftly perceived, and faced, his son's defection—*You were more right than any of us, dear, because you thought with your heart.* This meant, in the context of those years—the harvest of which we have not done reaping—that Elizabeth Bentley and Matusow and Greenglass were also thinking with their hearts, and so were the friendly witnesses before the House Un-American Activities Committee, who threw their friends to the wolves, and so was Eisenhower, when he refused to intervene in the Rosenberg case. No crime had been proven against Ethel

Rosenberg: she was considered to have masterminded her husband's crimes, though, clearly, there could be no proof of this, either, nor can it be said that there exists any proof of her husband's crimes. Eisenhower, nevertheless, asserted that leniency toward Ethel Rosenberg would mean, simply, that, thereafter, the Russians would recruit their spies from among women. Music up, slow dissolve (exterior, day) to close-up of the Statue of Liberty, fade-out, the end.

My first encounter with the FBI took place in 1945, in Woodstock, New York, where I was living in a cabin in the woods. Neither of the two men resembled Van Heflin in the least.

It was early in the morning, they walked me out of the diner, and stood me against a wall. My color had already made me conspicuous enough in that town—this is putting it mildly indeed—and, from a distance, the townspeople stared. I had the feeling that they were waiting to be selected as members of the firing squad.

I had not the remotest notion as to why they had come looking for me. I knew of nothing which I could possibly have done to have attracted their attention. Much later in my life, I knew very well what I had done to attract their attention, and intended, simply, to keep on keeping on. In any case, once you *have* come to the attention of the FBI, they keep a friendly file on you, and your family, and your friends.

But, on this morning, I was terribly frightened, and I was desperately trying to keep one jump ahead of them—to guess what it was before they revealed it. If I could guess what it was, then I might know how to answer and know what to do.

It developed that they were looking for a boy who had deserted from the Marines. I knew no one answering that description, and I said so. They conveyed, very vividly, what they would do to me if I did not tell them the truth—what they could do to smart niggers like me. (I was a smart nigger because I worked, part-time, as an artists' model, and lived in an artists' colony, and had a typewriter in my shack.) My ass would be in a sling—this was among the gentler warnings. They frightened me, and they humiliated me—it was like being spat on, or pissed on, or gang-raped—but they made me hate them, too, with a hatred like hot ice, and all I knew, simply, was that, if I could figure out what they wanted, nothing could induce me to give it to them.

They showed me a series of photographs. From their questions, I realized that they were talking about something that had taken place in the city, during my last visit there. I had spent a lot of time in the restaurant, where I was still occasional waiter. And I had been to a party, briefly, with some friends of mine. One photograph rang a distant bell in my memory: and they saw this. I had seen the face somewhere, but I could not remember where. And, now, my problem was to remember where I had seen the face, and then double lock the memory out of their reach.

And, eventually, I *did* remember. The boy's name was Teddy. I had met him at a party, with some friends of mine—who were, really, friends of his; had seen him, in fact, only once, and very briefly. If I could scarcely remember his name, he would certainly have the same difficulty with mine, and, if he was a fugitive from justice, he would scarcely take a chance on coming to hide in my cabin.

I knew the name now, and I was determined not to reveal it. It was no part of my duty to help them trap the cat, and, no doubt, he had his reasons for deserting the Marines. But the interrogation was rugged, ruthless, and prolonged, and, eventually, the name slipped out: "Well, there was Carmen, and me, and Joe, and Teddy—"

"Teddy? Is this Teddy?"

I cursed myself, for, of course, they had known the name all along. My utterance of the name had confirmed something, and I had been helpful to them, after all. This frightened me in a new way, in a way that I had never been frightened before. I could see, suddenly, that they could keep me against this wall, under this sun, for the foreseeable future, and, finally, whatever I knew would be dragged out of me. But, in fact, thank God, or somebody, all I knew about the boy was his name. I did not even know his last name. And the afternoon wore on, with threats and curses. They came to my cabin, and searched it—I felt that they had searched it before.

When the interrogation was finally over, one of them took out a nickel and dropped it into my palm. With this nickel, the moment I had any news of Teddy I was to call him. I'd be a mighty sorry nigger if I didn't. I took the nickel, and I assured him that I would certainly call him the moment I had any news of Teddy. I thought, You can bet your ass I'll call you. Don't piss, don't shit, don't fuck, until I call you: do nothing till you hear from me.

They left me, finally, haunted the cabin, and roamed the town for two days. Teddy never appeared. I never spent the nickel, I threw it away.

Teddy was turned in. This, I learned much later, in New York, during my visit in 1952. One of the friends at that long-gone party really knew Teddy, and the FBI had come to see him, too, and had also given him a nickel. I was having dinner with this friend one night, and he told me, in the casual course of conversation, that he believed that Teddy had stolen his typewriter, and this had made him so angry that he had gone downstairs, to the drugstore, and dropped the nickel in the slot, and turned the deserter in.

Well. Perhaps he would have turned him in, anyway—human beings, including you and me, are capable of anything, and *I* might have turned him in. Being human, I certainly have no guarantee that betrayal is not among my possibilities, and, indeed, betrayal takes so many forms that I know myself to have been guilty of betrayal more than once. But I do not think that my friend—with whom I never broke bread again—would have spoken of it so lightly had it not been for the moral climate of the time. The artifacts of the time had helped create this climate, and the artificers of the time had become accomplices to this unspeakable immorality. I was an artificer, too, facing, therefore, a heavy question. I loved my country, but I could not respect it, could not, upon my soul, be reconciled to my country as it was. And I loved my work, had great respect for the craft which I was compelled to study, and wanted it to have some human use. It was beginning to be clear to me that these two loves might, never, in my life, be reconciled: no man can serve two masters.

THREE
WHERE THE GRAPES OF WRATH ARE STORED

> I found a leak in my building,
>   and:
> my soul has got to move.
>   I say:
> my soul has got to move,
> my soul has got to move.
>
> —SONG

AT THE TOP of 1968, over the vehement protests of my family and my friends, I flew to Hollywood to write the screenplay for *The Autobiography of Malcolm X*. My family and my friends were entirely right; but I was not (since I survived it) entirely wrong. Still, I think that I would rather be horsewhipped, or incarcerated in the forthright bedlam of Bellevue, than repeat the adventure—not, luckily, that I will ever be allowed to repeat it: it is not an adventure which one permits a friend, or brother, to attempt to survive twice. It was a gamble which I knew I might lose, and which I lost—a very bad day at the races: but I learned something.

Fox was then resolving the Cuban-American tension by means of a movie called *Che!*. This enterprise gave us Omar Sharif, as Che Guevara, and Jack Palance, as Fidel Castro: the resulting vaudeville team is not required to sing, or dance, nor is it permitted, using the words very loosely, to act. The United Fruit Company is not mentioned. John Foster Dulles is not mentioned, either, though he was the lawyer for said company, nor is his brother, Allen, who was the head of the CIA. In the person of Che, we are confronted with a doomed, romantic clown. His attempts to awaken the peasants merely disturb them, and their goats: this observation, which is inexorably and inevitably true on one level, is absolutely false on the level at which the film uses it. In the person of Castro, we are confronted with a cigar-smoking, brandy-drinking maniac: a "spic," as clearly unsuited for political responsibility as the nigger congressmen of *The Birth of a Nation*.

Since both the film for which I had been hired, and *Che!* were controversial, courageous, revolutionary films, being packaged for the consumer society, it was hoped that our film would beat *Che!* to the box-office. This was not among my concerns.

I had a fairly accurate idea of what Hollywood was about to do with *Che!*. (This is not black, bitter paranoia, but cold, professional observation: you can make a fairly accurate guess as to the direction a film is likely to take by observing who is cast in it, and who has been assigned to direct it.) The intention of *Che!* was to make both the man, and his Bolivian adventure, irrelevant and ridiculous; and to do this, furthermore, with such a syrup of sympathy that any incipient Che would think twice before leaving Mama, and the ever-ready friend at the bank. Che, in the film, is a kind of Lawrence of Arabia, trapped on the losing side, and unable, even, to understand the natives he has, mistakenly, braved the jungles to arouse. I had no intention of so betraying Malcolm, or *his* natives. Yet, my producer had been advised, in an inter-office memo which I, quite unscrupulously, intercepted, that the writer (me) should be advised that the tragedy of Malcolm's life was that he had been mistreated, early, by some whites, and betrayed (later) by *many* blacks: emphasis in the original. The writer was also to avoid suggesting that Malcolm's trip to Mecca could have had any political implications, or repercussions.

Well. I had never before seen this machinery at such close quarters, and I confess that I was both fascinated and challenged. Near the end of my Hollywood sentence, the studio assigned me a "technical" expert, who was, in fact, to act as my collaborator. This fact was more or less disguised at first, but I was aware of it, and far from enthusiastic; still, by the time the studio and I had arrived at this impasse, there was no ground on which I could "reasonably" refuse. I liked the man well enough—I had no grounds, certainly, on which to dislike him. I didn't contest his "track record" as a screenwriter, and I reassured myself that he might be helpful: he was signed, anyway, and went to work.

Each week, I would deliver two or three scenes, which he would take home, breaking them—translating them—into cinematic language, shot by shot, camera angle by camera angle. This seemed to me a somewhat strangling way to make a film. My sense of the matter was that the screenwriter delivered as clear a blueprint as possible, which then became the point of departure for all the other elements involved in the making of a film. For example, surely it was the director's province to decide where to place the camera; and he would be guided in his decision by the dynamic of the scene. However: as the weeks wore on, and my scenes were returned to me, "translated," it began to be despairingly clear (to me) that all meaning was being siphoned out of them. It is very hard to describe this, but it is important that I try.

For example: there is a very short scene in my screenplay in which the central character, a young boy from the country, walks into a very quiet, very special Harlem bar, in the late afternoon. The scene is important because the "country" boy is Malcolm X, the bar is Small's Paradise, and the purpose of the scene is to dramatize Malcolm's first meeting with West Indian Archie—the numbers man who introduced Malcolm to the rackets. The interior evidence of Malcolm's book very strongly suggests a kind of father-son relationship between Archie and Malcolm: my problem was how to suggest this as briefly and effectively as possible.

So, in my scene, as written, Malcolm walks into the bar, dressed in the zoot-suit of the times, and orders a drink. He does not know how outrageously young and vulnerable he looks. Archie is sitting at a table with his friends, and they watch Malcolm, making jokes about him between themselves. But their jokes contain an oblique confession: they see themselves in Malcolm. They have all *been* Malcolm once. He does not know what is about to happen to him, but they do, because it has already happened to them. They have been seeing it happen to others, and enduring what has happened to them, for nearly as long as Malcolm has been on earth. Archie, particularly, is struck by something he sees in the boy. So, when Malcolm, stumbling back from the jukebox, stumbles over Archie's shoes, Archie uses this as a pretext to invite the boy over to the table. And that is all there is to the scene.

My collaborator brought it back to me, translated. It was really the same scene, he explained, but he had added a little action—thus, when Malcolm stumbles over Archie's shoes, Archie becomes furious. Malcolm, in turn, becomes furious, and the scene turns into a shoot-out from *High Noon,* with everybody in the bar taking bets as to who will draw first. In this way, said my collaborator (with which judgment the studio, of course, agreed) everyone in the audience could *see* what Archie saw in Malcolm: he admired the "country boy's" guts.

We are to believe, then, on the basis of the "translated" scene, that a group of seasoned hustlers, in a very hip Harlem bar, allow a child from the country whom nobody knows to precipitate a crisis which may bring the heat down on everybody, and in which the child, by no means incidentally, may lose his life—while they take bets. West Indian Archie is so angry that a child stepped on his shoes that he forgets he has all that numbers money on him, and all those people waiting to be paid—both above and below the line. And, furthermore, this was not at all what Archie saw in Malcolm, nor was it what I wanted the audience to see.

The rewritten scene was much longer than the original scene, and, though it occurs quite early in the script, derailed the script completely. With all of my scenes being "translated" in this way, the script would grow bulkier than *War and Peace,* and the script, therefore, would have to be cut. And I saw how that would work. Having fallen into the trap of accepting "technical" assistance, I would not, at the cutting point, be able to reject it; and the script would then be cut according to the "action" line, and in the interest of "entertainment" values. How I got myself out of this fix doesn't concern us here—I simply walked out, taking my original script with me—but the adventure remained very painfully in my mind, and, indeed, was to shed a certain light for me on the adventure occurring through the American looking-glass.

Lady Sings the Blues is related to the black American experience in about the same way, and to the same extent that Princess Grace Kelly is related to the Irish potato famine: by courtesy. The film pretends to be based on Billie Holiday's autobiography, and, indeed, Billie's book may make a very fine film one day: a day, however, which I no longer expect to live long enough to see. The film that *has* been made is impeccably put together, with an irreproachable professional polish, and has one or two nice moments. It has absolutely nothing to do with Billie, or with jazz, or any other kind of music, or the risks of an artist, or American life, or black life, or narcotics, or the narcotics laws, or clubs, or managers, or policemen, or despair, or love. The script is as empty as a banana peel, and as treacherous.

It is scarcely possible to think of a black American actor who has not been misused: not one has ever been seriously challenged to deliver the best that is in him. The most powerful examples of this cowardice and waste are the careers of Paul Robeson and Ethel Waters. If they had ever been allowed really to hit their stride, they might immeasurably have raised the level of cinema and theater in this country. Their effect would have been, at least, to challenge the stultifying predictable tics of such overrated figures as Miss Helen Hayes, for example, and life, as one performer can sometimes elicit it from another, might more frequently have illuminated our stage and screen. It is pointless, however, to pursue this, and personally painful: Mr. Robeson is declining, in obscurity, and Miss Waters is singing in Billy Graham's choir. They might have been treated with more respect by the country to which they gave so much. But, then, we had to send telegrams to the Mayor of New York City, asking him to call off the cops who surrounded Billie's bedside—looking for heroin in her ice cream—and let the Lady die in peace.

What the black actor has managed to give are moments— indelible moments, created, miraculously, beyond the confines of the script: hints of reality, smuggled like contraband into a maudlin tale, and with enough force, if unleashed, to shatter the tale to fragments. The face of Ginger Rogers, for example, in *Tales of Manhattan,* is something to be placed in a dish, and eaten with a spoon—possibly a long one. If the face of Ethel Waters were placed in the same frame, the face of Little Eva would simply melt: to prevent this, the black performer has been sealed off into a vacuum. Inevitably, therefore, and as a direct result, the white performer is also sealed off and can never deliver the best that is in him, either. His plight is less obvious, but the results can be even more devastating. The black performer knows, at least, what the odds are, and knows that he must endure—even though he has done nothing to deserve—his fate. So does the white performer know this, as concerns himself, *his* possibilities, *his* merit, *his* fate, and he knows this on a somewhat less accessible and more chaotic and intimidating level. James Edwards, dead at the age of fifty-three, in a casting office, was a beautiful actor, and knew, at least, that he was an actor. Veronica Lake was a star, riding very high for a while there: she also died in relative obscurity, but it is doubtful that she knew as much.

The moments given us by black performers exist so far beneath, or beyond, the American apprehensions that it is difficult to describe them. There is the close-up of Sidney Poitier's face, for example, in *The Defiant Ones,* describing how his wife, "she say, be nice. Be nice." Black spectators supply the sub-text—the unspoken—out of their own lives, and the pride and anguish in Sidney's face at that moment strike deep. I do not know what happens in the breasts of the multitudes who think of themselves as white: but, clearly, they hold this anguish far outside themselves. There is the truth to be found in Ethel Waters's face at the end of *Member of the Wedding,* the Juano Hernandez of *Young Man with a Horn* and *Intruder in the Dust,* Canada Lee, in *Body and Soul,* the Rochester of *The Green Pastures* and *Tales of Manhattan,* and Robeson in everything I saw him do. You will note that I am deliberately avoiding the recent spate of so-called black films. I have seen very few of them, and, anyway, it would be virtually impossible to discuss them as films. I suspect their intention to be lethal indeed, and to be the subject of quite another investigation. Their entire purpose (apart from making money; and this money is not for blacks; in spite of the fact that some of these films appear to have been, at least in part, financed by blacks) is to stifle forever any possibility of such moments—or, in other words, to make black experience irrelevant and obsolete. And I may point out that this vogue, had it been remotely serious, had a considerable body of work on which to draw—from *Up From Slavery* to *Let Me Live,* from *The Auto-Biography of an Ex-Colored Man,* and

Cane, to *Black Boy* to *Invisible Man* to *Blues Child Baby* to *The Bluest Eye* to *Soledad Brother.* An incomplete list, and difficult: but the difficulty is not in the casting.

My buddy, Ava Gardner, once asked me if I thought she could play Billie Holiday. I had to tell her that, though she was certainly "down" enough for it—courageous and honest and beautiful enough for it—she would almost certainly not be allowed to get away with it, since Billie Holiday had been widely rumored to be black, and she, Ava Gardner, was widely rumored to be white. I was not really making a joke, or, if I was, the joke was bitter: for I certainly know some black girls who are much, much whiter than Ava. Nor do I blame the black girls for this, for this utterly inevitable species of schizophrenia is but one of the many manifestations of the spiritual and historical trap, called racial, in which all Americans find themselves and against which some of us, some of the time, manage to arrive at a viable and honorable identity. I was really thinking of black actors and actresses, who would have been much embittered if the role of Billie Holiday had been played by a white girl: but, then, I had occasion to think of them later, too, when the tidal wave of "black" films arrived, using such a staggering preponderance of football players and models.

I had never been a Diana Ross fan, and received the news that she was to play Billie with a weary shrug of the shoulders. I could not possibly have been more wrong, and I pray the lady to accept from me my humble apologies—for my swift, and, alas, understandably cynical reaction. For, indeed, the most exasperating aspect of *Lady Sings the Blues,* for me, is that the three principals—Miss Ross, Billy Dee Williams, and Richard Pryor—are, clearly, ready, willing, and able to stretch out and go a distance not permitted by the film. And, even within this straitjacket, they manage marvelous moments, and a truth which is not in the script is sometimes glimpsed through them. Diana Ross, clearly, respected Billie too much to try to imitate her. She picks up on Billie's beat, and, for the rest, uses herself, with a moving humility and candor, to create a portrait of a woman overwhelmed by the circumstances of her life. This is not exactly Billie Holiday, but it *is* the role as written, and she does much more with it than the script deserves. So does Billy Dee, in the absolutely impossible role of Louis McKay, and so does Richard Pryor, in a role which appears to have been dreamed up by a nostalgic, aging jazz *aficionado.*

The film begins at the end, more or less: titles over, we watch a series of sepia stills of Billie being fingerprinted, and thrown, alone, into a padded cell. We pick up, then, on a gawky colored girl, alone in the streets of Harlem. She has been sent by her mother to a rooming house, which turns out to be a whorehouse. She does not stay there long—packs her bags, and gets dressed, in fact, as a particularly horny and vocal client is getting undressed. She has seen Louis in this establishment, or elsewhere: in any case, she has seen him. She later meets him again, in a dive where she is one of the singers, and where the singer is expected to pick up money off the tables with her, ah, sexual equipment. Billie cannot do this, which has its effect on the two men in her life, Louis, and Piano Man (Richard Pryor). It is at this point that Piano Man dubs her "Lady," and it is at this point that she has her first date with Louis. A few frames later, she is the black singer with a white band, touring the South. (Billie went on the road with Artie Shaw, but the film version of this adventure is not in Billie's book.) On the road, she encounters the Ku Klux Klan, and sees a lynching. One of the members of the band has been offering her drugs, but she has always refused. After the lynching—an image, and a moment, to which we shall return—she succumbs to the friendly pusher, and returns to New York, hooked. Louis tries to get her off drugs, but does not succeed. Desperate for a fix, she pulls a razor on him, to force him to give her her works; after which he asks her to leave his house. Her mother dies, she gets busted—I think, in that order—Louis returns, and helps bring her back to the living. He also realizes that she needs her career, and helps her to begin again. Since she cannot work in New York, they end up on the Coast, with Piano Man. Eventually, Louis has to leave, on business, and to arrange her date in Carnegie Hall. Left alone with Piano Man, she decides that she wants to "cop," and sends him out to buy the junk. They are broke, and so she gives him a ring, which he is to pawn, to pay for it. Piano Man cops, all right, but doesn't pawn the ring, and doesn't pay for the stuff, and is, therefore, beaten to death before her eyes. The patient and loving Louis comes to the Coast, and brings her back to New York, where she scores a triumph on the Carnegie Hall stage. As Billie is singing *God Bless the Child*, and as thousands cheer, we learn, from blow-ups of newspaper items behind her, of her subsequent misadventures, and her death at the age of forty-four. And the film fades out, with a triumphant Billie, who is, already, however, unluckily, dead, singing on-stage before a delirious audience—or, rather, two: one in the cinema Carnegie Hall, and one in the cinema where we are seated.

It is not every day that a film crams so much cake down one's throat, and yet leaves one with so much more to swallow.

Now, it is not easy enough to say that the film really has nothing to do with Billie Holiday, since the film's authority—and, therefore, its presumed authenticity—derives from the use of her name. It is not enough to say that the film does not re-create her journey: the question is why the film presents itself as her journey. Most of the people who knew, or saw, or heard Billie Holiday will be dying shortly before, or shortly after, this century dies. (Billie would now be sixty years old.) This film cannot be all that is left of her torment and courage and beauty and grace. And the moments of truth smuggled into the film by the actors form a kind of Rosetta stone which the future will not be able to read, as, indeed, the present cannot.

In the film, we meet Billie on the streets of New York. But we do not know that she was raped at ten, sentenced, as a result, to a "Catholic institution" where she beat her hands to "a bloody damn pulp" when she was locked in with the body of a dead girl. We do not know that she was virtually raped at twelve, and that, at thirteen, she was a "hip kitty." We do not know, from the film, that when she refuses to sleep with the horny and vocal Big Blue, he has her thrown in jail: we know nothing, in fact, of the kind of terror with which this girl lived almost from the time that she was born. The incident with Big Blue is reduced to low comedy, much as is the scene with Billie's mother when she tries on the extravagant hat. Billie's testimony concerning the meaning of this hat is not in the film: "all the big-time whores wore big red velvet hats then—she looked so pretty in it"—nor is the fact that it is the mother who had bought the hat, because "we were going to live like ladies." In the film, Billie auditions as a dancer, and is terrible, and she says so in the book. It is also during this audition that the piano player saves her by snarling, "Girl, can you sing?" and so she sings for the first time in public, and this turns out to be the beginning of her career.

But the scene, as recounted by Billie, and the scene as translated in the film have nothing whatever in common. In the film, for no immediately discernible reason, except, perhaps, ambition, Billie drops into a nearby club, and asks for an audition. She is dressed as Hollywood—though it should certainly know better by now, God knows—persistently imagines cheap whores to dress. She joins the chorus line, disastrously, ending with her black bottom stuck out—after which, etc., she sings, etc.

Billie's testimony is that she and her mother were about to be evicted in the morning and that it was as "cold as all hell that night, and I walked out without any kind of coat." She hits a joint, she is indeed allowed to dance, but solo, "and it was pitiful." Before they throw her out, the piano player does indeed say, " 'Girl, can you sing?'—So I asked him to play 'Trav'lin' All Alone.' That came closer than anything to the way I felt." And: "when I left the joint that night, I split with the piano player and still took home fifty-seven dollars—I went out and bought a whole chicken and some baked beans."

The scene, in the film, is far from being an improvement on Billie's testimony, and it has two curious results, neither of which is vouched for anywhere in Billie's book. One is the invention of Piano Man, who, according to the film, remains with Billie until his death. According to the book, she scarcely ever sees him again, nor, according to Billie's evidence, does he ever become one of her intimates. It is conceivable, of course, however preposterous, that this figure is meant to suggest a kind of distillation of Lester Young: but I do not have the heart to pursue that line of inquiry. The other result is that the club-owner, a white man, becomes one of Billie's staunchest supporters, and closest friends. The book offers no corroborating evidence of this, either, though Billie speaks with great affection of such people as Tony Pastor and Artie Shaw. But absolutely none of these people are even suggested in the film—these people who were so important to her, along with Pigmeat Markham, and "Pops" Armstrong, and Charlie Barnet—or the jazz atmosphere of that period of Billie's life, and our lives. The film suggests nothing of the terrifying economics of a singer's life, and you will not learn, from the film, that Billie received no royalties for the records she was making then: you will not learn that the music industry is one of the areas of the national life in which the blacks have been most persistently, successfully, and brutally ripped off. If you have never heard of the Apollo Theatre, you will learn nothing of it from this film, nor what Billie's appearances there meant to her, or what a black audience means to a black performer.

Now, obviously, the only way to translate the written word to the cinema involves doing considerable violence to the written word, to the extent, indeed, of forgetting the written word. A film is meant to be seen, and, ideally, the less a film talks, the better. The cinematic translation, nevertheless, however great and necessary the violence it is compelled to use on the original form, is obliged to remain faithful to the intention, and the vision, of the original form. The necessary violence of the translation involves making very subtle and difficult choices. The root motive of the choices made can be gauged by the effect of these choices: and the effect of these deliberate choices, deliberately made, must be considered as resulting in a willed and deliberate act—that is, the film which we are seeing is the film we are intended to see.

Why? What do the filmmakers wish us to learn?

Billie is very honest in her book, she hides nothing. We know the effect of her father's death on her, for example, and how her father died, and how, ultimately, this connected with her singing of "Strange Fruit." We see her relationship with her mother: "I didn't want to hurt her, and I didn't—until three years before she died, when I went on junk." We know, from her testimony, that she was in love with the husband who turned her into a junkie, and we certainly know, from her testimony, that she loved the Louis who did his best to save her. I repeat: her testimony, for that is what we are compelled to deal with, and respect, and whatever others may imagine themselves to know of these matters cannot compare with the testimony of the person who was there.

She testifies, too: "I had the white gowns, and the white shoes. And every night they'd bring me the white gardenias and the white junk. When I was on, I was on and nobody gave me any trouble. No cops, no treasury agents, nobody."

"I got into trouble," says Billie, "when I tried to get off."

Let us see what the film makes of all this: what we are meant to learn.

Billie's father is not in the film, and is mentioned, I think, only once: near the end of the film, when she and Piano Man are high—just before Piano Man is murdered—and they both crack up when Billie says that her father never beat her because he was never home.

In the book, her father is a jazz musician, mainly on the road, who, eventually, leaves home, divorces, and re-marries. But, when he was in town, Billie was able to blackmail him into giving her the rent money for her mother and herself. And she cared about him: "it wasn't the pneumonia that killed him, it was Dallas, Texas. That's where he was, and where he walked around, going from hospital to hospital, trying to get help. But none of them would even so much as take his temperature, or let him in [but] because he had been in the Army, had ruined his lungs and had records to prove it, they finally let him in the Jim Crow ward. By that time, it was too late." And, later: "a song was born which became my personal protest—'Strange Fruit'—when [Lewis Allen] showed me that poem, I dug it right off. It seemed to spell out all the things that had killed Pop."

This is quite forthright, and even contains, if one dares say so, a certain dramatic force. In the film, on the southern road, Billie leaves the bus to go relieve herself in the bushes. Wandering along the countryside, Billie suddenly sees, on the road just before her, grieving black people, and a black body hanging from a tree. The best that one can say for this moment is that it is mistaken, and the worst that it is callously false and self-serving—which may be a rude way of saying the same thing: luckily, it is brief. The scene operates to resolve, at one stroke, several problems, and without in the least involving or intimidating the spectator. The lynch scene is as remote as an Indian massacre, occurring in the same landscape, and eliciting the same response: a mixture of pious horror, and gratified reassurance. The ubiquitous Ku Klux Klan appears, marching beside the bus in which the band is riding. The band is white, and they attempt to hide Billie, making, meanwhile, friendly gestures to their marching countrymen. But Billie, because of the strange fruit she has just seen hanging, is now beside herself, and deliberately makes herself visible, cursing and weeping against the Klan: she, and the musicians, make a sufficiently narrow, entirely cinematic escape. This scene is pure bullshit Hollywood-American fable, with the bad guys robed and the good guys casual: as a result, anyway, of all this unhealthy excitement, this understandable (and oddly reassuring) bitterness, Billie finally takes her first fix, and is immediately hooked.

This incident is not in the book: for the very good reason, certainly, that black people in this country are schooled in adversity long before white people are. Blacks perceive danger far more swiftly, and, however odd this may sound, then attempt to protect their white comrade from his white brothers: they know their white comrade's brothers far better than the comrade does. One of the necessities of being black, and knowing it, is to accept the hard discipline of learning to avoid useless anger, and needless loss of life: every mother and his mother's mother's mother's brother is needed.

The off-screen Billie faced down white sheriffs, and laughed at them, to their faces, and faced down white managers, cops, and bartenders. She was much stronger than this film can have any interest in indicating, and, as a victim, infinitely more complex.

Otherwise, she would never have been able to tell us, so

simply, that she sang "Strange Fruit" for her father, and got hooked because she fell in love.

The film cannot accept—because it cannot use—this simplicity. That victim who is able to articulate the situation of the victim has ceased to be a victim: he, or she, has become a threat.

The victim's testimony must, therefore, be altered. But, since no one outside the victim's situation dares imagine the victim's situation, this testimony can be altered only after it has been delivered; and after it has become the object of some study. The purpose of this scrutiny is to emphasize certain striking details which can then be used to quite another purpose than the victim had in mind. Given the complexity of the human being, and the complexities of society, this is not difficult. (Or, it does not appear to be difficult: the endless revisions made in the victim's testimony suggest that the endeavor may be impossible. Wounded Knee comes to mind, along with "Swing Low, Sweet Chariot," and we have yet to hear from My Lai.) Thus, for example, ghetto citizens have been heard to complain, very loudly, of the damage done to their homes during any ghetto uprising, and a grateful Republic fastens on this as a benevolent way of discouraging future uprisings. But the truth is, and every ghetto citizen knows this, that no one trapped in the ghetto owns anything, since they certainly do not own the land. Anyone who doubts this has only to spend tomorrow walking through the ghetto nearest to his.

Once the victim's testimony is delivered, however, there is, thereafter, forever, a witness somewhere: which is an irreducible inconvenience for the makers and shakers and accomplices of this world. These run together, in packs, and corroborate each other. They cannot bear the judgment in the eyes of the people whom they intend to hold in bondage forever, and who know more about them than their lovers. This remote, public, and, as it were, principled, bondage is the indispensable justification of their own: when the prisoner is free, the jailer faces the void of himself.

If *Lady Sings the Blues* pretended to be concerned with the trials of a white girl, and starred, say, the late Susan Hayward

(*I'll Cry Tomorrow*) or Bette Davis (*A Stolen Life*) or Olivia de Havilland (*To Each His Own*) or the late Judy Garland (*A Star Is Born*) or any of the current chicks, Billie's love for her father and for the husband who so turned her on would be the film's entire motivation: *the guy that won you/has run off and undone you/that great beginning/has seen its final inning/*: as desperately falsified, but in quite another way. The situations of Lana Turner (in *The Postman Always Rings Twice*) or Barbara Stanwyck (in *Double Indemnity*) or Joan Crawford (in almost anything, but, especially, *Mildred Pierce*) are dictated, at bottom, by the brutally crass and commercial terms on which the heroine is to survive—are dictated, that is, by society. But, at the same time, the white chick is always, somehow, saved or strengthened or destroyed by love—society is out of it, beneath her: it matters not at all that the man she marries, or deserts, or murders, happens to own Rhodesia, or that *she* does: love is all.

But the private life of a black woman, to say nothing of the private life of a black man, cannot really be considered at all. To consider this forbidden privacy is to violate white privacy—by destroying the white dream of the blacks; to make black privacy a black and private matter makes white privacy real, for the first time: which is, indeed, and with a vengeance, to endanger the stewardship of Rhodesia. The situation of the white heroine must never violate the white self-image. Her situation must always transcend the inexorability of the social setting, so that her innocence may be preserved: Grace Kelly, when she shoots to kill, at the end of *High Noon,* for example, does not become a murderess. But the situation of the black heroine, to say nothing of that of the black hero, must always be left at society's mercy: in order to justify white history and in order to indicate the essential validity of the black condition.

Billie's account of her meeting with Louis McKay is very simple, even childlike, and very moving. Louis is asleep on a bench, a whore is lifting his wallet, and Billie prevents this, pretending that Louis, whom she has never seen in her life before, is her old man. And she gives Louis his wallet. Anyone surviving these mean streets knows something about that moment. It is not a moment which the film can afford, for it conveys, too vividly, how that victim, the black, yet refuses to be a victim, has another source of sustenance: Billie's morality, at that moment, indeed, threatens the very foundations of the Stock Exchange.

The film does not suggest that the obsolete and vindictive narcotics laws had anything to do with her fate: does not pick up the challenge implicit in her statement: *When I was on, I was on, and nobody bothered me. . . . I got into trouble when I tried to get off.* Neither does it suggest that the distinction between Big Business and Organized Crime is like the old ad, which asks, *Which twin has the Toni?* The film leaves us with the impression, and this is a matter of choices coldly and deliberately made, that a gifted, but weak and self-indulgent woman, brought about the murder of her devoted Piano Man because she was not equal, either to her gifts, or to the society which had made her a star, and, as the closing sequence proves, adored her.

There was a rite in our church, called *pleading the blood*.

When the sinner fell on his face before the altar, the soul of the sinner then found itself locked in battle with Satan: or, in the place of Jacob, wrestling with the angel. All of the forces of Hell rushed to claim the soul which had just been astonished by the light of the love of God. The soul in torment turned this way and that, yearning, equally, for the light and for the darkness: yearning, out of agony, for reconciliation—and for rest: for this agony is compounded by an unimaginable, unprecedented, unspeakable fatigue. Only the saints who had passed through this fire—the incredible horror of the fainting of the spirit—had the power to intercede, to "plead the blood," to bring the embattled and mortally endangered soul "through." The pleading of the blood was a plea to whosoever had loved us enough to spill his blood for us, that he might sprinkle the soul with his love once more, to give us power over Satan, and the love and courage to live out our days.

One of the songs we sang comes out of the last of the Egyptian plagues, the death of the firstborn: *when I see the blood, I will pass over you.* (There is a reason that blacks call each other "bloods.") Another of the songs is, at once, more remote, and yet more present: *somebody needs you, Lord, come by here!*

I had been prayed through, and I, then, prayed others through: had testified to having been born again, and, then, helped others to be born again.

The word "belief" has nearly no meaning anymore, in the recognized languages, and ineptly approaches the reality to which I am referring: for there can be no doubt that it is a reality. The blacks had first been claimed by the Christian church, and then excluded from the company of white Christians—from the fellowship of Christians: which taught us all that we needed to know about white Christians. The blacks did not so much use Christian symbols as recognize them—recognize them for what they were before the Christians came along—and, thus, reinvested these symbols with their original energy. The proof of this, simply, is the continued existence and authority of the blacks: it is through the creation of the black church that an unwritten, dispersed, and violated inheritance has been handed down. The word "revelation" has very little meaning in the recognized languages: yet, it is the only word for the moment I am attempting to approach. This moment changes one forever. One is confronted with the agony and the nakedness and the beauty of a power which has no beginning and no end, which contains you, and which you contain, and which will be using you when your bones are dust. One thus confronts a self both limited and boundless, born to die and born to live. The creature is, also, the creation, and responsible, endlessly, for that perpetual act of creation which is both the self and more than the self. One is set free, then, to live among one's terrors, hour by hour and day by day, alone, and yet never alone. *My soul is a witness!*—so one's ancestors proclaim, and in the deadliest of the midnight hours.

To live in connection with a life beyond this life means, in effect—in truth—that, frightened as one may be, and no matter how limited, or how lonely, and no matter how the deal, at last, goes down, no man can ever frighten you. This is why blacks can be heard to say, *I ain't* got *to do nothing but stay black, and die!*: which is, after all, a far more affirmative apprehension than *I'm free, white, and twenty-one.* The first proposition is changeless, whereas the second is at the mercy of time, weather, the dictionary, geography, and fashion. The custodian of an inheritance, which is what blacks have had to be, in Western culture, must hand the inheritance down the line. So, you, the custodian, recognize, finally, that your life does not belong to you: nothing belongs to you. This will not sound like freedom to Western ears, since the Western world pivots on the infantile, and, in action, criminal delusions of possession, and of property. But, just as *love is the only money*, as the song puts it, so this mighty responsibility is the only freedom. Your child does not belong to you, and you must prepare your child to pick up the burden of his life long before the moment when you must lay your burden down.

But the people of the West will not understand this until everything which they now think they have has been taken away from them. In passing, one may observe how remarkable it is that a people so quick and so proud to boast of what they have taken from others are unable to imagine that what they have taken from others can also be taken from them.

In our church, the Devil has many faces, all of them one's own. He was not always evil, rarely was he frightening—he was, more often, subtle, charming, cunning, and warm. So, one learned, for example, never to take the easy way out: whatever looked easy was almost certainly a trap. In short, the Devil was that mirror which could never be smashed. One had to look into the mirror every day—*good morning, blues/ Blues, how do you do?/ Well I'm doing all right/ Good morning/ How are you?*—check it all out, and take it all in, and travel. The pleading of the blood was not, for us, a way of exorcising a Satan whom we knew could never sleep: it was to engage Satan in a battle which we knew could never end.

I first saw *The Exorcist*, in Hollywood, with a black friend of mine, who had his own, somewhat complex reasons for insisting that I see it: just so, one of my brothers had one day walked me into the film, *The Devils,* which he had already seen, saying, cheerfully, as we walked out, *Ain't that some shit? I just wanted you to see how sick these people are!* Both my friend and my brother had a point. I had already read *The Devils;* now, I forced myself to read *The Exorcist*—a difficult matter, since it is not written; then, I saw the film again, alone. I tried to be absolutely open to it, suspending judgment as totally as I could. For, after all, if I had once claimed to be "filled" with the Holy Ghost, and had once really believed, after all, that the Holy Ghost spoke through me, I could not, out of hand, arbitrarily sneer at the notion of demonic possession. The fact that I had been an adolescent boy when I believed all this did not really get me off the hook: I can produce no documents proving that I am not what I was.

My friend and I had a drink together, after we had seen the film, and we discussed it at some length. He was most struck by the figure of the young priest: he found the key to this personage in a rather strange place, and his observation haunted me for weeks. Father Karras confesses, at one point, that he has lost his faith. "So, we must be careful," David said to me, "lest we lose our faith—and become possessed." He was no longer speaking of the film, nor was he speaking of the church.

I carried this somewhat chilling admonition away with me. When I saw the film again, I was most concerned with the audience. I wondered what they were seeing, and what it meant to them.

The film, or its ambience, reminded me of *The Godfather,* both being afflicted with the same pious ambiguity. Ambiguity is not quite the word, for the film's intention is not at all ambiguous; yet, hypocrisy is not quite the word, either, since it suggests a more deliberate and sophisticated level of cunning. *The Exorcist* is desperately compulsive, and compulsive, precisely, in the terror of its unbelief. The vast quantities of tomato paste expended in *The Godfather* are meant to suggest vast reservoirs of courage, devotion, and nobility, qualities with which the film is not in the least concerned—and which, apart from Brando's performance, are never present in it. (And, at that, it is probably more accurate to speak of Brando's *presence*, a pride, an agony, an irreducible dignity.) *The Exorcist* has absolutely nothing going for it, except Satan, who is certainly the star: I can say only that Satan was never like that when he crossed *my* path (for one thing, the evil one never so rudely underestimated me). His concerns were more various, and his methods more subtle. *The Exorcist* is not in the least concerned with damnation, an abysm far beyond the confines of its imagination, but with property, with safety, tax shelters, stocks and bonds, rising and falling markets, the continued invulnerability of a certain class of people, and the continued sanctification of a certain history. If *The Exorcist* itself believed this history, it could scarcely be reduced to so abject a dependence on special effects.

In Georgetown, in Washington, D.C., a young movie actress is shooting a film. She is forthright, and liberated, as can be gathered from her liberated language. The film she is making is involved with a student uprising—in the book, she describes it as "*dumb!*": in the film, one of her lines suggests that the students work within the system. This line, however, is neatly balanced by another, which suggests that the political perceptions of this film-within-a-film may owe a great deal to Walt Disney.

Before this, we have encountered the aged priest, who will become the exorcist, digging in the ruins of northern Iraq. This opening sequence is probably the film's most effective, ruthlessly exploiting the uneasiness one cannot but feel when touched by the energy of distant gods, unknown. It sets up, with some precision, the spirit of the terror which informs the Christian-pagan argument: it may be something of a pity that Ingmar Bergman could not have guided the film from there. However, Max von Sydow, the exorcist—rather like Marlon Brando, in *The Godfather*—having been exhibited, is now put on ice, and, if we wish to await his return, we have no choice but to see the end of the movie.

The horror of the demonic possession begins with what sound, to the heroine, like rats in the attic. Her daughter's dresses are misplaced. Room temperatures change, alarmingly and inexplicably. Furniture is mysteriously moved about. Her daughter's personality changes, and obscenities she has never used before become a part of her speech. (Though she overhears the mother using some of them: over the trans-Atlantic telephone, to her father, who is estranged from her mother.) The daughter also plays around with a ouija board, and has made a friend in the spirit world, called Captain Howdy. The mother worries over all these manifestations, both worldly and otherworldly, of the mysteries now being confronted by her growing daughter with all of the really dreadful apathy of the American middle class, reassuring herself that nothing she has done, or left undone, has irreparably damaged her child; who will certainly grow up, therefore, to be as healthy as her mother and to make as much money. But, eventually, at a very posh Georgetown party, of which her mother is the hostess, this daughter comes downstairs in her nightgown, and, while urinating on the floor, tells a member of the party that he is going to die. After this, her affliction, or possession, develops apace.

The plot now compels us to consider a Jesuit priest, young, healthy, athletic, intelligent, presumably celibate, with a dying mother, and in trouble with his faith. His mother dies, alone, in a dingy flat in New York, where he has been compelled to leave her, and he is unable to forgive himself for this. There is the film director, a drunken, cursing agnostic, other priests, psychiatrists, doctors, a detective—well: all people we have met before, and there is very little to be said about them. One of the psychiatrists is nearly castrated by Regan, the daughter, who has abnormal strength while in the grip of Satan. Along with the mumbo-jumbo of levitating beds and discontented furniture and Wuthering Heights tempests, there is the moment when the daughter is compelled by Satan to masturbate with a crucifix, after which she demands that her mother lick her, after which she throws her mother across the room, after which the mother screams, after which she faints. It develops that the film director, dead in a mysterious accident, has actually been pushed: by Regan, through her bedroom window, to his death: again, while in the grip of Satan. All else having failed, the aged priest is called from his retreat to perform the exorcism: the young priest is his assistant. The strain of exorcising Satan proves too much for the aged priest, who has a heart attack, and dies. The young priest, still mad with guilt concerning the death of his mother, taunts Satan, daring him to stop picking on helpless little girls, and enter *him*. Satan does this with an eagerness which suggests that he, too, is weary of little girls and hurls the priest through the bedroom window, to his death, and, also, presumably, to eternal damnation; as to this last point, however, I really cannot be clear.

The young priest is tormented by guilt, and especially in reference to his mother, throughout the film: and Satan ruthlessly plays on this, sometimes speaking (through Regan) in the mother's voice, and sometimes incarnating her. And Satan also plays on the guilt of Regan's mother—her guilt concerning her failed marriage, her star status, her ambition, her relation to her daughter, her essentially empty and hypocritical and totally unanchored life: in a word, her emancipation. This uneasy, and even terrified guilt is the subtext of *The Exorcist,* which cannot, however, exorcise it since it never confronts it.

But this confrontation would have been to confront the devil. The film terrified me on two levels. The first, as I have tried to indicate, involved my deliberate attempt to leave myself open to it, and to the extent, indeed, of re-living my adolescent holy-roller terrors. It was very important for me not to pretend to have surmounted the pain and terror of that time of my life, very important not to pretend that it left no mark on me. It marked me forever. In some measure I encountered the abyss of my own soul, the labyrinth of my destiny: these could never be escaped, to challenge these imponderables being, precisely, the heavy, tattered glory of the gift of God.

To encounter oneself is to encounter the other: and this is love. If I know that my soul trembles, I know that yours does, too: and, if I can respect this, both of us can live. Neither of us, truly, can live without the other: a statement which would not sound so banal if one were not endlessly compelled to repeat it, and, further, believe it, and act on that belief. My friend was quite right when he said, *So, we must be careful—lest we lose our faith—and become possessed.*

For, I have seen the devil, by day and by night, and have seen him in you and in me: in the eyes of the cop and the sheriff and the deputy, the landlord, the housewife, the football player: in the eyes of some junkies, the eyes of some preachers, the eyes of some governors, presidents, wardens, in the eyes of some orphans, and in the eyes of my father, and in my mirror. It is that moment when no other human being is real for you, nor are you real for yourself. This devil has no need of any dogma—though he can use them all—nor does he need any historical justification, history being so largely his invention. He does not levitate beds, or fool around with little girls: *we* do.

The mindless and hysterical banality of the evil presented in *The Exorcist* is the most terrifying thing about the film. The Americans should certainly know more about evil than that; if they pretend otherwise, they are lying, and any black man, and not only blacks—many, many others, including white children—can call them on this lie; he who has been treated *as* the devil recognizes the devil when they meet. At the end of *The Exorcist,* the demon-racked little girl murderess kisses the Holy Father, and she remembers nothing: she is departing with her mother, who will, presumably, soon make another film. The grapes of wrath are stored in the cotton fields and migrant shacks and ghettoes of this nation, and in the schools and prisons, and in the eyes and hearts and perceptions of the wretched everywhere, and in the ruined earth of Vietnam, and in the orphans and the widows, and in the old men, seeing visions, and in the young men, dreaming dreams: these have already kissed the bloody cross and will not bow down before it again: and have forgotten nothing.

ST. PAUL DE VENCE
JULY 29, 1975

ACKNOWLEDGMENTS

Nobody Knows My Name
Acknowledgment is made to the following publications in whose pages these essays first appeared. *The New York Times Book Review* for "The Discovery of What It Means to Be an American" (January 25, 1959); *Encounter* for "Princes and Powers"; *Esquire* for "Fifth Avenue Uptown: a Letter from Harlem" (July, 1960), reprinted by permission; *New York Times Magazine* for "East River Downtown: Postscript to a Letter from Harlem" (which appeared as "A Negro Assays the Negro Mood," March 12, 1961); *Harper's Magazine* for "A Fly in Buttermilk" (which appeared as "The Hard Kind of Courage," October, 1958); *Partisan Review* for "Nobody Knows My Name: a Letter from the South" (Winter, 1959) and "Faulkner and Desegregation" (Winter, 1956); Kalamazoo College for "In Search of A Majority" delivered there as an address; *Esquire* for "Notes For A Hypothetical Novel" (delivered as an address at the third annual Esquire Magazine symposium on the "Role of the Writer in America" at San Francisco State College, October 22, 1960); *The New Leader* for "The Male Prison" (which appeared as "Gide As Husband and Homosexual," December 13, 1954); *Esquire* for "The Northern Protestant" (which appeared as "The Precarious Vogue of Ingmar Bergman," April, 1960), reprinted by permission; *The Reporter* for "Eight Men" (which appeared as "The Survival of Richard Wright," March 16, 1961); *Le Preuve* for "The Exile" (February, 1961); and *Esquire* for "The Black Boy Looks at the White Boy" (May, 1961), copyright © 1961 by Esquire, Inc., reprinted by permission.

The Fire Next Time
"Down at the Cross" originally appeared in *The New Yorker* under the title "Letter from a Region in My Mind". "My

Dungeon Shook" originally appeared in *The Progressive*, Madison, Wisconsin.

The Devil Finds Work
Grateful acknowledgment is made to the following for permission to reprint previously published material: Alfred Music Publishing Co. Inc. and Hal Leonard Corporation: Lyrics from "The Man That Got Away" from the motion picture *A Star Is Born*, lyrics by Ira Gershwin, music by Harold Arlen, copyright © 1954 (Renewed) by Harwin Music Co. and Ira Gershwin Music. All rights on behalf of Ira Gershwin Music administered by WB Music Corp. All rights reserved. Reprinted by permission of Alfred Music Publishing Co. Inc. and Hal Leonard Corporation. Countdown Media: Lyrics from "Sing Sing Blues" by Joseph Kuhn. Reprinted by permission of Countdown Media.